WHAT IF?™ 2

ESSAYS BY

JAMES BRADLEY

CALEB CARR

THOMAS FLEMING

JOHN LUKACS

GEOFFREY C. WARD

AND OTHERS

❧

Edited by

ROBERT COWLEY

WHAT IF?™ 2

EMINENT HISTORIANS IMAGINE
WHAT MIGHT HAVE BEEN

G. P. PUTNAM'S SONS

New York

WHAT IF? is a trademark of American Historical Publications, Inc.

G. P. Putnam's Sons
Publishers Since 1838
a member of
Penguin Putnam Inc.
375 Hudson Street
New York, NY 10014

Library of Congress Cataloging-in-Publication Data

What if? 2 : eminent historians imagine what might have been :
essays / by James Bradley . . . [et al.] ; edited by Robert Cowley.
p. cm.
Contents: Socrates dies at Delium, 424 b.c./Victor Davis Hanson — Not by a nose/Josiah Ober — Pontius Pilate spares Jesus/Carlos M. N. Eire — Repulse at Hastings, October 14, 1066/Cecelia Holland — The Chinese discovery of the New World, 15th century/Theodore F. Cook, Jr. — Martin Luther burns at the stake, 1521/Geoffrey Parker — If Charles I had not left Whitehall, August 1641/Theodore K. Rabb — Napoléon's invasion of North America/Thomas Fleming — If Lincoln had not freed the slaves/Tom Wicker — France turns the other cheek, July 1870/Alistair Horne — The Election of Theodore Roosevelt, 1912/John Lukacs — The Great War torpedoed/Robert L. O'Connell — No Finland Station/George Feifer — The luck of Franklin Delano Roosevelt/Geoffrey C. Ward — The War of 1938/Williamson Murray — Prime Minister Halifax/Andrew Roberts — The boys who saved Australia, 1942/James Bradley — Enigma uncracked/David Kahn — Pius XII protests the Holocaust/Robert Katz — VE Day—November 11, 1944/Caleb Carr — The Führer in the dock/Roger Spiller — No bomb: no end/Richard B. Frank — The Presidency of Henry Wallace/James Chace — A tale of three congressmen, 1948/Lance Morrow — What if Pizarro had not found potatoes in Peru?/William H. McNeill.
ISBN 0-399-14795-0
1. Imaginary wars and battles. 2. Imaginary histories. I. Title: What if? two.
II. Title: What if? 2. III. Bradley, James, date. IV. Cowley, Robert.
D25.5 .W44   2001   2001034919
355.4'8—dc21

Printed in the United States of America
1   3   5   7   9   10   8   6   4   2

This book is printed on acid-free paper. ∞

Book design by Michelle McMillian
Map and picture research by Sabine Russ
Maps © 2001 Jeffrey L. Ward
Endpapers: Detail of Bayeux Tapestry, Musée de la Tapisserie, Bayeux, France.
Copyright Erich Lessing / Art Resource, NY.

ACKNOWLEDGMENTS

I wish to express my special thanks to Byron Hollinshead and Sabine Russ at American Historical Publications, and to David Highfill at Putnam, for their assistance in all aspects of the development of this book.

R.C.

CONTENTS

List of Maps & Illustrations   *xiii*
Introduction by Robert Cowley   *xv*

Socrates Dies at Delium, 424 B.C.   ✦ *Victor Davis Hanson*   1
   The consequences of a single battle casualty

Not by a Nose   ✦ *Josiah Ober*   23
   The triumph of Antony and Cleopatra at Actium, 31 B.C.

Pontius Pilate Spares Jesus   ✦ *Carlos M. N. Eire*   48
   Christianity without the Crucifixion

Repulse at Hastings, October 14, 1066   ✦ *Cecelia Holland*   68
   William does not conquer England

The Chinese Discovery of the New World,
   15th Century   ✦ *Theodore F. Cook, Jr.*   85
      What the expeditions of a eunuch admiral might have led to

Martin Luther Burns at the Stake, 1521   ✦ *Geoffrey Parker*   105
   "O God, is Luther dead?"

If Charles I Had Not Left Whitehall,
   August 1641 ✦ *Theodore K. Rabb*   120
     As a starter, no English civil war

Napoléon's Invasion of North America ✦ *Thomas Fleming*   134
     Aedes aegypti *takes a holiday, 1802*

If Lincoln Had Not Freed the Slaves ✦ *Tom Wicker*   152
     The inevitable results of no Emancipation Proclamation

France Turns the Other Cheek, July 1870 ✦ *Alistair Horne*   165
     The needless war with Prussia

The Election of Theodore Roosevelt, 1912 ✦ *John Lukacs*   181
     Brokering an earlier end to World War I

The Great War Torpedoed ✦ *Robert L. O'Connell*   195
     The weapon that could have won the war for Germany in 1915

No Finland Station ✦ *George Feifer*   210
     A Russian Revolution without Lenin?

The Luck of Franklin Delano Roosevelt ✦ *Geoffrey C. Ward*   236
     Seven might-not-have-beens on the road to the presidency

The War of 1938 ✦ *Williamson Murray*   255
     Chamberlain fails to sway Hitler at Munich

Prime Minister Halifax ✦ *Andrew Roberts*   279
     Great Britain makes peace with Germany, 1940

The Boys Who Saved Australia, 1942 ✦ *James Bradley*   291
     Small events can have large results

Enigma Uncracked ✦ *David Kahn*   305
     The Allies fail to break the German cipher machine

Pius XII Protests the Holocaust ✦ *Robert Katz*   317
     Could the wartime pope have prevented the Final Solution?

VE Day—November 11, 1944 ✦ *Caleb Carr* 333
The unleashing of Patton and Montgomery

The Führer in the Dock ✦ *Roger Spiller* 344
A speculation on the banality of evil

No Bomb: No End ✦ *Richard B. Frank* 366
The Operation Olympic disaster, Japan 1945

The Presidency of Henry Wallace ✦ *James Chace* 382
If FDR had not dumped his vice president in 1944

A Tale of Three Congressmen, 1948 ✦ *Lance Morrow* 404
America without Nixon, Johnson, and Kennedy

What If Pizarro Had Not Found
Potatoes in Peru? ✦ *William H. McNeill* 413
The humble roots of history

LIST OF MAPS & ILLUSTRATIONS

MAPS

page

7   Boeotia and Attica, 424 B.C.; and Ancient Greece

28   The Battle of Actium, 31 B.C.; and The Roman Empire, 31 B.C.

72   The Battle of Hastings, October 1066

90–91   Ming Voyages of Exploration, 15th Century

138   The New New France

259   Hitler's Invasion of Czechoslovakia, October 1938

295   Pacific Theater, 1942; and Eastern New Guinea, 1942

337   The End of the European War, Autumn 1944

371   The Invasion of Japan, 1945–46

ILLUSTRATIONS

page

26–27   Actium: Empire Lost, Empire Established

53   The Decision That Made a Religion

76   Hastings: Futures in the Balance

109   Portrait of a Survivor

127   Charles I: A Study in Stubbornness

156   A Cause Not Lost

171   Unnecessary Adversaries

185   The Bull Moose Candidate

214   The God That Almost Failed

251   A Reluctant Leader?

283 Prime Ministers in Waiting

309 The Perfect Machine

320 The Fatal Choice

348 Last Hurrah

386 Wallace Takes a Back Seat

417 Harvesting History

ROBERT COWLEY

INTRODUCTION

One of the troubles with history as it is studied today is that people take it too seriously. I don't mean to say that history isn't serious business, or that history doesn't matter. History is not, to invoke the ghost of Henry Ford, "the bunk." We need history. "Life must be lived forward," the philosopher Kierkegaard observes, "but can only be understood backwards." But that understanding should not be treated like an exigent dose of milk of magnesia. I have real qualms about the way history is dispensed.

The solemnity of history assails us from the time we are schoolchildren. We are force-fed history as social studies, an approach in which all races, nationalities, and sexes are given equal time: Everyone must be included, no one can be offended. This surrender to special interests is not just distorting but boring. History involving great people or pivotal events is out of fashion. Broad trends, those waves that swell, break, and recede, are everything these days. We are left with the impression that history is inevitable, that what happened could not have happened any other way, and that drama and contingency have no place in the general scheme of human existence.

What is too often lost is a sense of history as narrative, a vast and ever-evolving novel. A young woman I know was taking a course at an Ivy League university about women in pre-Revolutionary America. After we'd discussed matters such as compensation and race and gender roles, I casually asked if she had ever read Francis Parkman. "Who's Parkman?" she asked. I would have been more both-

ered by her answer if I didn't know that the best historians today tend not to be just fine writers but engaging storytellers. There is no reason why history can't entertain, especially when the object is to turn people on to a subject whose presentation at some point early in their lives may have turned them off. Parkman, remember, was the quintessential storyteller.

These thoughts bring me to the present volume, the sequel to What If?, *which appeared two years ago. The time has come for a new set of answers to the historian's favorite secret question. That first book was entirely military. Armed confrontation provides counterfactual history with its most natural arena—but it is by no means the only one. Nonmilitary events also have a place in any examination of what might have happened. Consider four moments of the greatest magnitude in human history, as we do in these pages. What if Jesus had not been crucified and Pontius Pilate had decided to set him free? What if Martin Luther had been burned at the stake for his heretical views—and what if his chosen instrument of combat, the printing press, had not yet been invented? What if, more than half a century before Columbus, Ming emperors had not called back the huge fleets of the eunuch admiral-explorer Zheng He but had allowed him to continue his voyages along the African coast? What if the Chinese and not the Spanish had discovered the New World? Or what if, in 1917, the Germans had not sent Lenin to Petrograd on the famous "sealed train"—what if he had arrived in Russia too late to lead a successful revolution?*

But consider too a seemingly trivial rebuff that would have enormous consequences, namely the rejection of Franklin Delano Roosevelt's offer of marriage to a beautiful debutante (who happened to be a Republican). There is also the phenomenon we might call a reverse counterfactual. Suppose, as William H. McNeill does, we were to subtract something as ordinary but essential to our everyday lives as the potato. How very different history might have been.

The reader will find an ample share of military might-have-beens; they are, quite simply, irresistible. Josiah Ober has love, under the sponsorship of Antony and Cleopatra, winning out at Actium. William doesn't conquer at Hastings and the Franco-Roman world that he represents loses more than a battle in Cecelia Holland's essay. Hitler follows his instincts and not the pleas of Neville Chamberlain to preserve peace in our time, invading Czechoslovakia in October 1938. The result, Williamson Murray tells us, would undoubtedly have been a general Euro-

pean War but a war that soon would have put Germany at a disadvantage. But two years could make all the difference. Andrew Roberts asks, what would have been the result if Lord Halifax and not Winston Churchill had become prime minister of Great Britain in 1940, as nearly happened. Would the Cold War have been averted and a million lives saved, Caleb Carr suggests, if Eisenhower had not "turned off" George S. Patton's gas early in the fall of 1944? Richard B. Frank explores the possibility that Japan might have tried to hold out, with disastrous consequences for the world, if we had not dropped two atomic bombs.

That these scenarios have entertainment value is undeniable, but their purpose is also to provoke. There is no better way of understanding what did happen in history than to contemplate what very well might have happened. Counterfactual history has a way of making the stakes of a confrontation stand out in relief. It can point out the moment that was truly a turning point—or the moment when the shading of an event edged from unfortunate to tragic. Plausibility is the key. Every day we make choices that, insignificant as they may seem at the time, can alter our lives, sometimes in drastic and unforeseen ways. History is merely the sum of millions of human decisions—which may be the decision to elevate the one person who makes the decisions for all of us. But history too may depend on a single accident—which has the power to abrogate all those thousands and millions of individual decisions. What if the arrow that killed the English King Harold at the Battle of Hastings had missed? What if, in February 1933, Giuseppe Zangara, bent on assassinating the president-elect, Franklin D. Roosevelt, had shown up at the Miami rally a few minutes earlier? These are the things that can't be quantified, no matter how diligently some historians try to change an art into a science. The only fixed rule of history is that there are no rules. This very rulelessness is what makes the study of history so full of surprise and fascination.

WHAT IF?™ 2

VICTOR DAVIS HANSON

SOCRATES DIES AT DELIUM, 424 B.C.

The consequences of a single battle casualty

That the foundations of the Western intellectual tradition may rest on a military moment is a notion that some may find unsettling; its potential consequences are even more so. According to Victor Davis Hanson, philosophy as we know it was "nearly aborted"—his verb is hardly too strong—one late autumn afternoon in 424 B.C., in "an accidental battle in a failed campaign in a backwater theater of the Peloponnesian War," the twenty-seven-year-long struggle between Athens and Sparta. At the Battle of Delium, a ragtag Athenian contingent confronted a larger force from Thebes, an ally of the Spartan confederacy. One middle-aged infantryman from Athens was Socrates, a philosopher whose reputation was as yet uncertain. Service in war was an obligation of citizenship, and Greek men from the ages of eighteen to sixty could expect to experience in their lifetimes at least two or three episodes of concentrated terror; Socrates had already fought in two campaigns. What if he, like several hundred of the men he fought with at Delium, had been ridden down and skewered as he tried to flee to Athens? What if Socrates had not lived another quarter of a century, the period of his greatest influence? Or if he had not been alive to meet, and teach, the young Plato—who, without Socrates, might have become a politician or a poet and not a philosopher? Beyond leaving an excessive number of corpses to rot, that encounter at Delium may have decided nothing. Still, if it had counted one more Athenian victim, as Hanson says, "the entire course of Western philosophical and political thought would have been radically changed."

1

VICTOR DAVIS HANSON is a professor of classics at California State University, Fresno, and the author of eleven books on subjects ranging from Greek military and rural history to the history of warfare and contemporary agriculture. His most recent books are *The Land Was Everything*, *The Soul of Battle*, and *Carnage and Culture*.

A NIGHTMARISH RETREAT

THE CLASSICAL GREEKS saw no contradiction between a life of action and contemplation, even in the extreme polarities between military service and philosophy. War, the philosopher Heraclitus says, is "the
father of us all." Plato proclaims that fighting "always exists by nature between every Greek city-state." A number of Greek writers, thinkers, and
statesmen fought in the phalanx. The lyric poet Archilochus was killed in
battle on the Aegean island of Thasos. The poets Tyrtaeus, Alcaeus, and
Callinus, the playwrights Aeschylus and Sophocles, the democratic leader
Pericles, the historian Thucydides, and the orator Demosthenes all took
their slot in the files of the phalanx or on the banks of a trireme. At the
siege of Samos (440 B.C.), Melissus, the Samian philosopher and student of
Parmenides, led his ship into battle against Pericles' fleet. Sophocles was
also at sea there, among the elected high command of Athenians who came
to enslave the island. The philosopher and mathematician Archimedes
died in the storming of Syracuse, in his final hours employing his novel military machines against the Roman besiegers.

It is not so surprising, then, that Socrates, the father of Western ethical
philosophy, and veteran of the fighting in the campaigns of Potidaea and
Amphipolis, found himself in a most dangerous place in the fall of 424 B.C.
The aging forty-five-year-old hoplite fled for his life from an abject infantry
disaster near the small border sanctuary of Delium, one nondescript, pot-
bellied, middle-aged soldier amid a routed Athenian ragtag force of old
men, irregulars, resident aliens, and inexperienced youth.

Delium, an accidental battle in a failed campaign in a backwater theater
of the Peloponnesian War (431–404 B.C.), is a little-known and little-

3

studied event. Nevertheless it was an unmitigated Athenian military disaster—the largest infantry battle fought near Athens since Marathon sixty-six years earlier, and a catastrophe in which nearly 15 percent of all Athenian infantrymen assembled there were killed in a few hours. No doubt an even far larger number were wounded or captured.

In the seventh year of the Peloponnesian War, the Athenians wished to end their two-front conflict with the Peloponnesians to the south and the Thebans to the north, and so in fall 424 B.C. they invaded Boeotia on their northern border. Unfortunately, they had devised an overly ambitious and unworkable plan of combined naval and infantry maneuvers in hopes of deploying two separate contingents inside Boeotia at the front and rear of a Theban army. The contemporary historian Thucydides records that the Athenian general Demosthenes had sailed earlier during the summer, intending to raise democratic insurrection throughout the Boeotian countryside by an unexpected amphibious landing. Then, aided by partisans, he was supposed to make his way east toward the sanctuary and small village of Delium—on the very day the other general, Hippocrates, and his Athenian hoplites, among them Socrates, marched out from Athens.

The idea was to crush the Thebans between two pincers, and thereby turn the entire Boeotian countryside into a democratic satellite of Athens in its war against Spartan oligarchy. But Demosthenes' naval assault to the west at the coastal Boeotian town of Siphae was timed too early. Once his plans were betrayed to the Boeotians, he was of little value in drawing off opposition from the Athenian land troops marching up from the south, and so he gave up the campaign. The result was that Socrates and his friends lost the element of surprise, were without help, and were soon to be confronted by the main army of an aroused and angry Thebes.

Hippocrates, a young nephew of Pericles and the general in charge of this rather motley expeditionary force, quickly turned his men toward home, stopping to have his Athenian infantry occupy the sanctuary of Apollo at Delium, cutting down surrounding vineyards and in general cannibalizing nearby farmhouses for the flotsam and jetsam with which to build his barricade. After ravaging the countryside, Hippocrates left a small force at the now garrisoned Delium and then led some 7,000 heavy infantrymen a few thousand yards back home toward the border of Attica.

When the Theban army finally arrived, the Athenians were ready to disband and apparently felt the campaign had failed—much to their relief. Thucydides says that a large throng of unarmed citizens and foreigners had followed the Athenian hoplite infantry from home, but had earlier dispersed, leaving few to stay with the army. In contrast, the Thebans had at least 7,000 hoplites, but also 10,000 light-armed troops, 1,000 cavalry, and an additional 500 skirmishers. When the battle commenced, Socrates and his friends would find themselves outnumbered by over two to one.

Without warning, the pursuing Theban army suddenly came up over a small hill and caught the assembled Athenian infantry off guard, still listening to a prebattle harangue from Hippocrates. Thucydides adds that water courses limited the field of operations. His description of the actual fighting is brief. Despite the uphill run, the Athenian right wing under Hippocrates nevertheless quickly cut down the Boeotian confederates opposite them on the enemy left. All along the Boeotian phalanx these panicked confederate allies fell back in the face of the Athenian upward assault. An Athenian victory looked certain. Yet at the same moment on the other side of the battlefield, the Theban general Pagondas and the reinforced Theban center and right wing held fast and soon went on the attack against the Athenian left. Delium thus unfolded as most typical hoplite battles of the age—a question of whether the strong right wing of an army could win the engagement before its own left weaker horn would collapse and lose it.

In fact, the unfortunate villagers of Thespiae on the extreme left of the Boeotian phalanx soon were at the point of annihilation from the Athenians under Hippocrates. Socrates was probably posted here along with his friends and associates—Laches (the eponymous subject of a Platonic dialogue), Alcibiades (his notorious young wayward student), and Pyrilampes (stepfather of Plato). Many in the army were middle-aged and well past forty (e.g., Socrates, Laches, Pyrilampes), perhaps because the campaign was envisioned as a short one while thousands of other frontline Athenian troops that late summer and fall were deployed elsewhere throughout the Aegean.

In any case, Thucydides tells us that in the first stage of the battle the Boeotian allies of Thebes in fact broke before the Athenian uphill charge, some trying to flee, others bumping into those attempting to fight and hang on. Meanwhile, far across the battlefield, Pagondas "gradually at first" pushed the weak Athenian left downhill and was systematically, as planned, clearing the battlefield through the advantage of favorable terrain and superior muscle. Only when the Thespian slaughter on his left horn threatened to pour Athenian hoplites to his own rear did Pagondas dispatch a reserve of Boeotian cavalry to the left to come up over the hill to the rear of the victorious Athenian right.

This was the key point in the entire battle. An apparent Athenian triumph was transformed into abject defeat in a matter of seconds. The successful Athenians under Hippocrates now wrongly surmised that an entirely new army was upon them. "On their sudden appearance over the hill," Thucydides writes, "the victorious Athenian wing thought an entirely fresh army had arrived, and thus simply took to panic." It was probably here—amid the stunned Athenians and their general who were suddenly transformed into panicked runaways—that Socrates began his famous trek back toward Athens.

Hippocrates was probably killed at this juncture, and soon the entire Athenian army took off at a run to the rear for safety—either nearby Mount Parnes, the fortified sanctuary at Delium proper and the refuge of Athenian triremes, or the woods in the flat Oropus borderland between Attica and Boeotia. Thucydides adds that some opportunistic enemy Locrian horsemen arrived for the spoils and now joined the Boeotian predators in the open-ended killing spree. Remember, there were already present over 10,000 light-armed Boeotians, in addition to 1,000 cavalry and another 500 peltasts, or skirmishers. With the Locrian reinforcements and the victorious hoplites, there may well have been a sizable swarm of 15,000 or so enemy pursuers, many of them either mounted or agile, lightly equipped auxiliaries. The routed Athenians, without much cavalry support or supporting

BOEOTIA AND ATTICA, 424 B.C.

Aegean Sea

N

Euboean Sea

Euboean Sea Oropus

Delium •

Thebes •

B O E O T I A

▲ *Mount Parnes*

SOCRATES' POSSIBLE
ESCAPE ROUTES

0 Miles 50

0 Kilometers 50

A T T I C A

• Athens

ANCIENT GREECE

Saronic Gulf

0 Miles 100 200

0 Kilometers 200

THESSALY

Euboean Sea

Aegean Sea

Thermopylae •

Delium

BOEOTIA Oropus

Thebes •

▲ *Mount Parnes*

• Athens

ATTICA

N

PELOPONNESUS

Sparta

MESSENIA •

LACONIA

Ionian Sea

© 2001 Jeffrey L. Ward

skirmishers, and struggling to fling away their heavy armor, were vastly out-numbered, slower, confused, and in many cases lost in the growing twilight.

Socrates wisely avoided both the route to Delium and the high ground of Parnes, and so found safety in a third way through the forested Oropus. The disaster of this "home guard" must have quickly taken on mythic pro-portions and been recounted constantly throughout Athens: Hippocrates, nephew of Pericles, stepbrother of Alcibiades, and general of the army, killed; Alcibiades' bravery during the retreat soon to inaugurate his mete-oric political career; Laches' less than courageous behavior in the flight from Delium foreshadowing his demise at the subsequent battle of Manti-nea (418 B.C.), where he also fled the field; and Plato's own stepfather and great-uncle, Pyrilampes, captured when Plato was but a mere toddler.

In three later dialogues—*Laches*, *Symposium*, and *Apology*—Plato makes direct mention of Socrates' gallantry in the flight, how he backpedaled and made an orderly withdrawal toward the borderland of Oropus, accompa-nied by both Laches and Alcibiades. Indeed, in *Laches*, Socrates is made to lecture about the proper technique of attacking and fending off blows when in isolated combat, with a clear allusion to his own nightmarish experience after Delium. In this dialogue of the same name, Laches brags of Socrates that "if others had been willing to be like him, our city would now be up-right and would not then have had such a terrible fall." In the last speech of his life, Socrates reminds his accusers in Plato's *Apology*—his defense to a criminal prosecution on trumped-up charges of impiety that led to his ex-ecution—that in three terrible battles he had kept rank and not left his po-sition. And in Plato's *Symposium*, Alcibiades gives a description of the acute danger in which Socrates found himself during the general rout after Delium:

> I happened to be riding, he was serving as a hoplite. As the army was scattered he was retreating with Laches when I happened on him; at first sight I told them to keep their courage up as I told them I would not abandon them. Then I had even a finer view of Socrates than at Potidaea. For my part I was less afraid since I was mounted. First off I noticed how much more in control of his senses he was than Laches,

and how—to use your own phrase, Aristophanes—he made his way there just as he does here in Athens "swaggering and glancing sideways." So he looked around calmly at both his friends and the enemy; he was clearly giving the message to anyone even at a distance that if anyone touched this man, he quickly would put up a stout defense. The result was that he and his partner got away safely. For it is true that attackers do not approach men of this caliber but instead go after those fleeing headlong.

Centuries later, Plutarch, in his life of Alcibiades, also recalls this widely circulated story that Alcibiades rode past Socrates and his isolated contingent who were in dire straits. But in Plutarch's version, Alcibiades' mounted presence saves the life of Socrates as the enemy "was closing in and killing many." In his *Moralia*, Plutarch adds a slightly different twist—that Socrates' choice of escape alone saved him and his friends, as most other Athenians who headed over the mountains were ridden down and slain, while those who reached Delium were eventually besieged.

The disparate ancient evidence, nevertheless, points to two salient facts about Socrates' retreat—that Delium was a horrific Athenian catastrophe where hundreds were mercilessly hunted down and killed right on the border of Attica, and that Socrates' courage and good sense brought him out alive when most around him were killed. Clearly the philosopher himself was nearly almost ridden down and speared in the chaotic rout.

When we add the macabre fact that the corpses of over 1,000 Athenian dead—no doubt the majority hunted down in the dark and found randomly for miles without armor and with stabs to the back—were collected by the enemy, but then left to rot in the autumn sun for nearly three weeks, the flight from Delium must have been ingrained in the collective Athenian and Boeotian memory as a grotesque event in which human detritus littered well-traveled local paths. Again, we have no idea how many thousand more eventually died of their wounds or were captured.

In the fall of 424 B.C., the forty-five-year-old Socrates came within a hair's breadth of being killed. Had the middle-aged philosopher been speared by an anonymous Locrian horseman, or if his small band had been overtaken by pursuing Theban infantry, or if he had chosen to flee toward either Delium or Mount Parnes, where most of his terrified comrades were killed, the entire course of Western philosophical and political thought would have been radically altered.

SOCRATES WITHOUT PLATO

Would Socrates' ideas have survived without Plato? Plato, approximately forty-two years Socrates' junior, was probably about five at the time of the battle of Delium. Had Socrates been killed, then the entire nature of Plato's dialogues would have been radically changed and with it the nature of Western thought itself. Even had a mature Plato written philosophical treatises, his dialogues—if there were to be any dialogues at all, since the original genre is patterned directly after Socratic oral dialectic—would have largely been non-Socratic both in form and content. In his autobiographical *Seventh Letter,* Plato says that he was naturally gravitating toward a life of politics until his association with Socrates, and his disillusionment over the philosopher's execution prompted him to turn to philosophy and reject an active life in government.

Much of Plato's singular literary genius draws inspiration from the magnetic character of the aged Socrates, who wandered the streets of Athens, engaging the strong, smug, and secure in tough question-and-answer sessions, and who in the process made such an impression on the adolescent Plato. Plato probably came under Socrates' tutelage sometime in his twenties, roughly in the last decade of the Peloponnesian War (e.g., 410–404 B.C.); the popular tradition relates that before their meeting, Plato was more interested in politics and poetry than philosophy. The influence of the elder Socrates on the young student remained profound until the old man was executed when Plato was twenty-eight.

Socrates is the chief interlocutor in the majority of the Platonic dialogues and the hero of the masterpiece *Apology,* which chronicles his final defense on charges of impiety and moral corruption before an Athenian jury. Socrates' concern that philosophy should deal with ethics, not mere natural inquiry or cosmology of earlier formal speculation, characterizes nearly all of Plato's early work. The idea in Plato that from knowledge comes virtue, and that morality can be taught through rational choices and the suppression of desire, seems to be derived from the thought and actual practice of the historical Socrates. And the notion of Socratic duality— men have souls whose integrity they must not endanger by a surrender to the appetites; the world we sense and live in is but a pale imitation of a divine and perfect counterpart—forms the basis of Plato's investigations into morality, language, the hereafter, politics, and the fine arts.

Quite clearly, had Socrates been killed that evening in autumn 424 B.C., Plato would never have had any firsthand association with the philosopher. Plato's interest in philosophy—if he even would have eventually developed such an interest from other contemporary thinkers—would have had little to do with Socrates. The latter himself wrote nothing; he founded neither a school nor institutional framework to keep alive his work. Socrates received no money for his teaching. The question then arises—in a world where Socrates never met Plato, would we now know anything about the itinerant philosopher and his thoughts at all?

Could there have been any other contemporary record of Socrates without Plato? Our other main source of Socrates' thought is preserved in the works of the historian and essayist Xenophon, whose dialogues *Memorabilia, Apology, Symposium,* and *Oeconomicus* feature Socrates as the main questioner on topics as varied as love, agriculture, politics, and his own career as combatant against the sophists. But like Plato, Xenophon also grew up under the influence of a post-Delium Socrates. He was born sometime around 430 B.C., and was probably at most a year or two older than Plato, making him only six or seven when Socrates was nearly killed at Delium. Consequently, a Socrates dead when Plato was five and Xenophon six or seven, rather than both in their late twenties, makes it likely that none of the works of either Plato or Xenophon would have centered around the lively presence of Socrates as interlocutor, their tough questioner and role model who serves as the fountainhead of their own ideas.

The famous orator and educator Isocrates claimed to be an adherent of

Socrates and he is mentioned favorably in Plato's *Phaedrus* as a star student of the old philosopher. But Isocrates was born in 436 B.C., eight years before the battle of Delium, making him nearly a generation younger even than both Plato and Xenophon. Had Socrates been killed in 424 B.C. when Isocrates was still a boy, the older philosopher would probably have had no indirect influence on the young orator, whose thought seems derivative from Socrates, especially the latter's disdain for radical democracy. It would have robbed Isocrates of any indirect knowledge of a quarter century of Socratic anecdotes and teaching, and his ideas probably would have had little place in Isocrates' massive corpus of work, which was influential in its criticism of both the sophists and radical democracy.

How, then, would we know anything of Socrates' thought without the testimony of Plato and Xenophon? Aristotle, of course, refers to Socrates often, but much of what he criticizes is derived from Plato and Xenophon, inasmuch as he was born (384 B.C.) twelve years after Socrates was executed (399 B.C.). We can assume that a Socrates dead at Delium would also have played almost no role at all in Aristotle's own thinking for a variety of reasons: There would have been no mention of Socrates in either Xenophon or Plato; Socrates would have died not twelve but instead thirty-seven years before Aristotle's own birth. Moreover, a dead Socrates would have been deprived of a final twenty-five years of life in which his own thinking reached maturity. These were the years that gave his ideas a chance to filter through talk of the dinner party or the symposium and private recollection of the last quarter of the fifth century B.C. in Athens. Most likely, a dead Socrates at Delium would not even have appeared by name in Aristotle's entire corpus—much of which gains its power for its deliberate posture against the politics and theology of both Socrates and Plato.

Were there other writers and philosophers besides Xenophon, Plato, Isocrates, and Aristotle who might have captured for posterity Socrates' unique ideas before he marched out at Delium? Thucydides, the contemporary historian and chief source for the battle of Delium, does not mention Socrates in his history at all, an omission that sometimes puzzles scholars. We also have no public or private Athenian inscriptions that mention him by name. Instead, there survive in association with Socrates only a few names of other philosophers who, like Xenophon and Plato, were self-proclaimed followers of the unique Socratic emphasis on philosophy as ethics, and who dedicated themselves to ensuring his memory as a great man who fought, rather than joined, the contemporary sophists, who unlike Socrates took money for their instruction and advocated moral relativism and situational ethics rather than an absolute code of good and evil that might transcend conditions of the moment. The chances, however, that any of these writers would have developed a sizable Socratic corpus of work had the philosopher died in 424 B.C. are small, if nonexistent.

The rather obscure Antisthenes, for example, may have been the same age as Socrates, and even known him well before Delium. Fragments of Antisthenes' work survive and suggest he was especially interested in the Socratic lifestyle, or at least the need for the man of contemplation to set himself apart from society and the temptations of the flesh. But we should doubt that Antisthenes would have kept alive the ideas of a middle-aged, rather than seventy-year-old, Socrates. For one thing, he seems to have written largely to combat Plato, and thereby may have not authored anything had Plato never met Socrates. Plato names Antisthenes as present at Socrates' last hours, and much of what little we know about his work seems prompted by Socrates' martyrdom and the fate of philosophical stalwarts who oppose the mob. Had Socrates died at Delium, then, Antisthenes would not have found his striking model of principled resistance to the ignorant crowd. Finally, we have only fragments of Antisthenes' work: Although he seems to have been known to Aristotle and a few others, the chances that his work in changed circumstances would have survived classical antiquity seem remote. There is no reason to think that had Socrates died at forty-five rather than seventy, we would know any more of him through Antisthenes than the tiny scraps of his work we now possess.

Aeschines of Sphettos wrote seven Socratic dialogues. The theme of many of them, apparently, was a defense of Socrates' association with the dissolute Alcibiades. None of these dialogues survives, except for a few fragments and quotations. But since Aeschines was roughly the same age as

Plato and Xenophon, like the latter two, he met Socrates only *after* Delium—and thus probably would not have devoted his life to a philosopher who did not write and whom he would never have met. In short, without a direct Socratic connection, we have little reason to believe any of Aeschines' work would have survived had Socrates died in 424 B.C.

Phaedon of Elis is just a name. Mere scraps of quotations of his two Socratic dialogues are extant. A near contemporary of Plato and Xenophon, he too was a small boy at the time of Delium. Nothing remains either of the work of Aristippus or Cebes, who both purportedly wrote panegyrics of Socrates. Thus we are left with the conclusion that most Socratic followers who were inspired to write about their mentor did so only after meeting him in the period *after* the battle of Delium—when they were of an age to wander along after the itinerant interlocutor. Many adherents seem to have been prompted to write after Plato began his early dialogues surrounding Socrates' death, either to enhance or reject the Platonic testimony. Socrates' other admirers, whose works are essentially lost, seem to have been influenced especially by his last courageous stand against his accusers in 399 B.C., in addition to the striking contrast between the grandfatherly philosopher and their own youthful zeal and impressionability. But in any case, the works of these lesser-known Socratics were either scarcely known or not highly regarded, and so there is no reason to believe they would have survived had Socrates died a quarter century earlier.

We are left with an inescapable conclusion: Almost everyone who wrote anything about Socrates and his thinking came of age *after* the battle of Delium. Socrates' influential students seem to be nearly all acquaintances from his late forties, fifties, and sixties. Had he died at the battle in 424 B.C., the later Western tradition of philosophy would probably have known almost nothing positive about either his life or thought.

We do, however, have at least one contemporary source for the life of Socrates who knew him well *before* the battle of Delium, a critic who has left us a gripping portrait a mere year after the battle—the dramatist Aristophanes. The picture of Socrates in his *Clouds* (423 B.C.) is not pretty, but a vicious caricature of a middle-aged huckster. Indeed, because of

Aristophanes' influential status, and since he portrayed Socrates on the stage before thousands of Athenians, both Plato and Xenophon spent their entire lives trying to counteract that apparently commonly embraced Aristophanic portrait of Socrates as sophist.

Some scholars have suggested that Socrates' hagiography in the works of both Plato and Xenophon was partly meant as a response to the vehemence of Aristophanes' earlier slander. Other comic poets—Ameipsias and Eupolis especially, whose works are now lost, but who were widely popular during the 420s—also caricatured Socrates on stage and reinforced the devastating portrayal of Aristophanes, whose lasting vilification so bothered Plato and Xenophon.

In Aristophanes' comedy *Clouds*, often considered his masterpiece and produced on the stage in 423 B.C., Socrates is the worst of the sophists, a leader of that infamous collection of slick tricksters who made a living by filling the heads of an idle rich elite with word games and relativist morality, and who were purportedly responsible for the cultural decline of Athens and its increasing lethargy and decadence during the long war with Sparta. In the drama, Socrates attempts to "make the weaker argument stronger." He is a windbag, whose superficial cleverness with words is attractive to untrained minds who are willing to pay for a foolish veneer of learning.

So influential was Aristophanes' invective that in the last speech of his life, as reported in Plato's *Apology*, Socrates attempts to defend himself from the popular prejudice incurred from the attacks of the comic poets. One tradition has it that he watched the comedy, and purportedly stood up during a presentation of *Clouds* to assure the audience he was not bothered by the caricature—an opportunity that also would never have transpired had he died along with hundreds of his comrades a year earlier at Delium.

Without Plato's and Xenophon's earlier acquaintance with Socrates, neither writer would have had any zeal to counteract the more prevailing Aristophanic view. Unlike themselves, the playwright at least had met and known Socrates for a good many years. It is highly likely, then, that our present-day Socrates would largely have remained a creation of Aristophanes and thus survived in history as little different from the notorious

Gorgias, Hippias, Protagoras, and other sophists whose writings are lost, but whose reputations have generally been sullied by nearly all their contemporaries. Socrates would not have been the hero of Plato and Xenophon, impressionable youths who both idealistically worshipped the aged philosopher whom they watched at seventy be unjustly killed by an ignorant mob. Instead, he would have remained the rascal of the cynical and jaded Aristophanes, joining the scoundrels Cleon and Alcibiades, whose reputations as knaves par excellence were cemented forever on the Athenian comic stage. Had Socrates died that afternoon in 424 B.C., whatever and whoever he was until the age of forty-five when he stalked the battlefield of Delium would mostly be unknown and of little interest to us outside the rather devilish creation of Aristophanes.

Finally, it is impossible to gauge the development of Socrates' own thought at age forty-five, inasmuch as he wrote nothing, and Plato's work gives us almost no clue to any chronological evolution in Socratic reasoning. Nevertheless, there is some evidence that his real development as a first-class thinker came during the last twenty-five years of his life, when he attracted the best minds of Athens to his side, such as Alcibiades, Agathon, Plato, Xenophon, and Isocrates. Other near-contemporaries of Socrates, who appear in Plato's dialogues as his close friends are, curiously, often non-Athenian—Phaedon of Elis, Echecrates of Phlius, Simmias and Cebes of Thebes, Aristippus of Cyrene, Euclides and Terpsion of Megara. And these men are interested not so much in ethical questions, but rather in natural philosophy and cosmology—especially Orphic thought, the teaching of Pythagoras, the ontology of Parmenides, the natural inquiry of Empedocles, and the radical views of Anaxagoras. When and where did Socrates meet these other disciples, who seem somewhat different from his later and more famous Athenian adherents?

Perhaps before the outbreak of the Peloponnesian War (431 B.C.), Socrates was even better known outside of Athens, and as an itinerant natural philosopher in the earlier pre-Socratic tradition of speculating about the nature of matter, the cosmos, and the soul. Later, with the outbreak of the war and the difficulty of these former associates to travel freely and to live in Athens (Elis, Thebes, and Megara were all at war with Athens), an older and more Athens-bound Socrates turned his attention increasingly away from these earlier concerns of cosmology to personal ethics, rhetoric, and politics—issues of vital interest as he watched his home city tear itself apart in open assembly during the war. A new following among wealthy, young, and impressionable Athenians suggests a more mature Socrates in his late forties and fifties, who traveled less and focused his philosophy on more germane concerns of everyday life. Thus, not only would we have known little about Socrates had he died in the darkness of Delium, but what little information that would have survived would suggest to posterity a picture of a rather obscure natural philosopher, who only very recently had turned his attention to ethical inquiry inside Athens, and so caught the attention of Aristophanes and the comic poets. The original faultline of Western philosophy—pre-Socratic as cosmology and natural inquiry; Socratic as ethical and moral thought—would never have existed.

PLATO WITHOUT SOCRATES

Can we speculate about Plato's own career without the influence of Socrates? If we would now know very little of Socrates without Plato, what would we know of a non-Socratic Plato, of a philosopher who never met Socrates at all? His most famous treatises—*Euthyphro, Apology, Crito,* and *Phaedo,* the tetrad that surrounds the trial and death of Socrates—would vanish. But even more important, at least a third of Plato's earliest work, the so-called Socratic dialogues, would probably not have been written or at least not written in their present form. Scholars have spent the past century trying to arrange Plato's thirty-one dialogues into some sort of chronology by date of composition—a difficult task given that Plato probably wrote over a fifty-year period and told us little about his own life as an author. But on stylistic grounds, philosophical content, and contemporary references to historical events there is now a rough consensus of "early" work (*Apology, Crito, Laches, Lysis, Charmides, Euthyphro, Hippias Major* and *Minor, Protagoras, Gorgias,* and *Ion*) written in Plato's thirties and forties (i.e., 390s

B.C.), which are rather distinct from twelve subsequent "middle" dialogues (written in the 380s and 370s B.C.) and a final eight "late" works (composed in the 360s and 350s B.C.)

The first group of dialogues are usually considered to deal primary with moral issues and the need to establish proper definitions of ethical problems—in contrast with Plato's middle and later interests that turn to metaphysics, ontology, and epistemology. In addition, Socrates is the primary figure of Plato's first eleven dialogues, but he seems to fade somewhat in importance in later texts; indeed, in the *Laws*, considered one of Plato's last treatises, he does not appear at all. Some scholars even believe that Plato began his early dialogues while in his twenties, at a time when Socrates was still alive (e.g. 408–399 B.C.). In any case, it seems likely that at least eleven of his most important works were written within a decade and a half of Socrates' death, employed Socrates as chief questioner, and dealt with concerns made famous by Socrates during the last years of his life. Had Plato never met Socrates, then these eleven dialogues either would not exist or would not exist in their present form.

Plato's middle and later dialogues, in contrast, when the memory of Socrates was decades past, show increasing interest in the work of Parmenides, Protagoras, and Empedocles, and draw directly on their notions of causation, change, sensation, cosmology, and reincarnation. Like the younger Socrates, Plato seems to regard these earlier thinkers—who unlike Socrates wrote substantially—the most influential philosophers of the Greek tradition. As Plato matured, as the memory of life and conversations with Socrates dimmed, and as the value of the written philosophical texts of others was more appreciated, Plato seems to have diverged from Socrates in important areas of philosophy and to have drawn on these earlier giants. Thus an irony arises: The philosophical interests of the elder Plato resemble somewhat the thought of the younger Socrates, suggesting that the last two decades of Socrates' life were an exceptional period in the history of Greek philosophical thought, devoted far more to the practical and ethical, and attuned to debunking the false knowledge prevalent in the streets of Athens. Had Socrates died at forty-five in 424 B.C. at Delium, it is likely that at least a third of Plato's most interesting work would either be gone or not exist in its present form. Rather, his entire corpus might better resemble his middle and later dialogues and thereby belong more to the mainstream of Hellenic cosmological and ontological speculation.

Finally, Plato seems to have sensed that Delium was a momentous event in Socrates' life, one that was related over and over to the younger student by a variety of associates. Not only is the battle mentioned three times in his work, but there are a number of veiled allusions that arise unexpectedly elsewhere as well. In the utopian *Laws* and *Republic*, the nightmare of Delium is never far away; both the disgrace of the Athenian loss and the Theban sacrilege in the battle's aftermath offer implicit lessons for the military reformer. In the *Laws*, for example, Plato urges regular peacetime military drill, regardless of weather, and lasting for an entire day (Delium atypically took place in the late afternoon of November). All residents—men, women, and children—are to join in, but in an ordered and disciplined manner (surely unlike the chaotic mass levee at Delium). There, as in the *Laches*, soldiers are to learn set moves to avoid individual blows. Such exercise will be especially valuable when the fighting is fluid "and the ranks broken and it is necessary to fight one on one, either in pursuing after someone who is defending himself or in retreating yourself and beating off the attack of another"—as Socrates must have learned at Delium.

In his utopia of the *Republic* the infamous retreat and carnage of Delium also drew his attention. Fathers (does he have his stepfather Pyrilampes in mind?) are to take their sons out to the battlefield to make them watch the fighting, with the guarantee that the "older guides" can direct them away in safe retreat "if the need arises." Those who are caught alive (again, like his stepfather?) are not to be ransomed but left to the desires of the enemy. In contrast, the courageous—i.e., the Socratic—shall be given military prizes for their heroism. Plato continues that the dead shall not be stripped nor desecrated, and insists that the corpses of the defeated must be returned to their countrymen for a decent burial (in contrast to the notorious Theban behavior). Nor should the Greeks (as the Thebans did after Delium) display the weapons of the defeated in sanctuaries as dedicatory offerings, but instead regard such desecration as a "pollution." Although Plato himself may have seen brief military service for two years during the Corinthian

War (394–95 B.C.), his discussions of war in large part draw on the experience of Socrates and are predicated on both his presence and survival at Delium.

SOCRATES' DEATH AT DELIUM AND THE LATER WESTERN TRADITION OF PHILOSOPHY AND POLITICS

One of the most moving texts in Western literature is Plato's *Apology*, the account of Socrates' final rebuttal before his peers in the Athenian jury. The influence of Plato's version of the speech has been enormous in the past two and a half millennia. Two fundamental traditions in the practice of Western philosophy followed from that majestic defense. First, is the accepted notion that society will kill those who question its authority and values, and thus the role of the true philosopher is properly to be tragic, inasmuch as an outsider he will inevitably meet with the revenge of the masses if he remains true to his ideas. Second, democracy—not oligarchy or autocracy—killed Socrates. In large part because of the trial and execution of Socrates, Athenian democracy suffered a terrible reputation among subsequent political and philosophical thinkers, from Cicero to Machiavelli to almost every subsequent major philosopher, until the late eighteenth-century revolutionaries in France and America.

In addition, the early Christian apologists of late antiquity, many responding to the renewed interest in Socrates among the Neoplatonist renaissance, who emphasized the mystical nature of Plato's work, found the parallel with the martyr Jesus especially unmistakable—both men were teachers who wrote nothing but were quoted widely by a close cadre of disciples; both were dragged before the mob, publicly humiliated, and then executed by lesser men who represented a frightened and paranoid establishment. In the early Christian apologists' view, Socrates' courageous end—and his advocacy of preferring to be hurt rather than to hurt others—was confirmation of his prescience: he surely had a blessed premonition of Jesus—and therefore, like Jesus, preached that we do not die with our bodies, but rather have an eternal soul that lives on after us. Socratic thought, via Plato, became critical to the early exegesis of the Christian Church.

Thus, there would have been no image of Socrates as pre-Christian pagan martyr had he died at Delium. Rather than a tragic man of conscience, he would have been a rather nondescript Athenian patriot and sophistic thinker who died during a bloodbath. In that sense, Socrates would have been embraced by, rather than at odds with, Athenian democracy. Nor would we have such a negative appraisal of Athenian democracy itself, had it honored Socrates as a fallen warrior of 424 rather than executed him as the perceived subversive agitator and tutor to the right-wing revolutionaries of 404 B.C. who for a time overthrew the government. Most of the animus of the democracy toward Socrates did not, as alleged, derive simply from his radical philosophizing as much from charges that his former students and associates toppled democratic government while he stood idly by.

In conclusion, Socrates fought in three battles, but it is his brush with death at Delium that captured the popular imagination of contemporary Greeks, a battle that was a nightmarish slaughter right on the border of Athens. That obscure battle has had a number of other ripples in Greek history: the shameful treatment of the Athenian dead later prompted Euripides' tragedy *Suppliants,* a play in which the Thebans are chastised for not burying the corpse of Polynices; Thebes itself underwent an artistic and architectural renaissance from the sale of the vast Athenian booty looted after the battle; and Alcibiades might have never convinced his peers to sail to Sicily nine years later without the heroic capital the young firebrand earned in his first battle at Delium.

Yet perhaps the chief significance of the battle is the philosopher's close escape from Theban pursuers. On that autumn late afternoon in 424 B.C., Western philosophy as we know it was nearly aborted in its infancy. Had Socrates been speared or ridden down by the enemy, today we would know almost nothing about him. The philosophical tradition would claim him only as an early and rather obscure cosmologist and natural philosopher in the tradition of Pythagoras, Parmenides, and Empedocles—or perhaps a budding sophist. But unlike his other contemporaries, there would not even be fragments of Socrates's own written work.

There would have been no Platonic or Xenophonic Socrates. Plato's own work—even if Plato would have gone on to write about philosophy without the tutelage and inspiration of Socrates—would be far different and probably exist as rather abstract utopian and technical theory with far less concern with everyday ethics or politics in general. A large percentage of Xenophon's work would never have been written. *Clouds* by Aristophanes, not the *Apology* by Plato, would be the sole source of information about Socrates the man, a character not much different from the other rogues who inhabit the Athenian comic stage. A dead Socrates at Delium would mean today there would not be a book in any library or bookstore on Socrates, and Plato himself might be as little-known to the general reader as a Zeno or Epicurus.

More important, Socrates' death at seventy—why and how he was killed—have had fundamental repercussions in the Western liberal tradition. Had he fallen to a spear thrust in the twilight of Delium in middle age and not been led away by a jeering and ignorant mob as an old man, the entire image of the philosopher would be radically different today, and the heritage of democracy far brighter. Twenty-five hundred years after the birth of Athenian democracy, much of the abstract criticism of popular government, ancient and modern, derives from the logic and emotion of Plato—whose political instincts were formed by the life and death of Socrates. In addition, the easy association between Socrates, martyr and founder of Western thought, and Jesus, who died on the cross to establish Western religion, would also not be so obvious. Neoplatonism as the early Church understood it through Plato would have had no ethical foundation without a live Socrates after 424 B.C. Quite simply, had a Locrian horsemen ridden down Socrates that late November afternoon, our present ideas about both Christianity and democracy would be radically different.

JOSIAH OBER

NOT BY A NOSE

The triumph of Antony and Cleopatra at Actium, 31 B.C.

To what extent does love exert a role in counterfactual history? Some would dismiss that as a purely Gallic question. Indeed, Josiah Ober notes here, the seventeenth-century French philosopher Blaise Pascal opined that if the Egyptian queen Cleopatra had possessed a less comely nose, "the whole face of the earth might have been changed." Would unpleasing looks have kept the soldier-politician Mark Antony, one of the most powerful men in the known world, from losing his heart to her, thus taking the first steps on the path to defeat at Actium and, as a consequence, the elevation of the first emperor of Rome, his rival Octavian Augustus? Was love the culprit?

To Pascal (and earlier, Shakespeare), the answer couldn't be clearer. "He who would fully know human vanity has but to consider the causes and effects of love," Pascal wrote in his Pensées. The causes of an infatuation might be trifling but the effects could be fearful, moving "earth, princes, armies, the whole world." Pascal was no doubt being hard on love, as well as on Antony and Cleopatra, but such concerns have made for an enduring tale of human folly. Why not say it? Cleopatra, apparently, was no beauty. Was this the nose that launched a thousand ships? No matter. She had other more fetching attributes. According to the Greek biographer Plutarch, who wrote within a century of Actium, "Her beauty (as it is reported) was not so passing, as unmatchable as other women, nor yet such as upon present view did enamor men with her; but so sweet was her company and conversation that a man could not possibly but be taken." Cleopatra

23

was captivating in another respect. Sex in the ancient world had its practical uses, as golf does in ours. In the ornate tents, barges, and bed chambers of the high and mighty, deals were made and alliances, political and dynastic, were cemented: Lack of virtue was its own reward, and Cleopatra was for much of her life a winner.

No Actium? No gilt-edged suicides? Ober considers some of the alternatives. With Antony and Cleopatra securely enthroned and their progeny guaranteed a future, their capital, Alexandria, might have been the other eternal city of the world. The whole evolving nature of religion would have been different: remember, Actium was fought in 31 B.C., at the threshold of the Christian era.

JOSIAH OBER, the chairman of the Department of Classics at Princeton University, is the author of *The Anatomy of Error: Ancient Military Disasters and Their Lessons for Modern Strategists* (with Barry S. Strauss), *The Athenian Revolution*, and *Political Dissent in Democratic Athens*.

O N A BARREN HILL on the western coast of Greece, above the site of the ancient city of Nicopolis ("Victory City") and some seventy-five kilometers by sea southeast of the popular Greek island of Corfu, there stands a unique and seldom-visited ancient monument. The monument takes the form of a low parapet, well built of massive stone blocks. On the face of the wall the occasional visitor who stumbles upon this place is struck by the deep and peculiar cuttings. Careful work by archaeologists has shown that the cuttings were specifically designed to accommodate the sawn-off ends of great oared warships; when the monument was still intact the wall bristled with delicately arched and highly decorated wooden ship sterns. This is a monument to a great naval victory.

The wall is Roman, dating to the age of the emperor Augustus. The ships that were mutilated to create this monument once belonged to Mark Antony. The monument was built by Antony's one-time partner, brother-in-law, and rival for the role of chief man in the Roman empire: Octavian, later to be called Augustus Caesar, the first emperor of Rome. Octavian Augustus erected this monument and founded the city of Nicopolis as lasting memorials to his most important naval victory, the Battle of Actium (31 B.C.), at which Antony—along with Antony's ally and lover, Queen Cleopatra VII of Egypt—was decisively defeated. Actium richly deserves its reputation as one of the turning-point battles of Western history.

Actium was not the first important battle fought between armies of Romans on Greek soil. As part of the Roman province of Macedonia, Greece had served as unwilling host to several sanguinary clashes between Roman citizen-armies, led by ferociously ambitious Roman politician-generals. Greece had the unhappy distinction of marking the boundary between the western Roman Empire, centered in Italy and extending to Spain, and the eastern Roman Empire, which extended well into Anatolia (modern

ACTIUM: EMPIRE LOST, EMPIRE ESTABLISHED

The Italian Renaissance artist Neroccio de' Landi did this fanciful tempera of the Battle of Actium, where Octavian (who would soon proclaim himself the Emperor Caesar Augustus) defeated

Turkey) and as far east as Syria. Cornelius Sulla had consolidated his position by victories in Greece in the mid-80s B.C. before returning to Italy to smash the supporters of Marius. Then Julius Caesar had crushed his rival, Pompey the Great, at Thessalian Pharsalus, in northeastern Greece. Next, at Macedonian Philippi, Octavian and Antony, at that time still allies, had eliminated the threat posed by Julius Caesar's assassins, the "Liberators," Brutus and Cassius. But Actium was the finale.

At Actium, Octavian defeated his last serious rival and so could finally proceed with his master plan: No longer would the aristocratic Senate dominate an ancient republic; rather the Senate would now be a rubber stamp for a new imperial form of government, a kingdom in all but name in which true power would be vested (if still somewhat covertly) in a single man. Actium also spelled the end of 300 years of Macedonian rule over an independent Egypt. After the battle, Octavian pursued Antony and

Antony and his ally and lover, the Egyptian queen Cleopatra.

(Neroccio de' Landi, 1447–1500, and workshop, *The Battle of Actium*. North Carolina Museum of Art, Raleigh, Gift of the Samuel H. Kress Foundation)

Cleopatra to Egypt. When Cleopatra committed suicide by asp bite rather than accepting the fate of passively marching in Octavian's triumphal parade, the last of the great Hellenistic Greek kingdoms passed into the control of the Roman state. Or, more precisely, into the private estate of the Roman emperor.

With Octavian's victory at Actium, the Roman conquest of the eastern Mediterranean was complete, and the long reign of the Roman emperors was inaugurated—for good (Claudius, Marcus Aurelius) and for ill (Caligula, Nero). And ever since, historians have speculated: Must it have gone that way? After all, Octavian, for all his political acumen, was not noted for his military talents; whereas Mark Antony was among the most skillful generals of his day. Antony brought a vast army and an imposing navy to Actium. How are we to account for Octavian's victory in this epoch-making confrontation? What factor might have tipped the scales of

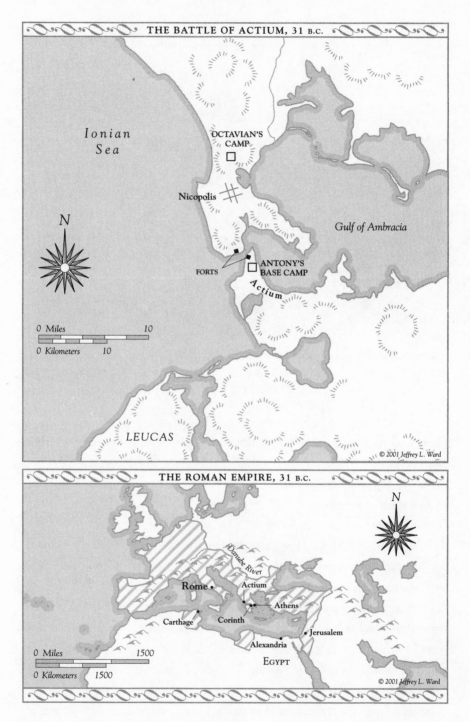

THE BATTLE OF ACTIUM, 31 B.C.

*Ionian
Sea*

OCTAVIAN'S
CAMP

Nicopolis

N

Gulf of Ambracia

FORTS

ANTONY'S
BASE CAMP

Actium

0 Miles 10

0 Kilometers 10

LEUCAS

© 2001 Jeffrey L. Ward

THE ROMAN EMPIRE, 31 B.C.

N

Danube River

Rome

Actium

Athens

Carthage

Corinth

Jerusalem

Alexandria

EGYPT

0 Miles 1500

0 Kilometers 1500

© 2001 Jeffrey L. Ward

war in the other direction, and what might the world have looked like in the aftermath of an Antonine victory?

In one of the most celebrated counterfactual speculations in Western literature, Pascal suggested (in his *Pensées*) that if Cleopatra had been born with a somewhat larger nose, Mark Antony would have defeated Octavian at Actium, and thus the entire course of Roman imperial history (and so, of Western civilization) would have been altered. Pascal's classic "what if?" is predicated on the assumption that Antony was madly in love with Cleopatra, and that his wild passion for her fatally clouded his judgment as a general and a politician. Love, then, was the key factor in Antony's miscalculations in the years leading up to the decisive encounter on the western coast of Greece: Rome was saddled with a long series of emperors because Antony lost his heart over a cute nose.

Pascal's whimsical thought experiment is memorable, enjoying all the parsimonious elegance of "for want of a nail . . ." yet with the added elements of romance and tragically flawed historical characters. Ironically, however, the ancient accounts of Cleopatra do not describe her as a great beauty. Plutarch, who wrote biographies of both Julius Caesar and Mark Antony, claims that Cleopatra's musical voice and great force of character rendered her delightful company, but the biographer notes that she was not particularly good-looking. Indeed the only surviving contemporary portraits of her, on coins minted under Cleopatra's own authority in Egyptian Alexandria, depict the famous queen with a sharp jutting chin and a very prominent hooked nose.

Yet even if we leave out the most obviously problematic elements of Pascal's scenario (the assumptions that male passion must be stimulated primarily by a woman's physical beauty; that women with large noses cannot be regarded as beautiful; and thus that Antony would not have been passionately misled by a large-nosed Cleopatra), his counterfactual is subject to correction on its most basic (and perhaps most attractive) grounds: that is, on the notion that the course of human history was changed by romantic love.

There is no doubt that Antony and Cleopatra were physically intimate (he acknowledged as legitimate his three children by her), or that they contracted a lasting and fateful alliance. But a properly critical reading of the ancient sources leads quickly to the conclusion that there is little reason to suppose that Antony's failure at Actium was a product of foolish infatuation. The real story, patiently restored by a generation of Roman historians, is less elegant, perhaps less romantic, but more satisfyingly complicated and ultimately more historically interesting. The real story of the events leading up to the great battle of Actium suggests that Pascal was right in suggesting that Octavian's victory was far from inevitable—but quite wrong to predicate that somewhat unlikely victory on the biological accident of a petite nose.

The decades leading up to the battle of Actium featured some colorful historical characters, but the era was haunted by a pale ghost: the spirit of Julius Caesar. Caesar had precipitated the second phase of Rome's civil wars when he crossed the Rubicon in arms in 49 B.C. He subsequently defeated his rivals in a series of brilliant campaigns, only to end up assassinated by a group of his closest friends on the Ides of March 44 B.C. Caesar had never declared himself emperor, but the assassins had feared that he was about to do so. He had certainly prepared the way for a new form of government in Rome, one that would take account of the dramatic growth of Roman power and the outstanding political importance of those who could command the loyalty of Rome's highly trained legions. Caesar rose to power on the strength of his undeniable military genius. He had built a reputation as an indomitable warrior, having fought successfully on disparate battle grounds: from naval incursions on the coasts of Britain to prolonged sieges in the towns of Gaul to great set battles in Germany, Greece, and Anatolia to running street fights in Egyptian Alexandria.

It was during Caesar's mopping-up campaign in Alexandria in 48 B.C. that the tough-minded fifty-two-year-old civil warrior had encountered twenty-one-year-old Cleopatra VII, who was then in the middle of her own civil war with her brother and sometime husband, Ptolemy XIII. Cleopatra and her brother were descendents of Ptolemy I, a Macedonian nobleman who had fought for Alexander the Great. After Alexander's death in 323 B.C. Ptolemy I seized the throne of Egypt by force of arms. The throne had been occupied by his linear descendants ever since—and they had taken up the practice of brother-sister marriage early on in order to ensure that ruler-ship of Egypt would remain a Ptolemaic family affair. Not surprisingly the family was not a happy one and young Cleopatra immediately grasped the advantages to be gained by contracting an alliance with the de facto ruler of the most powerful state the ancient world had ever seen. Accordingly, she arranged an introduction (reportedly by having herself smuggled into Caesar's apartments concealed inside a carpet). Making a quick assessment the situation, Caesar declared for Cleopatra. Ptolemy XIII was soon dead and with Caesar's legions behind her, Cleopatra was named undisputed queen of Egypt. She accompanied Caesar on a well-publicized tour down the Nile and, hardly coincidentally, the son she subsequently bore was nicknamed Caesarion—Little Caesar.

No doubt Julius Caesar found the young heiress to the throne of the Ptolemies attractive, but Egypt was much too important a place to allow ro-mantic sentiment to decide questions of long-term leadership. As a leading Roman aristocrat, Caesar had a wide choice of sexual partners, and he was much too serious a politician to throw his support behind anyone he re-garded as less than fully competent. Cleopatra was young, indeed, and a woman, but she had all the other prerequisites to be a successful client-ruler at the fringes of Roman authority. She had the right Ptolemaic bloodline, and so was likely to be accepted by her Egyptian and Greek-speaking sub-jects. And she had demonstrated in the civil war that she had the ruthless determination to do whatever was necessary to gain and hold power: she would never be swayed by family sentiment to spare a potential rival.

But Cleopatra had more than birthright and ruthlessness, she had an es-pecially clear apprehension of what it took to rule the diverse peoples of Egypt—native Egyptians, Greco-Macedonians, and Jews were only three of the most prominent ethnicities. Each ethnic group resident in Egypt had its own historical relationship to the Ptolemaic throne and its own religious rituals. Several had their own quarter in the thriving capital city of Alexan-dria, and their own strongholds in the vast agricultural hinterland formed by the annual flooding of the Nile. Unlike any of her monolingually Greek-speaking royal ancestors, Cleopatra learned at least some of the multiple languages used in her kingdom: she was the first Macedonian ruler of Egypt to speak Egyptian. Cleopatra was intensely aware of the complex set of political, social, economic, and especially religious roles that a successful ruler of Egypt (and client of Rome) would be required to play. And she played these with great finesse: appearing in Egyptian costume in the guise of the goddess Isis for her native Egyptian subjects, promoting Dionysian festivals for the Greeks, and leaving the Jews alone to practice their distinctive rites.

Cleopatra clearly grasped two vital political facts from the very beginning: First, in the age of Julius Caesar (and his successors) the single key factor in the flourishing of Egypt (and thus the ruler of Egypt) was retaining the favor of Rome—and this meant gaining and retaining the favor of powerful Romans. In Caesar's Rome, politics were very personal indeed—alliances were often made on the basis of kinship. And thus whatever she actually felt for Caesar (and there is no reason to deny that she found him good company: Caesar was a highly cultured man and a brilliant speaker as well as a great general), Cleopatra's best move was to contract an alliance with Rome's most powerful man. If possible, it should be the sort of intimate alliance that would result in progeny. Caesar might never acknowledge, in public and in Rome, that he had a son by the Egyptian queen. But Romans were very serious about ties of blood, and Caesar might be expected to look favorably upon a line of succession that would place his own bastard son on the throne of Egypt.

Second, Cleopatra realized that Egypt was both valuable and a potential problem to the Romans because of its wealth and relative security against invasion by land or sea. That wealth and defensible location helped the Ptolemaic rulers of Egypt to weather the fierce and protracted wars of succession that had dragged on for long generations after the death of Alexander. The Romans, for their part, had demonstrated an almost inexhaustible capacity to tap the accumulated wealth of the ancient world—paying the legions, sponsoring the festival games, and feeding the growing population of Rome took a huge amount of money. That constant appetite for wealth had contributed to the complex process by which Rome had absorbed much of the Mediterranean world, and all of the other great Hellenistic kingdoms, into the empire as provinces. Egypt, still technically independent, was a tempting prize. But also a dangerous prize: every Roman province required a provincial governor, and the competitive Roman aristocrats who dominated the Senate had long been worried about allowing any one of their number to take control of what might quickly become a private fiefdom. And so, Egypt had remained independent, but that independence required playing the game of Roman politics with skill, while making it clear that Egypt's wealth was always available to Rome (or to the right Romans) without the necessity of a war of annexation.

The bottom line, for Julius Caesar, was that Cleopatra was a good choice as queen of Egypt, from every perspective: good for Rome, and good for Caesar. That she was delightful company and bore him a son was icing on the cake, no doubt very tasty icing, but never to be confused with the cake itself.

The assassination of Julius Caesar in 44 B.C. threw many career plans into violent disarray and opened up a whole new field of play. The assassins quickly discovered that their "liberation" of Rome from "Caesar the tyrant" was much less popular with the other Romans than they had hoped. They quickly retired to the eastern empire, where they sought to raise money and recruit legionary armies. The most startling single career move was made by Octavian, Caesar's nineteen-year-old adopted son, who got the news of the killing while studying in Greece. Octavian reacted quickly. Sailing to Brundisium on the heel of Italy, he proceeded by road to Rome, picking up a huge retinue of his adoptive father's mustered-out troops along the way. Octavian arrived in Rome as a young man to contend with: that is to say, as a young man at the head of a personal army. Meanwhile, Mark Antony, one of Caesar's most promising lieutenants, had set himself in the forefront of the pro-Caesar loyalists—in part with a rousing public speech in the forum, made famous by Shakespeare ("Friends, Romans, countrymen . . ."). But Antony had dangerous enemies in the Senate, and he soon found himself declared a public enemy and embroiled in a war against senatorial forces in northern Italy. Octavian was dispatched by the Senators (who supposed they could use the youth to their own ends) to help the generals fighting against Antony. But Octavian and Antony found they had interests in common (for the time being at least). In conjunction with a third, well-armed partisan of Caesar, Marcus Lepidus, they joined their forces, forming the Second Triumvirate (the First Triumvirate, an alliance of Julius Caesar, Pompey the Great, and Marcus Crassus, had dominated Roman politics in the 50s B.C.).

The first duty of the triumvirs was to take revenge upon the assassins, who had by now assembled a considerable force in the East, in large part by extorting "taxes" from the unhappy provincials and by squeezing the client kingdoms of the East. Cleopatra, whose own early career had been so closely tied to Caesar's ascendant star, found herself in a very difficult position. Should she declare openly for the triumvirs and defiantly refuse to allow any fragment of the wealth of Egypt to be sent to build the armies of the so-called Liberators? Or should she play a more subtle game and wait to see who emerged as Rome's next preeminent strong man? In the end, she fended off the most pressing of the financial demands of the Liberators with pleas, not of loyalty to Caesar's memory, but to poverty: It seems that Egypt was suffering from both famine and disease and this prevented her from sending the assassins the ships and men they demanded. Meanwhile, Cleopatra covertly raised her own fleet and set out to sea, ostensibly to bring aid to the triumvirs. But bad weather intervened and the fleet returned to Alexandria without making contact with either friend or foe. Cleopatra was straddling the fence, waiting for the next decisive move in a game that would decide her own fate and that of Egypt. She saw that she could not yet hope to influence the game's outcome and the realization taught her an important lesson: Cleopatra would not again willingly allow herself to be a pawn, passively awaiting what fate might bring.

The forces of the triumvirs, well generaled by Antony (Octavian conveniently fell ill and so missed the military action), were victorious at Philippi. In the aftermath of the battle Antony and Octavian effectively divided control of the empire between them, with Antony taking as his primary sphere the East and Octavian the West.

There were scores to be settled in that summer of 41 B.C. Those Roman clients who had aided the Liberators must be punished; those who had resisted would be rewarded. But what of those who had sat on the fence? Just how they would fare would be up to one-sided negotiations with the new master of the Roman East. And so Mark Antony, stationing himself at Tarsus (in Cilicia on the southeastern Mediterranean coast of Anatolia), summoned the queen of Egypt to answer charges that she had secretly aided the cause of the Liberators.

Thus was set the stage for one of the most famous meetings in history: Cleopatra arrived at Tarsus on a sumptuous barge, invited Antony to dinner, and quickly persuaded him that (whatever she had done or had not done during the war between the triumvirs and the Liberators), he would be much better off with her as an active ally than as a deposed client-ruler. Presumably Antony and Cleopatra became lovers at that time; certainly Antony spent the winter in Alexandria, as the queen's guest. But as in the case of Caesar and Cleopatra, the sexual attraction was only one aspect of a larger political game, a game that would determine the course not just of individual careers, but of the Western world.

Antony needed the active support of the wealthy ruler of Egypt to defend and pursue his own and Rome's interests on two fronts. in the East, Antony was concerned with the expansionist tendencies of the Parthians, a bellicose semi-Hellenized people whose loose-knit kingdom stretched from Mesopotamia and the mountainous highlands of Persia eastward into central Asia. The Parthians had taken advantage of the disruptions of the Roman civil wars to push into Roman-occupied Syria, and their incursion potentially threatened the security of the entire eastern empire. The Parthians were a military force to be reckoned with: in 52 B.C. at Mesopotamian Carrhae they had handed Julius Caesar's triumviral colleague, Marcus Crassus, one of the worst and most humiliating defeats of recent Roman military history. Parthian mounted archers had chopped Crassus's infantry to shreds in the open plains of Mesopotamia. The legionary standards, the sacred "Eagles," that were lost at Carrhae had never yet been recovered. There was no doubt that a major campaign against the Parthians must be a central feature of Antony's Eastern sojourn; and no question but that it would be a difficult and expensive campaign. But events in Italy soon complicated the immediate goals (raise money [especially from Egypt], gather and train troops, shore up tottering client states, plan an invasion route that would avoid the open plains, and force the Parthians to come to terms). While Antony had been occupied in the East, some of his relatives had taken it upon themselves to raise an army and attack forces loyal to Octavian. Worse yet, they made a mess of it; the "Antonine" forces were besieged and compelled to surrender in midwinter of 40 B.C.

Antony was thus pulled in two directions: He was eager to begin operations against the Parthians, but if he did not want an open break with Octavian (a break that could only lead to more civil war, and so to more inroads on Roman-held territory by the Parthians), he must go to Italy and take the lay of the land. When he got there he found a complicated situation; along with everything else, one of the sons of Pompey the Great, Sextus Pompey, had raised a navy and was emerging as an independent military factor, potentially threatening Italy's vital lines of supply. Sextus knew that there had been trouble between the triumvirs and offered Antony an alliance against Octavian. But Sextus was an unsavory character with no reputation for sticking by his agreements. Antony stuck by Octavian, sealing their renewed alliance by marrying his partner's sister, Octavia. The de facto division of the empire was renewed as well, with Octavian inheriting the responsibility for looking after matters in Italy, and Antony taking on full responsibility for the Parthian threat. While still in Rome, Antony proved his loyalty by intervening when Octavian was threatened by a mob furious over elevated taxes. Meanwhile, Antony's loyal lieutenant, Ventidius, was pushing the Parthians out of Syria. Antony could return East with a sense of being on top of things; accompanied by his new wife he took up residence in Athens and began preparations for the great Parthian campaign. It appeared, for a while, as if the Second Triumvirate might prove durable.

That appearance was deceptive. Octavian's ambition was not limited to the western empire, but he needed to rack up some dramatic military victories if he were to prove himself Antony's equal in the eyes of the Romans—and especially of the legionaries. Octavian did not have a brilliant military mind; his greatest skills were in the area of politics and shaping public opinion. But he also proved highly adept at attracting talented and loyal people to his side. Among his most important "human resource assets" was Marcus Agrippa, a member of an obscure Roman family who proved to be outstanding at organizing and conducting large-scale naval operations.

Octavian set his sights on Sextus Pompey; crushing the last independent naval operation in the Mediterranean, and thereby assuring his own capacity to control the vital grain supply to the city of Rome, would be a public relations coup. But it would take some doing, not least because Antony was opposed to making war on Sextus, with whom the triumvirs had signed a pact. Ignoring his partner's requests that he desist military operations, Octavian launched an ambitious campaign against Sextus. He immediately ran into difficulties, losing many of his ships to the sudden and violent storms that plague Mediterranean shipping. Despite his irritation, Antony refused to take advantage of Octavian's weak position; instead of backstabbing, he came to Italy and offered his brother-in-law substantial material support. Yet Octavian proudly refused; Octavian knew that he would never cement a reputation as a victorious general if he remained in Antony's shadow. And so the campaign against Sextus continued with ever-higher taxes raised from an increasingly disgruntled Roman population. Antony began to perceive the shape of things to come: The triumvirate would survive only until Octavian felt ready to make his bid for the entire empire.

In 37 B.C., Antony finally turned his full attention to the Parthian campaign, an operation that had been delayed due to his abortive attempt to help out Octavian at the nadir of the campaign against Sextus. Despite their agreement to share Italy as a neutral military recruiting ground, Octavian clearly intended to block any attempt his erstwhile partner might make to raise funds or men in Italy. If he were to take on the Parthians, Antony needed to raise massive funding in order to recruit and train a really big army. And this meant a return to Egypt and Cleopatra.

The queen was ready to negotiate and a deal was struck: She would pay for his legions; Antony in turn granted Cleopatra control of certain client-territories under Roman control and he recognized as legitimate his twin children by Cleopatra: Alexander Helios ("the Sun") and Cleopatra Selene ("the Moon"). Cleopatra was by now in an even stronger position than she had been after the birth of Caesarion (now a boy of ten, and still very much in the succession picture): she was the consort of and the mother of the children of the most important Roman in the East. Cleopatra had played her key cards—Egypt's wealth and her own reproductive capacity—with great skill. If Antony fulfilled his promise as a general, the future of independent Egypt—and the future of its new/old line of Romano-Macedonian rulers—looked very rosy indeed.

The year 36 B.C. would prove decisive: Octavian's renewed campaign against Sextus Pompey and Antony's grand invasion of Parthian Mesopotamia unrolled in parallel dimensions, the one on sea and the other over land. But, contrary to all expectations, whereas Octavian's campaign went like clockwork (thanks to the careful advance planning of Agrippa), Antony's campaign against the Parthians proved to be an unmitigated disaster. The route of invasion, through Armenia and down the headwaters of the Tigris to the heart of Parthian territory, was well thought through—carefully avoiding the open desert terrain that had doomed Crassus at Carrhae. But the departure of the expedition from its Armenian base was unaccountably delayed, forcing Antony to push his infantry ahead of his siege-train in the march south. His ill-defended siege-train was captured by the highly mobile Parthian cavalry. And deprived of his siege engines, Antony failed to capture the key stronghold of Phraaspa, where he probably intended to winter his troops. The client-king of Armenia suddenly withdrew his vital cavalry units. The king of the Parthians refused to be bluffed into turning over the lost Roman standards. In the course of an inglorious Roman retreat north, the "finest army that any commander of that epoch gathered together" (Plutarch) was routed by the Parthians. Antony had lost some two-fifths of his force, perhaps 32,000 men total, mostly to hunger, weather, and disease.

Octavian's glorious naval victory and Antony's disastrous overland failure laid the groundwork for the decisive encounter at Actium five years later.

Antony's options narrowed considerably after his expedition into Parthia. The loss of men, material, and especially prestige in the eyes of his fellow Romans represented very serious setbacks. Before the Parthian disaster, Antony had been able to play a variety of roles simultaneously; now he would have to make some choices. It was no longer possible for him to act at once as Octavian's cooperative partner in the management of the Roman Empire, Octavian's sometime rival for supremacy in the Roman state, and a freelance potentate in the Hellenistic East. At least one of those roles would have to be dropped, and another would have to be prioritized. Antony's subsequent actions elucidate his decision: the facade of cooperative partnership was dropped and the role of Hellenistic dynast became primary. The rivalry with Octavian would continue, but now it would be carried out in terms of the forces of the East, led by Antony and financed by Cleopatra, versus the forces of the West, led by Octavian and financed by Roman taxpayers. Antony's decision was finalized by his refusal to accept fresh troops and supplies offered by his wife, Octavia: the troops were too few, the supplies too parsimonious in comparison with those he could expect from Egypt.

Acting very much as a Hellenistic dynast, Antony moved quickly to shore up his alliances with the lesser dynasts of Asia, especially the king of Media, who might prove an effective counterweight to the expansionist Parthians. He also moved decisively against the treasonous king of Armenia, defeating the Armenian forces in battle and capturing the king himself, who was taken back to Egypt in silver chains. In the aftermath of that victory, Antony held a grand celebration in Alexandria. It had overtones of the official Roman general's Triumph—a sacred victory parade that could only be celebrated in Rome. Moreover, again acting in his role as Hellenistic dynast, he formally granted control over various Asian territories to his young children by Cleopatra. Caesarion was declared joint ruler with his mother over Egypt.

In Italy, Octavian, master of spin, saw that Antony was playing into his hand. The grants of Asian territory, the notorious "Donations of Alexandria," could be sold to the Roman audience as proof positive that Antony had "gone Eastern" and had renounced his primary loyalty to "the Senate and People of Rome." Antony still had many partisans in Rome who clung to the memory of Antony as Caesar's loyal comrade. But Octavian's verbal attacks cleverly shifted attention from Antony to Cleopatra herself. Antony was not to be depicted as a monster, but as the drink-and-love besotted dupe of a diabolically clever and limitlessly ambitious Eastern witch. Octavian concocted a story to the effect that Cleopatra hoped to rule over the entire Roman Empire, establishing her sway over the city of Rome itself. And thus, loyalty to Antony could be recast as treason against Rome. Realizing the growing danger, the pro-Antony senators fled East. With their departure, Octavian enjoyed undisputed control of Rome. Among his first actions was to seize Antony's will from the Vestal Virgins, the sacrosanct priestesses in whose care Antony had left his testament. Portions were read out to the rump-Senate of Octavian supporters: among its scandalous provisions was Antony's request to be buried in Egypt, next to his queen. Proof positive, screamed the propaganda machine, that Cleopatra had seduced Antony into renouncing his Roman heritage.

By 32 B.C., there was no further doubt that the Roman civil wars had entered their next "hot" phase and both sides gathered their forces. With Cleopatra's financial backing, Antony was able to raise an impressive force: some nineteen legions—about 75,000 men, including veterans of the campaigns of Philippi and Parthia; 25,000 auxiliary infantry (non-Roman troops raised from around the Eastern empire); 12,000 cavalry; 500 heavy oared warships; and 300 merchant ships to carry supplies. Antony could not use this mighty force to invade Italy: that would play all too readily into Octavian's story about "Cleopatra the would-be Queen of the World." But it must have been with serious misgivings that Antony took up a defensive position at Actium and awaited Octavian's attack: The "defensive position in Greece" strategy made sense in terms of forcing his opponent to stretch supply lines across the Adriatic, but it had recently proved fatal to the hopes of Pompey the Great and the Liberators.

Fatal as well, as it turned out, for Antony. Octavian's campaign of disinformation mounted a crescendo: the war was a patriotic crusade. Not, of course, against his old friend Antony, but against the terrifying seductress Cleopatra. "All Italy," Octavian later boasted, "of its own volition, swore an oath of loyalty to me." Exaggeration to be sure, but indicative of the tenor of Octavian's public relations effort, an effort that eventually proved corrosive to the loyalty of many of Antony's fighting men and his key senatorial supporters. Antony's problem with maintaining morale in the face of Octavian's hostile propaganda was compounded by Cleopatra's presence in his own camp. As Antony's paymaster and most important ally, she meant to keep a close eye on operations. And we may suppose that her decision to put herself in the center of the action was sealed by the shadow of the period after the death of Julius Caesar, when she had had no choice but to sit on the fence, nervously awaiting the outcome of military events over which she had no control. But the Romans in Antony's camp understood none of this. They increasingly found it hard to deny that there might be some truth in Octavian's charges: Maybe that woman did have some unnatural hold over their commander. And if so, who were they really fighting for after all? For his part, Antony was finding that his role as Hellenistic dynast made it extremely difficult to work with traditional Romans—men who were used to giving commands to oriental potentates, not taking commands from them.

Meanwhile, on Octavian's side, Agrippa was displaying his usual efficiency as an admiral. The fleet headed out from Brundisium, via Corcyra, to establish a primary base at the future site of Nicopolis; Antony's main camp was due south, just across a narrow strait, on the Actium peninsula. By quickly establishing a secondary naval base in a harbor south of Actium, Agrippa bottled up the better part of Antony's warships in the Ambracian Gulf. Meanwhile, Antony's own attempts to force a land battle by using his cavalry to cut off Octavian's camp from its water supply fell short. The campaign was stalemated: Antony dared not offer battle by sea, nor Octavian by land. But defections and disease were decimating Antony's forces; time was clearly on Octavian's side.

By September 2, 31 B.C., Antony was desperate. His only hope of extricating himself from the increasingly dire situation was by risking open battle at sea with his 230 remaining ships. The resulting battle was hard fought, but Octavian had many more ships and the numbers told against Antony's forces. In the afternoon, as the wind came, a squadron of some eighty ships led by Cleopatra's flagship broke through the screen of enemy warships, raised sails, and made a dash south for Egypt. With Antony following, they made good their escape. Octavian's partisans would later say that Cleopatra's flight from the battle was precipitous; but it is more likely that the breakout was carefully planned. Cleopatra's ships, like Antony's, had deliberately carried sails into battle; normally ancient oared ships entered battles stripped of their heavy sails.

Despite Antony's escape, Octavian had won the battle, and decisively. Antony's land army broke camp and withdrew in good order through Macedonia. Octavian the politician knew enough not to press the issue. Rather than challenging Antony's intact land force to battle, he opened negotiations with them; Antony's defeated forces would be bought off. Octavian could afford it. With the whole of the wealthy Eastern empire about to fall to his hands, he had no further reason to worry about money. And fall it quickly did. Antony made no serious attempt to defend Egypt against the invasion that soon followed. He committed suicide by sword. Cleopatra, now Octavian's captive, followed her lover's example by deploying the famous asp. Egypt with all its material and cultural riches became Octavian's personal possession. The eastern and western ends of the Roman Empire were now reunited under the authority of a single man. Octavian was eventually given the name "Augustus Caesar" by his grateful subjects, and the age of the emperors began.

But none of this might have come to pass if the events had proceeded somewhat differently in the year 36 B.C.

Antony's failure at Actium had nothing to do with the size of Cleopatra's nose, and everything to do with the military disaster he suffered in Parthia in 36. It was the loss of men, arms, and prestige that precipitated his fatal decision to embrace the role of Hellenistic dynast, and thus to take on Cleopatra as an ally of equal standing—rather than treating Egypt as a client kingdom, which would enjoy a tenuous independence only for so long as it pleased Rome. That decision cannot have been made lightly—Antony knew enough Roman history to grasp just how hard it would be for an Eastern potentate (even one born Roman) to challenge the sway exercised by the city on the Tiber.

But what if Antony had been more successful in Parthia? There is every reason to suppose he could have been: He was a fine general, his large army was in excellent condition, and his basic strategy (securing Armenia, invading via the Tigris headwaters) was subsequently used successfully by Roman imperial generals. The Parthians would come to terms if pressed; they later turned over the lost standards in a negotiated settlement to one of Octavian's generals—a diplomatic coup that Octavian never tired of trumpeting.

Antony's key error in 36 seems to have been in the timing of the expedition's launch. We will never be able to penetrate the fog of Octavian's propaganda sufficiently to explain why in fact the expedition left Armenia so late in the campaigning season. But let us suppose that Antony had been just a bit more prescient in 38 B.C., and saw then that it would be a waste of time to seek to deflect Octavian from striking at Sextus Pompey. Let's suppose that he saw that it would be a further waste of time to seek to aid Octavian after the disastrous first naval campaign against Sextus. Let us suppose, then, that in 38 and 37 Antony stayed sharply focused on his own impending campaign against the Parthians, putting all of his considerable talents and energies into launching his forces as early as possible in the campaigning season of 36. If the departure had been on time, he would not have been constrained to leave his siege-train defenseless during the southern march. The stronghold of Phraaspa would have fallen to superior Roman siege craft before winter. And thus, there would have been every reason for the pragmatic Parthians to negotiate a deal similar to the one they in fact eventually negotiated with Octavian.

A victory in Parthia in 36 would have dramatically expanded Antony's subsequent options. The return of the standards lost by Crassus would have wiped away the shame of one of the greatest losses ever suffered by Rome's legions. Octavian could not possibly have denied his partner the right to celebrate a grand Triumph in Rome. The prestige of defeating the barbarous Parthians would have more than counterbalanced Agrippa's civil-war successes against Sextus Pompey in the eyes of the Roman people. Antony would have no difficulties recruiting men wherever he pleased. There would have been no realistic possibility of keeping him out of Rome—if, indeed, he wanted to spend time extending his influence in the city. But by the same token, there is no necessary reason to suppose that he would have chosen to spend the rest of his career in Italy.

"Marcus Antonius Parthicus—Mark Antony, Victor over the Parthians" might well have chosen to spend most of his time in the East. There can be little doubt that Antony genuinely enjoyed his life in Alexandria, including the company of Cleopatra. She was in every sense his intellectual peer, and had lived an exciting life in which her successes and failures were direct products of her own decisions. She had a bright sense of humor and was overall splendid company for a man with Antony's background and tastes. In brief, she was a good deal more interesting than most of the Roman women Antony would have known. And Alexandria was a genuinely fascinating, highly cultured city. Defeating the Parthians would have allowed Antony to enjoy Alexandria and Cleopatra's company on his own terms. Whatever their assumed level of equality when in private, he could have maintained a "properly" Roman political distance from the queen of Egypt in public. There would have been no need for the politically embarrassing spectacle of the "Donations of Alexandria"—at least not until Octavian had been dealt with once and for all.

Octavian would indeed need to be dealt with: Julius Caesar's adopted son was simply too ambitious, too power hungry to have allowed Antony to remain at a level of genuine parity. Eventually, and probably sooner than later, there would have been a break between them: the Battle of Actium (or some simulacrum thereof) was bound to be fought. Because Antony lost to the Parthians, events in the five years after 36 B.C. went almost entirely in Octavian's favor, and they fed his increasingly strident campaign of propaganda and disinformation. But that campaign of words and images would have had much less to work with had Antony been successful in Parthia. Rather than the sad dupe of Cleopatra, Octavian would be taking on the man who was unquestionably the premier general of his age. Even with the aid of Agrippa, master of naval operations, Octavian would be hard-pressed to come up with a winning strategy against such a figure and the high-morale army he would command. Even as it actually took place, the Actium campaign was not an easy victory for Octavian. Going up against an army and a general that did not suffer from the "Cleopatra factor" would have been a far greater risk.

Had Antony defeated Octavian's forces at Actium—most likely by forcing a land battle—he would need to return to Italy for at least a while. Like

Sulla in 86 B.C., Antony would need to mop up pro-Octavian forces. And he would need to arrange political matters in Rome to his own liking.

What might his arrangement have entailed? There is not much reason to suppose that Antony shared Octavian's monarchical vision for the Roman Empire—it is more likely that Antony would have purged the Senate of Octavian's partisans and packed it with his own. But then he might have left the aristocracy to rule (within the bounds set by the military strongman of the hour), as it had throughout the period of the Republic. Antony might have divided his time between Rome and Alexandria, between working to ensure the continuity of a stable "Antonine" aristocracy in Rome and establishing Egypt and its queen at the center of a stable group of quasi-independent client states in the East. On this model, Egypt would not have become a Roman province, nor would (for example) Judea. Cleopatra (and her heirs) would dominate the southeastern Mediterranean culturally and economically, careful never to act in any way that might appear to threaten Rome's supremacy. Antony had realized (and would teach his own political heirs) that active rulership of this very tricky part of the world—with its mosaic of religious commitments and cultural traditions—was best left to the Macedonian descendents of Ptolemy I, who had spent generations developing techniques for maximizing revenues while minimizing cultural conflicts.

The long-term historical effects of such an arrangement in the eastern Empire, especially if we imagine the politically astute, multilingual, culturally sophisticated Cleopatra as its behind-the-scenes architect, would have been profound. Mediterranean culture and commerce would have revolved around two great poles—Alexandria and Rome. Interchange between the two would have been constant and intense: Roman exposure to Greek culture would be primarily mediated through the multicultural filter of Egypt's capital city.

Egyptian-speaking Cleopatra would see that the weak point in Ptolemaic social policy had been the segregation of Egyptian and Greek cultures. In her own person she was a cultural fusionist, and with the Roman military to restrain open expressions of resentment on the part of any of her Greek subjects who felt that equity for Egyptians threatened their own privileges, Cleopatra would have been able to make significant inroads in the traditional exclusion of ethnic Egyptians from active participation in the life of the city.

Among the most striking social developments, especially from the perspective of traditional Romans, would be the relatively greater freedom enjoyed by women in Egypt. Under Ptolemaic rule, native Egyptian women, mostly living outside of Alexandria, had retained their traditional rights: they could go into law, inherit real estate, and operate businesses in their own name. Now that pattern of relatively greater gender equality could spread into the capital city. Among the Alexandrian elite, Cleopatra's own example would have provided the model for an expansion of educational, cultural, perhaps even political opportunities for women. An openly multicultural society in which women took on some of the roles traditional Romans had always supposed were uniquely the preserve of men, would have been highly attractive to certain Greeks and Romans—Antony's tastes in culture and society were hardly unique. Egypt would continue to benefit from the talents of immigrants eager to find a place in the relatively open culture that contrasted so starkly with most of the societies that had so far flourished around the Mediterranean basin. The culture that would have emerged within a few generations after Actium might indeed begin to look remarkably "modern" to the eyes of twenty-first-century readers.

Meanwhile, the "Egyptian zone" of the southeastern Mediterranean would remain a center of religious innovation—and a hotbed of imaginative interfaces between religion and state. The early Ptolemies had proved themselves to be open-minded and inventive in the religious sphere, creating a composite state religion based on the god Serapis, which had blended Greek and Egyptian elements. Cleopatra had strongly encouraged identification of herself with the highly popular Egyptian goddess Isis, but she was happy to mix the rituals associated with a variety of deities into the frequent religious celebrations in which she and Antony participated.

If Antony had won at Actium, Jesus of Nazareth, born just a short generation after the battle, would have come to manhood in a very different society—one administered by highly trained professional Ptolemaic bu-

46

reaucrats, rather than nervous Roman amateurs like Pontius Pilate. Those Ptolemaic bureaucrats would have had a much closer sense of how Jerusalem politics worked: they might well have found some solution to local concerns about a self-proclaimed messiah that would not have required his crucifixion. They might, for example, have arranged for him to move to Alexandria, where the sophisticated, hellenized local Jewish population would not be scandalized by his audacious ideas. So Jesus might have grown old, gathering to himself a following attracted by his socioreligious message rather than by a dramatic martyrdom. If so, Christianity would have developed quite differently and Alexandria, not Rome, would be its center.

If the new religion found quick and wide acceptance within the realm, the flexible heirs of Cleopatra would have found a place for it in the festival life of the city, perhaps eventually putting Serapis on the back burner and (like the Roman emperor Constantine in the fourth century A.D.) promoting Christianity as the favored state religion. Let us suppose, for a moment, that Caesarion, son of Julius Caesar, had succeeded his mother on the throne, and (keeping it all in the family, as the Ptolemies were prone to do) had married Cleopatra VIII Selene, daughter of Antony and Cleopatra. They in turn might have had a daughter, who would surely (following highly conservative Ptolematic naming practice) also be named Cleopatra. This hypothetical Cleopatra IX might have come to the throne at the time that Christianity was officially incorporated into the Egyptian state religion, a religion in which the queen of Egypt must of course be a central figure. And so we might imagine that a woman with a remarkable ancestry, granddaughter of Julius Caesar, of Mark Antony, and (twice over) of Cleopatra VII, would become Founding High Priestess—"Lady Pope" of the Universal Alexandrian Church of Jesus the Uncrucified.

In any event, the world we live in would be very different, and perhaps not worse, if the stone-wall monument above Nicopolis had displayed pieces of the warships of Octavian rather than of those lost by Mark Antony at the battle of Actium.

CARLOS M. N. EIRE

PONTIUS PILATE SPARES JESUS
Christianity without the Crucifixion

Take away the crucifixion and you have erased the central moment of the Christian religion. Is it blasphemous to wonder what would have happened if Pontius Pilate, the Roman procurator of Jerusalem, had not ordered Jesus of Nazareth to be nailed to a cross but had spared him? What sort of life might Jesus have led? And, more important, how might the faith that he founded have developed and what sort of influence might it have had? How might the Romans have turned it to their advantage?

That new religion, speculates Carlos M. N. Eire, the chairman of the Department of Religious Studies at Yale University, would have been monotheistic but hardly Christianity as we know it. In essence, it would have been a form of Judaism, but a form that persecuted those who disagreed with its interpretation of Jesus: those who refused to accept him as a prophet or, conversely, those who believed him to be the Messiah—in other words, the people we now know as Jews and Christians. For Rome, a crucifixionless Christianity might have been a blessing, as Eire explains, because such an official state religion could have helped the empire survive into our own time. Still, what would our world be like without an Easter or a Christmas?

CARLOS M. N. EIRE is the T. Lawrason Riggs Professor of History and Religious Studies at Yale University and chairs the Department of Re-

48

ligious Studies. He is the author of *War Against the Idols: The Reformation of Worship from Erasmus to Calvin* and *From Madrid to Purgatory: The Art and Craft of Dying in Sixteenth-Century Spain*. A memoir of his childhood during the Cuban Revolution, *Kiss the Lizard, Cuban Boy,* is forthcoming.

THE PRISONER STOOD before the procurator, bruised and bleeding, his hands bound, and his head ringed with thorns. A crude crown, made by Roman soldiers.

A zero, ringed with thorns, on the head of this rabbi.

The crowd kept calling for crucifixion, but the procurator hesitated and stalled. He couldn't pass sentence. Not that sentence. Not yet. Maybe there was some other way to save this prisoner from death. He had already pronounced him innocent, and so had Herod, the local "puppet" king who ruled over Galilee, the prisoner's homeland.

He kept thinking about that message his wife had sent him, urgently, by means of a servant. Like many Romans, the procurator placed a lot of faith in dreams, especially those that spoke directly to present affairs. Dreams were messages from the gods. And here, in godless Judaea, where they worshiped only one measly deity who was very touchy, and overly jealous, the gods had spoken to his wife.

He couldn't get the message out of his mind, not just because it was troubling, but also because his wife was such a good conduit for messages from the gods. She didn't garble the messages, or get them wrong. She was good at it. Better than most.

"Have nothing to do with that righteous man," the message read, "for today I have suffered much over him in a dream."

He had already tried to free this prisoner by offering the crowd a choice between him and the notorious rebel Barabbas. Much to his chagrin, the crowd had chosen freedom for the accused murderer instead of the rabbi.

And the crowd called for the rabbi to be crucified, again and again.

Accursed place, this Palestine, to which he had been sent. How he longed for those balmy summer evenings in his native Tarraco, in Iberia, on the shores of Mare Nostrum—Our Sea, the Mediterranean. No better place on earth.

He had already ordered a severe scourging for the prisoner, thinking this would satisfy the crowd's thirst for punishment. Then he ordered that the rabbi be paraded before the crowd, arrayed in a gorgeous purple cloak—an ironic joke from Herod—with that stupid crown on his head. Maybe these morons would get the joke and leave the poor man be.

Pilate yelled to the crowd, "Behold your king!"

But the crowd still called for crucifixion. Morons, all of them.

His own judgment and conscience weighed in heavily against giving in to the crowd. And then there was message about the dream. He couldn't dismiss that so easily. No. Not at all.

Pilate spoke: "You brought me this man as one who was perverting the people; and after examining him before you, behold, I didn't find this man guilty of any of your charges against him."

The crowd yelled more loudly: "Crucify him! Crucify him!"

Pilate pronounced him innocent again. And the crowd grew increasingly hostile. "Crucify, crucify him!" Pilate spoke a third time: "Why? What evil has he done? I have found in him no crime deserving death; I will therefore chastise him and release him."

The crowd yelled all the louder. The noise unnerved Pilate, but his conscience unnerved him even more. If he were to release this man, would he have a riot on his hands? What would be the best thing to do here? Spare the life of an innocent man, who posed no threat to the empire, or sacrifice that life for the sake of peace in Jerusalem?

He hated riots. All that property damage. All those corpses, and all those casualties. He hated to lose any of his soldiers, especially.

He hated the thought of having to face his wife too and of having to tell her that he had disregarded her dream. He heard her voice in his own head, speaking clearly and very loudly from the future, any time some misfortune should befall them: "See! See! It's all your fault: I told you not to crucify that man in Jerusalem!" That was it. Yes. That clinched it.

Over the roar of the crowd, Pilate shouted at the soldiers as loudly as he could: "Release the prisoner. Release him now! Forget any additional pun-ishment. He's suffered enough. Release him and escort him back to Galilee. Now!"

He placed his hand on the rabbi's shoulder as he walked by, and neither man said a word. Jesus looked Pilate straight in the eye with a look of total bewilderment. Pilate looked away and stared at his hand—the one with which he had touched Jesus. He stared at it for a minute or so, and at the blood on it. He called for water. "I need to wash my hands," he said to one of the guards.

The crowd went wild, but nothing much happened. A few tried to start a riot, but the soldiers took care of that quickly. Roman soldiers knew how to handle such situations. This was an easy crowd to control, compared to others they'd seen. A few cracked skulls, some broken bones, a few punc-ture wounds. A little bit of blood. That's all. The crowd dispersed within an hour.

Pilate went home early and told his wife about the hard day he'd had and how much he'd appreciated that message she sent him.

It turned out to be a beautiful, sunny spring afternoon. Pilate and his wife drank three jars of wine that evening. Wine from Italy they'd been sav-ing for a special occasion. They toasted the glowing sunset in that godless land, thanked the gods for their messages, fell asleep early on their dining couches, and snored so loudly that the slaves began to laugh and woke them up.

And Jesus of Nazareth returned to Galilee, under escort. There, out in the hinterland, he continued to teach and preach, and to cure the sick, and astound the crowds that flocked to him like sheep. Every now and then he showed up in Jerusalem, especially at Passover—that is, until that rebellion against Rome when the Jerusalem temple was destroyed. After that, he stopped coming to Jerusalem.

Many around him thought Jesus was the Messiah, the savior promised by God to the Jewish people, and he did his best to keep them guessing. Some proclaimed this message, up until the day he died, crucified by his own ag-ing body and its 1,001 infirmities.

And after his death? What?

THE DECISION THAT MADE A RELIGION
Pontius Pilate (second from left) discusses the fate of Jesus, in a fourteenth-century fresco by Giotto. Pilate would elect to crucify the troublesome religious leader, thereby presenting the Christian religion with its central unifying moment.

(Giotto di Bondone, 1266–1336, detail from *The Mocking of Christ*, Scrovegni Chapel, Padua, Italy. Alinari/Art Resource, NY)

• • •

What if Jesus hadn't been nailed to a cross at Pilate's orders? What if he had lived a long, long life? Or even just ten more years? Or one? What if his person and message had been interpreted differently, as they surely would have been?

These are impertinent questions for a believing Christian—questions only an impious dog would dare ask, as John Calvin might have said in the

sixteenth century. Believing that the world was saved through the crucifixion of Jesus is central to the Christian faith. For any believing Christian
this counterfactual exercise is the ultimate blasphemy. The answer any traditional Christian theologian would have to give to our "what if?" question
is quite simple: If Jesus hadn't been crucified, there would have been no redemption from sin and death, and the entire human race would be headed
straight for hell.

Rewriting history with a different Jesus is a daunting enterprise. If you alter the central figure of the Christian religion, what might you end up with?

Religion is such an unpredictable factor in history, perhaps one of the
most unpredictable. It is not entirely rational. Its very nature is to seek
transcendence, and the coincidence of opposites. Paradox is always key.
Sometimes, especially in the case of the Christian religion, the deepest and
largest claims of truth are those that are most radically paradoxical.

This means that if you deal with the wild card of religion in any historical narrative and try to rewrite history, you are balancing on a high
tightrope, and often without a net. Finding "facts" to tweak in religious history is not easy. Even single events, which could be considered pivotal
facts, such as the crucifixion of Jesus, do not lend themselves readily to a
counterfactual approach. This is because religion necessarily involves beliefs, and beliefs are among the fuzziest of "facts."

Even the "minimal rewrite," that is, the changing of one small, highly
plausible fact, is hard to carry off with confidence in religious history. One
of the most common, and most plausible minimal rewrites in counterfactual history is that which kills off the protagonist earlier than he or she died
in real history. The proposition may seem simple enough—but not when it
comes to religion. Consider this: The minimal rewrite that kills off Jesus is
impossible, since it is the fact that he was killed prematurely that started
the Christian religion and remains the basis of an entire structure of belief,
the cornerstone of thousands of institutions.

Any fact related to Jesus, then, is embedded in a thick bundle of para-
doxes. Facts are inverted, folded into counterfacts, into beliefs. The prime
"facts" the historian has to work with in the story of Jesus and the religion
he founded are not bare historical facts, but beliefs. And here is the rub: Be-

liefs leave you with no clearly defined line between the objective and subjective.

Religion is all about interpretation.

And a figure such as Jesus of Nazareth is like a lightning rod that attracts
interpretations. To speculate on what might have happened if anything at
all had been different in the story of Jesus and his followers is to sail in an
infinite ocean of possibilities.

So, what if Jesus had lived to a ripe old age? Or even just one year longer?

It could have happened, easily enough. Pontius Pilate did not have to
condemn Jesus to death by crucifixion. This is what all the gospel accounts
tell us. And the prime reason might have well been a procurator's desire to
heed the warning given to him by his wife, for a complex set of reasons—or
perhaps for a reason as simple and mundane as a husband not wanting to
give his wife yet another chance to nag him for the rest of his life.

So, what might have happened if Pilate had listened to his wife?

Flash forward one year.

Jesus is still attracting huge crowds wherever he goes. It's not just what
he says, but what he does that draws people to him. Especially the healing.
When word comes that Jesus is near, the afflicted as well as the healthy
flock to him. He moves from town to town, as always, never staying in any
one place too long. Many of his relatives still think he is insane, but have
given up on rescuing him from his delusions. Mary, his mother, remains at
his side much of the time, and still supports and encourages him.

He still depends on twelve disciples to help him with his mission. Judas
has been replaced by another man, handpicked by Jesus. As always, all
twelve of them are confused and perplexed. What is Jesus trying to do?
What is going on?

Jesus himself has a very clear sense of who he is and what he needs to do,
but awaits the direction of the Father he always mentions. The Father
doesn't always reveal His intentions, so Jesus goes from town to town healing the sick, preaching the coming of the Kingdom of God, expelling
demons from those who are possessed by them, and, occasionally, it is rumored, raising people from the dead.

Jesus asks himself: "What happened last year?" He thought then that going to Jerusalem at Passover would have been the turning point, the ushering in of the Kingdom of God. He was ready to suffer and die. He didn't like the idea, but he was ready. He had even told his disciples he would be killed. Maybe the Father had heeded one of his prayers on the night he was arrested? "Father, if you are willing, remove this cup from me; nevertheless not my will, but yours be done."

The Father always acted in mysterious ways. When and how would his Kingdom come? He kept telling the disciples that even he, Jesus, didn't know. Only the Father knew.

But he knew he had to go to Jerusalem again at Passover. He had to. Maybe this time he'd be killed. He didn't know what would happen, but he had to go where the Father led him.

It was so different now. There was much less talk about the Messiah among his followers. Last year's arrest had shaken them up. They had all fled. Even Peter, their leader, had turned tail and denied him, as Jesus knew he would. The arrest, and the torture, and the trial had made many redefine their Messianic hopes, and their view of Jesus. Could the genuine Messiah allow himself to be handled so roughly, and come so close to death? Many were now saying that Jesus was merely a great prophet: another Elijah, another John the Baptist.

Jesus listened to what people said. He always did. And many believed he could read their minds.

So he went to Jerusalem again, not knowing exactly what would happen and yet knowing, in that peculiar way of his. This time, thanks to Pilate, no harm came to him. He preached the Kingdom, expelled demons, and healed the sick. And all of the religious elites who despised him could do nothing but wring their hands.

Those Roman soldiers were such good guards. Some were the very same men who had scourged him and beaten him up, but he had forgiven them, and they now had a very special affection for him.

He knew he had to descend into every hell, every single hell, and offer himself up in the place of every human bound by sin. But when would this happen? Not this year, it seems, he thought as he made his way back to Galilee with his disciples.

This scenario repeated itself many times over. Year after year he preached the Kingdom, celebrated Passover in Jerusalem, and waited for the Kingdom to come. He sacrificed his life, hour by hour, day by day, ministering to his people, tirelessly, waiting for the sacrifice to be offered, for his blood to be spilled. Year after year, he received protection from the Roman authorities. They liked what he had to say, despite all his talk about a Kingdom to come. The Romans knew that all of this Kingdom talk is like that of followers of Mithras, or Zoroaster, or even the Egyptian mother-goddess Isis. Spiritual talk, that's all. He taught people to turn the other cheek and forgive their enemies. What a wonderful message to preach to a subject people! Anyone who preached docile submission must be protected, especially if he also encouraged people to pay their taxes.

"Render unto Caesar what belongs to Caesar. . . ."

Emperors Tiberius, Claudius, Caligula, and Nero will hear of this Jesus and heartily approve of having him protected and so will their immediate successors. If only other subject nations could have such a prophet and teacher! So what if Jesus and his followers refuse to worship the gods of the empire? There's plenty of room for that Jewish God in the pantheon of all divinities. No one in their right mind would think that the Jewish God could totally displace all the other gods that exist and are worshiped. So what if this sect balks at worshiping the emperor? Better to allow these people to teach and practice submission than to insist on worship of the emperor. Only that crazy Caligula really believed he was a god, anyway. The others knew better. Any wise Roman knows that Jesus is a gift from the gods—a strange one, since he denies their existence, but a gift all the same. The gods have a strange sense of humor.

By the time he is sixty years old, Jesus has many more followers than he can handle or control. There are so many different ways in which his message and work are being interpreted. So many ways to interpret what Jesus has said and done. So many ways to interpret that change he made in the

57

Passover dinner ritual, in which he distributed matzoh and wine and said, "Take this and eat; this is my body. Take this and drink; this is my blood. Do this in remembrance of me." So many ways to interpret the Kingdom, too, and the New Covenant.

He can manage his disciples, for the most part, and they, in turn, those who are under their care. But the chain of command, though clear enough, stretches too far. And there is plenty of fraying and breaking away beyond that tight, narrow chain. Too much.

At one end he has those who still proclaim him to be the Messiah. Among these there is a whole spectrum of beliefs. Some see him as a spiritual savior; some have no clue as to what he can accomplish, but worship and revere him; some see him as a king in the making—a king who will establish a new order on earth. At the other end, he has followers who hate Rome with a passion and are waiting for him to lead a revolt. To these followers, he is a political leader.

In between these two ends, there are almost as many interpretations of who he is as there are people who follow him. Some believe he is a messenger from the spiritual realm who has come to reveal secret knowledge about the structure of the universe, and to expose and defeat the evil that resides in matter. Some of the intellectuals approach him as a sage and the founder of a new philosophical school. Some believe that he is a great prophet who has come to extend membership in the Chosen People to gentiles. Some constantly change their minds as to what he is, or what he is going to do. All they care about is the healing he imparts to bodies, souls, and minds, or the power he has over demons.

The world is so full of demons. They are everywhere, desperately trying to turn earth into hell. And Jesus has power over them. The demons fear him, and obey him. They leap out of the bodies of the possessed screaming and writhing and foaming at the mouth, and cursing Jesus and his Father. The important thing is that Jesus makes the demons tremble, and obey, and desist.

The most amazing thing of all: Simply invoking the name of Jesus makes the demons flee. You don't have to be Jesus, or even one of his handpicked disciples. You don't have to be touched by him or be appointed to this task.

You don't have to know everything he's said, or to understand it, or even agree with it entirely. All you have to do is have faith in him, invoke his name, and those stinking, accursed fiends bolt back to the nether regions from whence they came.

So many followers, so many views. So hard to control all these people and what they think and say. So impossible.

And then there are those disciples who have fanned out to all corners of the earth. Disciples traversing the entire Roman Empire, even as far away as Iberia and Britain. Disciples beyond the boundaries of the empire. Disciples in Ethiopia. Disciples in Armenia. Disciples in Persia. Disciples as far away as Scythia, Colchis, and the Indus River Valley. Rumors of disciples having made it all the way to the Middle Kingdom of China. And all those disciples in Rome, the seat of power.

These disciples have made tremendous inroads among the Jews who are scattered all over the world: the Jews of the Diaspora. There are so many opinions, and so many teachers, but also so many new disciples. Day by day their number grows throughout the world, and not just among his own people.

By now, also, a very large number of his followers are not Jewish by birth. There are many gentiles who believe that they can be counted among the Chosen People if they worship Yahweh, the True God of Israel, without observing all of the ritual and dietary laws required in the covenant with Moses. Jesus, they believe, has come to announce a new covenant—one that makes all nations children of Abraham. These beliefs were already in place before Jesus came along with his so-called new covenant. Jews had been carrying out missionary activity of this sort before, but now, with the presence of Jesus, and the wisdom he imparts, and the Kingdom he promises, and the cures and exorcisms effected in his name, the missionary activity has a keener sense of purpose. And Saul of Tarsus: what a dynamo, what a wonderful apostle to the gentiles!

Jesus loves to read Saul's letters. The man is truly inspired. By the time Jesus is sixty-six or so, all hell has broken loose on his corner of the earth. The Zealots in Palestine have openly rebelled against the Roman powers. A terrible war has swept over the land. In the end, the Jewish uprising is crushed. Jerusalem is besieged and captured by the Roman forces. The temple is destroyed, reduced to mere rubble. That gorgeous temple, gone, just as he had foreseen so many years ago. The very seat of God's presence on earth demolished. No more place to offer sacrifices to Yahweh, as required by His Law. So many Jews killed. Jerusalem, it is rumored, is awash with the blood of the slain. He knew it would happen, but that doesn't make the news any easier to bear.

Jesus is spared by the Romans. They know they can count on him to keep teaching submission and nonviolence.

Jesus weeps and sobs uncontrollably by the shores of the Sea of Galilee. He has managed to find a lonely spot where he can be by himself. Well, almost by himself. He always keeps some of his favorite disciples near him. That John, especially; he is the sweetest of them all, and the best friend anyone could ever hope to have. John is nearby, and Jesus can hear him weeping too. And those women. None of them are there now, but how could he live without them? They make life bearable when it is at its most unbearable, and they help to make him wiser. They are so far ahead of the men, and the men are too slow to realize it. They fill his life. He loves them so. No women at this spot, this time, though. Better not to let the women know you are crying uncontrollably. A few tears are fine: they can witness that, and have witnessed it hundreds of times, but unrestrained sobbing is another thing. No, that would reveal far too much and would cause more misunderstandings. Every tear is already counted and interpreted in so many ways. What would happen if the women saw this torrent, this infinite sea of tears that merges with all the water in the world, turning each and every drop into a grain of salt.

What if that one woman he loves more than all the others—the one who has so filled his soul for all these years—were to see him crying like this? No. She shouldn't see it. She might not be able to bear it. But John will understand. He always does.

There are really so few people he can trust and rely on. As they all fled once, so could they all flee again. All but John, and the women. Sometimes an awful thought crosses his mind too. Can he trust the Father? Can he rely on Him? Can he, really?

Abhorrent thoughts cross his mind all the time. He is tempted, sorely tempted, as are all human beings. Such an intolerable burden at times, the mind and the body. Wanting this, shunning that. So many appetites. So much that is forbidden, with good reason. So much that is unknown. So much that has to be taken on faith. So much mystery in history.

Such a disaster, such a holocaust. Was this the ultimate sacrifice that would usher in the Kingdom? The temple destroyed one more time, one final time? The end to animal sacrifices, forever? The Ark of the Covenant nowhere to be found? The Jewish people slaughtered yet another time, dispersed to the four winds?

Jesus cries out, as he has taught everyone to do: "Father, dear Father, our Father, who art in heaven, thy Kingdom come, thy will be done, on earth as it is in heaven."

What will his many, many followers say and do now? What shall he do now?

Fast forward, another thirty years or so.

Jesus is ninety-seven years old, and very frail. He can barely see now: he who once healed the blind. Cataracts. He can barely walk: he who once made the lame dance. His hearing is still fine, though. The Word incarnate, as John calls him, can hear just fine. He suffers from arthritis, and his mind is somewhere else most of the time. On some days he doesn't even recognize his favorite disciple, John, who is nearly as old as he is, but still attends to his needs. Jesus' disciples think that his mind is in heaven most of the day and night. He suffers terribly from a hernia that can't be repaired, and from constant indigestion, and a bladder he can no longer control. His hands and feet are so numb sometimes that he can't feel them at all. He looks as old as he feels too: thin, white hair, wrinkled, nearly transparent skin, spots all over his body, blue veins snaking all over too. No teeth left with which to chew.

He who healed so many has chosen not to heal himself, it is rumored.

Jesus wakes up to good news on the last day of his life on earth. He receives word that a woman he healed as a little girl more than sixty-five years ago has come to visit him with some of her great-grandchildren. Many still believe he didn't simply heal her, but actually brought her back from the dead. He loves her visits, and the thought of seeing her again makes him rise from bed eagerly, for a change.

He thinks about the numbers that his disciples toss at him all the time: so many disciples here, so many there. He has followers all over the world, most of whom consider themselves members of the Chosen People. His followers don't all agree. As a matter of fact, more often than not the various sects are at each others throats. Jesus thinks of what might happen once he dies.

He knows what will happen. He's been praying for it not to happen since that awful Passover night, when he begged the Father not to take his life, the night before he was tried and tortured by Pontius Pilate.

"Holy Father, keep them in thy name, which thou hast given me, that they may be one, even as we are one."

He has been praying for it not to happen for over sixty years. He knows that all the divisions that exist already will only grow worse once he's gone. But he doesn't stop praying for it not to happen.

The Father works in mysterious ways.

So many people are now worshiping the one true God and following the spirit of Law of Moses rather than its letter. So many gentiles turned into Chosen Ones, spiritual children of Abraham. So many of them, in so many different places. In Rome alone, the numbers are amazing. In Alexandria, that most learned of cities, there are so many intelligent followers trying to make sense of his message according to the structures of thought invented by Greek philosophers. So many bright scholars trying to fuse Moses, Jesus, Plato, and Aristotle.

The future looks dim and promising at the same time. He is convinced that his physical death is not the end at all, but only the beginning. He thinks back on all his years on earth, ponders his long, long life, and all the pain and joy.

He has spent so much time these last few years reliving his childhood in Nazareth. Does he really talk about the carpentry shop that often? John, ever so thoughtful, has taken to bringing him baskets full of sweet-smelling sawdust. "Nothing like sawdust," says Jesus.

Jesus sleeps with the sawdust next to his head.

This is not what he expected. Not at all. He knew he'd have to empty himself, spend himself totally. But, this? Betrayed by Judas once upon a time. Yes, that was awful, but easier to comprehend. Betrayed by his own body now, and by the Father, maybe. That is not so easy to understand.

So much accomplished. So little accomplished.

He thinks of his visitor that morning. He can't wait to see that little girl, now a great-grandmother, and, as ever, he is eager to embrace the children.

It is then that he suffers a massive stroke, alone in his room, alone with the Father, and the Spirit he is always talking about too, the Spirit he so desperately wants to see take over the world.

"My God, My God, why have you forsaken me?"

Jesus dies within two minutes, his blood spilled, finally, inside his own head. No one is there to see him die, or hold his hand. It is John and the little girl turned great-grandmother who find the corpse. "Oh, look, he's asleep," says the old woman.

Jesus receives a humble, discreet burial, as he had requested many times.

No one, however, will be able to find his body after it is buried. It vanishes from the grave, mysteriously. John and his disciples are accused of stealing and hiding the body, but they claim they buried it properly. Those who witnessed the burial will speak up in their defense.

Three days later, though, some will claim to have seen him alive. The rumors will spread like wildfire. Most who claim to have seen him are in Palestine, but reports will later surface all over the known world. In Rome itself; in Colonia Agrippina, on the Rhine River; in Toletum, in Iberia; in Athens; in Carthage; in Edessa; in Seleucia, near ancient Babylon; in Nubia; far, far away in Varanasi, on the banks of the Ganges River; and even farther away, walking on the Wan-Li Cha'ng-Ch'eng, the so-called Great Wall of the Middle Kingdom. All of the reported sightings say that the resurrected Jesus looks as if he's thirty-three years old again.

And, oddest thing of all, no one dares to claim that they have a relic taken from his body.

Flash forward, about 230 years. The Emperor Constantine is seated on his imperial throne, taking part in the dedication of a new synagogue and shrine to the Apostle John, whose body has been brought to Rome. Constantine is about to make his conversion official. He is almost ready to undergo baptism, the rite of initiation into the New Covenant. He is about to become one of the Chosen Ones, as soon as Passover rolls around, in a couple of months.

This is a remarkable synagogue that Constantine has built, the grandest building in all of Rome. Imagine, having the body of the Apostle John, right here in Rome. Imagine all the pilgrims that will flock to this shrine, and all the miracles that will take place there. Imagine all the honor that will spill over to the emperor who built the shrine, brought the body to Rome, and was there at its consecration.

Constantine congratulates himself for having decided not to build that new capital city out east, on the site of that fishing village, Byzantium. What a dumb idea that was, in the first place. Good thing he didn't listen to those Greek advisers.

Constantine has put imperial muscle to work in unifying all of the followers of Jesus. All of those wrangling sects. Too many of them. Too untidy for the religion of the state. Unseemly for the Chosen People to disagree so much. Calling all of the chief rabbis together at Milan was one of the best ideas he ever had all on his own. They came up with a list of beliefs and defined the Truth for all time. Jesus has been proclaimed a prophet. The greatest prophet of all time. His New Covenant promises to make anyone who is baptized one of the Chosen People. The Messiah is yet to come, at some point in the future. Jesus has helped pave the way for him who will redeem and transform the earth for good. These New Covenanters think of themselves as God's Chosen Ones, since they worship Yahweh, but they despise those Jews who don't accept the teachings of Jesus and still follow the Law of Moses. They also despise those followers of Jesus who proclaim him to be the Messiah, and believe him to have been resurrected. The central rituals of the Chosen Ones are baptism, and the celebration of the New Passover meal, which is celebrated weekly, on the Sabbath. The council has also approved the veneration of the relics of Jesus and those of anyone who has led a holy life. Every synagogue is to have at least one relic enshrined under the pulpit from which the Scriptures are read.

Now that all of this has been defined, Constantine's troops can get busy closing down the synagogues of all those who don't believe the Truth as defined at Milan. Now all of his subjects will share the same faith, and be as one, just like the Prophet and Teacher Jesus, and the Father. Now his troops can descend upon those few misguided souls who still believe that Jesus was the Messiah, and that he rose from the dead. Deluded fools, turning Jesus into the Son of God. Now his troops can also go after those Jews who refuse to pay any attention at all to Jesus. Retrogrades, ignoring Jesus and following Moses instead. Now all those who believe falsely can be wiped off the face of the earth, for the glory of God and the well-being of the Chosen People and their empire.

A little persecution should take care of all those who believe what is wrong.

With the emperors residing at Rome, the western half of the empire remains strong and vibrant in every way, and the Roman cities of Western Europe grow and flourish undiminished by attacks from Germanic tribes. The German barbarians are held back east of the Rhine and north of the Danube and are gradually civilized by the missionaries that the Roman emperors send across the border. The same happens with the Scots and Picts, and the Celts of Ireland. The eastern half of the empire remains as strong as ever too, so the empire remains intact for a few more centuries, until the armies of the prophet Mohammed wrestle away much of the Near East and all of North Africa.

Centuries after Constantine, Roman civilization dominates all of the European continent, including those client states of the former barbarians that were outside the Constantinian borders of the empire, as far north as the Urals. All of these people profess belief in the One God of the ancient Jews. Anyone who doesn't agree with the orthodox religion defined by the rabbis, and approved by the Roman state, is persecuted, even in the client states of northern and eastern Europe. The evolution of the Roman Empire into a loose federation of nation states takes centuries, but is more or less complete by the year 1700 after the birth of Jesus. An evolved form of Latin remains the lingua franca of the entire continent, thanks to its use in all the rituals of the state religion. As to those lands discovered across the Atlantic

Ocean by the client state of the Norsemen in the ninth century, they will be Roman too. Conquered bit by bit, those two continents will be converted to the Roman religion, all the way down to Tierra del Fuego, by the year 1400. Missionaries make their way to Asia too, and contact with the East becomes ever stronger. Around 1250, Australia and New Zealand are discovered and colonized by the Chinese, who have learned a few lessons from the discoveries of the Norsemen.

But all that is in the distant future. Meanwhile the whole world has woken up and found itself Chosen, or so it seems. Chosen Ones, members of the New Covenant revealed to Jesus by God, according to the Council of Milan. Even those barbarian tribes north of the empire's borders are beginning to accept the new religion from Palestine and Rome, and they are becoming ever more civilized and docile. The old gods are dying fast. The old elite families of Rome continue to cling to the old religion, and the simple people mix the old with the new, but there is no denying the fact that the world has been transformed.

The temples to the old gods are vanishing quickly. Many have been turned over to the worship of the One Jewish God, Yahweh. The sayings of Jesus, and the narratives that tell of his life, are now being given the same attention by learned men as the writings of the greatest philosophers. Men and women are flocking to the desert to live lives of prayer and self-denial, just like the Essenes of old, the Jewish sect that had spawned John the Baptist, and influenced Jesus himself. Gladiators are a thing of the past, as are most of the old, cruel games of the arena. Crucifixions? Forget it. They've gone the way of wild orgies.

Some are very, very unhappy about the sexual ethics of this new religion. Will anyone ever be able to have any fun again?

As Constantine watches the long, intricate consecration ritual, he ponders the reconstruction of the temple in Jerusalem. Should he do it soon? Should he do it at all? This new Synagogue of John the Apostle in Rome is so nice, and it has cost so much to build. Isn't this enough for now? Isn't it enough that he has also brought to Rome the bed in which Jesus died, and the clothes he was wearing that final morning, along with all of his meager surviving wardrobe, and those coffers full of his hair and nail clippings?

And what about that most precious relic of all, the golden flask containing all the tears that Jesus ever shed, so lovingly collected by the women who followed him around all the time? Isn't all of this enough for now? Should he give in to the nearly endless requests he receives from all around the known world and rebuild the temple?

Constantine imagines what honor would devolve upon him if he were to rebuild the temple. He could go down in history as another Solomon, or maybe surpass him in fame.

The Temple of Constantine? It sounds so good. Maybe he should also move the capital of the empire from Rome to Jerusalem? Or, better yet, why shouldn't the temple be rebuilt at Rome instead of Jerusalem? Rome: the New Jerusalem? He should ask his advisers. He should ask the chief rabbis too. And he should check with his wife, first. Maybe she's had a dream?

CECELIA HOLLAND

REPULSE AT HASTINGS, OCTOBER 14, 1066
William does not conquer England

*Hastings may come down to us mainly in the form of delicious trivializations like
1066 and All That (the "All That" being the rest of British history). But there
is no getting around the date: The battle was one of those encounters—Salamis,
Saratoga, Gettysburg, and D day come to mind—that, by determining futures,
truly deserves to be called decisive. Hastings, in spite of (or perhaps because of)
the mythic overlays of the victor's history, has the quality of good fiction, replete
with the confrontation of two dominating protagonists. Here were two determined
opponents, Harold Godwinson, who had occupied the English throne for a matter of months, and the man who came from across the Channel to wrest the crown
from him: William the Bastard, duke of Normandy, known to posterity as the
Conqueror. Not just a straightforward brawl in the typical medieval manner,
Hastings was one of those rare struggles in which different styles of war-making
face off: the defense-minded English infantry taking on the cavalry shock tactics
favored on the Continent—although William also relied on archers and infantry
(it was, a Norman knight later said, "a strange kind of battle"). Add to that another quality of a well-made plot, suspense, with an outcome that didn't become
clear until the very end.*

*There was more, evident now as it was not a millennium ago. At that battle-
field in October 1066, Cecelia Holland points out, two rival worlds collided. The
one that emerged victorious would dominate not just the next English centuries but
those of the Continent as well. England at the time belonged to a Scandinavian-*

centered sphere of influence that extended from the Viking fortress towns of Russia to the precarious settlements of Vinland on the North American coast (roughly from Newfoundland as far south as Maine). Opposed was the Franco-Roman world that William represented. He too was descended from Vikings, though his forebears had been settled for a couple of centuries in the country at the mouth of the Seine. Warriors with a knack for the political main chance, the Normans (from Normanni, Northmen*) would carve out principalities as far away as Italy and the Holy Land. England, with its growing population, its grain, and its fine harbors, was the potential cornerstone for a Europe dominated either by the North or the South.*

What if Norman arrows had not killed Harold and his brothers? What if the English infantry had stood firm behind its shields, and the waning light of an autumn afternoon had left them, and not William, masters of the field? Would the sequel of the battle have been played out, not that December in Westminister Cathedral, where William was crowned king of England, but at a later date in the woodlands of America?

CECELIA HOLLAND, one of our most acclaimed and respected historical novelists, is the author of more than twenty books.

I N THE NIGHT word came to Duke William that the English army was approaching down the road from London. It was mid-October, with daylight precious, and William wasted none of it. At once he roused himself and his men and began to get ready. In his hurry, in the dark, he put on his hauberk backward, which several of the men around him were ready to interpret as a bad omen.

William brushed the matter off—as he had dismissed his stumbling, a few days earlier, when he first set foot in England and fell flat on his face. "I have seized England with both hands," he cried then, turning foul into fair.

William had been working for years toward this day, plotting and scheming and arranging. Yet not even he could have guessed that the battle he was about to fight would become one of the most famous in history, or that the victory would decide the fate of Europe for centuries.

With his officers, most of them friends or kinsmen, William heard Mass and took Communion. He hung sacred relics around his neck. The blue banner that the pope had consecrated for him fluttered out on the day's first breeze, and in the cool gray of the English dawn William led his army, some 7,000 men, out to meet Harold Godwinson and his army, to settle the issue between them.

This issue was the crown of England. William's claim to the throne was specious at best, but he could take advantage of the circumstances. After centuries of struggle against the Danes and Norse, England's leadership was decimated. Now the Danes and Norse had momentarily lost their grip and the kingdom was ripe for the taking. The English king, Edward the Confessor, who had died late in 1065, had left no son to succeed him; and Edward's mother had been Norman, William's great-aunt Emma. William had even been able to extort oaths and promises of support from Edward's chief man,

Harold Godwinson himself, the most powerful earl in England, when some years before Harold came luckily into William's hands in France.

The problem with all this effort was that the English crown was elective. When old saintly Edward died, the kingdom's council of elders turned to Harold Godwinson, whom they knew and who was half Saxon, anyway, if not of the house of great Alfred, and made him king. William proclaimed Harold a usurper and an oathbreaker—hence the relics and the blessed banner—and now the Norman duke was coming to get what he wanted.

On the day of the Battle of Hastings, William of Normandy was thirty-nine, a big, hot-tempered, shrewd, and vigorous man who had survived a terrifying childhood, wooed his wife by roughing her up, and mastered his whole duchy at the point of a sword. For his purposes he had assembled what was for the times an enormous force. Besides his own Normans, who had been fighting under his leadership for years, he had contingents of knights and infantry from Brittany, Belgium, and France, even from as far as Italy, including a corps of archers, who led the army down the road as it marched inland. After them heavier armed foot soldiers tramped along, wearing helmets and hauberks, the thigh-length mail coats the knights also wore, and carrying spears and swords. In the back of the army, with his knights, where he could see everything before him, William himself rode beneath the blue banner.

When the fighting started, William did not hold back and direct the action from a distance, like a modern general. William charged and struck and took blows like the rest of his men. In the end, as it had been all his life, he won or lost by the power of his own right arm.

Now he and his army climbed the road up a long hill. As his first ranks reached its crest, they looked out and saw the English.

Before them the road fell away to cross a narrow, marshy valley. Opposite, the land rose again into a treeless ridge, flanked on either side by swamp and forest. As William's army came up over the first hill, they could see the English in a mass pushing up through the forest onto the long height of that treeless ridge.

The road ran on across the valley, up that ridge, and on to London,

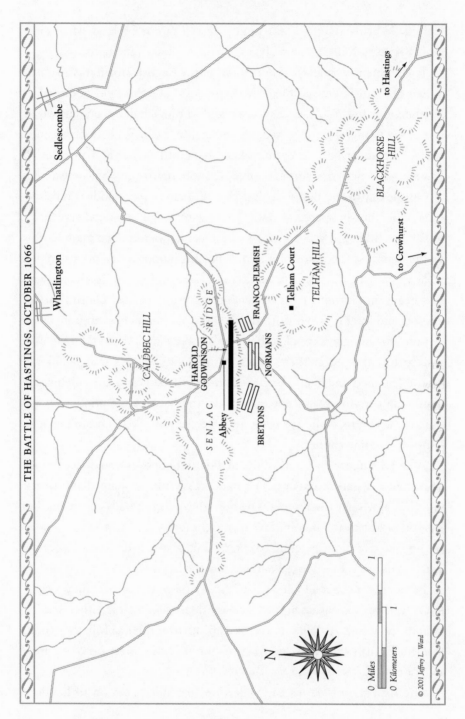

THE BATTLE OF HASTINGS, OCTOBER 1066

Sedlescombe

Whatlington

CALDBEC HILL

HAROLD
GODWINSON

SENLAC RIDGE

Abbey

FRANCO-FLEMISH

NORMANS

BRETONS

Telham Court

TELHAM HILL

BLACKHORSE HILL

to Hastings

to Crowhurst

N

0 Miles   1
0 Kilometers   1

© 2001 Jeffrey L. Ward

England's heart. If William could take London, he could claim to hold the kingdom of England. But now, across the height of the ridge, where the road crossed, the English were building a wall of shields and bodies, to keep William of Normandy out.

There were thousands of these English, including a core of Harold God-winson's own war band, his housecarls, bound to him by a personal com-mitment, and fighting under his gilded and jeweled banner, whose figure was a fighting man. Harold's two warrior brothers were part of this war band, and with the rest of these experienced, well-trained, and well-equipped soldiers formed the center of the shield wall.

Most of the other Englishmen were peasants, farmers and herdsmen, the fyrd, or militia, of the kingdom, bound by long tradition to arm themselves and answer Harold's summons for a set length of time, around a month. They could fight well, but they were untrained and not battle hardened and many had only a stick or a club to fight with.

Harold's army was stout and brave, but one-dimensional, without cav-alry or archers. The housecarls carried tall shields, axes, and spears, but no bows; although they rode to the battlefield, they dismounted to fight. This limited what they could do. Yet on this day what they could do seemed good enough. On the crest of this hill King Harold had chosen an excellent position, making the most of his strengths.

The English army was a tough outfit. William's was the second invading force they had faced in less than four weeks. Halfway through the previous September, Harald Hardraada, the king of Norway, had landed with a siz-able force in the north, near York, to take up again the endless Norse proj-ect of harrying England. Harold Godwinson had gathered his housecarls and marched up to meet him, picking up contingents of the fyrd as he went.

Harald Hardraada—the hard-counsel, or ruthless—was one of the most famous warriors in Christendom, a veteran of battles from Constantinople to Norway. He had with him his personal war band and several other free-lance contingents of warriors, plus some rebellious English, and when a lo-cal army came out to challenge him, Hardraada's force made short work of them. Overconfident, Hardraada sent most of his men back to his ships and waited around at Stamford Bridge to receive the homage and hostages of the city of York, which had prudently gone over to him at once.

Harold Godwinson and his Saxon army got to Stamford Bridge before the homage. They caught the Norse king by surprise and annihilated him. When the rest of his army came up in support, too late, Harold crushed it also. Now, ranged up across the London road on Telham Hill, Harold Godwinson and his English army were ready for Duke William.

This day the sun was high on the hills of southern England. With blasts of horns, William's army advanced across the narrow valley toward the ridge; swamp on the left and forest on the right kept them from flanking Harold's position. William sent his archers up the slope first, to shower the English with arrows; shooting uphill and against the massive shield wall, the archers had little effect, and they fell back as the heavier infantry moved forward. Behind them, William's mounted knights spurred their horses to a gallop.

From the shield wall came the roars and screams of the English. Taking advantage of the height of their position, they threw spears and axes and stones fixed to chunks of wood onto the approaching Normans. The infantry faltered under this hail. William, in the center, charged his knights up into the hard fighting—his men chopping with swords, hurling and jabbing with spears crashing their horses into the shield wall. The massive line of interlinked shields held against them. The English yielded nothing. Crowded together, fighting hand to hand and uphill, surrounded by a deafening din, the Norman duke's whole army began to waver. Then, on the left, suddenly, his men turned around and ran away, down the hill.

Wails of despair rose. The disorderly rout spread rapidly throughout the Norman army. Even William, in the center of the line under his blue banner, had to fall back, and suddenly, he was down.

In the confusion the rumor flew from mouth to mouth that the duke was dead. In a wild panic the Norman army fled away down the hill into the valley, scattering across it, and on the height above them, some of the English broke ranks and rushed after.

But William was not dead. His horse had been killed, but he commandeered another, bounded into the saddle, pulled off his helmet, and galloped along the scattered fleeing ranks of his army, shouting, "Look at me! I am alive, and I will be the victor, with God's help!"

Seeing him, the panicking men began to slow, to hold their ground. William gathered them swiftly and brought them around into a counterattack on the English streaming after them down the hill. All across the field, the faltering Normans saw their duke leading this new charge and swung to join it. The Englishmen spilling down the steep slope had lost their tight formation; the Normans rode them down from either side, broke them into fragments, and wiped them out piecemeal, while Harold Godwinson and the bulk of his army stayed on the hill above.

Harold Godwinson had missed his best chance to win the battle. Had the entire English army charged when William's men fled away, they could well have swept the Normans back, prevented them from regrouping, and harried them into the sea. In fact only the untrained fyrd had charged down from the height after the fleeing Norman army. In the center of the line, the housecarls stayed put.

Possibly they did not attack because no one ordered them to. In the center, under the banner of the fighting man, where the initial fighting had been heaviest, where William and Harold had fought, Harold's two brothers now lay dead, killed in that first terrific clash. Perhaps it was the loss of this leadership that held the housecarls back. Whatever the reason, Harold remained where he was, and now William brought his men under control and turned toward the shield wall again.

"Then an unusual kind of combat ensued," says William of Poitiers, "one side attacking in bursts and in a variety of movements, and the other rooted in the ground, putting up with the assault."

For the rest of the day, the Norman duke poked and probed at Harold's shield wall. Since the disorderly flight of the first attack had come to such a good conclusion, he staged another such retreat, perhaps two, luring the English down the hill each time to be hacked up when the Normans turned on them. The day wore grimly on. The ground was scattered with the bodies of men and horses; the carcasses began to get in the way of the fighting men. The fight looked like a standoff. The English were bleeding steadily, but so were the Normans, and Harold's housecarls stayed solid in the cen-

HASTINGS: FUTURES IN THE BALANCE

The Bayeux Tapestry depicts the events surrounding the Battle of Hastings in 1066, which earned William, the duke of Normandy, the name "the Conqueror." In the section shown here, one of William's commanders (left) wields a club to prevent the flight of Norman cavalrymen, after a rumor has circulated that William has been killed in the battle against King Harold's English troops.

(Section of the Bayeux Tapestry, ca. 1080. Musée de la Tapisserie, Bayeux, France. Giraudon/Art Resource, NY)

ter behind their interlocked shields and held the hill and the road to London. One of the longest battles in medieval history was still grinding on with no resolution. Night was coming. One way or another, it had to end soon.

Hastings was more than a struggle between two determined men. At that battlefield in October 1066, two rival worlds collided, and, going in, the momentum actually favored not William of Normandy but Harold Godwinson.

England in 1066 was part of the great northern community that included Norway and Sweden, Novgorod and Kiev in Russia, Denmark, Iceland, the Faeroes, Scotland and the Orkneys, Greenland, Vinland the Good, and even Spitsbergen, above the Arctic Circle. Northern kings and adven-

turers had been taking England apart for centuries, and the English resistance had shaped the kingdom of Alfred the Great into a realm facing
north. This northern attachment was deep and strong. Norse kings had
ruled York for generations; and some fifty years before the Battle of Hastings, Canute the Great, king of Denmark, overran the whole of England,
was crowned its king, and ruled it successfully for twenty years as the cen-
terpiece of an empire stretching all around the North Sea.

England was saturated with Danish culture. A good deal of England still
lived under Danish law. Many people spoke the Danish tongue as much as
they spoke English. Harold Godwinson himself was a symbol incarnate of
this wedding of Northerner and English. Godwine, his father, had risen to
prominence under Canute, in the power vacuum left by the death and exile of the English royal house, and had married a Danish woman, so Harold
was half Dane. In many ways Harold's brief rule was a continuation of
Canute's as much as the Saxon kingship. The housecarls who held the ridge
against William of Normandy were an innovation of Canute's, a war band
formed on the Danish model.

The bonds between England and the Northern sphere of influence went
far beyond the political. Anglo-Saxon weekdays were Tir's day and Woden's
day and Thor's day, not Mercury's day and Mars' day as it was in neighboring France, a country under a long and heavy Roman influence. *Beowulf*,
the great classic of old English, written in Northumbria, portrays a world
straight out of the Eddas, the traditional Norse poetry telling of warriors
and darkness and grief. The English church, while Christian, paid little attention to the pope; Harold Godwinson had been crowned by an arch-
bishop who was under an anathema from Rome. The English economy was
tied to the vital North Sea trade routes: English goods went in Norse and
Danish hulls across the North Sea to Danish and Swedish trading cities.
The English spoke a Germanic language, heavily salted now with Danish
words, not the Latin-based language of France, Italy, and Spain. From
the perspective of 1066, England belonged more to Scandinavia than to
the southern, Franco-Roman world across the stormy Channel.

This Scandinavian-centered northern economic empire reached the
apex of its energy and power around this time. At mid–eleventh century

the long ships were still visiting Vinland, even if the Norse and Danes had not been able to establish a permanent colony there, and their trade routes to the east, through Sweden, reached all the way to Constantinople.

In 862, the Viking Rurik built the Baltic stronghold of Novgorod; his successor Oleg conquered Kiev; and in the tenth century great fleets of dragon ships sailed the Black Sea, headed for Constantinople. The tremendous natural defenses of the World City daunted them, but they came back, to trade and to hire their swords out to the Byzantine army. Harald Hardraada himself fought Saracens in Sicily under the legendary Byzantine general George Maniakes. Thus Viking trading outposts at Novgorod and Kiev gave Greater Scandinavia access to the East, to the Silk Road, and thus to the whole of Asia.

No one man ever ruled this vast complex, although many tried. The first fierce boom of the north, with its individualism, its legalistic mind-set, its practical ingenuity, was in many ways an equal opportunity employment, a rapidly expanding mosaic of free farms and independent earldoms and petty kingdoms, a few cities. The century before Hastings had produced a handful of ambitious kings, who in 1066 were still struggling to get it all under one crown. For a few decades Canute had ruled the core of this empire, Denmark and Norway—from England. Harald Hardraada, with his connections back through Sweden to the Russian cities, clearly had the same project in mind.

But in the next few centuries the Northern empire retreated. The physical circumstances changed: After a warm spell around 1000 A.D., the climate in the North Sea grew steadily worse. Drift ice floated remorselessly down across the sea-lanes linking the Northern land posts. Where once Viking settlers had grazed cattle in Greenland, now the snow lay on the ground all year round. The Northerners gave up the effort to colonize Vinland, eventually lost Greenland, and even nearly Iceland, as the huge burst of energy that had flung itself out of every fjord and every vik for 300 years subsided and shrank back to its homeland. Novgorod and Kiev became more steadily Slavic than Scandinavian; even the Varangian guard of the Byzantine emperors, named for the Russian Vikings who had first filled its ranks, became mostly made up of Englishmen.

If the North had kept its grip on England, with its growing population, its grain, and its southern, open harbors, might they not have been able to sustain the effort? Then the changing climate might have driven them to expand, not contract. Searching for better land, better lives, they might have built homes in Vinland, spread their colonies down that coast, and linked the whole, Vinland, Greenland, with sea-lanes south of the danger of ice. Following the coast of Vinland southward they would have come on good harbors, better farmland, the best fishing in the Atlantic—prizes worth confronting the native peoples—or, better, since they had no such huge technological edge as the later Spanish and English—coming to terms with them.

Thus, with England as the cornerstone of a sprawling Northern empire, the European migration to the Continent on the western edge of the Atlantic could have begun much earlier than it actually did. What kind of society would the Northerners have built there? Not, surely, a kingdom. Much of the colonization of the North Atlantic Rim was done by Danes and Norse fleeing from the oppressions of greedy brutal kings. The Northern colonies in Vinland and beyond would most likely have been, at least at first, republics, like Iceland, ruled through an Althing, or general assembly. If Harold Godwinson had won the Battle of Hastings, a republic of Europeans could have appeared on the western continent 500 years before 1776—without a revolution.

And without the destruction of the native peoples. The Norse and Danes enjoyed a slight technological edge over the native tribes they encountered, but hardly a decisive one. They would have had to work out some modus vivendi with the tribes they found in the New World, and in one nation, perhaps, the Mohawk, they would have met a people much like themselves—enterprising, agressive, with a certain inclination to popular government. Perhaps a blended culture might have arisen in the dark forests and lakes of the New World—a Viking-Mohawk republic, the westernmost edge of the Empire of the North.

Perhaps at some point one dynasty would have taken all this broad Northern community under a single crown. More likely the great sprawling quiltwork of settlements, farms, jarls, and little kings and republics would have formed a commonwealth, allowing for the Northerners' practical creativity at law and government. The whole community would be bound together by the vital energy of trade, and everywhere the Norse and Danes would encounter other peoples, challenges, ideas to fertilize their continued growth. Snorri Sturlusson could write sagas about the wars with the Mohawk. Buffalo robes and tobacco might sell briskly in Constantinople, and Chinese tea might find its way to the Mississippi. Dragon ships might sail on the Great Lakes, seeking a passage west, carrying crews half native, half Norse. What they charted might have found its way eventually into a Chinese map.

Such a power, connecting the North Atlantic and Baltic Sea and reaching down through Russia to the eastern Mediterranean itself, would have presented a formidable challenge to the rest of Europe. Compared with this Greater Scandinavia, this Northern empire, fueled by a huge trading community stretching across half the world and tied at Constantinople into the whole hub of Asian trade, Latin Europe in 1066 had little to offer.

Latin Europe, in fact, was at its nadir. Centuries of ruinous wars and invasions had battered the little continent into shocked fragments. The popes were struggling to assert some kind of political control over the Western emperor and the rash of little kings; but the territory was lawless and the ox-cart economy slow. England was in fact the richest kingdom of Europe, France a minor power. So in mid–eleventh century, Latin Europe did not look like it was maturing into much of anything. The great Crusades, the counterassault on the Moslem world, were thirty years away; farther still in the future lay the magnificent creative outpouring of the twelfth century, the Gothic bloom of the High Middle Ages.

That splendid future might have never happened. The talent that raised Chartres and founded the University of Paris could very well have gone to embellish courts in Oslo and London and Kiev, draining France and Italy of their creative juices. The German states already shared culture and language with the Scandinavians, and their connection with the Latin world was always uneasy, always complicated by the illusion of the empire. Their interest would easily swing north, toward that great lifeline of trade, that familiar way of life, away from Rome. The pieces of the old Mediterranean world could have become mere satellites of the Empire of the North. If Harold Godwinson had won that October day in 1066, England might have been the keystone of another civilization entirely.

But Harold Godwinson was up against a different breed of Viking.

William of Normandy was descended from Rollo, or Rolf, or Rou, a Norse adventurer who in the tenth century seized the broad rolling lands around the mouth of the River Seine. The king of France, making a virtue of reality, granted him the title of duke and gave him a French princess for his wife. In return, Rollo kept other marauders out of the Seine and away from Paris. The duchy came to be called Normandy, the Northman's country. Rolf's men married local women and produced a hybrid strain, the Normans.

These Normans were tough, hardy, good fighters, and above all, cunning politicians. They fought all over Europe, in Anatolia, in the Holy Land, and everywhere they built states. Norman freebooters, drifting down to Italy in the eleventh century, conquered Sicily, and turned it into the most efficient kingdom in Europe. Norman Crusaders built the principalities of Antioch and Edessa. After the Battle of Manzikert, a Norman mercenary tried to build a country of his own in eastern Turkey. Normandy itself throve, with courts and laws and active dukes who did justice and kept the peace.

In 1026 or close to it the then duke's teenage brother Robert saw a girl wading in a stream and fell in love. Being of noble blood he could command this peasant girl to him, and he did. Their son was born in 1027 or 1028, in his father's castle, but grew up in the house of his mother's father, the tanner Fulbert, in Falaise, where perhaps he acquired the earthy manner that distinguished him all his life. Soon after William was born, Robert, still barely twenty, succeeded his brother as duke of Normandy.

He became known as Robert the Magnificent, and Robert the Devil. He never married, and when, seven or eight years after becoming duke of Normandy, he abruptly decided to go on crusade as penance for his sins, he presented his court with William as his heir.

"He is little, but he will grow," Robert is alleged to have said, and he made his nobles swear homage and accept him. The boy was seven years old. Then Robert rode away on crusade and never came back.

The duchy fell into anarchy. A boy duke could do no justice and command no peace. Every castle was an armed fort, most of them hostile to the boy duke. He grew up under a succession of guardians, men as rough and violent as his enemies. Four of these guardians in succession were murdered, one before young William's eyes; a courtier grabbed the child and hustled him off to hide in the wretched hovels of the village while his enemies hunted him through the castle with swords in their hands.

Yet the boy throve. He grew up strong, blunt, wily, and sober, gifted with the two chief medieval virtues: iron piety and a strong arm. When he was nineteen, half his vassals rose against him in favor of another claimant to the duchy. William made this revolt into the fulcrum of his career; he put down the rising by force of arms, killed or drove out the worst of the nobles, subdued the others, and had the whole country firmly under his control by the time he was twenty-two. Almost immediately, he cast his eyes on England, where his cousin Edward the Confessor was king.

Edward favored Normans. And he was childless. The only heir left to the great line of Alfred was living in Hungary. William began laying the groundwork for a claim to the English crown.

He visited England. He got Edward to make him a vague promise of the throne. When Harold Godwinson was shipwrecked off the coast of Brittany, William went in person to rescue him from the predatory locals and bullied him into taking an oath of allegiance. After Harold had sworn what he assumed was a personal oath, standing before what seemed a plain altar, William whipped back the cloth to reveal a huge collection of relics, making the oath, at least in William's eyes, inviolate.

At last the old king died, giving him his chance. When Harold Godwinson was elected king, William got the pope to consecrate his cause and bless his banner, and then he sent out a general call for fighting men, promising them land in England—if they won. His reputation, and their own greed, brought thousands to assemble on the Channel coast.

There they stayed, idle. William spent the months after Edward's death feverishly building and commandeering boats, gathering over 600, enough to transport his army. But the wind blew foul all that summer, preventing them even from leaving harbor, much less making the treacherous Channel crossing. William fumed and prayed, his army grumbled, the summer wore on into autumn. What would later come to be known as Halley's Comet blazed enigmatically across the sky. Everybody knew that portended some great deed to be done, the rise and fall of kings. But the wind augured otherwise.

William resolved to move his fleet and his army up the coast, to a point where he could catch a west wind for England. This little voyage along the coast was hazardous enough; several boats were wrecked, and a few men drowned. Still the wind blew from the south. William ordered prayers and fasts. He had all the relics he could find paraded along the seashore. At last the wind relented, swung around, filled his sails. The duke of Normandy and his little fleet bobbed away over the Channel. He had only been there a few days when word reached him of Harold Godwinson's approach.

Now, on the battlefield, William was looking failure square in the face. The daylight was fading. He was running out of time. Above the long slope, littered with bodies of men and horses, Harold Godwinson and his shield wall still held the height, his great gaudy banner furling and unfurling above him. Everything, all the scheming and plotting and politics and blood, came down to one final charge.

William had been resting and saving his archers since their first useless round of fighting. He brought them up again and ordered them to shoot in volleys, lifting their bows high so that the arrows would fall straight down on the shield wall. Under the cover of these arrows, William flung his whole army up the hill one last time.

Floods of arrows rained down on the English. Suddenly Harold Godwinson staggered back, clutching at an arrow in his eye. The shield wall gave way, and Norman horsemen poured through, hacking and hewing at the English as they went. Harold went down, and the English broke. Their lord was dead, the day was lost, and they began to flee into the forest. William pursued them into the night, but except for a few pockets of defiance, English resistance to him was over. The road to London was open. On Christ-mas Day 1066, William of Normandy was crowned king of England in Westminster.

Few battles in all of history have been as decisive as Hastings. The out-come of those bloody hours on October 14, 1066, was to wrench England from the northern axis of Scandinavia and the North Sea around to a pro-found involvement with the Southern, Latin world. Henceforth the Northern world waned, and the Latin world blossomed into the glory of the High Middle Ages and the Renaissance. Hastings deserves its reputation as the greatest battle in English history, and a major turning point in the his-tory of the world.

THEODORE F. COOK, JR.

THE CHINESE DISCOVERY OF THE
NEW WORLD, 15TH CENTURY

*What the expeditions of a eunuch
admiral might have led to*

We do not think of China as a nation of seamen explorers, adventurers who probed distant oceans, and for the most part that assumption is correct. There was, however, one brief interval in its history, early in the Ming dynasty at the beginning of the fifteenth century, when China was the preeminent maritime power in the world. These were the years when the Ming emperor Zhu Di—the emperor of the reign known as Yongle, or "Perpetual Happiness"—dispatched armadas of several hundred vessels that carried as many as 37,000 men: His giant "treasure ships," which were up to 400 feet long and over 150 wide, may have been the largest wooden ships ever built. (By comparison, Christopher Columbus's flagship, the Santa Maria, was one-fifth as long, a mere eighty-five feet.) The principal Ming naval commander was a shadowy figure named Zheng He, a man of imposing size, strength, and personal magnetism, whose most enduring characteristic was his lack of manhood. A confidante of the emperor, the eunuch admiral had first served as a soldier in the civil war that brought Zhu Di to the throne. Between 1405 and 1433, Zheng He led seven expeditions into the Indian Ocean basin, reaching Madagascar and the eastern coast of Africa and venturing into the Persian Gulf and the Red Sea; some of his ships may have visited Australia. As Theodore F. Cook, Jr., writes, he "must rate as one of the monumental figures in any Age of Exploration."

The first emperors of the dynasty that would rule China for almost three centuries (1368–1644) were activists, rough-hewn warriors, and builders eager to establish a Chinese presence (and their claim to legitimacy) far beyond its borders. But increasingly the Ming rulers retreated into the Forbidden City, the imperial palace built by Zhu Di in Beijing; some hardly ventured outside its high walls during their entire lifetimes. The real power fell to a retinue of palace-bound civil administrators, many of them eunuchs, who did their utmost to restrict contact with the rest of the world. First the expeditions were called off; later, shipbuilding itself was banned. Enemies of Zheng He even burned his accounts of his voyages.

But how much would history have changed if the Ming emperors had not turned inward—if they had decided instead to continue the great effort that Zheng He had initiated? China had the ships, the navigational technology, and the experience to bring its influence and its civilization to parts of the world that the West would soon dominate. That domination did not have to happen. It is not inconceivable that the Americas—which would not have been known as such—might have been discovered by a Chinese admiral, a successor to Zheng He, decades before Columbus. Would historians talk about the Rise of the East?

THEODORE F. COOK, JR., is professor of history at William Paterson University of New Jersey and an authority on the history of Asia. He is, with Haruko Taya Cook, the author of *Japan at War: An Oral History*.

THE "AGE OF DISCOVERY," the "Era of Exploration," the "epoch of European Expansion and Colonialism," have introduced generations of students to the seafaring exploits of navigators, who, from about 1450 to 1600, first set out onto the Western Sea—the great Atlantic Ocean—and then traversed all the oceans of the world. Yet in the previous half-century, nearly fifty years before the Portuguese caravels sent out by Henry the Navigator crossed the equator on the Atlantic coast of Africa going south, and three-quarters of a century before Vasco da Gama finally reached Calicut in India in 1498, Chinese fleets were poised at the edge of their own explored seas on the other side of Africa. Ready to spread Chinese civilization—economic, cultural, political, and moral values bound together—into what Europeans seemed to regard as their realm of exploitation, Chinese naval forces, sent forth by the Ming emperor himself, had the capability of thrusting themselves into the maelstrom of the history of Western European history as never before.

In the former port of Changle in Fujian Province, on China's southeastern coast, a tablet was erected in 1432 by Zheng He, China's "Admiral of the Western Sea" that evoked a view of the wider world seldom associated with the Middle Kingdom:

We have traversed more than one hundred thousand *li* of immense waterscapes and have beheld in the ocean huge waves like mountains rising sky high, and we have set eyes on barbarian regions far away hidden in a blue transparency of light vapors, while our sails, loftily unfurled like clouds day and night, continued their course [as rapidly as] a star, traversing those savage waves as if we were treading a public thoroughfare.

• • •

Raised to commemorate the seven great expeditions the admiral had organized and led out to the edges of the Indian Ocean Basin beginning in 1405, the tablet is as much a monument to the spirit of adventure, the thrill of ocean sailing, and the experience of a generation of Chinese seamen who shared their admiral's thrill at visiting lands far from their Chinese home as it was a personal proclamation. In many ways, it was to serve as an epitaph both to the admiral himself and to China's great age of sail. Even before the admiral himself died, the dynasty that had sent him forth was implementing a policy that would call back his fleets, undo the web of diplomatic, trade, and cultural relations he had woven over almost three decades, and, by the time of the arrival of Europeans in numbers in the waters of the Indian Ocean, literally reduce his magnificent sea charts and shipbuilding techniques to ashes.

Yet need it have been so? What if China had discovered Europe?

Zheng He (1371–1433) must rate as one of the monumental figures in any Age of Exploration. His origins and personal history were surely as convoluted and exceptional as the biographies of a Bartholomeu Dias, Vasco da Gama, Christopher Columbus, or Ferdinand Magellan. Moreover, his career was tightly intertwined with the rise to power of the third Ming emperor, Zhu Di, the "Yongle" (or "Perpetual Happiness") Emperor, who ruled China from 1402 to 1424. The emperor entrusted to Zheng He the critical mission of leading what became seven stupendous maritime expeditions between 1405 and 1433. These voyages took him and the name of China into what is today called the South China Sea, through the Strait of Malacca, and past the kingdoms that sought to trade on their geographical control what they saw as "the navel of the world." He was to sail beyond into the Bay of Bengal, to Ceylon, up the Malibar Coast of India to the fabled cities of Cochin and Calicut, to the aptly named Arabian Sea—with its ancient sea route linking India to Mesopotamia and Arabia—into the Red Sea, and by land even unto Mecca. Elements of the fleets sailed down the coast of East Africa, past Zanzibar, perhaps as far as Mozambique and Madagascar. There is some evidence that elements of Chinese fleets may even have touched the northern coasts of Australia after calling at the eastern extremes of the Spice Islands.

The future admiral's origins could hardly have been less auspicious or more difficult. Stories of his youth all agree on the essentials of what was to be an extraordinary rise to power. Born in the land-bound province of Yunnan in southwest China to Muslim parents in this region conquered by Kublai Khan in 1253 to '54, and ruled as a Yuan dynasty province under a Mongol prince until the fall of that dynasty, Zheng He was ten years old when General Fu Youde, sent to subjugate the region for China by the first Ming emperor, completed another of his tasks by gathering a number of boys to be sent to the court for service as eunuchs, a class of public servant most highly prized by the Chinese court. Selected for his alertness and courage by the general himself and marked a "candidate of exceptional qualities," after enduring the excruciating agony of castration by knife (which traditionally removed both penis and testicles), the boy was assigned to the retinue of one of the emperor's sons, the Prince of Yan (Zhu Di's title during his father's reign), at the capital of Nanjing. Trained for military service, largely because of his height, powerful build, and imposing presence, Zheng He served on maneuvers along the northern frontier of China and later in battles of the civil war that culminated with his patron, Zhu Di, deposing his nephew and making himself emperor in 1402.

As one of the most trusted associates of the new Son of Heaven, the eunuch was chosen to create and lead a Ming fleet, augmenting already formidable naval forces engaged in the southern seas. It likely seemed a wise diplomatic gesture to dispatch a Muslim Believer rather than an Infidel as plenipotentiary in sea-lanes then dominated by Arab merchant sailors and to the many countries that were Muslim-ruled. Naval experience was apparently less important than loyalty, although Zheng He soon demonstrated organizational skills and leadership abilities; what was described as an "awesome physical presence," must also have justified the emperor's choice. For a eunuch to command a fleet, or army for that matter, was not unusual in Ming times. Indeed major commands were often entrusted to such men. Yet both Zheng He's success and his closeness to his sovereign were eventually to provoke great jealousy and resentment.

MING VOYAGES OF EXPLORATION, 15TH CENTURY

Voyages of Zheng He (1402–34)

Vasco da Gama voyages (1492–99)

Magellan and del Cano voyages (1519–22)

Possible Ming voyages of exploration

GREENLAND

NORTH AMERICA

Atlantic Ocean

Pacific Ocean

Acapulco

Panama

Lima

SOUTH AMERICA

N

Puerto San Julián

Strait of Magellan

Cape Horn

0 Miles   2000   4000

0 Kilometers   4000

© 2001 Jeffrey L. Ward

91

Why the expeditions were ordered is less immediately obvious than the choice of their commander. Their significance must be understood within the broader context of Ming history. Zhu Di became the Yongle Emperor at age forty-two, taking over leadership of the dynasty that his father, Zhu Yuanzhang, the Hongwu Emperor (r. 1368–1398), had founded. The Great Progenitor of the Dynasty, as the founder was styled, had led a successful military rebellion and then military overthrow of the Yuan, or Mongol dynasty, in 1368. A poor peasant who restored native Chinese to the imperial palace by ousting the Mongols and their entourage of Central Asian non-Chinese officials and Chinese sycophants willing to serve at the bottom of the Mongol bureaucratic hierarchy, the Hongwu Emperor's official portrait, now held in the National Museum of China in Taipei, captures his coarse features with his jutting chin, his explosive energy, and potential for violence. The long and bitter battles against the Mongols had entailed military campaigns throughout China and its peripheral regions, and Zhu Di was at the center of these campaigns once he attained his majority.

Zhu Di's usurpation of power from his nephew, and his Shakespearean ambition and simultaneous self-doubts about the morality of his acts, has long fascinated students of what has been called the "Second Founding of the Ming." Using as pretext "the defilement of his father's inviolable institutions" and proclaiming that it was "his duty to rescue the dynasty from the evil ministers exerting undue influence on a young ruler," Zhu Di seems to have sought to equal or surpass the achievements of his illustrious father. Although the former emperor probably perished in the fire that destroyed his palace on July 13, 1402, when Zhu Di's armies stormed Nanjing, his death could not be confirmed absolutely. Fearing that supporters of his nephew might find allies in areas outside the control of the Imperial Government, whether among Mongols yearning for revenge, in the nether reaches to the south, or even across the seas, the Yongle Emperor appears to have decided to make his reign known throughout Asia, to demonstrate that he was now the legitimate ruler of China. Moreover, he determined to invite their rulers to visit his court to offer tribute. His dispatching of fleets under Admiral Zheng He was an essential part of this mission.

• • •

What did these "fleets" sent out by Ming China look like? Was it really possible that China could have threatened the coming European domination of the Age of Sail? Indeed, judging from the way China seems to be perceived even today, casual historians of the era may be surprised to learn that China in the first years of the fifteenth century was arguably the world's preeminent maritime power. At the command of the Ming emperors were among the largest and best-equipped fleets the world had yet known.

No more comprehensive description of the expeditions lead by Zheng He exists in English than Louise Levathes's *When China Ruled the Seas: The Treasure Fleet of the Dragon Throne, 1405–1433.* Not only did her book bring this extraordinary period in Chinese history to the attention of the wider scholarly and popular world, but her peerless description of the eunuch admiral's world helped rescue from obscurity the grand maritime tradition of China.

China's fleets would have seemed to the Europeans of their day to be gigantic armadas, composed of myriad vessels of undreamt-of size and sophistication. The hardy caravels of the Portuguese or Spanish that made the epic voyages of the last years of the fifteenth century would have been dwarfed by the great "treasure ships" at the heart of the Ming fleet, and surpassed in size and capabilities by many of the other ships in the fleets. Zheng He sailed with an array of vessels specializing in all the needs of expeditions that would sometimes number as many as 37,000 men. He had horse ships, capable of carrying horses both from China for his forces or back in the tribute trade. He had supply and provision vessels, freshwater transport ships especially designed for missions in little-known seas near arid lands. He also had at his command a formidable fleet of combat ships including "floating fortresses," armed with cannon and other weapons well suited for bombardment of recalcitrant enemies, troop transports for his substantial land army, and smaller, faster vessels capable of warding off and running down pirates. They were coordinated at sea by a complex system of flags, drums, gongs, and lanterns, intended to allow the ships to remain in communication with one another, and to relay vital information about navigational or other dangers easily and reliably.

In 1402, the Yongle Emperor ordered his admiral to begin assembling a fleet to dominate the Indian Ocean. By 1420 it had become an imperial armada consisting of about 3,800 ships, 1,350 of which were major vessels capable of combat. Of the combat ships, some 400 were large oceangoing floating fortresses and perhaps as many as 250 were giant "treasure ships." The precise size and shape, as well as rigging and alignment of sails of these ships, which seem to have had as many as nine masts, has long been a topic for debate among students of naval architecture. Not only did the Ming fleets contain vessels larger in size than any wooden ships ever built, but they were extraordinarily seaworthy. They were equipped with the latest technology available, including magnetic compasses, sternpost rudders, detailed maps and charts, compartmentation belowdecks, and staggered masts, so placed as to better capture the wind, with sails of the strongest cloth available. In size, the ships dwarfed their European counterparts. Some displaced 1,500 tons, five times the displacement of the ships Vasco da Gama sailed to India.

Whole provinces were mobilized to build these ships. The effort engaged the minds and skills of the technological cream of the state. More than 400 households of carpenters, sail-makers, and shipwrights were transferred from the maritime regions to the shipyard at Longjiang, and thus perhaps between 20,000 and 30,000 specialists were brought together in one great nexus of shipbuilding expertise. Two shipyards were run at Nanjing—one for the normal boats and one for the huge "treasure ships." The dockyards at Longjiang included seven dry docks, most capable of handling ships 90 to 120 feet in width, with two extra-large ones, 210 feet wide, that could accommodate hulls the size of the treasure ships at the heart of the fleet.

While Western historians often claim that knowledge of wind and sea currents in the fifteenth century was considerably more advanced in the West, thanks to the Portuguese and Dutch, the great caveat must be to add "in the waters they knew." For the Chinese, the regular monsoons of the Indian and Southeast Asian waters, the extensive experience of their own countrymen, and the myriad merchants calling in Chinese ports helped make the charts used by Zheng He marvels of simplicity and practical application. Few have survived to the present day, of course, but they reportedly allowed the admiral to calculate a course accounting for wind, tide, currents, and expected weather, from any major port to any objective, reliable to within hours.

The voyages themselves spanned the period from 1405 to 1433. Zheng He began by making a base at Malacca, from which he could operate into the Indian Ocean. From there he traveled to Ceylon, Siam, Bengal, on to Hormuz and down the east coast of Africa. He forged alliances and used force where necessary. The treasures brought back to China included *quilin*, supposedly sacred animals we would call giraffes, zebras, and other exotic African beasts. These were precisely the kind of signs from nature, the "auspicious animals," that the tradition of Chinese dynastic cycles forecast would appear to indicate Heaven's sanction of a ruler's virtue.

On the first voyage, from 1405 to 1407, for example, Zheng He's fleet consisted of 317 ships accompanied by almost 28,000 armed troops. Many of these vessels were mammoth, nine-masted treasure ships with four decks capable of accommodating 500 or more passengers, as well as massive stores of cargo. Measuring up to 124 meters (408 feet) long and 51 meters (166 feet) wide, these treasure ships were by far the largest marine craft the world had ever seen. On the first three voyages (1405–1407, 1407–1409, and 1409–1411), Zheng He took his fleet to Southeast Asia, India, and Ceylon. The fourth expedition (1413–1415), went to the Persian Gulf and Arabia, and later expeditions ventured down the east African coast, calling at ports as far south as Malindi in modern Kenya. Throughout his travels, Zheng He liberally dispensed gifts of Chinese silk, porcelain, and other goods. In return he received rich and unusual presents from his hosts, including the animals that ended their days in the Ming imperial zoo. Zheng He and his companions paid respect to the local deities and customs they encountered, and in Ceylon they erected a monument honoring Buddha, Allah, and Vishnu, a kind of interfaith Rosetta Stone. Zheng He generally sought to attain his goals through diplomacy. But a contemporary reported that Zheng He walked like a tiger and did not shrink from violence when he considered it necessary to impress foreign peoples with China's military might. He ruthlessly suppressed pirates who had long plagued Chinese and Southeast Asian waters, intervened in a civil disturbance to establish his authority in Ceylon, and made displays of military force when local officials threatened his fleet in Arabia and East Africa. These seven expeditions established a Chinese presence and reputation throughout the Indian Ocean basin. Returning from his fourth voyage, Zheng He brought envoys from thirty states who traveled to China and paid their respect at the Ming court. Thereafter, however, the voyages began to lose central support, and hence the momentum and scale of the next two were substantially curtailed.

At just the moment when Zheng He's fleets seem to have achieved their initial assignment, when China's culture was drawing the attention and respect of rulers and traders throughout the Indian Ocean basin, the expeditions suddenly came to an end. As Emily Mahon has pointed out, many historians have expressed the idea that with the shipbuilding and navigational technology evident in the treasure ships, the Chinese could have met Henry the Navigator in his Portuguese home port. Instead, they apparently turned away from exploration, resuming what Michael Wood has called "their traditional inward focus." The analytical methodology used by most Western scholars has been a negative historical comparison, a "why not?" approach. They ask why *didn't* China develop as the West did? Implicit in such investigations is the assumption that something went "wrong," that the decision made by China's leaders could not have been a reasoned choice made by open-minded men, but was instead one rooted in a cultural uniqueness, reflecting a lack of some vital emotional or economic ingredient that subsequent "Western" success in the first age of imperialism would demonstrate. These arguments will not be refought here, but instead some of the main reasons advanced for them need to be touched on before we look beyond to ask what might have been.

As Zhu Di settled into his imperial role, the need for expensive overseas prestige-building missions seemed to diminish; their fabulous expense was seen increasingly to be drawing off resources needed to meet challenges to security closer to home. When challenges on the northern border from the Mongols became more serious, Zhu Di ordered a reduction in the sea service after the fifth expedition, from 1416 to 1419. There was a single, much smaller sixth expedition in 1421, but Zheng He came back early for the dedication of the new Forbidden City in Peking, the Yongle Emperor's reconstructed northern capital. The admiral presided over a parade of auspicious *quilin*. Disaster struck soon after the dedication, however, when lightning caused a great fire, which severely damaged the new palace. The emperor interpreted it as an ill omen: Had his policies put the world out of balance? He manumitted a substantial number of taxes to reduce the financial burden on the people and temporarily suspended future voyages of the Treasure Fleet. Now old and sick, Zhu Di died in 1424 at the age of sixty-four while on campaign.

His successor was his studious elder son Zhu Gaozhi. No warrior, the new emperor began plans to reverse many of his father's policies including the heavy taxation for military campaigns and public projects. However, Zhu Gaozhi died (perhaps of heart failure, perhaps from poison) after only nine months as emperor, and was succeeded in turn by Zhu Zhanji (age twenty-six) in 1426. The fifth Ming emperor was a combination of his warrior, spendthrift grandfather and his scholarly, fiscally conservative father; his reign was a time of peace, prosperity, and good government. He commissioned Zheng He to accomplish a seventh and final treasure ship expedition in 1430, for increased prestige and restoration of the tribute trade. This was perhaps the largest expedition, with 27,500 men and perhaps 300 ships.

Yet in the mid-1430s, the Ming emperors decided to end the expeditions altogether. Confucian ministers, who mistrusted Zheng He and the eunuchs who supported the voyages, argued that resources committed to the expensive expeditions would go to better use if devoted to agriculture. Moreover, during the 1420s and '30s the Mongols mounted a new military threat from the northwest, and land forces urgently needed financial support. Scholars have blamed the introspective culture of the later Ming period for a decline in many branches of science and technology. Launched on command, China's awesome maritime effort was also shut down from the center. In 1436 an imperial decree forbade the construction of new seagoing ships; the large shipyards consequently deteriorated and naval personnel were reassigned. The ability to maintain the oceangoing ships disintegrated and zealous officials seeking to assure that the expeditions would never be repeated destroyed even the records of the fabulous journeys. Zheng He himself died in 1433, apparently during his last voyage.

By 1474 the fleet was down to one-third of its size in early Ming times; by 1503 just a tenth of its peak size remained. In 1500, it became a capital offense for a Chinese to go to sea in a ship with more than two masts without special permission. Later, officials were authorized to destroy the larger classes of ships. Private merchants and shipwrights fled the maritime provinces and the harsh punishments for engaging in international trade, some finding work along the Grand Canal, and many others establishing themselves in the overseas Chinese communities throughout Southeast Asia that had first become a major feature of the region in the early years of the Ming. Moreover, a suspicion that those engaged in the coastal trade were in contact with non-Chinese beyond the reach of central authority and had a penchant for smuggling led them to forbid coastal people from plying their trades legally. This led in turn to an explosion of piracy along the China coasts, with Taiwan as a major center of activity. This development, often blamed on "Japanese pirates" (who were mostly of Chinese origin) resulted in the population of whole districts being relocated away from the coast both to "starve the pirates" and to shut down smuggling, as well as to destroy the nautical skills needed to engage in it.

What had once been a great fleet operating in response to the Imperial Will had disappeared and become such a minor factor in regional affairs that in 1515 a Portuguese envoy archly remarked that "With ten ships the [Portuguese] Governor of India . . . could take the whole of the China coast." Quite a condemnation!

Need it have been so?

What if, instead of curtailing the great overseas expeditions as it did upon the return of the last of Zheng He's missions in 1433, China's rulers had instead rededicated themselves to bringing to the world beyond eastern and southern Asia the news of China's glorious civilization and extending to yet-unvisited places the benefits of association with the Ming Imperial Court and the Chinese World Order? What if the Chinese emperor, instead of following the advice of his Confucian counselors and fiscal conservatives to abandon what they saw as reckless and unprecedented maritime activity had instead allowed it to continue, or even expanded the effort? What if, rather than yielding to a call to return to the "natural course" of Chinese history through a xenophobic looking inward, China's rulers had run the risk of inviting universal acceptance with its potential rewards as well as its hazards? What kind of world might have resulted had the Ming fleets not been reined in?

Imagine a Chinese fleet, substantially smaller perhaps than Zheng He's last East Africa expeditions, but still dwarfing those of the Portuguese, making a reconnaissance down the coasts of South Africa below Mozambique, around the Cape of Good Hope, into the Atlantic—what would surely have been seen from China's perspective as a second "Great Western Sea." Certainly, there was little to hold their attention in this barren stretch of coast, though the ostrich and other animals that hailed from the area would surely have been welcome additions to the imperial menagerie. But, was there enough to provide incentive for an expedition of discovery, taking a Chinese squadron up the western coast of Africa to Guinea or the Portuguese Atlantic islands before the Portuguese arrived in force? Perhaps there would have been just enough to carry them into contact. Confronted with a Chinese fleet—even a smallish one—that had allies and clients along the Angolan, Congolese, and West African coasts, would the Portuguese have continued to see this route to the East as desirable?

It is of course hard to envision the Roman Catholic Church accepting Chinese fleets as anything but one more instrument of the Devil sent to torment Christendom. With the Turks ascendant in the Eastern Mediterranean, the Arabs still powerful in North Africa (though no longer dominant in Iberia), a significant, sustained pressure from the south by yet another alien force could hardly have seemed anything more than another test by God of the Catholic faith. Yet what could the Portuguese have done to prevent it in the middle of the 1400s? Historically, Portugal only fortified Fort Elmina on the Gold Coast of West Africa in 1482. One almost certain outcome of a Chinese appearance on the Cape of Good Hope or the waters of the Atlantic would have been a greatly solidified Chinese position within the Indian Ocean basin and a consequent sharp check on Portuguese expansion. Might not the worst horrors of the Atlantic slave trade been aborted by a halt to Portuguese expansion along the African coast at this early date?

The Iberian princes, still somewhat unsteady on their own thrones, may well have been even less inclined to back "mad adventures" than they were historically. Instead of an East Africa ruthlessly exploited by the Portuguese as they established their first footholds in Angola on the western coast and then in Mozambique on the eastern coast of Africa, Chinese-influenced African kingdoms, perhaps buoyed up in their ability to resist, might have been able to face the Portuguese down or call on their "overlord" for assistance. Rather than European exploitation of many areas in the East from bases in Goa, Malaya, and Singapore, and the East Indies, Chinese control of the Strait of Malacca, even indirectly via a system tributary states rewarded for their obligations to the Dragon Throne, would have been a tremendous asset to any Ming emperor, and a formidable obstacle to interloping European adventurers in the late fifteenth and early sixteenth centuries. A Chinese presence in Ceylon and the Indian coasts, besides further enriching the remarkable cultural diversity of those lands, could well have made local rulers less easily intimidated and less willing to accept the fortified outposts and depots the Portuguese established as a means of asserting their control over routes of trade. Simultaneously, there exists a distinct possibility that the course of Middle Eastern history might have been altered by a continued Chinese presence in the Red Sea near Egypt and in the Persian Gulf.

The westward explorations could have had a reverse effect. If Chinese and client merchants had been able to trade and sell goods in Africa and the West, that Iberian navigators would one day acquire only by sailing halfway around the world, China itself might have been transformed. Had the constraints and controls of state enterprise been loosened, the dividends could have been enormous. The revenue potential of trade with a world seeking the products of Chinese industry and creativity might have brought about something like a mercantile revolution.

Anyone contemplating the might-have-beens of this scenario must engage in the delightful fantasy of a Chinese discovery of America and a pre-

Columbian contact with its peoples. How far-fetched was such a possibility? Certainly it could not have happened until the Chinese had firmly established themselves along the western coast of Africa. Lacking concrete knowledge of a land mass to the west, they would not have had the incentive to brave the devilish currents of the South Atlantic. Moreover, the extensive logistical train that China's approach to naval expeditions had thus far required would not have been suited to a perilous jump into the unknown. But once the entire bulge of West Africa had been incorporated into a Chinese system, probes in the direction of the South American continent would have been more likely. One might imagine a European world in close contact with Chinese fleets along the maritime frontier of Africa forced into a grand strategic defensive in these waters just as it was in the eastern Mediterranean against the Turks, Europe would have had to leave exploration to the Chinese intruders.

An intriguing alternative to the western Africa-to-Brazil route of Chinese maritime expansion might have been a grand trans-Pacific expedition. This would most likely have utilized the northern route, sailing past the Ryukyus, calling at a now still hospitable Japan, and then setting out across the North Pacific to the Aleutians and Alaska. From there, an expedition would have continued down what Europeans would come to call the Canadian shore to California—and beyond. The Chinese could surely have used the trans-Pacific route at lower latitudes, the same one that Magellan's expedition would first exploit in 1521; but, as the Spanish found, while the cross-Pacific route from Mexico to the Philippines was reliable, the reverse direction was much more problematic due to the unreliable currents and vast expanses of empty ocean.

Either route to what would become known as the Americas might have brought peoples of all races of the world under Chinese influence, with local chieftains offering to accept the Ming Son of Heaven as distant overlord in exchange for the wonders of Chinese goods and Chinese recognition. Radically altered diplomatic, cultural, and military exchanges profoundly altering the history of conquest and exploitation that was the fate of the Americas, all raise intriguing possibilities for "Latin" America's course of development. Would the "pre-Columbian" [pre–Zheng He] kingdoms have been wiped out by the diseases of the Old World with the same relentlessness had Chinese been the visitors? Would the Chinese have introduced the horses, guns, and metallurgy, all of which, in the first third of the sixteenth century, might have helped the Aztecs and the Incas keep the Spanish at bay? Or would the Spanish and their militant Catholicism have prevailed, only later in the century? Would smallpox still have tipped the historical balance?

We can be relatively sure that whatever the possibilities for the Chinese beyond Africa, the continuation of maritime and diplomatic efforts in the Indian Ocean basin could have had a great impact on the development of the world along very different lines than the European Age of Discovery we have come to accept as the natural course of world history in the sixteenth century. The Chinese attitude toward the outside world was hardly open-minded, to be sure. Since ancient times, China's imperial rulers had not conceived of their state as a small part of a larger whole—one nation among many others—but as the core of world civilization, and their own place as the "Middle Kingdom," the natural order of Heaven. Chinese rule, when it occurred in such bordering lands as Korea or Vietnam, or even Tibet, could never be described as benign.

Nevertheless, the purveyors of Confucian civilization on the world stage were likely to be less inclined to enslavement of entire peoples than their Iberian brethren and Chinese were not as likely to attempt to cleanse ancient, but newly discovered, civilizations of their essential features and force on them alternative gods as they installed foreign conquerors as their direct rulers. How different the world might have been had the Chinese brought the Old World to the New for the first time.

A VISION AT THE GOLDEN GATE

As the envoy passes through the Grand Portal of the Outer Palace that dominates the heart of the great coastal city of Tongjing (Eastern Capital), a splendid square suddenly stretches before him, broken in the distance only by a mountain of gilded steps rising up beneath a canopy roof of brilliant crimson that seems to float above the earth. That, he has been informed, is where the carpeted path he now treads will take him. It is the Hall of Reception where he is to present himself to the representative of the Celestial Government assigned to receive him this day. Looming off to his right, astride the rocky isle that rises from the bay, is the Temple of the Eastern Heavens, reserved for prayers by the emperor himself should he ever visit this part of his world-spanning realm. Just visible beyond are brown hills, crowned by billows of fog that appear poised to pour down and close the mouth of the bay. The envoy can see the grand harbor below, its waters covered with a forest of many-masted ships riding at anchor, sails furled, their brilliant banners flapping in the wind.

The escorting official assigned to the envoy boasts that Tongjing's Square of Eastern Peace, with its high walls, rivals even the mighty Forbidden City compound of the Son of Heaven in Beijing itself, but his own eyes widen as he sees how it swallows up the thousands of attendants in their silks of myriad colors who cannot begin to fill its vastness. Ranks of soldiers stand arrayed in polished armor. They are armed with weapons of all description, strange knives at their belts, shining as they catch the sun, while a special cadre of uniformed men touch fire to gleaming barrels and flame and deafening noise belch forth in salute as each delegation arrives—no matter whether large in size like the bejeweled and jingling procession that has proceeded the envoy, said to have come from the far south, or few in number, humbly clad amongst all this grandeur as is the envoy's party. Huge beasts with godlike riders high above the ground seem either impervious to the booming, or are held in check by firm hands and gentle words. Behind the soldiers who line the entire path to the distant pavilion draped in imperial yellow stand blocks of scholarly civil servants in their academic robes, formed into regular lines, a mark both of the order and the grandeur of the occasion.

This is, after all, the first time that the newly arrived governor of the East, an Imperial prince, fourth son of His Majesty, will be receiving visitors from the many lands and peoples that span this continent. He will allow them to make their ritual supplication and bows of submission before he issues, in his father's name, the symbols of investiture to their chieftains, lords, and kings. A numbing drone, emitted by reed instruments, punctuated by the screech made by bows pulled across little boxes by a virtual army of musicians and the clash of metal disks, seems to delight the Chinese as much as it causes the envoy's teeth to clinch. And then, at last, as the envoy makes his way along the appointed path, he finds *himself quite near to small clusters of strange men whose faces are of colors not common in this land: They must be the ambassadors from far reaches of the world—even further away than his home—here to witness the ceremonies now under way.*

It is a life-changing moment for the envoy. In addition to the symbols of office he will receive, he knows he will be entrusted with the bejeweled badges of honor and the keys to the chests of the treasure that will be bestowed upon his people by the magnanimous Chinese throne. He is well pleased that he has been able to complete this part of his role as emissary, yet remains anxious about the long journey that lies ahead on his return. Starting out at the Golden Gate on the Great Bay that offers shelter from the Eastern Ocean, called "Pacific" only by those who have never known its furies, he will have to return across the broad desert, mighty mountains, and buffalo-filled plains to his forest home in the Iroquois Confederacy. His people have finally agreed to bond themselves to the wider Ming world, now counting among its friends, allies, and subjects, all the nations and communities from the Incas in far-off Peru, to the Mexican kingdoms of the Aztecs and their former rivals, since reconciled by the benevolent influence of the Great Son of Heaven.

GEOFFREY PARKER
_____

MARTIN LUTHER BURNS
AT THE STAKE, 1521

"O God, is Luther dead?"

The event that has long signaled the birth of Protestantism is Martin Luther's nail-
ing of his Ninety-five Theses to a door of the Wittenberg castle church on October 31, 1517, All Hallow's Eve. The theses themselves were hardly revolutionary
documents. The thirty-four-year-old professor of theology, an Augustinian
monk, argued that indulgences, paper certificates guaranteeing in the name of the
pope that sinners would not have to spend Eternity in Purgatory, should not be
given to those who simply made a pious donation. "Nailed" may be a bit over-
dramatic, though it has long been invested with the pound and rap of tradition; we
are dealing with a powerful symbol here. "Posted" is probably more in the spirit of
Luther's act, which was, as Geoffrey Parker notes, "the normal way of requesting a public debate." Luther at this point had not the least intention of breaking
with the Church. Once copies of the theses were printed up and circulated, however, a controversy whose repercussions might have remained merely local became widespread and their author a figure of sudden notoriety. The printing press
made Luther a celebrity, one of the first that media created. Indeed, if there had
been no such invention, could there have been a Luther? By the same token,
without a mass-produced Bible available to ordinary individuals, could Protestantism itself have existed? As he put it, every man could now become his own
priest.

Martin Luther was always blessed by good luck. He died in bed, not standing
upright on a pile of burning fagots, bound to a stake. What if death by fire had

been his fate when he was hauled before the Diet of Worms in 1521 and asked to recant views that had already led to his excommunication? What forms would Protestantism have taken if it had lacked the magnetizing force of a Luther? Could Protestantism, except as a scattering of dissenters, have even existed? Would his death, and the leadership vacuum created by it, have given the Catholic Church the breathing space that Rome needed? And what different directions might the history of sixteenth-century Western Europe have taken without the great schism of religion? The development of the New World might have been affected as well. To understand the stature of this rude, arrogant, yet frequently charming man, we need simply to contemplate his absence.

GEOFFREY PARKER is the Andreas Dorpalen Professor of History at Ohio State University and the author of such works as *The Dutch Revolt, Philip II, The Military Revolution, The Spanish Armada* (with Colin Martin), and most recently *The Grand Strategy of Philip II*. He is (with Robert Cowley) editor of *The Reader's Companion to Military History*.

ABOUT FOUR O'CLOCK on the afternoon of April 17, 1521, the ushers led Martin Luther, looking drawn and pale, before Emperor Charles V and the German Diet, meeting in the city of Worms on the Rhine. On a table in the center of the episcopal hall, next to the great Romanesque cathedral, stood a pile of Luther's books and pamphlets. A spokesman asked him two questions: Would he acknowledge the authorship of these books? And, would he recant all or parts of them? Luther, realizing that he would have no chance to state his views, requested twenty-four hours for reflection. The next day at about six in the evening he again entered the crowded episcopal hall, now illuminated by hundreds of candles. Facing the emperor, the princes, and the prelates, Luther delivered in a high clear voice a ten-minute speech in German, which he later repeated in Latin. When he had finished, the spokesman objected that he had still not given a simple answer as to whether he would recant or not. Luther paused and then replied defiantly:

> Since then Your Serene Majesty and Your Lordships seek a simple answer, I will give it in this manner, neither horned nor toothed. Unless I am convinced by the testimony of the Scriptures or by clear reason (for I do not trust either in the pope or in councils alone, since it is well known that they have often erred and contradicted themselves), I am bound by the Scriptures I have quoted and my conscience. I cannot do otherwise. Here I stand, may God help me, amen.

Pandemonium now broke loose in the hall. The emperor, angry and excited, rose to his feet and declared that he had had enough of such talk. The meeting broke up in chaos.

For a moment, Luther's fate hung in the balance: some Catholic zealots wanted to seize him and shouted "into the fire"—the traditional fate of heretics. Nevertheless, Charles V respected the safe conduct he had given Luther to attend the diet and even allowed him a few days of further discussion with theologians. Luther left Worms a free man on April 26. No sooner was he outside the city, however, than a group of masked men ambushed him and he abruptly disappeared. On hearing the news, the German artist Albrecht Dürer wrote in his diary: "O God, is Luther dead? Who will now explain the Gospel to us as clearly as he used to do?"

We now know (as Dürer did not) that the "kidnappers" were the soldiers of Luther's patron, Elector Frederick of Saxony, and that they took him in secret to one of Frederick's castles. There he grew a beard and spent one year disguised as a knight, "Sir George," while he worked on the greatest of his literary labors: a German translation of the New Testament. By the time Luther died in 1546, his vigorous, melodious version had appeared in 253 editions and formed the basis for several other vernacular translations. Thus William Tyndale's English Bible (and therefore the Authorized Version, into which much of it passed) stems directly from Luther's version. The reformer returned to Wittenberg in 1522 where, until his death twenty-four years later, his preaching, teaching, and writing shaped a Lutheran church with some five million members around the world today.

But what if, in April 1521, Charles V had listened to those who urged him to disregard Luther's safe conduct, on the grounds that "One does not keep faith with heretics"? A century before, another critic of the papacy, Jan Hus from Bohemia, had also received an Imperial promise of safety to come from Prague to Germany and defend his views, but it had been dishonored. The emperor who issued it watched him burn at the stake and then led a series of military campaigns to exterminate his followers in Bohemia.

Martin Luther, born in Saxony to a mining family, attended primary and grammar schools away from home. He took his bachelor's degree at the University of Erfurt in 1501 and his master's the following year, at age nineteen. In 1505, after a bolt of lightning almost killed him, he became an Au-

PORTRAIT OF A SURVIVOR

A rebel in middle age: Strong will and intelligence are captured on the face of Martin Luther in this contemporary etching.

(Lucas Cranach the Elder, 1472–1553, *Martin Luther*. SEF/Art Resource, NY)

gustinian monk, in gratitude for his survival. But he continued to study theology in his monk's cell and obtained his doctorate in 1512. Then he moved to Wittenberg, where he began to lecture on the Bible to students at the new university, founded by Frederick of Saxony, and to deliver sermons to the citizens as preacher in the town church.

Luther always saw teaching and preaching as crucial, and he continued to do both throughout his life. He also wrote to be heard as well as to be read, always addressing himself to "my readers and hearers." "The voice should be the soul of the word," he wrote. "Letters are dead words, speech is living words." He devoted great attention to finding the right words and, as he wrote, spoke the sentences aloud to himself until the stresses, pauses, cadences, and the sequence of vowels and consonants sounded just right. One of the mourners at the reformer's funeral paid tribute to his great linguistic gifts when he claimed that "Luther taught us to speak."

These communication skills would have made Luther a formidable authority on any subject, but gradually he focused on a particularly important issue for Christians: sin and salvation. How can the sinner be saved? His close reading of the Bible suggested that good works and insincere penance would not suffice: only complete faith in Christ could assure salvation. In 1517, Luther became concerned that a practice by some of his fellow priests, members of the Dominican Order, was leading Christians astray, offering them a false security. They toured Christendom distributing indulgences that promised the living and the dead, in the pope's name, remission of ecclesiastical penalties, and of time in purgatory, in return for a contribution toward the cost of rebuilding the basilica of St. Peter's in Rome. Although the local authorities forbade the Dominicans to offer indulgences in Wittenberg, they did so nearby, and members of Luther's congregation left town to acquire them.

When his sermons failed to halt the exodus, on October 31, 1517, Luther presented a set of ninety-five objections to the practice. His criticisms fell under three heads. Most attacked the Dominicans' failure to require any penance or inner contrition before issuing their indulgences; others argued that the Gospels provided everything a Christian needed to know for salvation; a few claimed that those who stifled the Word of God to make room for indulgences—even if granted by the pope—were the enemies of Christ. Luther posted his Ninety-five Theses on the door of a local church, the normal way of requesting a public debate at the time. He also sent them with a cover note to his ecclesiastical superior, who forwarded them to Rome, and he mailed copies to some friends, who published them all over Germany.

This provided Luther's first taste of widespread popularity, and he relished it—all the while professing that he had nothing to do with it. "It is a mystery to me," he noted (with a trace of smugness), "how my Theses, more so than my other writings—or indeed those of other professors—spread to so many places." The theses also provoked envy and enmity. The Dominicans who distributed the indulgences noted a fall in revenues and complained to the pope about Luther's criticisms; so in the summer of 1518 he received a summons to Rome to explain his objections.

Political calculations now rescued Luther, for the first but not the last time. When the papal summons arrived in Germany, its ruler, Emperor Maximilian of Habsburg, urgently desired to have his grandson Charles recognized as his successor. He therefore met at the city of Augsburg with those who would make the choice: seven Imperial Electors, including Frederick of Saxony, Luther's suzerain. Frederick, who had advanced large sums of money to the emperor in the past, asked Maximilian to allow Luther to address the pope's concerns in Augsburg instead of Rome. Grateful and anxious for Frederick's vote, Maximilian agreed.

Why did Frederick care? He met Luther face-to-face only once—at the Diet of Worms—and the two men never exchanged a spoken word. The elector, however, possessed unusual piety. In his youth he had undertaken a pilgrimage to Jerusalem and afterward began to collect relics. Some he purchased, others he exchanged for pictures by Lucas Cranach (his Court painter), and a few his agents stole. By 1520, his collection exceeded 19,000 items, ranging from some milk from the Virgin Mary's breast, some straw from the stable at Bethlehem, a piece of the burning bush, and some soot from the fiery furnace, to articles of merely local appeal like the beaker used by St. Elizabeth of Marburg, a medieval German saint. When the entire collection came out on display, the total time remitted from purgatory in return for pious prayers approached two million years. Frederick kept his collection, the largest in the world, in the castle church at Wittenberg—the very spot where Luther had posted his Ninety-five Theses—and he paid eighty-three resident priests to celebrate almost 10,000 masses annually on his behalf. These were precisely the sort of "false" religious practices that Luther abhorred and against which he would preach. In 1518, however, these differences lay in the future and Frederick sought to protect Luther, apparently out of a sense of "fair play" and, perhaps, because he did not wish to see one of his own "star professors" disgraced. He therefore not only provided overt protection against those who sought Luther's destruction, but also gave him covert advice through his legal experts.

Unfortunately for Luther, the senior papal representative at Augsburg was Cardinal Cajetan, general of the Dominican Order—a man unlikely to give way on the issue of indulgences. For four days in October 1518 the two men debated. The cardinal pointed out that several popes had proclaimed the efficacy of indulgences, forcing Luther to reply that "the pope is not above, but under the word of God" and could therefore err. The following month, at Cajetan's direction, the pope issued a decree ordering that everyone should obey his teaching on indulgences. This pushed Luther one step further toward an open confrontation with Rome. He read the document and announced in January 1519 that, since it offered no biblical support for its assertions, "although I will not reject it, I will not bow down before it." That same month, Maximilian died and Germany lacked any secular authority capable of keeping the "monk's quarrel" (as many considered it) within bounds.

Luther had intended his Ninety-five Theses to provoke a scholarly debate, and a prominent German theologian, John Eck, duly challenged him. In July 1519, the two met in an open forum at Leipzig in Saxony. Luther cited the teaching of the Greek Orthodox Church, which also condemned indulgences; Eck pointed out that Jan Hus had done the same. This horrified Luther, who had previously accepted that Hus died a heretic. Now he started to read the writings of the Bohemian reformer and was amazed at what he found. "Up to now I have held and espoused all the teachings of Jan Hus without knowing it," he told a friend. "We are all Hussites without realizing it." But Hus had criticized far more than indulgences: he had denied the power of the popes and exalted the authority of the Bible. Luther realized that he would have to do the same and wrote, early in 1520:

I am in deep turmoil since I can hardly doubt that the pope is the true Antichrist whom everyone has been expecting. Everything fits together too well—his life, his deeds, what he says and what he demands.

This proved too much for some of Luther's supporters and they now abandoned him. For many Germans, "Hussite" was equivalent to "rebel" or "priest-hater." In England, one of the few countries outside Bohemia where Hussite views had gained a following, King Henry VIII wrote a tract condemning Luther and his Hussite leanings (which led the pope to confer on Henry the accolade "Defender of the Faith," a title still treasured by English monarchs). More ominous, John Eck sent a detailed list to Rome of heretical views uttered by Luther during the Leipzig debate.

Luther now published tracts that set out his beliefs in detail and, by the end of 1520, he had published over thirty of them, printed in 400 editions, with combined sales of 300,000 copies. One of them, *Address to the Christian Nobility of Germany Regarding the Improvement of Christendom,* which called on princes and magistrates to reform the Church (since the pope clearly did not intend to do so), sold 2,000 copies in five days. His style became instantly recognized—when he authored an anonymous tract he had no doubt that "anyone who reads it, if he has seen my pen and my thoughts, must say: 'This is Luther'"—and his books flooded the market. The other outstanding writer of the day, Erasmus of Rotterdam, complained huffily that one could hardly find a book in Germany that was not either written by Luther or about Luther.

The tone of the debate also became sharper. In his *Address,* Luther claimed that, whether Hus was a heretic or not, he had been unjustly executed because heretics should be refuted with arguments and not with fire. He also argued that "the prime concern" of Christians

should be to live sincerely in faith and in accordance with Holy Scripture. For Christian faith and life can easily exist without the intolerable laws of the pope. In fact, faith cannot properly exist unless there are fewer of these Romanist laws, or unless they are abolished all together.

Luther's tracts stressed that the Bible could be read and understood by anyone without any need for a church hierarchy—or, in his memorable phrase, "Every man is his own priest." Eck, for his part, secured a papal decree in June 1520 that attributed forty-one separate doctrinal "errors" to Luther, ordered him to recant, and threatened him with excommunication if he did not. Six months later, Luther responded with a theatrical gesture: he ceremonially burnt a copy of the decree and, for good measure, threw a copy of the canon law into the flames as well. "As they would do to me, so I do to them," he wrote. The following month, the pope excommunicated Luther and called on Charles V, now emperor, to outlaw him.

Charles could not oblige. In July 1519, just as Luther and Eck began their debate, the electors met to choose a successor to Maximilian. They considered three candidates: Maximilian's grandson Charles of Habsburg, King Francis I of France, and Frederick of Saxony. Frederick refused to stand and threw his weight behind Charles, who was elected unanimously. In return, however, the new emperor promised not to outlaw anyone without a legal hearing. At Frederick's insistence, he therefore agreed to allow Luther to attend the Diet of Worms, scheduled to meet early in 1521, albeit in the expectation that the excommunicate would simply recant.

By then, however, the execution of Luther could no longer have silenced the growing chorus of open critics of the Catholic Church. Luther's prolific writings and his dramatic personal appearances all over Germany to defend his views had won numerous followers and, by 1521, Albrecht Dürer was not alone in regarding Luther as the most gifted exponent of a new kind of Christianity. But he was no longer the only one. Wittenberg experienced a religious revolution even without Luther. Under the leadership of another university professor and priest, Andreas Bodenstein von Karlstadt, radical preachers dispensed communion in both kinds, bread and wine, to the laity (the Roman Church allowed only bread), crowds smashed church images, monks left their monasteries, and priests began to marry. Radical prophets warned that the end of the world approached and called for social justice. Far to the south, the chief preacher of the city of Zurich in Switzerland, Huldrych Zwingli, noted with approval in his diary Luther's defiance of Rome and, in 1519, persuaded the city magistrates to ban indulgences. The next year, he received permission to preach "the gospel" as he wished, and all other clergy in Zurich followed his lead. While Luther hid in Frederick's castle, others advanced his cause.

What, then, if Charles V had tried to burn *all* these critics of the Roman Church? Once again, by 1521 it was probably too late for effective persecution. On the one hand, Luther's ideas had become too popular to suppress. Even Hus's teachings—spread only by word of mouth and in manuscripts until the invention of printing with movable type in the 1450s—survived his martyrdom. Repeated attempts to invade his native Bohemia and eradicate his followers failed ignominiously: The Hussites fought back and won. Printing, which Luther regarded as "God's highest and ultimate gift of grace, by which He would have his gospel carried forward," made it impossible for any German government to destroy all copies of all of Luther's works. Moreover, they had by then spread beyond Germany. By 1530, some thirty Lutheran tracts had appeared in Dutch translation, and three in English. On the other hand, experience would show that killing Protestants did not eradicate their beliefs. In 1523, Charles ordered two Netherlands monks to be burnt because they upheld Luther's teaching and refused to abjure—the first Lutheran martyrs anywhere—and in the course of his reign at least 2,000 more Netherlanders perished for their beliefs.

Nevertheless, Lutheranism (as well as the other persecuted Protestant creeds) continued to thrive in the Low Countries. In Switzerland, an armed attack on Zurich by her Catholic neighbors in 1531 resulted in the death of Zwingli in battle, but his faith lived on and even spread to other cantons. Finally, in Germany, the relentless persecution of the Anabaptists, groups of believers who separated from both the Lutheran and Zwinglian camps in 1522–23, failed to extinguish them. Their faith survived and their descendants (Mennonites and others) today number more than one million members in some sixty countries worldwide. There is no reason to suppose that even intense and protracted persecution would have extinguished Lutheranism either.

In any case, three political considerations precluded effective enforcement of Charles's decree of outlawry. First, the king of France, rankled by his failure to secure the Imperial title, concluded a series of alliances with

Charles's enemies and prepared to declare war. Rumors of a hostile coalition reached the emperor in Worms, and he begged the Imperial Diet to vote him funds with which to organize a coherent defense. It made no sense to antagonize Frederick of Saxony, one of the richest rulers, by outlawing Luther before approval of the taxes. Charles therefore issued his edict of outlawry in May 1521—a month after Luther's defiance—only when Frederick had left Worms. Second, on the empire's eastern flank, a new Ottoman sultan, Suleiman, advanced up the Danube and captured Belgrade after only three weeks' siege. This opened the plain of Hungary and, beyond, the Habsburgs' patrimonial lands, to Turkish raids. In 1529, Suleiman and his army laid siege to Vienna. Time after time, a Turkish offensive up the Danube (or the fear of one) led Charles to agree to tolerate Lutheranism in the Empire in return for Lutheran taxes and troops to defend Austria. In 1529, Luther composed his most famous hymn, "A Mighty Fortress is our God," for the Saxon troops who marched to save Vienna after Charles had granted a further period of toleration. Third, and finally, the emperor spent little of his reign in Germany. After the Diet of Worms, he decided to go to Spain in order to supervise the suppression of a major popular rebellion (the *comuneros*), and the enmity of France kept him there for the next seven years. He was in no position to enforce his decree of outlawry (or any other measure) in Germany.

Would Luther's death in 1521 have changed anything? Undoubtedly. To begin with, we would lack his powerful translation of the Bible, as well as most of his 3,100 other publications, which take up over 60,000 printed pages in the standard edition of his works. This would have weakened the Reformation in two distinct ways. First, the very popularity of Luther's works helped to harmonize the different dialects spoken in Germany. The first Basel edition of his German New Testament included a glossary of unusual Saxon terms for the benefit of southern German readers. Without later works to popularize Luther's style, the need for such aids might have continued, complicating the spread of anti-Catholic ideas. Second, and more obviously, without Luther's commanding authority, the various centers of anti-Catholic sentiment would have developed in isolation. Instead of a relatively unified Lutheran bloc in northern Germany and Scandinavia, there would have been a patchwork of states, each with their own creed. Perhaps a divided (or, rather, a more divided) Reformation would have proved unable to withstand a Catholic counteroffensive once Charles eventually made peace with the French and the Turks.

The impact of the Peasants' War of 1524–25, the greatest popular uprising in Europe between the rebellions of the 1350s and the French revolution, would certainly have been different. As it was, the peasants of southern Germany took many of their grievances straight from the teachings of Luther and Zwingli, and several of their leaders had been (and a few still were) his followers. Luther used his enormous authority both to distance the Reformation cause from the rebellion and to legitimize the brutal repression of the peasants. His most influential tract on the subject, with the bloodthirsty title *Against the Murdering and Thieving Hordes of Peasants*, commanded "everyone who can, to smite, slay and stab them, secretly or openly, remembering that nothing can be more poisonous, hurtful or devilish than a rebel." Without his firm, shrill voice, the peasant movement would have become more radical—and perhaps more popular—discrediting the cause of reform irreparably.

Predicting the impact of Luther's martyrdom at Worms beyond the 1520s becomes more hazardous. Let us consider, for example, the impact of a weaker Reformation camp on the Catholic Church. Perhaps burning Luther, and intimidating (though not eliminating) his supporters, would have lulled the papacy back into complacency, leading it to write off the few isolated Protestant enclaves just as it had written off Hussite Bohemia. Probably, then, later reformers (such as John Calvin) would still have divided Europe with new calls for reform. Conversely, however, a weaker and less abrasive Reformed movement might have proved easier for the Catholic Church to accommodate. Many sincere Christians, including Charles V, wished to end the schism and compelled Catholic and Protestant leaders to attend several meetings to resolve their differences. All of them failed, in part because of Luther's intransigence. Without him, perhaps papal negotiators could have reached an agreement with at least some of the Protestant leaders, healing the schism and reuniting all Western Christians under papal authority.

Without the great divide between Protestant and Catholic, certainly the history of sixteenth-century Western Europe would have been very different: no religious wars, no Dutch Revolt, no Thirty Years' War. The forces of a united Christendom might have held back the Turks at Belgrade or Budapest; the united forces of Charles V's subjects might have established Habsburg hegemony in Europe, precluding all settlements in the Americas by other Europeans. So just possibly: No Luther, no United States as we know it.

Luther might well have relished that extreme connection. As with the thunderbolt that narrowly missed him, he believed that the fate of his cause as well as his personal future rested solely in God's hands. In April 1521, he jauntily told the Diet of Worms, quoting the Acts of the Apostles:

> "If this is the counsel of men, this work will be overthrown; if it is of God, you will not be able to overthrow it." The emperor and the imperial estates are welcome to write that to the pope in Rome! I know that if my work is not from God, within three years, or even two, it will perish of its own accord.

A year later, as he rode back to Wittenberg to resume his duties as teacher and preacher, he felt vindicated and empowered. At Worms, Elector Frederick had found Luther "much too bold," but he had seen nothing yet. In 1522, his persistent carping persuaded Frederick to pack up his collection of relics, and later that year the elector and his entourage appeared at the Imperial Diet wearing a Lutheran slogan ("The word of God endures forever") on their clothes. In 1524, the emperor's sister Isabel went to Wittenberg to hear Luther preach and publicly took communion in both kinds. Before he died in 1525, Frederick also received both wine and bread at communion, a clear sign of his personal break with Rome.

That same year, Luther abandoned his monastic habit and married a nun, and shortly afterward he began to celebrate October 31, the day he had published his Ninety-five Theses, with a special toast. In his last years, he drank the toast out of one of the few surviving relics from Elector Frederick's collection—the beaker of St. Elizabeth of Marburg—symbolizing his victory not only over the pope but also over the emperor, the princes, and the prelates who had once sat in judgment upon him at the Diet of Worms. In 1546, he died serenely in his bed in the town where he was born sixty-two years before. His career offers one of the best defenses of the "Great Man" theory of history: that a single individual can decisively influence the course of human affairs. There might still have been a Reformation without Luther, but it would have taken a totally different form.

THEODORE K. RABB

IF CHARLES I HAD NOT LEFT WHITEHALL, AUGUST 1641

As a starter, no English civil war

"Charles I," Theodore K. Rabb remarks, "is the perfect exemplar of the truism that the personality and actions of a major historical figure can alter the course of events." Without Charles (who reigned from 1625 until he was beheaded in 1649), the English civil war probably never would have happened and Oliver Cromwell would have remained at home singing hymns and breeding horses. It was a war that changed nothing and everything. Cromwell's short-lived republican experiment died with him and the monarchy was restored, its powers apparently intact. But this was not the authoritarian monarchy of Charles, and would never be again. His son Charles II was a king who liked to rub shoulders with his sub-jects (and to take some of the fairer ones to bed). When his successor, James II, tried to revert to the old ways (and to the Catholic Church), he was sent packing.

But more than the monarchy had changed. An elected Parliament was now supreme, and rudimentary political parties were beginning to take form. Govern-ments could actually be voted out of office. "The basic elements of electoral democracy as we know them," Rabb writes, "gathered inexorable force in En-gland." By the end of the next century, a truer democracy, embodying the ideal of universal suffrage—not just the rule of the landed classes—would emerge in the rebellious British colonies across the Atlantic.

None of this might have happened had it not been for the devious obstinacy of Charles I. Since it was against his beliefs to compromise with Parliament, a con-frontation was inevitable. But as Rabb observes, there was one scenario, not at all improbable, that might have changed everything. It hinged on the recurring scourge of seventeenth-century Europe—the plague. In August 1641, Charles I headed north to deal with rebellious subjects in Scotland. Six days later, in a house just one hundred yards from his Whitehall Palace, the inhabitants came down with the usually fatal disease. What if Charles had delayed his trip by just a week—and had become a victim himself? The future, our past, might have assumed a considerably different shape, and not necessarily a democratic one.

THEODORE K. RABB is a professor of history at Princeton University and the author or editor of such notable works as *The New History, The Struggle for Stability in Early Modern Europe, Climate and History, Renaissance Lives,* and *Jacobean Gentlemen.* He was the principal historical adviser for the acclaimed and Emmy-nominated PBS television series *Renaissance.*

A MONG THE WARS, military campaigns, and individual battles that
can change the face of a continent, civil wars are often the most ago-
nizing. Though the landscapes they alter tend to be only within specific
countries, the intensity of the conflicts and the transformations that they
bring about can have long-term consequences that extend far beyond national borders. In the twentieth century, for instance, the effects of internal
strife were not restricted to Russia, Spain, China, or Vietnam, to name but
four of the most brutal instances. And the same can be said, in earlier centuries, of America in the 1770s or France in the 1790s.

The importance of these struggles is only enhanced if one considers how
easily they could have come out otherwise. What kind of world would we
have inherited had Lenin, Franco, Mao, Ho Chi Minh, Washington, or the
Third Estate lost their assaults on the existing order? Each had more than
one moment when their movements could have collapsed, sending history
into very different directions. And the argument holds even when a civil
war seems not to have shifted many landmarks, as appears to have been the
case with the upheavals that shook England in the 1640s and '50s.

Although armies were either on the march or trying to dissuade resistance for most of the period from 1640 to 1660 in England, they seemed to
leave little mark. The persistence of political structures had been notable in
the wake of previous English civil wars, such as the Wars of the Roses that
had raged some 150 years earlier, and at first sight the events of the 1640s
and '50s appeared to follow the same pattern. The monarchy, which for a
few years had ceased to exist, returned in 1660 with just about all of its
powers intact. Both the House of Lords and the Anglican Church, which
had been abolished, were restored; traditional powers in the counties were
resumed by the landed country gentry; and Parliament once again was both

summoned and dissolved at the command of the king. A few legal rights and practices had been reformed, but common law and the power of precedent were not significantly more authoritative than before. Nor were religious dissenters, on the whole, much more comfortable than they had been in the 1630s. And the many unprecedented ideas that had bubbled to the surface as the established order dissolved—from a belief in equal political rights for all men to the wish for complete freedom of the press—seemed to evaporate after 1660, their later influence impossible to predict. Behind the outward show, however, there had been a fundamental shift in political culture, reversing the drift toward authoritarianism that Charles I had represented.

During the civil wars that outcome could not have been predicted, because the voices of hope for a new future, represented notably by the poet John Milton, were often drowned out by the despair of those who regarded the disintegration of England's traditional institutions as a prelude to anarchy, redeemable only by a determined sovereign. Among the latter, the most acute observer was probably Thomas Hobbes, whose *Leviathan* may well be the most powerful response to civil war ever written. Deeply disturbed by the chaos that had forced him into exile, he published his masterpiece in 1651, just two years after the execution of King Charles I. Writing in the context of profound and unprecedented social uncertainty, Hobbes sought to define a political system that would have as its prime purpose the assurance of stability for all its citizens. The only logical possibility, he concluded, was an all-powerful sovereign, dedicated to the maintenance of order and capable of imposing his will without restraint.

Given the spread of absolutist doctrines and practices through much of the Europe in which Hobbes wrote—certainly in the France of Louis XIV, where his exile had taken him—his conclusions seemed to capture the spirit of his times. There was a relentless single-mindedness and a devastating finality in his dismissal of alternatives, which made his views less than popular (though hugely influential) in his own lifetime, but there could be no doubt that most of his contemporaries would have taken his side if faced with a choice between the might of centralized authority and the chaos of resistance to that authority. Hobbes may have written amid crisis, but his rethinking of the purpose of government has remained fundamental to political theory ever since.

Yet it was not a Leviathan-like king who returned to power in 1660. The Stuart dynasty had learned how dire could be the effects of arbitrary rule, and Charles I's son Charles II was determined to retain the affections of his subjects. Where his father had been remote and aloof, he mingled enthusiastically with the people of London. He went riding in Hyde Park; he frequented the theater; and the most famous diarist of the age, Samuel Pepys, reported that he was swept along so far by the crowd that gathered when the king was opening a new session of Parliament that he eventually found himself at Charles's elbow, reading along as the royal speech was delivered. Such mingling, and the political relationships it implied, would have been inconceivable under the autocratic Charles I or across the Channel in Louis XIV's France.

What this changed atmosphere reflected, however, was something more profound than clever public relations or a warm personality. It was the realization that, for all the apparent continuities, the country's political culture had been fundamentally altered by the experience of civil war. Thus, it is true that disabilities were again imposed on dissenters from the official Anglican Church. They were excluded from the universities and public office; forbidden to come too close to the capital, London; and made sufficiently uncomfortable that, as in the 1630s, a nonconformist like William Penn sought better prospects in the New World. But they were not hounded, directly persecuted, or prevented from observing their own forms of worship. A de facto tolerance was extended, and it embraced even a growing community of Jews, who had been forbidden to settle in England for centuries, but who now began to return in some numbers even though the formal legal prohibition had not been repealed.

This unwritten acceptance of new conditions also transformed the political system. So deep was the reaction to the bloodshed and upheaval of the midcentury that the English were determined to avoid such confrontation again. The troubles had wracked the Continent, too, where the Thirty

Years' War had devastated Germany, and where rebellions and open conflict had broken out from Portugal to Russia. The reaction of another acute observer, John Locke, was typical, if exaggerated, in that he hoped all means could be found to avoid repeating the "perpetual foundation of war and contention, all those flames that have made such havoc and desolation in Europe, and have not been quenched but with the blood of so many millions."

When, therefore, Charles II's brother and successor, James II, a committed Catholic, sought to reintroduce that hated and feared religion into his realm in the 1680s, he was removed from the throne in a bloodless coup, engineered by the leaders of English society, and known ever since as the Glorious Revolution. There was no need for battle or civil war, though it is possible that, had James decided to stand and fight rather than flee to France, his legitimacy might have enabled him, perhaps with compromise, to retain his crown. That, however, is another "what if?," and one whose main casualty would have been the disappearance from the romance of history of the valiant and hopeless Jacobite movement, which sought for decades to restore James and his descendants to the throne. In the event, James did flee, and his very surrender was an indication of how completely the English polity had changed since the 1630s: Parliament was now unmistakably supreme, and no monarch could flout its wishes or those of the landed classes it represented.

This new outlook found its champion and its most influential exponent in John Locke himself. In his *Second Treatise of Civil Government*, written before the Glorious Revolution, but not published until the new king, William III, was safely on the throne, Locke defined the political outlook that, as developed by his followers, has come to be known as liberalism. He was deeply influenced by Hobbes's theories, but he softened their implications so as to justify the establishment of a regime that, rather than exercising total control, took care (as did the English government of his day) not to ignore the concerns of its leading citizens. Where Hobbes had described the State of Nature before the invention of government—a brilliant and original intellectual construct—as hellish, shaped by the greed and cruelty of man into a war of all against all, leaving life "nasty, poor, brutish, and short," Locke argued that human reason was already operating in the State of Nature. When government was created, therefore, it was willingly set up so as to meet peoples' needs, not established in fear so as to protect its subjects from one another. Hobbes, determined to minimize resistance to authority, reserved just one right to the individual: protection of life. Locke, speaking for the self-assured landed gentry, expanded those rights to include not only life but also liberty and property.

From then on, the basic elements of electoral democracy as we know them gathered inexorable force in England. By 1700, nationwide political parties with distinct agendas were beginning to organize; there were contested elections that forced governments out of office; and a significant segment of the population felt itself entitled to influence the direction of events in the capital. The electorate was still small, but the assumptions about the nature of politics had changed dramatically in little more than half a century. And the momentum continued as the mother of Parliaments spawned countless imitators over the next 300 years.

This is a central story of modern history, and it is one of the crucial reasons that the West has had so powerful an influence on the rest of the world. But it could so easily have turned out differently. It may be that the democratic idea, which has its roots in ancient Greece, would eventually have flowered anyway. Other theorists, practices, and traditions could well have appeared. But this was the particular road that opened up, and one needs only a modicum of imagination to see how, in its earliest days, it could have turned into a dead end. For civil wars are times of such rapid change that even a slight shift in circumstances can have momentous results.

Charles I is the perfect exemplar of the truism that the personality and actions of a major historical figure can alter the course of events. Possibly because, as a young man, he had stayed at the Spanish court for a number of months, and had been able to watch an absolute monarch exercise total command of people and policy, Charles as king developed a haughty and dismissive view of the rights of his subjects. His reign began with four years of struggle with Parliament, at the end of which the House of Commons

CHARLES I: A STUDY IN STUBBORNNESS

Charles I of England, the foremost art collector of the seventeenth century, posed on horseback for this portrait by one of his favorite painters, Anthony Van Dyck. For Charles, compromise was never an option, and he would lose the English civil war (and his head). But what if he had been out of the picture?

(Anthony Van Dyck, 1599–1641, *Portrait of Charles I*. Louvre, Paris. Alinari/Art Resource, NY)

even sought to challenge his ancient right to dissolve the session. At that point, in 1629, he decided he had had enough, and for the next eleven years he ruled without Parliament. Distant and disdainful, he became a deeply unpopular figure, and when his authoritarian policies drove his Scottish subjects to revolt, the carefully constructed facade of imperturbable majesty collapsed around him.

Unable to finance an army to repel the Scots without parliamentary taxation, Charles was forced to recall the assembly in 1640, but the Commons, organized by a determined member of the landed gentry, John Pym, made demands Charles could not countenance, and he quickly dissolved what came to be known as the Short Parliament. As the crisis deepened, though, he was forced to give way again and to summon the so-called Long Parliament, which gained the right not to be dismissed without its own approval and was to sit until 1653. It was this assembly that led the revolution.

Most of the radical changes in the law, in political structures, and in the Church that the members of the Long Parliament decreed did not long survive the revolution. But the shock they delivered to the country's system of government was never forgotten, especially since the climax was an assault on the monarchy itself. Constantly deceived by a king who, despite defeat on the battlefield, regarded himself as bound by no promises or agreements, the parliamentarians finally lost all patience. The commander of their army, Oliver Cromwell, called Charles "a man of blood" for the deviousness and the plots that scuttled every compromise and repeatedly forced a renewal of the fighting. Finally, in January 1649, the king was executed after a trial whose legality he refused to recognize, and England became a republic.

By this time, many of the revolutionary ideas for which the period is remembered had come to the surface, most notably a demand for virtually universal male suffrage—a proposal that was not to be implemented for more than two centuries, but which has come to be seen as a pillar of modern democratic practice. And the execution also inspired the counter-theory of Hobbes's *Leviathan*. As for the structure of government itself, the major assault on tradition (the destruction of the authority of the Church of England, the aristocracy, and the monarchy itself) had taken place, and none of the many experiments tried over the next decade left a mark on England's polity. But might the intensifying conflict of the 1640s have been avoided? Could things have turned out otherwise, and if so, what would the consequences have been?

· · ·

One scenario requires no more than a slight adjustment in the incidence of the great scourge of seventeenth-century Europe, the plague. Nobody was immune to its dread assault. The only recourse was to flee from an outbreak and to hope that one escaped before the contagion spread to one's own home. That is indeed what happened, for example, in August of 1641, when Charles's relations with his subjects had reached a perilous moment.

With the armed threat from Scotland intensifying, the king left London for the north to face his rebellious subjects on August 10. Just six days later plague was discovered in a house in Westminster, near parliament. As Charles's adviser, soon to be secretary of state, Edward Nicholas, reported in October, the more hotheaded members of the Commons "wished rather that they should sit here at Westminster and die here together, but I believe Mr. Pym will find few (besides those of his juncto [faction]) of that opinion." The caution was only natural, but the proximity of the outbreak to the person of the king himself bears emphasizing.

Charles's splendid Whitehall palace was but a few yards from where parliament sat in Westminster. Tourists today flock to the palace's one remaining building, Inigo Jones's magnificent Banqueting House in Whitehall. Its ceiling, painted by Rubens, was commissioned by Charles to glorify his father, and in a supreme irony it was to be outside this house that the royal scaffold was to be erected in January of 1649. For most tourists these days, the site is a convenient stop, because at the end of Whitehall, perhaps a hundred yards away to the south, is Parliament Square. That was the trivial distance that would have separated Charles from the plague had he left for Scotland just one week later.

It happened that the plague of 1641 was a minor outbreak. In 1636 it had been quite serious, and the worst casualties of the century were to come in 1665. But the pestilence of 1641 could easily have been far worse; it was merely luck, and perhaps the weather, that restrained its virulence. And we know what its effects could have been. One has but to read Samuel Pepys's diary for 1665 to get a sense of its ravages. Many who were close to Pepys died, and as he traveled the streets of London, he encountered regularly the

stricken, covered in sores, and corpses. He was alternately fearful and resigned as he recorded what was "every day sadder and sadder news." He calculated that in one week some 10,000 had died of the plague, and in the
midst of it all he decided to draw up his will, "the town growing so un-
healthy that a man cannot depend upon living two days to an end." That
he made it through—on one occasion finding that he could escape the
stench of death only by chewing tobacco—was, he admitted, pure luck. His
terror at every report of illness or at any hint of a symptom, such as a
headache, was well-founded; only the stoicism he managed to muster in the
face of this most dreadful of the seventeenth century's scourges was unusual.

It is clear that, had the king succumbed in the summer of 1641, his children would probably have died as well, because the young were especially
susceptible to plague once it had entered a home. And the eradication of
the immediate Stuart dynasty would have had incalculable consequences.
For the heir would have been Charles's sister, Elizabeth, now in her mid-
forties, who in 1613 had married Frederick, the elector of the Palatinate, a
rich principality on the banks of the Rhine. This unfortunate couple had
become one of the saddest spectacles in the Europe of the day. When, just
six years after Elizabeth's wedding, the kingdom of Bohemia, which was
heavily Protestant, had revolted against its staunchly Catholic Habsburg
rulers, the rebels had turned to her husband, the leading Calvinist prince in
Germany, to take over the throne. Despite warnings from all his friends
that it was foolhardy to make common cause with rebels, the impulsive
Frederick, excited at the prospect of a royal crown, had accepted the offer.

The result had been total disaster. Before he had enjoyed even a year in
his new rank, Frederick and his supporters had been crushed by the Habsburgs and their ally, Catholic Bavaria, at the Battle of the White Mountain, just outside Prague. For the Czechs, this may have been merely one
in a series of subjugations that have dotted their history, but the defeat
loomed especially large because it signaled the final suppression of their religious unorthodoxy and placed them under Habsburg domination for 300
more years. And for Frederick and his family it was a catastrophe. Mock-
ingly referred to as the "Winter" king and queen thereafter, he and his wife

had to flee Prague ignominiously. Moreover, as punishment for his treason, the Habsburg Holy Roman emperor, who was his overlord, stripped him of the Palatinate; transferred his title as one of the seven electors of the empire (who elected each new emperor) to Bavaria; allowed Spain's Catholic army to occupy his lands; and forced him into exile.

The years that followed were utterly miserable. From his refuge in the Netherlands, Frederick became a rallying point for the Protestant resistance to the Habsburgs, but to no practical effect. Indeed, it became possible to end the Thirty Years' War in the 1640s only when a compromise was finally reached, allowing his family to return to the Palatinate and their electorate, while at the same time allowing Bavaria to keep a newly created eighth electorate. By then the Winter king was long gone: he had died during a surreptitious visit to the Palatinate in 1632, and his grave site has been unknown ever since. His widow, Elizabeth, was left to bring up in exile the survivors of the twenty children the couple had produced in just under twenty years of marriage.

That she had come through twenty childbirths, and was to live another thirty years, made Elizabeth an extraordinary figure in the Europe of her day. Pregnancies were highly dangerous in an age of easy infection and ineffective medicine, and it was almost unheard of to bring twenty of them to a successful conclusion. That, in addition, she was able to shoulder the huge burden of a fatherless family makes her one of the more remarkable women of the century. She had assistance for a few years from her brother, Charles I. And the sympathetic Dutch who were her hosts ensured that her exile was comfortable. Most important, she became a symbol for all Protestants, especially her English countrymen, of persecution by the Catholic leaders of Europe. Indeed, one of the accusations leveled at her father and brother by their more strident subjects was that they had betrayed not only the Protestant cause, but family duty, by doing nothing to restore Elizabeth to her lands and titles.

This was the woman who would have inherited the English throne in 1641 if that August plague had erupted just a week earlier, spread one hundred yards to Whitehall Palace, and carried off Charles I and his family. She would have reigned for twenty-one more years, and her oldest son, Karl Ludwig, who was to regain the Palatinate electorate in 1648, would have brought a German line on to the English throne half a century earlier than it actually arrived (with George I and the Hanoverians, whose title was to descend from Elizabeth's youngest daughter, Sophia). Elizabeth's most famous child, her third son, Rupert, a soldier who fought in the Thirty Years' War and later in Charles I's army, would doubtless have been a major figure in English society. But her most unusual daughter, also Elizabeth, who was a friend of Descartes and the abbess of a community of pious Lutheran women in Germany, would probably have led much the same life.

How might things have been different, however, for Elizabeth and for England? That there would have been no civil war seems almost certain. Parliament's power was secured by the summer of 1641, and the new queen would have been a heroine to the very rebels who were so suspicious of Charles I. There is little in her life to suggest that she would have encouraged the schemes and the confrontations that drew her brother into the fatal war with his subjects. The compromises that required so much shedding of blood might well have been achieved in peace. In particular, because of her Calvinist background, and her many years in the tolerant Netherlands—that "staple of sects and mint of schism . . . where not one so strange/Opinion but finds credit and exchange," in the words of the poet Andrew Marvell—Elizabeth would almost certainly have supported a more open and expansive religious settlement than the one that was reached in the 1660s.

It is possible that the more conservative elements in English society would have remained opposed even to the moderate settlement that could have been reached in the last months of 1641. They resented Pym deeply, as Nicholas's letter to Charles that autumn made clear. But Pym was not to live long, and in the absence of warfare it is implausible that Cromwell would have filled his shoes as a political leader. It is far more likely that he would have remained, as he had been until 1640, a retiring country gentleman, happy on his estates and in the practice of his Puritan beliefs.

Other radicals in Parliament might still have caused trouble, but without a civil war their influence would have been minimized. The voices of the dispossessed would have remained unheard, and the heritage of such ideas as universal male suffrage or freedom of the press (which Milton was soon to advocate) would have had to await their first champions, perhaps for more than a century. That neither Hobbes nor Locke would have felt the need to write about politics is perhaps the most dramatic change of all. The concept of the state, the definition of authority, and the quest for freedom as we know them today would have developed more slowly and possibly in entirely different forms. One hundred fifty years later, the absence of the precedent of a people trying and executing their king might also have affected the course of the French Revolution, not to mention the entire revolutionary tradition of modern Europe. The fact that England had not gone through the trauma, though, might have removed the restraint that helped make her a mere spectator during subsequent revolutionary upheavals.

Sometimes, however, it is the small detail that is especially telling about the contingencies that shape our ends. With Elizabeth on the throne, and dissenting faiths quietly accepted, there would have been no need for William Penn to emigrate to America. There might still have been a United States, but there would certainly have been no state named Pennsylvania. Move a plague just one week earlier, and have it travel no more than a hundred yards northward, and you shift the contours of both the little hillocks and the large ranges that determine history's wayward path.

THOMAS FLEMING

NAPOLÉON'S INVASION
OF NORTH AMERICA
Aedes aegypti *takes a holiday, 1802*

As we have seen in Theodore K. Rabb's essay about Charles I, disease can be history's great leveler, literally, and epidemics, those accidental force multipliers, have been responsible for more than their share of turning points—and might-have-beens as well. You think of the mysterious plague that decimated an all-conquering Assyrian army in front of Jerusalem in 721 B.C., a decisive moment in the religious history of the world; the flulike illness that ravaged Periclean Athens (and killed Pericles himself), helping to destroy Athenian power; or the smallpox that wasted Native American tribes and brought down two empires, the Aztec and the Inca. The list could go on. What if these epidemics had never happened, had broken out at a slightly different time or in a form less severe?

There may be no better example of the effect of disease on history than the yellow fever epidemic that largely wiped out a French army in Haiti in 1802 and presented the young United States, just twenty years after the Revolutionary War, with a matchless opening to the West. That was of course the Louisiana Purchase, the 868,000 square miles of the lands west of the Mississippi that Thomas Jefferson's representatives in France picked up for a bargain price of $15 million, or approximately four cents an acre. No longer would the United States be hemmed in by the Mississippi River and British Canada. New Orleans, the key trading city for the trans-Appalachian states and territories, would be ours. The westward movement (and with it, a half century of rancorous dispute over the spread of slavery) could begin.

But Thomas Fleming asks us to consider some of the alternatives, and ones that would have been altogether impossible without Aedes aegypti, the mosquito that carries yellow fever. Would a French-led Caribbean-American empire, a second New France, have taken shape? How would a Louisiana Territory in which slavery was banned have affected the United States? Might Napoléon himself have sought refuge in New Orleans—with a Waterloo in the bayous as the result?

THOMAS FLEMING is a historian whose many books include biographies of Thomas Jefferson and Benjamin Franklin; an account of the American Revolution, *Liberty!*; *Duel: Alexander Hamilton, Aaron Burr, and the Future of America*; and most recently, *The New Dealer's War: Franklin D. Roosevelt and the War Within World War II*.

EVERYONE AGREES THAT the 1803 Louisiana Purchase was the great triumph of President Thomas Jefferson's administration. In one stroke, the man from Monticello doubled the size of the United States. Few realize the so-called "greatest real estate deal in history" also solved one of the president's most unnerving problems: the possibility of a biracial Revolutionary French army in New Orleans—a presence that would almost certainly have changed the course of American history.

Even fewer know that the solution to this nightmare—and the origin of Jefferson's triumph—was largely the product not of clever diplomacy or glorious feats of arms, but of the existence of a tiny female creature known to scientists as *Aedes aegypti*—the mosquito that produces yellow fever. Breeding in pools of stagnant water in cities, towns, and army camps, *Aedes* triggered devastating epidemics in the Caribbean, South America, and tropical Africa, with death rates as high as 85 percent. At the turn of the nineteenth century, no one had any idea that this seemingly harmless insect was the source of such woe.

When Jefferson became president in 1800, he was still in the throes of his long love affair with the French Revolution—a romance so intense, he once declared he would have gladly seen the entire world depopulated rather than permit "that cause" to fail. This ideological fervor enabled Jefferson to dismiss the blood-soaked orgy of violence into which the historic upheaval collapsed—and its evolution into a virtual tyranny under the leadership of Napoléon Bonaparte. The new president was equally blithe about the nasty undeclared war the United States had fought with France during the last two years of President John Adams's administration, in which French warships and privateers had destroyed $12 million worth of American shipping—the equivalent of $600 million in modern money.

Also ready for diplomatic revision in Jefferson's White House was America's relationship with the republic that had been established on the island known variously as Hispaniola and Saint Domingue. Then as now it was divided into a French-speaking western third (the future republic of Haiti) and a Spanish-speaking eastern two-thirds (the future Dominican Republic), with a range of mountains as a geographical barrier between them. Spain had ceded the Spanish part of the island to France in 1795. For American merchants, Saint Domingue's wealthy upper class were prime customers. In 1790, before the French Revolution exploded, U.S. exports to the island, mostly food and lumber, amounted to $3 million, second only to the $6.9 million that the United States shipped to England. Small wonder that the island was considered the ultimate prize in the numerous wars the great powers fought in the Caribbean.

The French Revolution's cry of liberty, equality, and fraternity had reached Saint Domingue early in the 1790s. The precarious social mixture of royal officials, rich creole planters, middle-class storekeepers, and craftsmen and free mulattoes was sitting on a potential volcano of 400,000 black slaves, whose toil on the sugar plantations made the island France's most lucrative overseas possession. In 1793, war erupted between England and Revolutionary France—a conflict that roiled the politics of the United States for a decade. The two embryo parties, the Jeffersonian Republicans, forerunners of today's Democrats, and Alexander Hamilton's Federalists, forerunners of the Republicans, took opposite sides.

The British and their allies made very little headway against the French Revolutionary armies on land. But overseas, the British fleet proved a major advantage. Island after island of France's Caribbean empire fell to British amphibious assaults, an art they had mastered during the Seven Years' War (1754–61). In Paris, meanwhile, the radical Jacobins seized control of the French National Assembly. In 1794 they issued a declaration freeing all the slaves in France's overseas dominions. The move was motivated only partly by a belief in universal liberty. The French also hoped to trigger massive slave revolts in Jamaica and other English colonies and in the United States. By that time President George Washington had declared America neutral in the global war—with a distinct Hamiltonian tilt toward England.

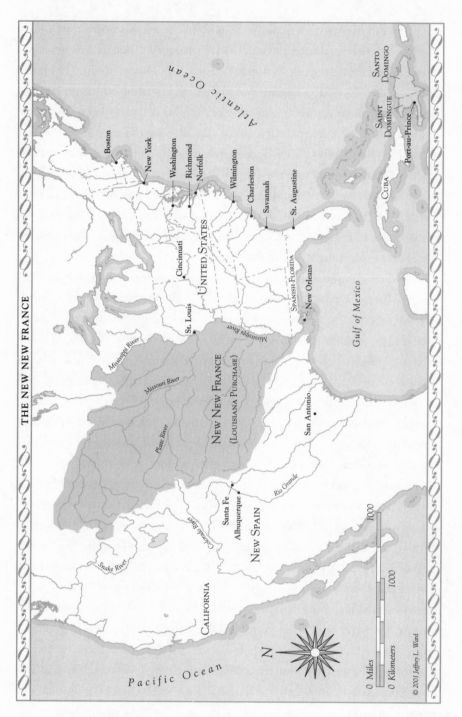

When news of the Jacobin decree reached Saint Domingue, a civil war of unbelievable ferocity exploded, with massacres of whites by blacks and vice versa, compounded by the invasion of a British army. Out of the turmoil emerged a charismatic black leader, Toussaint L'Ouverture, a figure who terrified slave owners in the American South. The Federalists in control of the American government took a different view. President John Adams and his secretary of state, Timothy Pickering, saw L'Ouverture as an opportunity to frustrate British and French imperialism in the Caribbean and maintain America's lucrative trade with Saint Domingue. They shipped L'Ouverture's army supplies and ammunition and at Alexander Hamilton's suggestion, sent his boyhood friend Edward Stevens, born on St. Croix, to the island's major port, Cap François, where he became L'Ouverture's trusted friend and adviser. The Adams administration even ordered the American fleet in the Caribbean to show the flag at Cap François. Without quite saying it, they urged L'Ouverture to declare independence.

Secretary of State Pickering performed masterfully in this delicate diplomacy, persuading jittery South Carolina Federalist slave owners to back him in Congress by producing evidence that the French government's representative in Saint Domingue, a demagogic Jacobin named Theodore Hedouville, had urged L'Ouverture to invade British Jamaica and the American South to foment slave uprisings there. But the black leader had refused to pursue this racist foreign policy.

Backed by American diplomacy and firepower, L'Ouverture routed the British army and became the de facto ruler of Saint Domingue. His troops quickly conquered the Spanish part of the island as well. Through Edward Stevens and Timothy Pickering, Alexander Hamilton was invited to advise the black leader on a constitution. True to his authoritarian instincts, Hamilton told L'Ouverture to appoint himself governor general for life—and enroll every able-bodied man in the militia. An assembly was also added to the government's structure, but it had no power to initiate legislation.

With driving energy, L'Ouverture invited whites and mulattoes to join him in restoring a semblance of prosperity to Saint Domingue. He banned slavery forever but persuaded the former slaves to return to the sugarcane fields to work as draftees in the service of the state. Unfortunately, he never trusted the slave-owning British and Americans enough to declare independence. He retained a frequently expressed loyalty to Revolutionary France, which had given his race their freedom.

When Napoléon Bonaparte seized power in Paris, followed within a few months by Thomas Jefferson's electoral triumph in 1800, Toussaint L'Ouverture was doomed. In Washington, D.C., the new American president urged the French chargé d'affaires, Louis Pichon, to tell his government that America was eager to help restore French rule in Saint Domingue. He advised France to make peace with England and send an army to crush the black rebels; "Nothing would be easier than to furnish your army and fleet with everything and to reduce Toussaint to starvation," Jefferson said.

Historians debate whether this ruthless reversal of American policy was rooted in Jefferson's eagerness to show his friendship for the new ruler of France or in his fear of a slave republic that would communicate dangerous ideas about freedom and equality to the restless blacks of the American South. It was probably a mixture of both motives. Napoléon had not yet made himself France's ruler for life. Jefferson was still able to view him as a legitimate heir of the Revolution. In September 1800, Virginia had been badly shaken by the aborted rebellion of Gabriel Prosser, a Richmond blacksmith, and his brother Martin, an itinerant preacher.

The Prossers, both free blacks, had organized slaves at funerals and secret religious meetings, using the language of the American Declaration of Independence and the French Declaration of the Rights of Man. The plan called for a march on Richmond from nearby plantations, a seizure of the state arsenal to equip a black army, and the massacre of all the white inhabitants except Methodists and Quakers, who opposed slavery. On the night of the rebellion, a storm washed out the roads to Richmond and the would-be rebels scattered. Before they could reorganize, the secret leaked and the Prossers and other leaders were promptly executed. But sporadic smaller slave revolts had continued to disturb the state for the next two years.

In Europe, Jefferson's election as president coincided with the exhaustion of the two superpowers, after eight years of global warfare. As peace negotiations began, Napoléon acted on Jefferson's invitation. In November 1801, the First Consul shipped a 20,000 man army to Saint Domingue, commanded by his brother-in-law, General Charles Leclerc. Unknown to Jefferson or anyone else, this expedition had another purpose. In March 1801, the Man of Destiny, as Napoléon liked to be called, had browbeaten his reluctant Spanish ally into retroceding the immense territory of Louisiana to France. It had been given to Spain as compensation for her losses in the Seven Years' War.

In secret orders, Bonaparte told Leclerc to transfer the bulk of the army to New Orleans as soon as he restored French supremacy in Saint Domingue, a task that Bonaparte estimated would take only six weeks. As for slavery, Napoléon thought it ought to be reimposed along with French rule, but he withheld judgment on that decision for the time being. The goal was the creation of a self-sufficient overseas empire. Louisiana would supply Saint Domingue and the other French islands with food at cut-rate prices, eliminating the need to buy from the Americans. The islands would produce sugar, coffee, and cotton to swell France's depleted exchequer. Ships of other nations would be excluded from this lucrative business.

A confident Leclerc arrived in Cap François in February 1802, and promptly went to work on "the gilded Africans," as Napoléon contemptuously called them. The size of the French fleet and army made L'Ouverture and his allies more than a little suspicious. It was much too large to be the mere escort of a delegation from Paris, reaffirming France's theoretical sovereignty. When Leclerc called on Henri Christophe, one of L'Ouverture's generals, to surrender the port city, he declined. Leclerc promptly attacked from land and sea. Christophe responded by burning Cap François and retreating into the country.

All-out war erupted throughout Saint Domingue. At first it seemed to go well for the French. The Spanish section of the island was quickly occupied with the help of the local population. Some black garrisons surrendered to oncoming French brigades. In ten days Leclerc had captured all the key coastal ports and forts and was preparing an offensive into the interior. But

L'Ouverture remained beyond his grasp, and another black general, Jean-Jacques Dessalines, rampaged through the countryside, slaughtering every white person he found—and any black who tried to help them.

An attempt at negotiations failed and on February 18, 1802, Leclerc launched an offensive against L'Ouverture's interior stronghold, Gonaïves. Advancing in four columns, the French discovered they had to wade through "fire and bayonets" for every foot of ground. Losses were heavy on both sides but the aggressive attack paid off when several black generals switched sides and supported Leclerc. The French commander combined force with lavish promises of money and power to those who joined him in a pacified Saint Domingue.

On February 23, L'Ouverture ambushed a French force of 5,000 men a few miles from Gonaïves. For a while the French teetered on rout. But their commander, General Donatien de Rochambeau (son of the general who was George Washington's partner at Yorktown) rescued the situation with a moment of bravado. Tossing his hat into the ranks of the oncoming blacks, he shouted: "My comrades, you will not leave your general's hat behind!" The French infantry wheeled and soon had L'Ouverture's men on the run. The next day Gonaïves went up in flames.

Leclerc was losing men—as many as two thousand in a single battle. Also, for the first time he noticed a strange illness creeping through his army. Soldiers weakened without warning; in a day they were too sick to walk. Then came black vomit, yellowing skin, convulsions, and death. But the French commander, as determined and as ruthless as his imperious brother-in-law, pressed his offensive, and soon other black generals— notably Henri Christophe—switched sides.

On May 1, L'Ouverture agreed to peace terms. He would give up power and retire with a respectable bodyguard to a plantation in the interior. His generals and officers would receive equivalent ranks in the French army, which soon became 50 percent black.

Why did Toussaint surrender? Probably because he learned that Napoleon had signed what seemed a definitive treaty of peace with the British at Amiens. This left him and his black army at the mercy of Bonaparte's vastly superior numbers and weaponry. The black leader capitulated, hoping to get the best possible deal from Leclerc. L'Ouverture's second in command, Dessalines, sullenly accepted similar terms on May 6.

But the war was far from over. Guerrilla resistance continued to flare throughout the interior of the island. Moreover, Leclerc was confronting other problems beyond Saint Domingue's horizon.

In the same first months of 1802, Jefferson and his secretary of state, James Madison, learned that the French now owned Louisiana. Next, the American ambassador in London warned them of Napoleon's plan to make Saint Domingue a mere way station on Leclerc's voyage to New Orleans. Jefferson's love affair with the French Revolution came to an abrupt end, under the influence of the cooler, more suspicious Madison and other advisers. Tench Coxe, a Philadelphia merchant who was heavily involved in the cotton business, warned that the United States could not "be too much on our guard against the consequences" of a French army in Louisiana.

When General Leclerc proclaimed a blockade of the Saint Domingue's rebel-held ports and asked Charge Louis Pichon to obtain American cooperation, the dismayed Frenchman encountered an American about-face that left him speechless. Jefferson and Madison informed him, presumably with straight faces, that they would not be able to starve Toussaint's army after all. The United States did not have the power to enforce an embargo against American merchants, who were making millions trading with the blacks. An agitated Pichon reported that he found Jefferson "very reserved and cold."

Secretary of State Madison told Pichon the United States would adopt a posture of "neutrality" if war broke out between the French army and the black rebels. That meant the French could seize American ships if they could catch them. But it also meant that the American government would not give Leclerc's army loans or credits to buy food and ammunition for his men. The French did not have enough warships to clamp a meaningful blockade on the island's thirteen ports and France was too far away to supply them with food.

A testy Leclerc tried to force American merchants trading with Saint Domingue to accept lower prices or promissory notes for their cargoes. They refused the notes, knowing that France was more or less bankrupt, and preferred to sell their goods to the rebels. Most merchants had deduced or otherwise learned Napoléon's plan to make trade with Saint Domingue an exclusively French affair. Profits, present and future, accentuated the American tilt to the rebels.

Next came an uproar from New Orleans that had a huge impact on Jefferson's attitude toward Leclerc's expedition. The Spanish, still in control of the port city, suddenly announced they were revoking the "right of deposit," which George Washington's administration had negotiated in 1795. Under this agreement, Americans were entitled to export cotton, farm produce, and other items of trade through New Orleans. When the right was revoked, an instant shout for war rose from the Western states, led by warrior politicians such as Andrew Jackson of Tennessee. Kentucky alone had a half million dollars in goods and crops on the Mississippi when the news of the revocation arrived.

General Hamilton warmly seconded this call for war in the pages of the New York *Evening Post*. In private letters he gloated over the dilemma Jefferson confronted. He had been elected deploring the large army and navy the Federalists had raised for the undeclared war with France and the taxes that supported the new military establishment. He had repealed the taxes and reduced the armed forces to a shadow. Now he was faced with "the great embarrassment of how to carry on a war without taxes."

When Jefferson tried to defuse the situation by sending James Monroe to France as an envoy extraordinary, Hamilton, writing in the *Evening Post* under the pseudonym Pericles, ferociously attacked the move. Hamilton recommended going to war immediately, before the French had time to ship an army to New Orleans. He called on Jefferson to triple the size of the pathetic 3,000-man regular army and muster a 40,000-man standby force of militia. The Navy should be strengthened and negotiations opened with England to "cooperate with us at a moment's warning."

Now the whole country, instead of a few administration insiders, knew the threat President Jefferson was confronting—and Hamilton had used it to portray the president in the worst possible light. Unfortunately, the details were essentially true. Jefferson had reduced the army and navy to a shadow. Worse, we now know, thanks to a chance to explore French and Spanish archives, Napoléon had on his secret service payroll men who could have made his conquest of the Mississippi valley a simple matter.

Brigadier General James Wilkinson, the commander in chief of the American army, received a secret annual stipend from Madrid (currently allied with France). Known to his Spanish handlers as Agent 13, Wilkinson had taken an oath swearing allegiance to Spain back in 1787. George Rogers Clark, conqueror of the Northwest Territory in the Revolution, was among the distinguished names on the French secret service payroll. Such allies might well have enabled Napoléon to add the United States to Holland and other nations of Europe that had become French satellites, with governments that obeyed orders from Paris.

By now President Jefferson was a very troubled man. Doing a hitherto unthinkable foreign policy somersault, he talked of "marrying ourselves to the British fleet and nation" to keep Napoléon out of Louisiana. It is unlikely that the British would have been eager to do business with a man who had vilified them for the previous decade.

Fortunately for the disturbed president, that aforementioned character, *Aedes aegypti,* was hard at work, decimating the French regiments. Noting Leclerc's growing weakness, a watchful L'Ouverture began intriguing for a comeback. But Leclerc was watching him too. Lured to a nearby plantation without his usual escort, the black leader was seized, thrown on a ship, and deported to France as a common criminal. There, Napoléon deposited him in a freezing fortress in the Jura Mountains, where L'Ouverture died a year later.

At this point Bonaparte made a truly egregious blunder. Pressured by refugee planters from Saint Domingue and by numerous merchants in Le Havre and other French ports who had grown rich on the slave trade, he decided to reimpose slavery. When word of this decision reached Saint Domingue in June 1802, the black masses rose in fury against the French and the black soldiers allied with them, triggering a new cycle of massacre and countermassacre. General Leclerc was stunned by the ferocity of the blacks' resistance. "They die with incredible fanaticism—they laugh at death; it is the same with the women," he said. The astonished French commander concluded he would have to kill everyone above the age of twelve, a policy he proceeded to put into brutal practice.

Weakened by a growing food shortage and a lack of water bottles and medical supplies, the French also found themselves fighting a losing battle with *Aedes aegypti*. Whole regiments died virtually en masse. Soon an appalling 60 percent of Leclerc's staff was dead. Finally, on November 2, 1802, the French commander himself succumbed.

American merchants continued their clandestine trade with the black rebels, shipping them guns and ammunition as well as food. The enraged French threatened to send captured blacks to America, where they would make good on Hedouville's plan to spread slave revolts throughout the Western Hemisphere. A grimly determined Napoléon poured in replacements and ordered General Donatien de Rochambeau to continue the struggle.

Reinforced by 15,000 men, Rochambeau seemed on his way to restoring French control of the island. He drove black rebels from all the chief seaports, cutting off most of their supply of guns and ammunition, and began launching devastating attacks into the interior. But in Europe events were unfolding that soon turned these victories into hollow triumphs. The British decided that their experiment with a purportedly peace-loving Napoléon was not working. France was exhibiting aggressive behavior in the Mediterranean and elsewhere. It soon became obvious to Napoléon that the war for world supremacy was about to resume.

With that near certainty in mind, the Man of Destiny rethought his plans for Louisiana. Without a fleet, he would be unable to defend the territory. Pichon reported that the cancellation of the right of deposit at New Orleans had turned American public opinion strongly against both France and Spain. That aroused the specter of fighting a war with the Americans, which he was unlikely to win, especially if war with England resumed and the British fleet interdicted support from France for Rochambeau's army.

Perhaps more important, Bonaparte needed money for his war machine. When Ambassador Robert R. Livingston visited him in early 1803 seeking to buy New Orleans and Florida, Napoléon suddenly asked him how much he would be willing to pay for all of Louisiana. The amazed ambassador was soon joined by special envoy Monroe, who could speak forcefully for President Jefferson. By July of 1803, they had bought 868,000 square miles of North America for $15 million, and Jefferson was able to proclaim a tremendous political triumph over Alexander Hamilton, who had solemnly predicted Napoléon would never sell Louisiana.

Napoléon continued the struggle to subdue Saint Domingue—stirring fears that he might repudiate the Louisiana deal. But the moment news of the declaration of renewed war with England reached the Caribbean, the British West Indies fleet made Saint Domingue target number one. The royal navy bombarded the French-held seaports and smuggled guns and encouragement to the rebels. A desperate Rochambeau told French chargé Louis Pichon the situation could be rescued only if he received a million francs a month to buy food and weaponry. Jefferson declined to help and American bankers were equally cold. In November 1803, Rochambeau, his army reduced to 8,000 men, retreated for a last stand in Cap François. With yellow fever continuing to ravage his ranks, he surrendered to a British fleet cruising offshore.

On January 1, 1804, the new black ruler, General Jean-Jacques Dessalines, who had long since switched back to the rebel side, proclaimed the island independent of France and declared it would henceforth be known by its Carib-Indian name, Haiti. Taking a French tricolor, Dessalines tore the white strip from the flag, a graphic illustration of his regime's racial policy. He proceeded to massacre all the remaining whites on the French part of the island. (The Spanish part of the island regained a precarious independence with the help of the British fleet.) Under Dessalines's personal direction, white men, women, and children were hacked and shot to death. It was a blunder that sent Haiti careening into isolation for decades—and banished all thoughts of emancipating slaves in the American South.

If Napoléon had been a true son of the French Revolution, with a genuine commitment to universal human rights, instead of a Corsican military genius with only minimal moral standards, he might well have succeeded in his original vision of using Saint Domingue as a first step toward the establishment of a Caribbean-American empire. The key to his possible success was a genuine alliance with Toussaint L'Ouverture and his black legions. Philadelphia merchant Tench Coxe knew whereof he spoke when he described Toussaint's soldiers as "military" with "habits of subordination" broken forever.

A worried Coxe envisioned the possibility of a "large detachment of republican blacks [being sent] to Louisiana, accompanied by the sudden emancipation of the blacks there." The result might well have been a race war on the American continent with barbarities that more than matched the gruesome horrors of Haiti. Out of the turmoil might have arisen an American warrior whose generalship matched L'Ouverture's, and whose ferocity matched Dessalines's—Andrew Jackson. Almost certainly, Old Hickory would have meted out to the blacks the fate he inflicted on the Creek Indian nation in 1814: extermination.

If Napoléon had established a biracial colony of free blacks and whites in Louisiana and avoided war with the United States, it would have put terrific pressure on the American South to begin a policy of gradual emancipation. President Jefferson was strongly in favor of this idea. Before Gabriel's Rebellion, he had drawn up a draft constitution for Virginia that would have freed all slave children born in the state after December 31, 1800. Even after Gabriel Prosser's attempted insurrection stoked white fears, the Man from Monticello continued to insist that gradual emancipation, instead of guns and whips and patrols, was the best way to defuse black anger.

If such a policy had prevailed, the United States would have been spared the national nightmare known as the Civil War, with its 600,000 dead. A biracial nation might have emerged a hundred years earlier than the one that is still struggling to heal the spiritual wounds of involuntary abolition and slavery's incalculable humiliations.

The grisly events in Saint Domingue combined with Gabriel's Rebellion to make this biracial dream untenable in 1804. Jefferson was a politician as well as an idealist and he soon found himself under terrific pressure from fellow Southerners to make sure Haiti remained isolated from the American South. His son-in-law, John W. Eppes, rose in Congress to declare that U.S. merchants should have nothing to do with people of a race Americans needed "to depress and keep down." Congress soon concurred and passed a law prohibiting all trade with Haiti, which Jefferson signed. Former secretary of state Timothy Pickering, now a U.S. senator from Massachusetts, attacked this measure, claiming that the Haitians were only guilty of having "a skin not colored like our own." It was, thanks to Napoléon and Dessalines, much more complicated.

An even larger possibility swirls out of this historical kaleidoscope. If Napoléon had followed a wiser, more moral policy and created a biracial Caribbean-American empire, when he was defeated in Europe and exiled to Elba, he might have fled westward from that island and found refuge in the still loyal colony of Louisiana, where the blacks of the French army would have welcomed him as an apostle of emancipation. His white troops would have been equally ready to rally to his standard.

The Spanish policy of closing New Orleans would have been long since revoked, stirring warm feelings for France up and down the Mississippi Valley. Napoléon's charisma would have electrified the fighting men of the west. It is hard for us to realize the fascination with which everyone regarded this larger-than-life figure. Newspapers reported his taste in food, women, clothes, horses, in rapt detail. Combine this hypnotic effect with a call to defend the rights of man against Perfidious Albion and you have the makings of a titanic confrontation.

The British, determined to hunt down the great predator, as they viewed Bonaparte, would have dispatched a huge fleet and army in pursuit of final victory. What might have happened? One can easily envision a battle of New Orleans in which Andrew Jackson performed as one of Napoléon's brigadiers. Also in the upper ranks of this force might have been another devotee of political power—Aaron Burr.

With the French firmly in control of New Orleans and the lower Mississippi Valley, there would have been no opportunity for Burr to launch his 1806 scheme to detach the western states from the Union and conquer Mexico. That gambit depended on intimidating an enfeebled Spain. But Burr's hatred of Thomas Jefferson and James Madison would have been no less intense. With his confederate, General James Wilkinson, who almost certainly would have thrown in his lot with Bonaparte, Burr might well have convinced Napoléon to launch a war of conquest to absorb Texas and

Mexico. By the time Napoléon arrived in New Orleans, Spain would no longer have been an ally. The lure of filling his exchequer with Mexico's gold and silver would have been all but irresistible. Moreover, General Wilkinson had something very tangible to offer—a collection of rare maps of the Southwest that would have enabled the Man of Destiny to invade Mexico from a half dozen possible routes.

But first, there was the ultimate battle with the English. How fitting, the Americans (and even Bonaparte) might have thought, that this decisive clash should take place in the New World, where the idea of liberty first flowered. The British would have been driven by a variant on this idea— here was a chance to stamp out once and for all the American perversion of that noble idea, British liberty, into the license of a rabble in arms to defy their lawful sovereign.

To command their forces in this revised battle of New Orleans, the British would not have sent any old general, picked out of the government's hat, to finish off Bonaparte and the Americans. They would have chosen their best man—Arthur Wellesley, the Duke of Wellington. Napoléon, fighting on unfamiliar ground, without the massed cavalry that so often shattered his foes at a battle's crucial moments, might have found himself at a severe disadvantage. The Russian debacle would have also shaken his self-confidence.

We can be certain that the Iron Duke would not have committed the blunders perpetrated by his impulsive brother-in-law, Major General Edward Pakenham, in the confrontation with General Jackson at New Orleans in January 1815. There would have been no suicidal frontal assault against massed French and American muskets. Wellington would have had the advantage of an overwhelming British fleet—something Pakenham's puny squadron never gave him. With full control of the Mississippi in his grasp, the British commander would have enfiladed the French-American barricades from the river, forcing the defenders to fight in the open against his battle-tried veterans.

A British victory, a Waterloo of the bayous, would by no means have been impossible or even improbable. Napoléon would have ended up on St. Helena with a steady diet of British arsenic, as he did in factual history.

George III's delighted ministers would have found themselves in control of the city that dominated the American heartland—with a force majeure claim to possession of the entire province of Louisiana. Up in New England, Senator Pickering and other Yankees, disgusted by fourteen years of Jeffersonian government, were discussing secession from the Union. They would have greeted the news of Wellington's triumph with gloats of grim satisfaction.

For a decade Pickering had been talking about negotiating a New England alliance with London, which would join the descendants of the Puritans with Canada and the Maritime provinces to create a nation capable of eventually dominating the continent, reducing Jefferson and his slavocrats to a humbled minority. The destiny of North America—and the world— would have been far different, if this political realignment had come to pass on Wellington's bayonets.

Such are the amazing possibilities negated by a tiny insect with an evolutionary compulsion to feast on humans' blood—and infect them with one of the world's deadliest diseases. With blind indifference, these buzzing creatures frustrated the dirtiest schemes and the noblest ambitions. On the Fourth of July, Americans, after toasting their heroes, might well raise a glass to *Aedes aegypti* as one of the unsung heroines of the republic.

TOM WICKER

IF LINCOLN HAD
NOT FREED THE SLAVES

The inevitable results of no
Emancipation Proclamation

*Abraham Lincoln's Emancipation Proclamation of September 22, 1862, which
declared slaves "forever free," is the supreme moral moment of American history.
"Lincoln's political artistry," Tom Wicker writes here, "assured that the Proclamation . . . would be seen as a justified war measure, as well as a great humanitarian deed." When he proposed it to his Cabinet that July, he argued that the
taking of the moral high ground "was absolutely essential to the salvation of the
nation." Though the North had won big victories in the West, the Civil War
closer to Washington seemed that summer to be turning in favor of the Confederates. They had stopped the Union in the outskirts of their capital, Richmond, won
a heady triumph at the Second Manassas, and now Robert E. Lee's Army of
Northern Virginia was preparing to invade Maryland and Pennsylvania. It would
make a scythelike swing that, if unchecked, might very well have ended in the capture of Baltimore and the isolation of Washington. Before he could issue his
Proclamation, Lincoln badly needed a victory, any kind of victory. What he got
on September 17 at Antietam—the famous bloodiest day in American history—
was a tactically drawn battle but a strategic victory, a combination that the war
produced again and again. Lee retired to Virginia, ending the invasion threat and
buying precious time for Lincoln. Five days later the president made his an-
nouncement.*

The Emancipation Proclamation was more than a visionary document; it was a strategically astute move, something too often forgotten. It "made the war appear to be a Northern crusade against slavery," Wicker writes, and from that point on, the European recognition that the Confederacy so desperately sought would seem "an endorsement" of slavery. But what if the moment of victory (or the illusion of one) had not come in time? In Wicker's unhappy scenario, it is not improbable that the proclamation would have gone unissued and the war would have ended in a negotiated peace brokered by England and France. "Neither the moral question of slavery nor the political question of secession would have been resolved." Slavery might have survived for decades more. But beyond slavery, the consequences of an unresolved Civil War might have persisted into our own time. The counterfactual stakes of the Emancipation Proclamation could not have been more potentially damaging.

TOM WICKER is a former *New York Times* Washington bureau chief and a columnist for the newspaper. Among his many writings on the Civil War is the novel *Unto This Hour.*

POLITICAL ANALYSTS, SOCIOLOGISTS, journalists, and historians agree that the "race problem" remains a virulent, underlying issue in American politics, local and national. How could it be otherwise? When black citizens retain a virtually genetic memory of centuries of enslavement, and when the fight against racial segregation, share-crop peonage, and voteless second-class status barely triumphed less than a half-century ago. When the "black ghetto" with its crime, poverty, unemployment, and hopelessness has become a permanent feature of urban life. When even middle-class blacks still suffer blatant discrimination in housing, health care, school and professional admissions, and a criminal justice system in which a black man is more than seven times as likely as a white to go to prison.

If black-white relations in America remain so largely tense and unsympathetic 137 years after Abraham Lincoln declared former slaves "forever free" and 135 years after Robert E. Lee surrendered the main Confederate army at Appomattox, who can say how hostile those relations might be had there been no Emancipation Proclamation, no "Great Emancipator," no successful war to end slavery, no constitutional amendments to give at least legal validity to the equality of all Americans of whatever skin color?

It seems altogether likely, if such were the case, that the "civil rights movement" of the fifties and sixties, coming earlier or later, would have been more violent and more violently resisted, that the "long hot summers" of black uprising that followed in the greatest American cities would have been even more destructive of life and property, and that our vast fortress prisons, in addition to giving "the impression of institutions for segregating the young black and Hispanic male underclass from society" (as the criminologist Norval Morris put it) would long ago have erupted in rage and resistance even more furious, on both sides, than was demonstrated at New York's Attica Correctional Facility in 1971.

As for other vital developments in the nation's chronic racial problem—the desegregation of the armed forces in 1949, the Supreme Court's school desegregation ruling in 1954, or the monumental post–World War II migration of blacks out of the South and into cities whose faces and futures were changed forever—of these and other events it can only be said with any certainty that they would not have happened as they did, or when they did, or under the circumstances that actually prevailed, had not a savage and terrible war forced our greatest president to the most important act in American history.

Abraham Lincoln did not set out, however, to free the slaves by proclamation. Not that he favored human bondage: "As I would not be a slave," he said, in one of his precise formulations, "so I would not be a master. This is my idea of democracy." Nor did Lincoln lack human sympathy and understanding. "He treated me like a man," said the former slave Frederick Douglass, after a White House visit in 1863. "He did not let me feel for a moment that there was any difference in the color of our skins."

That was in keeping with Lincoln's deep sense of human brotherhood. But his attitude toward Douglass, an educated and accomplished black man, did not connote a belief in the genuine equality of what Lincoln often called "separate races." Blacks, "suffering the greatest wrong inflicted on any people," he told an audience of free black leaders, yet were "far removed from being placed on an equality" with whites. Not only had they been ill-treated but a broader difference than exists between almost any other two races" would always cause "a ban" even upon blacks freed from slavery and treated well by white people.

When he became president of the United States in 1861, Lincoln *did* favor emancipation—but gradual and compensated. In his Cooper Union speech of February 27, 1860, which greatly aided his presidential campaign, he had quoted Thomas Jefferson as having said:

It is still in our power to direct the process of emancipation and deportation, peaceably, and in such slow degrees, as that the evil will wear off insensibly; and their places be, *pari passu*, filled up by free

A CAUSE NOT LOST

This elaborately decorated version of Abraham Lincoln's Emancipation Proclamation appeared not long after the Union president's order became official on January 1, 1863. Many regard the Proclamation as the supreme moral moment of U.S. history. Had it not been for a drawn battle, which Lincoln treated as the victory he sought, the opportunity might have been missed.

(Library of Congress)

white laborers. If, on the contrary, it [slavery] is left to force itself on, human nature must shudder at the prospect.

But slavery was "forcing itself on," even as Lincoln won the presidency, the Civil War began, and in his first years in office he seemed to be presid-

If Lincoln Had Not Freed the Slaves

ing over a losing military effort. As late as his annual message to Congress of December 1862 (*after* the "preliminary" Emancipation Proclamation had been issued in September), the president proposed a constitutional amendment providing that states abolishing slavery *before the year 1900* would be compensated in U.S. bonds; that any slave earlier freed by presidential proclamation should be permanently free and his or her former owners compensated; and that Congress should have power to spend money for the colonization of blacks in a foreign land.

This proposal, subsumed in the freedom that followed Emancipation's effective date of January 1, 1863, obviously came to naught. It nevertheless reflected Lincoln's oft-stated conviction that the Constitution gave neither the president nor Congress the power to seize citizens' property, including slaveholders' bondmen; as well as his belief that whites and blacks could not live together amicably. Blacks, therefore, should be sent to Africa or elsewhere to rule themselves. (Neither Lincoln nor anyone else proposed that *whites* should emigrate and leave the territory of the United States to blacks.) This attitude toward black-white social and economic relations was shared by most nineteenth-century white Americans (and a century and a half later still influences admissions, housing, and criminal justice practices in a supposedly integrated nation).

Presidents are not kings, however, and events through the first seventeen months of Lincoln's presidency were driving him toward emancipation. ("I claim not to have controlled events but confess plainly that events have controlled me," he later wrote in a wartime letter to Albert G. Hodges of Kentucky.) Not only were aggressive abolitionists, many of them influential Republican members of Congress, urging him to take action; the threat of European intervention on the side of the Confederacy was ever-present. The war itself was going badly enough that the president came to believe that he had to seek some more dramatic means of waging it, while still maintaining unity in the war effort.

On the other hand, an army faction around General George B. McClellan, and a substantial portion of Northern political opinion, resisted the idea of "revolutionary" warfare, as well as punitive measures against the "erring sisters" of the South. Emancipation, Lincoln himself feared, might shatter the tenuous federal unity in waging the war. (The four vital "border states"—Missouri, Kentucky, Maryland, and Delaware—that remained loyal to the Union themselves sanctioned slavery, as did the District of Columbia. Abolition was a loud but not necessarily a majority sentiment in the Union of the 1860s.)

By July 13, 1862, with McClellan's Army of the Potomac newly turned back from the gates of Richmond, Lincoln told members of his Cabinet that he had "about come to the conclusion that it was a military necessity, absolutely essential to the salvation of the nation, that we must free the slaves or be ourselves subdued."

In the 1864 letter to Hodges, he elaborated on his view in 1862:

When [early in that year] I made earnest, and successive appeals to the border states to favor compensated emancipation, I believed the indispensable necessity for military emancipation, and arming the blacks would come, unless averted by that measure. They declined the proposition; and I was, in my best judgment, driven to the alternative of either surrendering the Union, and with it, the Constitution, or of laying strong hand upon the colored element. I chose the latter.

On July 22, 1862, Lincoln acted on that choice and read to the Cabinet a first draft of the preliminary Emancipation Proclamation. His mind was substantially made up, he said, but he delayed publication on Secretary of State William Seward's advice that the proclamation might seem a "cry of distress" if issued on top of federal military defeat in Virginia.

Even then, with the proclamation already drafted, but while Lincoln waited for a Union military victory to make it public, he told the nation in a masterfully phrased open letter to Horace Greeley, the editor of the *New York Tribune*:

My paramount object in this struggle is to save the Union and is *not* either to save or to destroy slavery. If I could save the Union without freeing any slave I would do it; and if I could save it by freeing all the slaves I would do it; and if I could save it by freeing some and leaving others alone, I would also do that. What I do about slavery, and the colored race, I do because I believe it helps to save the union, and what I forbear, I forbear because I do *not* believe it would help to save the Union. I shall do less whenever I shall believe what I am doing hurts the cause, and I shall do more whenever I shall believe doing more will help the cause.

Within days, still another Union defeat, this time virtually on the outskirts of Washington—the second battle of Bull Run—again delayed the proclamation. "The bottom is out of the tub!" Lincoln lamented, when he heard the news. But he had been persuaded by Seward to wait until Union war progress made the Emancipation Proclamation seem more effective, and the president more in command.

If such a moment had never come, it's at least conceivable that Lincoln might never have issued the great document—and in the autumn of 1862, with Lee and the Army of Northern Virginia moving into Maryland in their first invasion of the North, and another powerful Confederate army marching into Kentucky toward the Ohio River, many in both North and South doubted, with reason, that such a moment ever would arrive.

If it had not, owing to a continuing Confederate victory trend, the war might well have ended in a negotiated peace. That would have been, in effect, a Southern success, with slavery surviving much as it was before Fort Sumter. Something like Lincoln's proposed Constitutional Amendment of December 1862 eventually might have been adopted; as wartime animosities in the states of the former Confederacy gave way to peacetime calculations of interest. History and economics ultimately would have argued for compensated emancipation.

The subsequent history of the nation, of course, would have been quite different—disastrously so.

We can only speculate about that, however; because, in fact, the moment *did* come—a moment, at least, that Lincoln could treat as if it were the longed-for victory. On September 17, 1862, within weeks of the Greeley letter, McClellan—briefly and reluctantly restored to command—fought the Battle of Antietam (called Sharpsburg in the South) just well enough to stop Lee and his invading army. McClellan was fatally afflicted, however, with what Lincoln in a cutting phrase called a case of "the slows"; so, unfortunately, the general and his army let the mauled and ragged Confederates escape back to Virginia.

Ever the adept politician, Lincoln nevertheless seized even this flawed moment. Five days after Antietam, the president called his Cabinet together again, read them a humorous passage from Artemus Ward, reminded them of the draft proclamation he had read aloud a few weeks earlier, and told them he did not wish their advice about "the main matter—for that I have determined for myself." Then he read the proclamation again, this time intending it for publication.

So the deed was done and after the long months of hesitation, emancipation was proclaimed—hardly a moment too soon. In December at Fredericksburg, Virginia, federal forces, then under Ambrose Burnside, suffered probably the most devastating defeat of the war. Simultaneously, perhaps the most propitious *military* moment for British recognition of the Confederacy was at hand.

Such a perhaps fatal (for the Union) diplomatic act was prevented by Lincoln's proclamation of September 22, 1862, to take effect on January 1, 1863. The Emancipation Proclamation precluded the possibility of European intervention because it made the war appear to be a Northern crusade against slavery (however tardily and reluctantly conducted). If a foreign nation had recognized and supported the Confederacy after emancipation, that nation's action would have been seen throughout the world as an endorsement of chattel slavery.

Despite his earlier doubts about the constitutionality of compelled abolition, Lincoln justified his proclamation as a war measure falling within the emergency powers of the president—and a powerful war measure it turned out to be. Not only did emancipation prevent foreign intervention by proclaiming a crusade for human freedom; it undermined the Confederate home and military fronts with slave unrest, labor depletion, and military desertion, causing many rebel soldiers to recognize that they were risking their lives and their families' well-being in "a rich man's war but a poor man's fight."

On the federal side, emancipation provided spiritual support for the cause of "Father Abraham," who was beginning to be seen as a symbolic moral leader. It also tapped a new and welcome source of manpower— 180,000 black troops serving in federal ranks by the end of the war in 1865. The document made Lincoln "the Great Emancipator" and ensured that his death would bring him the martyrdom and reverence he is accorded to-day, everywhere in the world—including the states of the old Confederacy.

Rightly so; for not only was the concept of emancipation morally and strategically powerful; but Lincoln's political artistry assured that the proclamation really would be seen as a justified war measure, as well as a great humanitarian deed. His timing, in the wake of Antietam, gave the document plausibility. It signaled the end of slavery everywhere in the nation, though legally it freed slaves only in states and parts of states then in rebellion against the Union—not in any place (the District of Columbia, for instance) where Lincoln had the immediate power to strike off their bonds.

Thus, whatever divisive effect a less considered, less well-timed proclamation might have had in the North was minimized. Even so, in the congressional elections of 1862, the Democrats made substantial gains.

The excess of the North's manpower, industrial strength, and military might over those of the Confederacy, together with stronger Northern political institutions and Southern dissension, might well have brought *eventual* Union victory, even without emancipation, even after European intervention.

That argument, however, overlooks the real possibility that continued Confederate military success, even in defense, might have sapped Northern morale, destroyed Lincoln's political support, and brought about his defeat in 1864 (when George B. McClellan was his Democratic opponent). In the long hindsight of history, it seems likely that the Northern public, tiring of an apparently unwinnable war, would have forced a negotiated peace at some point *before* those underlying Northern advantages could have had their likely effect.

Aside from what would have happened in the war itself had not Lincoln

freed the slaves as and when he did, the postwar and contemporary consequences are almost incalculable. What *would* have happened had the nation failed even in a great war to win the freedom of the black bondmen
and women of the wartime and antebellum South? And had a compromise
peace left the "peculiar institution" in place and its masters in their former
seats of power?

A few likelihoods, approaching certainties, can be suggested: Slavery
would have continued for a time in the old Confederate and border states,
though the increasing pressures of world opinion and of an inefficient and
wasteful labor system eventually would have brought about its end—probably gradually, and with compensation, as Lincoln and many other leaders
of goodwill once had envisioned, but to which the South had preferred war.

Had eleven undefeated Southern states returned to the Union, to Congress, and to American politics, neither the thirteenth Amendment, abolishing slavery, the fourteenth, guaranteeing equal protection of the laws,
nor the fifteenth, establishing the right to vote to persons of color and to
former slaves, would have been added to the Constitution—at least not for
decades, perhaps never.

The so-called "reconstruction" of the Southern states that actually did
take place after the historical Confederate defeat would not have been necessary or tolerated by an undefeated (counterhistorical) South. Freed
Southern blacks would not have enjoyed the temporary political and other
forms of power some gained in the "reconstruction" years after the war. Re-
sentful Southern whites therefore would not have felt it necessary to form
the original, terrorist Ku Klux Klan—with its hateful echoes into the
present.

If these events, taken together, had *not* happened, the decades of hostility between Southern whites and blacks (repressed but real, on both sides)
that had its origins in the post–Civil War years, and the racial repression
and segregation to which whites soon resorted, might have been avoided,
or at least softened. So might the long years in which a "solid South" voted
religiously Democratic, dominated Congress, and controlled—with the so-
called "two-thirds rule"—party presidential nominations.

These would have been paltry gains compared to other, inevitable developments. Had gradual and compensated emancipation ultimately prevailed—perhaps by the end of the nineteenth-century, as Lincoln had proposed in December 1862—the system of "sharecropping" by which the white South maintained virtual peonage, and the "separate but equal" rule of law that enforced racial segregation, no doubt would have evolved anyway—later, perhaps, but otherwise about as it actually did.

These were responses not so much to the end of the Civil War as to the end of slavery. They also were effective Southern efforts—mostly winked at by the rest of the nation—to maintain white supremacy even after defeat in war and military emancipation. There's no reason to suppose that the white South would not have devised the same or equally clever means, or worse, to continue white supremacy, even after having consented—under economic pressure—to gradual and compensated emancipation.

The *fact* of black political, economic, and social freedom—no matter how achieved—would have been resented and feared by whites (as in many ways it is today), and would have demanded perhaps even more forceful responses from the fearful. Even as it was, between 1882 and 1900 there were at least 100 lynchings of blacks a year, and by 1968 more than 3,500 African-Americans had been lynched. And there's certainly no reason to suppose that other Americans would have protested anymore strongly than, historically, they did—at least until prompted by resisting blacks themselves, as in the actual civil rights movement.

No Emancipation Proclamation? A compromise peace with slavery surviving the Civil War? The nation would have been tenuously and unhappily reunited in those circumstances, but not on the basis of victor and vanquished—only in an apparent stalemate in which both sides had achieved their essential war aims: continued slavery for the Confederacy, a restored Union for the government at Washington.

Neither the moral question of slavery nor the political question of secession would have been resolved. Gradual and compensated emancipation might have drained some of the urgency from the former, but the strained theory of a right of secession might well have remained troublesome even today—far more so than in actual contemporary circumstances, when occasional secession threats sound more than a little empty (owing precisely to that Union victory in 1865 to which the Emancipation Proclamation contributed so heavily).

Of all the consequences of a less salutary course of events in the 1860s— no compelled emancipation, no Union victory—the worst might well be the knowledge of the 12 percent of Americans who are black that their forebears were *not* freed from bondage by crusade, by the willingness of a generation "touched by fire" to sacrifice its lives and futures, by the greatness of a leader martyred not least for his proclamation of brotherhood. Instead they would live with the knowledge that the forces of bondage and oppression had prevailed—perhaps far into the twentieth century, if not permanently.

If black Americans could not take at least small satisfaction in what, in historical fact, *did* happen more than a century ago, what faith could they have in a nation to which their race was borne in chains? In a "democracy" that had failed, in its most fundamental test, to strike off those chains? In freedom itself, so long denied their ancestors, so boldly and belatedly won for themselves, from a reluctant and grudging majority?

In winning freedom for slaves more than a century ago, however, the nation finally accepted freedom for itself—though not without protest. In issuing the great proclamation, Lincoln responded not just to the pressures of his era but—as if to a vision—to the needs of later times, into the present and on into the future. His "justified war measure," taken for reasons so compelling in 1862, is even more vital to Americans today. It strengthened the Union war effort as desired—but, more importantly, it began the "unfinished work" that Lincoln was to define at Gettysburg: a "new birth of freedom" in a nation "conceived in liberty" but not yet devoted to it.

For white and black alike, that is still what he termed it—"the great task remaining before us."

ALISTAIR HORNE

FRANCE TURNS THE OTHER CHEEK, JULY 1870

The needless war with Prussia

The unification of Germany in January 1871, at the end of the Franco-Prussian War, was a central event of the nineteenth century; it would be the defining one of the twentieth. Its poisoned fruit produced three world conflicts (if you count the Cold War), and all manner of attending horrors, from the Stalinist purges to the Holocaust. Unification may have been bound to happen—and could have occurred without especially dire consequences—but was achieved prematurely through the unexpected humiliation of France, which left a spreading taint of bitterness, a kind of historical oil spill. The French ambassador's July visit to the Prussian king William, taking the waters at Bad Ems, and the king's refusal to give in to his provocative demands, was the inconspicuous beginning of a crisis. The somewhat doctored account of the meeting, known as the Ems telegram, that Otto von Bismarck, the Prussian chancellor, sent out hardly seemed a pretext for armed confrontation. But it was a perceived affront that Napoléon III, the French emperor, could not afford to ignore: two days later, on July 15, France was at war with Prussia and its client states.

The cause of the Franco-Prussian War may have been feckless and French preparation to fight chaotic, their strategy inviting disaster; yet the odds were not totally against France. Its army, though outnumbered, was based on a solid core of professional soldiers, who relied on weapons—notably a breech-loading rifle and a primitive but effective hand-cranked machine gun—that were superior to those of the Prussians. The early battles were close (in one, the French inflicted

8,000 casualties in less than twenty minutes). But the ailing French emperor allowed his army to be trapped at Sedan and was forced to surrender. In one of the most brilliant campaigns ever waged in Europe, one Napoléon I would have been proud of, the encirclement of Metz and Paris soon followed Sedan. For Prussia, 1870 was the year of the trap, not once but three times, something of a military tour de force. By the time the capital fell in January 1871, its population had been reduced to eating zoo animals and rats: starvation and not Prussian artillery led to its surrender. But for France and the rest of the world, the most potentially lethal trap of all, though one that would not be sprung for another generation, was a unified Germany, with its military growing in overconfidence.

The lamentable record of what did happen brings us inevitably to what might have happened. What if the French had won those early battles, as they nearly did, and had forced a stalemate? Would the various German principalities have held together without the quick-drying cement of victory? (Some, remember, had fought Prussia a few years earlier.) What if France had acquiesced to unification as a quid pro quo for German concessions and a peace in which neither side was a victor—a peace in which Alsace and Lorraine would have remained French? How different would Germany have been without a fatal dependency on the myth of an all-conquering military? How different, too, would the world have been without a century of antagonism between France and Germany?

There is, of course, another, simpler scenario, the simplest of all, which Alistair Horne suggests in the chapter that follows—namely, that Napoléon could have done nothing, that he might have ignored the bait of the Ems telegram. In which case, the predominant cause for World War I—the loss of Alsace-Lorraine—would have been removed; and no World War I would have meant no Hitler, and no World War II. Horne's counterfactual may take a fanciful turn but the facts are closely and logically reasoned. A hint: In this case, the medium really was the message.

ALISTAIR HORNE, a Cambridge University Litt D., is the author of seventeen books. He has been awarded the British CBE, and has been made a Chevalier of the French Légion d'Honneur for his historical writings, which include *The Price of Glory: Verdun 1916; The Fall of Paris: The Siege and the Commune, 1870–1;* and *How Far from Austerlitz? Napoléon 1805–1815.* He is currently completing *Seven Ages of Paris.*

I N JUNE 1870, the newly appointed British Foreign Secretary, Lord Granville, gazed out with satisfaction on the world scene and claimed—with reason—that he could not discern "a cloud in the sky." In all his experience he had never known "so great a lull in foreign affairs." In Paris, Emperor Napoléon III's prime minister, Emile Ollivier, echoed Granville by declaring that "at no period has the maintenance of peace seemed better assured." Indeed, peace seemed to be in the air everywhere. Over Europe as a whole such a spring of content had not been seen for many years. As summer developed, however, it became a particularly trying one; in fact one of the hottest in memory. From several parts of France there were reports of drought, with the peasants praying for rain and the army selling horses because of the shortage of fodder; but then, what urgent need was there for cavalry when there was absolutely no threat of war on the horizon? Nevertheless, it was the kind of summer, not unlike those fateful summers of 1914 and 1939, when tempers frayed.

Even so, who in July 1870 could have predicted that within a matter of weeks the emperor of France, Napoléon III, would be deposed and seeking refuge in England; that Paris would be besieged and within a few months starved into surrender, while proud France herself lay prostrate and suing for peace with Bismarck's Prussians; and that the whole balance of power that had regulated Europe so meticulously since Waterloo in 1815 would be fundamentally altered?

At the beginning of July 1870, a small cloud passed across the sun—but it seemed only a very small cloud. For the past two years the throne of Spain had been vacant, following the deposing of the unsatisfactory Queen Isabella. One of the possible candidates was a German princeling, Leopold of Hohenzollern-Sigmaringen. He was a good Catholic, father of a family, and his brother Charles had recently accepted the crown of Romania with-

out anyone objecting. The idea of the Hohenzollern Candidacy had originated in Spain; Leopold's kinsman, King William I of Prussia, had agreed to
it—but only with considerable reluctance—but regarded it as purely a family matter. When his bombastic chancellor, Otto von Bismarck, however,
picked up the ball and ran with it, Paris rose up in alarm. It was the thought
of having German princes on the Pyrenees frontier as well as the Rhine;
though historians could have reminded French statesmen that, by filling
the Spanish throne with a Bourbon prince less than two centuries previously, this kind of hegemony was almost exactly what Louis XIV had sought
to impose on Europe.

So violent was the storm in France, egged on by inflammatory articles in
the Paris press, that the Hohenzollern Candidacy was promptly withdrawn.
Relieved, Lord Granville chided the French government for resorting to
such strong language, and the British press returned to themes of Queen
Victoria dispensing prizes in Windsor Park. But the furor in Paris continued
to mount dangerously. Napoléon III was a tired and sick man, with a large
stone growing in his bladder, and certainly not the match of his illustrious
uncle. His foreign policies had been thwarted at every turn, coming up
against two of the most adroit and dangerous statesmen of the nineteenth
century: Bismarck in Prussia, and Cavour in Italy.

In nearly two decades of absolute rule, as one way of diverting French
minds from the loss of their essential liberties, Napoléon had brought huge
prosperity to France. This had become an acceptable substitute for the majority of Frenchmen—though only temporarily. Under his famous Prefect,
Baron Haussmann, he had remodeled Paris. The railway network increased
from 3,685 kilometres to 17,924, so that all of a sudden the Riviera—
formerly the haunt of only a few eccentric English at Cannes—became a
Parisian resort. Telegraph lines radiated out all over the country, and shipbuilding expanded as never before. Mighty banking concerns like the
Crédit Lyonnais and the Crédit Foncier were established, the latter especially designed to stimulate the vast new building programme. "*Enrichissez-
vous*" (Get rich) was the slogan of the era, and a new wealthy bourgeoisie
had arisen. Yet at the same time the gap between rich and urban poor had
widened drastically. In Paris there was menacing discontent, at times with

echoes of 1789; worse still, and more dangerously, despite (or perhaps because of) his attempts at liberalization, France was bored with Napoléon III— *la France s'ennuyait.*

As at many other times in French history, hotheads clamored for the distraction of a successful adventure abroad. If the emperor needed such a success, no one was pushing him harder than his Spanish-born empress, Eugénie, who took the opportunity to remind her husband of Prussia's lightning victory over Austria in 1868, which was widely regarded as a humiliation to French foreign policy. Pointing to their heir, the Prince Impérial, she declared dramatically: "This child will never reign unless we repair the misfortunes of Sadowa."

Meanwhile, France's heavy-handed foreign secretary, the Duc de Gramont, held a personal grudge against Bismarck for having once described him (not unreasonably) as "the stupidest man in Europe," and he now began to adopt a plaintive, hectoring tone toward Prussia. It was not enough that the Hohenzollern Candidacy had been retracted, Prussia had to be humbled for her presumption. Accordingly, Gramont sent the French ambassador in Berlin, Count Vincent Benedetti, to badger the king at Bad Ems, where he was taking the waters. Benedetti was received with the greatest courtesy by King William, who had no desire (any more than his fellow German rulers) for war, observing that the unification of Germany would be "the task of my grandson," not his. (That grandson would be Kaiser Wilhelm II, who would lead a united Germany into World War I.)

This was, however, not the view of Bismarck, who was in no way determined to wait two generations, and who calculated that a war with France would provide the essential mortar required to cement together the existing, rather loose structure of the German federation into a unified nation— dominated, of course, by his native Prussia. But the *casus belli* would have to be most carefully selected, so as to cast France in an unfavorable light among the other nations of Europe—but also with Prussia's own German allies. As he once remarked, "A statesman has not to make history, but if ever in the events around him he hears the sweep of the mantle of God, then he must jump up and catch at its hem."

With the French now bent on pressing for diplomatic victories, Bis-

marck, twisting the knife in the wound, saw his chance. Irritated by Benedetti's importuning at Bad Ems, the benign old king refused to give a guarantee that the Hohenzollern Candidacy would never arise again, and
declined a request for a further audience. A telegram giving an account of
the interview was duly dispatched to Bismarck in Berlin. Bismarck saw "the
mantle of God"; without actually fudging the text, as he has often been accused of doing, he sharpened the tone of the dispatch before passing it to
the Berlin press—and the world.

As edited by Bismarck, it stated that the king had "decided not to receive the French Ambassador again, and sent to tell him through the aide-
de-camp that his Majesty had nothing further to communicate to the
Ambassador."

Even with Bismarck's editing, certainly when compared with the diplomatic language that was to prevail during the Cold War in the second half
of the twentieth century, the famous Ems Telegram hardly seems to have
constituted a *casus belli*. But Bismarck had his ear well tuned to the prevailing tone in Paris. Frenzied crowds surged through the streets shouting
"*À Berlin!*" In one of the rashest claims in all military history, the French
commander in chief, Marshal Leboeuf, encouraged the hawks with his foolish declaration that the army was "ready down to the last gaiter-button."
(Wits remarked that this was largely true, as there were no gaiters in stock
anyway.) Now, on receipt of Bismarck's telegram, urged on by his empress
and Gramont, fired by the ever shriller Paris press, Napoléon III took the
plunge.

On July 15, France declared war—in a state of exhilaration, recalling
Napoleon I's repeated successes beyond the Rhine, and expecting a repeat
performance. But, through Bismarck's cunning, she found herself at once
branded as a frivolous aggressor. As the *Illustrated London News* declared,
"The Liberal Empire goes to war on a mere point of etiquette," and this was
precisely how opinion, in America as in Europe, saw the new conflict. In
the severe judgment of a leading British expert on the Franco-Prussian
War, Sir Michael Howard: "Thus by a tragic combination of ill-luck, stu-
pidity, and ignorance France blundered into war with the greatest military

UNNECESSARY ADVERSARIES

The Franco-Prussian War may have been an avoidable confrontation, but it was one that would shape the history of the world. Here, a dejected Napoléon III of France (left), captured with his entire army at the battle of Sedan on September 2, 1870, meets with the victorious Prussian chancellor, Leopold von Bismarck.

(Hulton/Archive)

power that Europe had yet seen, in a bad cause, with her army unready and without allies."

In sharp contrast, the Prussian military machine was superbly ready, superbly equipped and led, and well tested in battle. Within eighteen days of mobilization, Bismarck and his German allies were able to field an unheard of force of 1,183,000 men. For France, military disaster followed on military incompetence. On September 1, a sick and defeated Napoléon III surrendered to King William of Prussia at the head of his army in Sedan. On the fourth, a stunned Paris greeted the news first with horror, then with a mixture of delight. As the empress fled to England, the mob invaded the Tuileries Palace where they found all the pathetic signs of an unintended departure; a toy sword half-drawn on a bed, empty jewel cases strewn on the floor, and on a table some bits of bread and a half-eaten egg. The end of the empire was proclaimed, and a new republic formed in the Hotel de Ville. Momentarily there reigned an atmosphere of unrestrained carnival; it was a sparkingly sunny day, no blood had been shed, and all Paris now turned out in its Sunday best to celebrate the most joyous revolution it had ever had. Automatically it was assumed on the street that—now that the emperor and his bellicose regime were gone—the victorious Prussians would return home and leave France alone.

Not so. A bitter four-month siege lay ahead, followed by an even more savage civil war as the Commune de Paris took over. By the summer of 1871 peace returned. But France was in financial ruins; much of proud Paris in physical ruin. Under Bismarck's harsh terms, France lost two of its fairest and richest provinces, Alsace and Lorraine. The nation would never forget. Forty-four years after the Ems Telegram, France would go to war to regain them, bringing the whole world with her into a new catastrophe. The whole world equilibrium would be fundamentally altered, and a second, even more terrible world war would be fought before some semblance of the pre-1870 Europe could be rediscovered. From the moment at Ems in the torrid July of 1870 was born all the evils of our twentieth century, which would scourge our planet with two terrible, and—worse than terrible—unnecessary world wars. Unnecessary, that is, if somehow war between Prussia and France could have been avoided that summer; if the Ems Telegram had never been sent—or, better, conveniently overlooked in Paris.

Could it have been otherwise? Well, yes it could, and this is one way a peaceful outcome might have happened.

In June 1870, Napoléon III is miraculously cured of the enormous—and debilitating—stone in his bladder by a brilliant young English doctor, passing it out of his system. He is still only sixty-two, and suddenly seems quite rejuvenated. Apart from his trust in medicine, at various times in his career he had sought advice from a greatly acclaimed Parisian *occultiste*, or medium, Allan Kardec—his real name, Hippolyte Léon Denizard Rivail. (To this day you can find Kardec's Stonehenge-like grave in famous Père

Lachaise cemetery [section 44], still kept heaped with the flowers of fans—apparently hoping to transfer to themselves his psychic powers. Supposedly his darkened bronze effigy also exudes a special appeal for the sexual fetishist; as the guidebook will tell you, a certain part of the body shines brightly, thanks to the caresses of sterile women. Kardec died in 1869, the year before the Ems Telegram—but for our purposes we will give him a few more years of life. And if it wasn't Kardec, it could have been another medium like him.)

So, cured of his disabling physical malady, Napoléon III goes off secretly to Kardec's Paris apartment to seek his help in the crisis that was brewing with Prussia. Could he, for instance, summon up the spirit of his illustrious uncle, Napoléon the Great, and ask him what he would do under the circumstances? Accordingly, in a darkened room, the medium's table begins to heave and levitate. All of a sudden the air is filled with an imposing presence; then a violent *coup de pied dans le derrière* [kick in the rear] suddenly propels the emperor across the room, throwing him flat on his face. (This seemed to confirm a popular joke much realized by Parisian wits and opponents of Bonapartism.) A voice out of the ether, with a strongly Corsican accent, fulminates:

"You fool, *tus es imbecile!* You're getting everything wrong. Even worse than I did. Why don't you call up that slimy old Talleyrand? He's a horrible old rascal, 'shit in a silk-stocking,' I once called him—but if only I had listened to him and gone for peace, instead of war, after the Treaty of Tilsit in 1807, I would never have had to face Wellington at Waterloo."

The bruised nephew goes away and thinks about it, then returns to Kardec the following day. "Get Talleyrand, *et tout de suite!*" A smooth, oily voice comes across the firmament:

"Yes, *Sa Majesté*, your uncle is absolutely correct. Alas, if only he had listened to me, you wouldn't be in this kind of mess now—but he forced me to resign after Tilsit."

"So, what should I do with that tiresome bully, Bismarck?"

"First of all, sack Garmont. Bismarck was being too kind when he called him 'the stupidest man in Europe.' You and I can run French foreign policy by ourselves. Then replace Benedetti in Berlin."

"By whom?"

"Well, what about that annoying hack, the opposition leader Adolphe Thiers? I know he's caused you a lot of trouble—but I always used to say, bring the troublemakers in, don't let them fester outside. He's quite sympathetic to the Prussians, at least they think so. He's a canny politician, he'd be able to tie Bismarck in knots, wrong foot him. After all, what is Bismarck but an overweight Kraut bully? And he's got plenty of other problems at home on his agenda. But, first, you must get rid of the hard-liners."

"What about the empress?"

"Well, *Majesté*, really she's your problem."

The emperor, always keen on the ladies and still with a hankering after the beautiful Italian countess of Castiglione (to whom he once gave a 422,000-pearl necklace, plus Fr 50,000 a month pin money), has an inspiration. Eugénie is frigid, but there were rumors that her virtue had once lapsed when opening the Suez Canal in 1869, just the previous year, when she had fallen for the sexy khedive of Egypt. He, Louis-Napoleon, could speak to his lawyers in the morning. After all, his uncle had divorced the magical Josephine and gotten away with it.

Talleyrand continues:

"Above all, *bin* that telegram of Bismarck's. Ignore it—it doesn't mean a thing, or at least don't let it. Remember what I used to say in your uncle's time—*surtout point de zèle* ['not too much zeal']."

"I know," says the emperor, ruefully, "and my favorite motto was always *Il ne faut rien brusquer* ['never rush things'], but the Impératrice would never listen to me . . . So, what next?"

"Reconvene my Congress of Vienna, which I put together in 1814 to save France—and Europe—when your uncle was sent to Elba. I don't want to boast, but it did give Europe fifty-five years of peace—and, with all those balls, the delegates had a devilish good time in Vienna while it lasted. As I say, Bismarck's got a lot of other things on his agenda, all sorts of problems at home to distract him—keep him talking, for months, if possible; then he'll lose momentum—and that'll be the end of him.

"Remember what Wellington used to say about you, *Sa Majesté*, *votre oncle*—a conqueror is like a cannonball, it has to go on; once it comes to rest, that's the end of it. That nice, cozy old king of Prussia, William, hates and fears Bismarck and his policies and would love to get rid of him. So wrong foot Bismarck."

"That's all wonderful advice, Monsieur Talleyrand; as a man of peace, you really should have been a bishop."

"But I was, *Majesté*, I was. . . ."

Talleyrand disappears, leaving behind an aroma of snuff, incense, and expensive perfume. Emperor Napoléon III returns to the Tuileries Palace, determined to take Talleyrand's helpful advice. It is July 14. His hand is greatly strengthened by an urgent dispatch just arrived from Granville in London, pressing France to do nothing drastic. This has a considerable effect when read out to the imperial ministers meeting in Council. Precariously the "doves" in the government seem to have gained the ascendancy. Under Louis-Napoléon's pressure rash thoughts about mobilization are shelved. That evening he summons to the Tuileries first Thiers, the opposition leader (and his principal political opponent), together with Thiers's leading left-wing followers. He urges them to take a bipartisan line and support his new drive for peace. Remember Talleyrand, he exhorts them! Thiers and his team agree—provided Louis-Napoléon's prime minister, Emile Ollivier, will tow the line. Next the emperor calls in Ollivier. Ollivier, a forty-five-year-old lawyer with a Republican background, had only been brought in that January to herald a new "Liberal Empire," and one of his first acts, as a man of peace and moderation, had been to cut France's excessive burden of arms expenditure. Over the past weeks he had been sitting on the fence, uncomfortably, as regards the Hohenzollern crisis, inclined toward conciliation but buffeted by the hawkish head of the army, Marshal Leboeuf, and Louis-Napoléon's sabre-rattling empress. Now, with the emperor's new—and surprising—change of heart, together with the promised support of Thiers, his former Republican ally, he is happy to climb off the fence and join the "Peace Party."

That night in the Tuileries, Louis-Napoléon has a furious row with the bellicose Impératrice. Recalling their passionate tryst in a grotto of Cairo's Gezira Palace of the previous fall, she reckons that there, in Egypt, at least, was a monarch who would obey her whims; and richer than Napo, too. She makes her plans, while Louis-Napoléon makes his.

The next day, July 15, in the Corps Législatif, Thiers—as good as his word—rises to denounce war. "Do you want all Europe," he challenges the hawks with forceful eloquence, "to say that although the substance of the quarrel was settled, you have decided to pour out torrents of blood over a mere matter of form?"

Thiers is followed by Ollivier, who—declaring that he cannot accept the responsibility of war *"d'un coeur léger"* ("with a confident heart")—wins over the Assembly with his proposal to launch an international appeal to a Congress of Powers.

The crisis of 1870 is over. Empress Eugénie takes the next available boat from Marseilles. Napoléon III heaves a sigh of relief, and—in his newly rejuvenated vigor—sends a note to his old love.

Paris remains tense for a few days. There are anti-Prussian demonstrations, but after a few troublemakers shouting *"À Berlin"* have been shot or sent to Devil's Island, calm is restored. Prime Minister Ollivier and his liberally inclined supporters are triumphant. Gramont retires to his estates in the provinces, in voluntary exile. Benedetti, by now the former ambassador to Berlin, is given the Latin American desk in the Quai d'Orsay, where he writes minutes (which no one reads) on conflict between Bolivia and Peru. Napoléon III persuades the Great Powers to convene a new Congress of Vienna, which he leads with distinction. In London, Foreign Secretary Granville heads for Scotland and the grouse, delighted that once more the skies are truly cloudless.

Henceforth Britain, and Queen Victoria, will do anything for Louis-Napoléon's new, prudent France (she, anyway, remembered how, on a visit to Paris in the '50s, she had found the emperor more attractive than any man since poor Albert). The whole world is impressed by France's cool-headed statesmanship; leaders suddenly recall the aggressiveness of Frederick the Great, rather than the successive ravaging of Germany by Louis XIV and Napoléon I. Bismarck is no longer the flavor of the month anywhere.

There is no war.

As clever old Talleyrand predicted, the new Congress of Vienna drags on into 1872. Bismarck has been humiliated, if not routed—totally wrong footed and made to appear before the world as a blustering bully, and a threat to the concert of nations. In Berlin the doves prevail; the king, who had certainly never wanted to be promoted to kaiser of a united Germany, returns to a quiet life at Potsdam, growing grapes in the conservatories built in a rare moment between wars by his ancestor, Frederick the Great. Moltke's huge army is progressively stood down, so that more money can be spent on education and roads. The 50 percent of Germans who are Roman Catholic rejoice that the march toward domination by Protestant Prussia, which once seemingly inexorable, is now halted. Once Bismarck had his impetus over the Hohenzollern Candidacy removed, like Wellington's cannonball, he and his policies are rendered pointless. Again, as Talleyrand predicted, he had plenty on his agenda—and problems—at home to occupy his mind. Like all bullies, once resisted, he collapses.

As soon as he decently can, good King William "drops the pilot"; full of unheeded resentment, the "Iron Chancellor" retires to his estates at Varzin, resuming his voracious diet of eleven hard-boiled eggs for breakfast, plus plates loaded with Reinfeld ham, goose with olives, and Varzin wild boar. A forgotten man, Bismarck dies in 1898 of gluttony (exacerbated by acute constipation) and disappointment.

In the meantime, Catholic Bavaria has formed a customs union with its neighbor, Catholic Austria, thereby providing a powerful counterweight to Prussia in the German-speaking world. In the west, the discovery of vast deposits of iron in Alsace-Lorraine (which, of course, continue to belong to

France) and coal in the neighboring Rhineland Ruhr led to a transfrontier coal-and-steel pool, the beginnings of a European Common Market. This is strongly backed by U.S. commercial interests, and contributing massively to overall European prosperity, thereby eradicating one of the main causes of war.

And what of America in all this? General Ulysses S. Grant comes to power in 1868 for two terms, on a campaign slogan of "Let us have peace." Having on his conscience the deaths of more men in the recent War between the States than any other general, he is so appalled by the prospects of a similar carnage in Europe that, renouncing the strictures of the Founding Father, George Washington, he commits the United States to playing a far-reaching role in European affairs. The brilliant U.S. ambassador in Paris in 1870, Elihu B. Washburne, is appointed secretary of state, and under his guidance the United States assumes a leading influence in the new Congress of Vienna. Under the Washburne Plan, there is widespread economic cooperation between the United States and Europe, with Washington offering troops in case of an outside threat—for instance, from an expansive, czarist Russia.

U.S. forces and mediation are indeed very nearly needed in 1898, when a serious conflict breaks out in Africa between Britain and a new, powerful France, called by historians the Fashoda Incident—Europe's ugliest moment since 1870. Pushing the claims of their rival empires, French troops under General Marchand, marching all the way across Africa, running up against the British forces on the Nile at Fashoda. Thanks to U.S. intervention, however, war is once more averted.

At the same time, Britain finds a new ally in the shape of King Frederick III's Prussia, now feeling distinctly inferior to the new France. Married to Queen Victoria's daughter, "Dear Vicky," Frederick had always been pro-British. He inherited the throne from his father, William I in 1888, and (instead of dying after a few months from cancer of the throat, possibly caused by all the stress of the Franco-Prussian War), lives to a ripe and fulfilling old age of eighty-three. Casting aside Bismarck's silly (and dangerous) notion that his map of Africa lay in Europe, under the Gute Fritz [b. 1831] as he was nicknamed, Prussia is now happy to accept, in return for her support, some tidbits of the British Empire south of the Sahara. As contemporary historians note, enlightened and benevolent colonialism in Africa continues into the twenty-first century—much to the benefit of the residents.

To gain him administrative experience, and quiet the aggressive impulses of a troubled heir born sadly with a withered arm, Frederick sends the prospective Wilhelm II to German South-West Africa—where tragically he succumbs to malaria. Frederick's fun-loving grandson, nicknamed "Little Willie" by the English, takes over in Berlin as Wilhelm II—instead of commanding an army at Verdun in 1916. Under him, emulating his uncle, Edward VII, Berlin becomes the *gai Paris* of Eastern Europe.

In France, the heir of Napoléon III, the beloved "Prince Impérial," having no need to seek refuge in England, does not join the British army to get killed by Zulu spears; instead he becomes a studious young man at the Polytéchnique, dim but peace-loving and succeeding his father in the Tuileries in 1875, but with most of his hereditary powers shorn by Republican politicians.

Meanwhile, in 1889, a boy, called Adolf, is born in the small Austrian town of Braunau, to the lower-middle-class Hitler family. He takes up painting, but nobody buys his pictures; called up into the Austro-Bavarian army, he manages to avoid the inconclusive border skirmishes that ensue after the assassination of an archduke in Sarajevo. In Berlin, the Prussians view with some pleasure the discomfort of their rivals to the south; in St. Petersburg, the czar rattles his sword, but a few brisk dispatches from President Teddy Roosevelt (reelected in 1912, he defeats an ineffectual Princeton professor named Wilson), and the newly formed North Atlantic Treaty Organization (NATO)—nothing quite as rude as the Ems Telegram—suffice to keep the lid on the kettle. Returning to Braunau, young Adolf gets involved in local politics, isn't elected as he is too far-out right wing and anti-Semitic; prosperous Austro-Bavaria has no time for that kind of nonsense. He dies, unknown and unmourned, in the arms of his mistress, Eva, of apoplexy while on a trip to Berlin in the spring of 1945. His dreadful paintings are eventually bought up by London's Tate Modern—along with a lot of other junk; which is why we remember the name of Hitler.

. . .

So there is no Great War, no Second World War—and no Holocaust. Such notional events were indeed utilized in a far-fetched, prophetic novel from the imagination of a little-known English science-fiction writer called H. G. Wells. But the critics panned the excessive fantasy that the peace-loving Americans could conceivably wipe out two cities in smiling Japan with bombs made from a handful of atoms. It was recalled that Wells, with his fevered imagination, had also previously written a book that was equally way-out—about the world being invaded by men from Mars; hence his novel, *1945 and All That*, was dismissed as just too fantastical by a tranquil twentieth century, which had come to regard itself evolving as an extension of the "perfectible" eighteenth.

A lovely, Arcadian dream perhaps; and possibly it takes too little into account the inbuilt aggressiveness and greed of the human race, which will one day wreck our planet. But impossible? No! All this from France's refusal to get overexcited about the Ems Telegram? Why not? Great events so often have tiny beginnings; and think of Ulysses' famous speech in *Troilus and Cressida*:

> . . . untune one string,
> And, hark! what discord follows; each new thing meets
> In mere oppugnancy. . . .

JOHN LUKACS

THE ELECTION OF THEODORE ROOSEVELT, 1912

Brokering an earlier end
to World War I

That Theodore Roosevelt could have recaptured the Republican nomination for president in 1912—and with it certain victory in the November election—is not fantasy. Even the unseating of a president in his own party, William Howard Taft, was possible, and Roosevelt almost brought it off. TR, who had spent his first four years out of office writing books and hunting big game in Africa, had become increasingly disenchanted with his handpicked successor: He described Taft as "a flubdub with a streak of the second-rate and the common in him." (The final break came over the Taft administration's prosecution of U.S. Steel, a trust whose formation Roosevelt had previously consented to. The antitrust suit seemed to imply that TR had countenanced an illegal monopoly.) Making the famous statement that his "hat was in the ring," he took the primary route against Taft. (Nationwide presidential primaries were one of the central planks of a program he called a "New Nationalism.") TR won ten out of twelve contests—he even took Taft's home state, Ohio—and beat the president by more than a million votes; he came to the August Republican convention in Chicago with 278 delegates. Though TR was clearly the choice of the party's rank and file, Taft was backed by the powerful GOP regulars. The outcome was practically settled before the convention, in a battle over the seating of pro-Roosevelt delegates, who might have given their leader the fighting chance he needed. As we know, the regulars won, but it was a Pyrrhic victory.

In John Lukacs's scenario, TR shows up at the convention to spellbind it. In

actuality he was prevented from doing so, but he did go on to preside over the for-
mation of his new Progressive Party—which, in the election, would capture more
votes than the Republicans, though two million less than those of the victorious
Democratic candidate, Woodrow Wilson.

What would have happened, Lukacs asks, if TR had been elected for a third
term? As far as his domestic policies were concerned, they may not have been rad-
ically different from those of Wilson. But Roosevelt would have asserted Amer-
ica's role in the First World War much earlier, intervening on the side of the Allies
as early as 1916. (By that time, TR, a champion of universal military training,
would have had an army ready to fight—"the military tent where they [men of dif-
ferent backgrounds] sleep side by side," he once said, "will rank next to the pub-
lic school among the great agents of democratization.") It was Roosevelt, after all,
who had brokered the end of the Russo-Japanese War with the Treaty of
Portsmouth in 1905 and who, the following year, had supported the Algeciras
Conference, at which the statesmen of the great European powers had settled the
crisis over Morocco. He would not have acted less positively in the world crisis af-
ter 1914.

This chapter and the next present two scenarios, both plausible, that might
have led to variant outcomes for the First World War. (Lukacs gives us what aca-
demics call a "second-order counterfactual"—which is to say that after big
changes a familiar pattern of history would reassert itself.) Both scenarios turn on
the personalities of two individuals, in the first case Roosevelt, and in the second,
the German chancellor in the early years of the war, Theobold von Bethmann-
Hollweg. They are counterfactual case studies in the active and passive uses of
power.

But let us start with Lukacs's proposition: that TR had been able to gain the
Republican nomination.

JOHN LUKACS, an emeritus professor of history at Chestnut Hill College, Philadelphia, is the author of many books, among them *The Duel*, *The Hitler of History*, *The Thread of Years*, and *Five Days in London, May 1940*. He lives in Pennsylvania.

HISTORIANS HAVE PAID insufficient attention to Theodore Roosevelt's triumphant third-term campaign in 1912. His landslide victory in November overshadowed the complicated story of his nomination at the Republican National Convention in Chicago four months earlier. They also ought to have at least asked the question: What if not Roosevelt but Wilson had been the president of the United States at the time of World War I in Europe?

The Roosevelt nomination in Chicago in August 1912 was by no means a foregone conclusion. Most of the leading Republican politicians and, perhaps more importantly, the managers of the convention, wanted President Taft for a second term for many reasons, the prime one having been their distrust of Theodore Roosevelt and their dislike of his Progressive ideas. (This counted more against TR than the accusation of his departure from George Washington's traditional reluctance to seek the presidency for the third time; after all, TR had not chosen to run for a third term in 1908, and there was the recent example of Grover Cleveland, who had sought, and won, the presidency after a four-year interruption.) Well before the convention met in Chicago the Credential Committees of the Republican National Committee succeeded to "contest" pro-Roosevelt delegates in various states. Intimates also had a general impression that TR was no longer his old self. Henry Adams had met him on a Washington street in December 1911 and wrote that Theodore "looked bigger and more tumbled-to-pieces," that his manners were "more slovenly," that he showed some "mental enfeeblement." However, that was not the impression the nation had, especially when reading TR's statement to the press even before his declaration in Columbus, Ohio: "My hat's in the ring! The fight is on and I'm stripped to the buff!"

And when Roosevelt appeared on the floor in Chicago, breaking the un-

written custom of presidential candidates keeping away from the convention until they are nominated, the roar of his supporters drowned out much
of the opposition—as well as the careful preparations of the managers,
which included the presence of 1,000 Chicago policemen and strands of
barbed wire hidden beneath the bunting of the platform, to prevent Roosevelt enthusiasts from rushing up there to claim it. Breaking with yet another unwritten custom, on the third day of the convention, during a hot
and, for once, milling rather than roiling crowd, Roosevelt suddenly rose
and began speaking from the floor. There was an unaccustomed tide of silence; and his high-pitched voice soothed and inspired, rather than fired up
the mass. "Now I am but a voice in a crowd," he said, "but allow me to
think out loud. What I am going to say may represent the inner convictions
and the patriotic inspirations not only of Republicans but of the great majority of my countrymen." What he said and how he said it impressed hundreds of delegates, and even some of his opponents. This was not a speech
from a bully pulpit; it breathed the music of a realistic idealism. It was the
psychic turning point of the convention. His once friend and ally, and his
former secretary of state, Elihu Root, had deserted him, being the august
chairman of the convention and siding with the orthodox party; but now
Root, too, had to turn around or, rather, adjust the timings of his gavel. He
thought that he had to allow giving the platform to at least two speakers
nominating Roosevelt—who was then nominated by a majority.

The rest we know. He triumphed over Woodrow Wilson with more than
two million majority. He carried nearly every state in the North and West,
and even two states in the South. He picked the Pennsylvania conserva-
tionist Gifford Pinchot for his vice president (a favorite of his who had
been dismissed by Taft) and Albert Beveridge for his secretary of state.
Elihu Root wanted that job and would have been a natural for it; but TR,
though not an especially vindictive man, could not forget Root's association with the Taftite financiers of the Republican party.

The Roosevelt who rode to his inauguration with Taft next to him in the
largest motor car Americans had yet seen in March 1913 was more corpu-
lent and less physically fit than before. This was visible in some of the pho-
tographs and in the flickering newsreels in the movie houses, but it did not

THE BULL MOOSE CANDIDATE

When ex-President Theodore Roosevelt was denied the Republican nomination in 1912—after handily carrying the primaries—he ran as the presidential candidate of the Progressive Party; its adopted symbol was the fierce, proud bull moose. Above, TR hitches a ride on a temporarily co-operative animal.

(Underwood & Underwood/CORBIS)

seem to matter. He had a popular mandate as great as he had in 1904. There was another difference. There was a considerable similarity in the propositions that he and his opponent Wilson represented; in one way or another, both of them were Progressives. Roosevelt—and the nation, and the world—believed that his main agenda, indeed, that perhaps his only important immediate agenda, was domestic. He ran it through Congress and the various state legislatures with remarkably little trouble. They consisted of four pieces of legislation: the establishment of a national income tax; of the direct selection of senators; of the admission of one very large south-western state, "Arizona," uniting the Arizona and New Mexico territories (against the wishes of most of the latter's inhabitants); and of the prepara-tion of a new immigration law, establishing more stringent measures than heretofore, and a yearly maximum quota (though not a national quota sys-tem) of allowable immigrants. Except for the second, these laws, including the income tax law, came to fruition without the need for a constitutional amendment. Only the new immigration legislation (which Roosevelt in-sisted was essentially a regulation, not necessarily in need of detailed con-gressional approval) was still pending when World War I erupted in Europe in 1914.

On June 15, 1914, two weeks before the assassination of the Archduke Franz Ferdinand in Sarajevo (which Roosevelt immediately denounced as "a heinous crime committed by terrorists"), Roosevelt stood in a cloud of steamy heat at the Gatun Locks, opening the Panama Canal, of which he was both godfather and father. That was a moment of apotheosis, a monu-ment to him and to the America he represented, the Big Brother of the en-tire Western Hemisphere. (The pejorative sense of those two words would not appear until George Orwell's 1984, more than a generation later.) TR—sometimes having had to face down his often cantankerous and im-perialist secretary of state, Beveridge—had already demonstrated his ability in conducting foreign affairs, together with his strong and measured es-pousal of American national interests. Thus during the Mexican civil war of 1913 his stern warning from the White House was enough to bring about a sudden (though temporary) halt of the anarchy in Mexico City and Vera Cruz, establishing thereby a guaranteed protection of American and British interests. Contemplating another murderous anarchy in Haiti in early 1914, he intervened and sent the marines to maintain law and order in Port-au-Prince, after which he negotiated the permanent establishment of a U.S. Navy base at Petit Goave, similar to that at Guantánamo in Cuba, against the wishes of Beveridge, who preferred putting all of Haiti under American jurisdiction, somewhat like Hawaii or the Philippines. But Bev-eridge was not only cantankerous and an alcoholic; he was also getting old. In June 1914, Roosevelt replaced him with Bainbridge Colby. Colby was a decent minor statesman but not a particularly willful one. As is the case with so many powerful leaders, TR would often act as if he were his own secretary of state. That Beveridge's final letter of resignation had reached TR at his breakfast table on June 28—in the same hour when 4,000 miles away the fatal shots rang out in Sarajevo—was proof of what Chesterton once said, that "coincidences are spiritual puns."

There was a duality in Theodore Roosevelt's first reactions to the European War. (The phrase "World War" became current only a year later, mostly employed by American newspapers and Germans.) He was appalled by the German invasion of neutral Belgium, and said so to his circle; at the same time he assured his friend, the German ambassador to Washington, that the United States was neutral. He made a few public statements extolling the differences of the New from the Old World; but privately he was disgusted with the behavior of many Americans in Europe, who were scurrying homeward in a panic and demanding the protection of every possible American authority. But soon Roosevelt's duality began to melt away. "They all miscalculated," he said to his friends, meaning the various European governments and General Staffs; this will be a long war. And therefore the United States must ready itself for all emergencies. In addition to its superb navy, TR ordered the rapid building up of the army, calling in ringing voices for Patriotic Volunteers. First to Plattsburgh, New York, then to 125 other training camps across the nation flowed two million young American men, ready to be drilled at arms. Roosevelt's recent opponent, Woodrow Wilson, said that he was "proud to speak out against educating our youth for Armageddon." Roosevelt privately (and not so privately) said that Wilson was "an abject coward." Then, in a famous speech, he spoke against "the craven fear of being great." (A phrase that Winston Churchill would employ thirty years later, warning the British people of new dangers on the morrow of VE Day in 1945). Incidentally, TR appreciated the young Churchill, with whom he had entered into a confidential correspondence already in 1914; and he expressed his regret when Churchill's imaginative thrust into the Dardanelles had failed and when Churchill had to resign as First Lord of the Admiralty.) In April 1915 a German submarine sank the *Lusitania*. TR did not mince words: "Murder on the high seas!" he exclaimed. When Henry Ford hired and sent his Peace Ship packed with pacifists and all kinds of odd people into the North Sea later that summer, TR dismissed Ford as "an ignorant mechanic." Less than one year after the outbreak of World War I, Roosevelt seemed to have concluded that the prestige of the United States was great enough to make its voice heard, and that its power was great enough for the European Powers to weigh its effects at once. In an important speech in Boston in November 1915, he said that "the United States cannot be indifferent to the firestorm ravaging Europe, and *especially* not to what happens in the Atlantic Ocean and on its Western European shores."

This was the first definite indication that Roosevelt would not accept an eventual German domination of Western Europe or an eventual German preponderance in the North Sea. He knew that such an American policy, including its prospect of drawing closer and closer to the European War on the side of Britain (and of France) against Germany had many opponents besides Ford's pacifists: German Americans, Scandinavian Americans, Irish Americans, Jewish Americans (the latter mostly emigrants from the Czarist Russian empire whose numbers were considerable, and perhaps growing). In Milwaukee a man tried to shoot him; the bullet fortunately only grazed his neck. "Don't touch him!" TR shouted. The potential assassin was a German American; Roosevelt thought it best to call him an anarchist. The episode redounded in his credit. Still, aware of the rising tide of anti-Roosevelt opposition in the approaching presidential election, he weighed the alternatives. Should American intervention come before or after November? By the spring of 1916, he chose the first option. "The people will not want to change horses [he meant *this* horse and *this* horseman] in midstream." He was right; he was renominated, easily, for a fourth term. ("My last!" he exclaimed.) He won the presidency, defeating Wilson again—though with a lesser majority than four years before. Illinois, Wisconsin, Michigan, and California went to Wilson—in the latter Roosevelt's earlier ally, Hiram Johnson, had turned bitterly against him.

But all of this happened after Verdun, and after the Somme, and—more important—after Presidential Order Number One, issued by Roosevelt in March 1916, ordering the navy to enter the Eastern Atlantic and the

North Sea, protecting and escorting merchant ships sailing those waters (including ships not only from the United States but from the entire Western Hemisphere, and merchantmen carrying arms and munitions to Britain and France); and ordering the establishment of an American navy base in Rotterdam (after the German government had threatened the Netherlands government for having allowed the transfer of transatlantic goods to Britain). At the end of May, the German Naval High Command thought it best not to interfere with a chain of American destroyers patrolling the Dutch coast and the North Sea—which contributed to the strategy of the British victory over the German High Sea Fleet off Jutland at the end of May. Immediately after his reelection in November 1916, Roosevelt sent a three-point note to each of the warring powers in Europe. (When its contents became known, his enemies—and, of course, some German newspapers—called it not the Roosevelt Corollary but the Roosevelt Effrontery, but no matter.) It was a state paper of the greatest importance. The government of the United States, Roosevelt declared, proposes one, the cessation of all hostilities in Europe and on the high seas within a month; two, the return of all armies and Powers to their state frontiers of July 1914; three, the convocation of a Peace Congress in The Hague three months after the armistice, with the United States represented together with all other Powers. None of the governments of Europe had expected such a definite proposal, not even the British. The world was stunned and startled. The cartoonist of a Hearst paper in New York drew TR, with the sun behind him, rising as Augustus Caesar over the tribes of the world.

Cautiously and slowly the British, and very reluctantly the French (and the Russian and the Italian) governments expressed their inclination not to reject the proposal; surprisingly so did the Austrian government, to the distaste of Germany, which did reject it. Indeed, on January 31, 1917, Berlin announced the resumption of unrestricted submarine warfare; within three days, five American merchant ships were sunk in the Western Approaches to the British Isles. Immediately, Theodore Roosevelt went to Congress and asked for a declaration of war against Germany. After a very brief debate he got it. By that time much of the new American army—armed, trained, drilled by the two million Plattsburgh-type graduates who were now second lieutenants and sergeants, suitable leaders of a four-million-man draft army that Roosevelt had organized after shoving a draft bill through Congress the previous year—were crowding and milling in the Eastern ports, ready to sail for France. The swiftness and the size of this unprecedented movement from the New World to the Old—a reversal of the movement of peoples across the Atlantic during the four previous centuries—was such that the German government announced the temporary suspension of submarine warfare against American vessels. That was the first crack of the German resolve. The second came in April 1917, when a brief advance of the American First Division lodged along the Argonne-Meuse line was sufficient for the Germans to attempt a cautious withdrawal of about six miles in front of the British in Flanders and of the French on both sides of Verdun. On the first of May the German Catholic Center party and the new German Democratic party joined the Social Democrats in the Reichstag to request that the imperial government consider the Roosevelt Three-Point Declaration—provided that it was still valid. Late that night Roosevelt—who was not in the best physical state—received this news from a telegram brought to the White House. "I had a very good sleep," he declared to his family the next morning. "I will tell that, yes, it *is* still valid; but they'd better pull up their pants and get moving at once."

They did. The British and the French were abashed—a little: they hoped that with more and more American troops on the way the Germans would collapse sooner rather than later. But they had to go along, and so did the Germans. In the highest war councils General Ludendorff and Admiral Tirpitz were voted down; and as soon as the Social Democrats declared that they did not insist on the proclamation of a German republic, William II was advised to abdicate in favor of his son. A German constitutional monarchy came thus into being. The armistice was signed on May 15 and the fighting came to an end. The Hague Peace Congress met on August 4, 1917, three years to the day after Britain had declared war on Germany. Theodore Roosevelt had sailed to Rotterdam aboard the USS *New York*, diplomatically avoiding a landing in Britain en route. Despite the objurgations and insistences of minor Powers, the 1914 frontiers were restored everywhere (except for Alsace and Lorraine, which reverted to France), with the provision that The Hague International Court of Justice (an old project of Roosevelt's) examine all requests for indemnities and frontier problems within five years, through a series of international commissions, in each of which Americans would be represented. TR's presence—and influence—towered over all others during the Peace Conference. Yet domestic opposition to his policies (especially among many Republicans) went on to prevail.

Before that, in March 1917, a revolution had broken out in St. Petersburg. The czar abdicated. Roosevelt who, as we have seen, had plenty on his plate at that moment, still deemed it necessary to pay considerable attention to the developing events in that vast country. Less than a week after the abdication of the czar, Roosevelt declared that "it is in the interests of the United States and of the entire civilized world that law and order should prevail within the Russian Empire." The Russian military then—encouraged by the Three-Point Declaration, allowing them to reoccupy the territories they had lost to the Germans during three years of war—was instrumental in installing a new monarch, the former Archduke Michael I, as czar of the Russians, under the conditions of a constitutional monarchy that was then affirmed by a transnational referendum. TR and the Secret Service were aware of revolutionary movements in Russia, including agitators and agents abroad. They took a few measures against them. Thus Lev Bronstein (alias "Trotsky"), an agitator and former movie extra on Long Island, attempting to return to Russia, was nabbed by Canadian agents in Halifax and brought back to Brooklyn, while the Swiss federal police in Zurich made sure that V. I. Ulyanov (alias "Lenin") and his friends would not be allowed to cross the frontiers of Switzerland. The third leading "Bolshevik," a mustachioed Caucasian by the name of I. V. Dzhugashvili (alias "Stalin") chose to abandon his subversive affiliations and became a highly efficient agent of the newly formed Russian State Police.

Of course The Hague Tribunal was not able to bank the fires of nationalist and revolutionary agitation everywhere. Bloody skirmishes and wars broke out in Transylvania, Bohemia, South Tirol, Trieste, along the Italian–Austrian, Austrian–Czech, Hungarian–Romanian, Bulgarian–Turkish, and Turkish–Arab frontiers. Some of these were settled, others were not, and flared and festered for a long time. The authority of The Hague Tribunal was considerable, but its powers were, after all, limited—especially when its American representation was gradually withdrawn after 1920, during the Hoover and Coolidge administrations. In 1918, a stern Rooseveltian warning stopped Japan from resuming its war and conquest of China; in the same year, agitation in Ireland against British rule was gathering speed; and the hottest place in Europe was Poland, whose people rose against both German and Russian occupation—that is, for the restoration of the frontiers of 1914—with creditable success. Roosevelt was unwilling to assert American intervention in some of these conflicts—for which he was more and more frequently criticized by his domestic opponents. The Democrats made considerable advances in the November 1918 congressional elections.

Roosevelt had not begun to weigh the question of his eventual successor when—suddenly and tragically—in January 1919 he died. That he was one of the greatest—and perhaps *the* most influential—of American presidents few people doubted, including his adversaries. His task was not finished; as we have seen, agitation and disturbances went on in Europe and in the Near East, but also in the cities and industries of the United States. But his greatest achievement was his establishment of a philosophy of American world relations, of a foreign policy that rested on geographical and national realities rather than on "international" illusions; on the recognition that the freedom of the entire Atlantic region, including that of Western Europe, was in the prime interest of the United States (as it had been of Britain). This was in profound contrast to the ideological vision of his former opponent Wilson, another Progressive, with his Fourteen Points and the War to End All Wars. For Roosevelt three points were enough; and he also knew that wars cannot be abolished by legislation or by the nonexistent powers of an illusory League of Nations (about which he was less sanguine than about the International Court of Justice).

And yet, as the wise (and melancholy) proverb says, God Writes Straight With Crooked Lines. In 1920, the anti-Roosevelt Republicans swept back into power. Their presidential candidate, Herbert Hoover, made sure it was known that he was a Progressive; indeed, he was (and felt) much closer to Wilson than to the Theodorian tradition. Slowly, gradually, the Wilsonian ideology of international relations grew more attuned to American intellects than the Rooseveltian vision of the Western world (which his intellectual critics called "The Theodorian *Realpolitik*": a shorthand and inaccurate summary phrase). There was also the isolationism of "America First," the future leader of which was to be Taft's son, a Republican senator from Ohio. The Republicans governed the country for another twelve years, until the bankruptcy of their financial and social policies became increasingly evident. In 1932, the American people gave their overwhelming support to Franklin Delano Roosevelt, Theodore's young cousin. He was a Democrat.

By that time it had begun to appear that the thunderous success of the 1917 Roosevelt Declaration notwithstanding, Europe—and the world—could not be turned back to 1914. In the 1920s, a former Italian Socialist who had turned nationalist, Benito Mussolini, became the dictator of Italy, reducing the king to the role of a figurehead. Ten years later a former German soldier and artist, Adolf Hitler, became the leader of a German popular movement, rejecting the conditions of The Hague settlement, and especially the reluctant German acquiescence in the existence of an independent Polish state. The War to End All Wars was a mirage, the League of Nations was an illusion; Germany was rising and arming again, and a second world war was in the wings. Few men saw this clearer than Theodore Roosevelt's erstwhile correspondent, Winston Churchill; but these were events we need not recount, as they are only too well known to us.

We know that in another sense, too, the world of (or before) 1914 could not be restored. The symptoms of the breakup of the old and largely bourgeois order of the Hundred Years' Peace before 1914, were there well before that year—in letters and art and fashions and music and mores and manners and social unrest, signs and clouds and antennae registering then. James Joyce and Ezra Pound had succeeded William Dean Howells and Edward Arlington Robinson (who had been TR's favorite contemporary novelist and favorite contemporary poet, respectively); ragtime and the tango were already raging in 1914, to be followed by jazz and the Charleston; the women's suffrage movement was rising almost as fast as the hems of women's skirts; "socialist" and "radical" had become positive words among the intelligentsia, even more exciting than "progressive." In 1913, TR was among those who denounced the "art" displayed at the New York Armory Show; he was acclaimed by the New York bourgeoisie, many of whom were howling outside. Fifty years later, at the anniversary of the same Armory Show, the descendants of these philistines were inside the Armory, mumbling their approval of "nonrepresentative art." *Toujours ça change, toujours c'est la même chose.* The more things change, the more they remain the same. Do they? Yes; and no.

ROBERT L. O'CONNELL

THE GREAT WAR TORPEDOED

The weapon that could have won
the war for Germany in 1915

Few events lend themselves as poignantly to counterfactual scenarios as the First World War. A certain amount of wishful thinking is involved, the understandable urge to wipe out the multiple catastrophes, traumas, and political disasters that the conflict spawned. But more than just historical wishful thinking confronts us. It is conceivable that, with a small number of slightly changed, yet altogether plausible, tips of the dice, some of the nastiest sequels of the late century might have been avoided, or at least rendered less extreme. The most familiar turning points, as Robert L. O'Connell observes, focus on the early months, and the majority arrive at the same conclusion: Germany could have won—no, should have won— a war that was still a continental power struggle and not yet a worldwide one. Once the trench stalemate set in, most historians agree, the might-have-beens diminished, with odds on a German triumph lengthening as the years went on. O'Connell, who has written extensively on the history of armaments, does not share that view. He maintains that we have overlooked the one weapon that could have genuinely altered the strategic balance in Germany's favor, sooner rather than later. That weapon was the submarine.

What if the submarine had not been held hostage to the German government's fear of United States involvement, at least early on, when the Great Neutral was not even prepared to be prepared? Berlin did announce a campaign of unrestricted submarine warfare at the beginning of 1915, but as yet it did not have a U-boat fleet large enough to make that campaign truly effective. Had an all-out U-boat construction program been initiated at that time, O'Connell argues, and had the effort to isolate the British Isles not been abandoned as a result of the furor over the May sinking of the Lusitania and the loss of 128 American lives, Germany might well have been able to bring the Allies to the peace table within a year. The Battle of the Somme would not have been for Germany the beginning of an attritional mudslide downward but the ending of the Western Front bloodbath, in which the Allied fighting spirit would be broken once and for all.

One person stood in the way—and counterfactual history has a way of etching in relief otherwise inconspicuous figures. The blandly malign presence who emerges in the pivotal months after the wasted opportunities of 1914 is that ultimate bureaucrat, the German chancellor Theobald Bethmann-Hollweg. He, as much as anyone, was responsible for Germany's defeat. When the chief of staff, Erich von Falkenhayn, informed him in December 1914 that the war was no longer winnable, Bethmann-Hollweg answered that the people (by which he probably meant the kaiser) would not stand for a negotiated settlement—thereby sentencing a generation of Europeans to death. In the months that followed, it was Bethmann-Hollweg who also lobbied against unrestricted submarine warfare— but at what price? Without him, O'Connell writes, "everything might have been different."

In the event, Germany did turn again to unrestricted submarine warfare at the beginning of 1917. The results were, for a time, spectacular, but it was already too late. The main effect was to bring a more energized United States into the war, with the promise of fresh and practically limitless cannon fodder. That was an offer the Allied warlords would never refuse.

ROBERT L. O'CONNELL is the author of *Of Arms and Men: A History of War, Weapons, and Aggression; The Ride of the Second Horseman: The Birth and Death of War; Sacred Vessels: The Cult of the Battleship and the Rise of the U.S. Navy;* and the forthcoming *Soul of the Sword,* an illustrated history of weapons. He has also written the novel *Fast Eddie,* based on the life of Captain Edward Vernon Rickenbacker. O'Connell lives in Charlottesville, Virginia.

I T MAY BE COINCIDENTAL, but it is suggestive nonetheless that the interest among serious historians in counterfactual analysis basically corresponds with the rise of a dramatically new way of looking at the physics of complex systems, known popularly as chaos theory. In both pursuits a key operative principle is the sensitivity of any complicated chain of events to small changes in initial conditions, symbolized by the whimsical notion of a butterfly flapping its wings in Tokyo changing the weather over Washington two weeks later.

Since there are few areas of human endeavor more chaotic and more subject to chance occurrence than warfare, it has become a logical focal point in the counterfactual analysis of history, the venue of greatest leverage, where the smallest changes can plausibly bring the biggest results. But there are broader issues involved. However tragic or ridiculous or outmoded our propensity for organized violence, wars matter; like few other events, they have the capacity to change things fundamentally for good or ill. Plus, the science of complex systems informs us in a very convincing way that nothing is inevitable, or even necessarily probable. On the surface of events, history simply happens, a roll of the dice or rather an accumulation of rolls. So it is far from trivial to examine the alternatives. What might have been not only *really* might have been; but also could have been profoundly important.

World War I was arguably the pivotal event of the twentieth century, the historical train wreck responsible for the Bolshevik revolution and world Communism, the Second World War, the Cold War, and all the cataclysm surrounding these phenomena. As such it has exerted a magnetic attraction on counterfactualists. Intuitively they have been drawn to the earliest stages of the conflict, exploring initial conditions on the political front (What if the Russians had not mobilized first; or the British had declared their neutrality?) and the first key operational decisions (What if Moltke had not weakened the German right flank?).

Nevertheless, a case can be made that the tragic consequences of the Great War actually flowed primarily from the unintended effects of weapons technology. More than anything it was the characteristics of available armaments that enforced the stalemate that slaughtered ten million soldiers and made a mockery of rational political and military calculations, along with the leadership responsible for them. Yet 1914's card deck of death machinery does not seem, on the face of it, a promising playground for counterfactualists, being packed with high-powered artillery, machine guns, and barbed wire, which only served to bog down the action; aircraft so underdeveloped that they amounted to little more than a diversion for the suffering entrenched masses, and vast fleets of surface ships enthralled to giant dreadnought battleships so specialized and vulnerable that they were inherently indecisive. In the entire stack there was but one wild card, a joker so misplayed that historians have largely dismissed its influence, except in the negative sense of being responsible for American belligerency and Germany's ruin. Yet it could have been otherwise. The kaiser's submarines, had they been used relentlessly against Britain's commerce, could have changed everything.

Few expected much, but unlike other warships, the submarine proved surprisingly effective right from the earliest stages of hostilities. Barely a month passed before a German submarine managed to sink its first man-of-war, the light cruiser HMS *Pathfinder*. Just two weeks later, on September 23, U-9 torpedoed and sank in rapid succession three British armored cruisers, *Cressy, Hogue,* and *Aboukir.* The ships were old and obsolescent, but they were large (12,000 tons each) and filled with sailors, most of whom died. The 1,459 fatalities were greater than the cost of Trafalgar, and constituted the worst wartime disaster the Royal Navy had suffered in nearly 300 years. As if this was not enough, the main body of the British fleet at Scapa Flow was so harassed by submarine sightings, both real and imagined, that in October it was forced to withdraw to the north coast of Ireland until a complex of booms and obstructions could be installed at its main base.

This may have bought some safety for the dreadnoughts of the Grand Fleet. But there were far easier targets available.

Eighteen months before the war began, Arthur Conan Doyle, the opium-smoking creator of Sherlock Holmes, published a novel called *Danger*, a prescient war fantasy describing an imbroglio between England and Nordland, a small imaginary European state. Lacking an effective fleet, Nordland's monarch is about to submit, when he is reminded of his eight submarines by John Serious, a resourceful naval officer. "Ah, you would attack the English battleships with submarines?" inquires the king. "Sire, I would never go near an English battleship."

Instead, he proposes to wage a merciless campaign against merchant shipping, striking at the island kingdom's greatest weakness, utter dependence on seaborne foodstuffs. Transports are attacked wherever they are found and without warning. "What do I care for the three mile limit, or international law?" growls Serious. In short order, England is pushed to the edge of starvation and forced to accept a humiliating peace.

Not surprisingly, *Danger* was basically dismissed by the English, especially those acting in an official capacity. The Germans found it intriguing, however, and it was brought to the attention of the naval staff and Grand Admiral Alfred Peter von Tirpitz, the patriarch of the fleet. Since Tirpitz and his colleagues were battleship advocates, and the only prewar intelligence estimate of what it would take to enforce a blockade against England called for 221 submarines (Germany entered the hostilities with only nine), it can be assumed that the scheme was still buried far back in their collective naval minds when the guns of August first roared.

Soon, however, everything changed. The great pendulum that was the Schlieffen Plan slowed to a halt, the fighting degenerated into trench warfare, and Germany accumulated in excess of half a million casualties in the first three months. At the same time, the oxymoronic High Seas Fleet barely ever ventured out of sight of land, utterly thwarted by the specter of England's dreadnoughts. Against this grim backdrop the submarine's early successes, though limited, were riveting to a high command looking for a quick way out. The public also liked the submarine, due in part to a carefully mapped propaganda campaign. More to the point, newspaper accounts indicate that a majority wanted the new and powerful weapon set against Britain's merchant shipping without restraint.

For the first months of the Great War, Germany held its submariners strictly to the time-honored prize rules of "detention and search" when they came upon merchant vessels at sea. The relevant international laws, formulated with surface vessels in mind, demanded that transports first be searched for contraband and only sunk after the passengers and crew had been safely put off into boats. In effect, this robbed the submarine of its key advantages of stealth and surprise, while forcing it to surface and operate under conditions that exposed the slow and vulnerable craft to greatly increased levels of danger. The chief reason for adhering to this self-defeating guidance was the Germans' fear of turning neutrals against them. And, although the already pro-British giant far to the West, the United States of America, was hardly foremost in their minds, it would soon loom large.

By the late fall of 1914 the scales of Teutonic policy were plainly tilting in a new direction. In early November the chief of the Naval Staff had decided to urge a program of unrestricted submarine warfare upon the chancellor and the emperor. On December 14, Admiral Tirpitz weighed in with a surprise interview given to the Berlin correspondent for the United Press in which he publicly questioned Germany's submarine policy. "What will America say if we open U-boat warfare against all ships sailing to England and starve it out?" It seemed less like a question than a taunt.

The German press and public were jubilant, but the chancellor, Theobald Bethmann-Hollweg, was appalled, believing the interview was entirely premature and inflammatory. Bethmann-Hollweg was a true insider. His career had been spent in the Prussian civil service and his skills were those of a bureaucrat—parochial manipulation and extreme persuasiveness in small groups. He had no particular grasp of military-technical issues, and his understanding of the submarine was purely that of a generalist. But on these grounds he could certainly see that the momentum for unleashing it was growing irresistible, and therefore avoided open opposition, at least initially.

The die was cast during the first days of February 1915, when Admiral

Friedrich von Ingenohl, the timid commander of the High Seas Fleet, was replaced by the more aggressive Hugo von Pohl. Although the new admiralissimo saw little prospect of going head to head with the Grand Fleet, he was utterly convinced that an underwater assault on British seaborne trade was the key to victory. Consequently, when the kaiser came to Wilhelmshaven on February 4 to review the fleet, Pohl demanded and got approval for declaring the waters around the British Isles a war zone. After February 18 any ship found there, including neutrals, would be sunk. (The inclusion of nonbelligerent vessels arose from the fact that the British Cunard liner *Lusitania* was spotted flying the stars and stripes in the Irish Sea on January 31.) For better or worse, the unrestricted submarine campaign was on.

Was it a good decision? Could it have won the war for Germany? The votes of historians have been decisively cast in the negative, based largely on what they perceive as the capabilities of the available submarines, and the political ramifications of the campaign itself. Both deserve closer examination.

Critical here was the belief that the Germans simply did not have enough undersea craft to do the job. The raw numbers do seem daunting. Whereas Great Britain entered the war with over twelve million tons of merchant shipping, Germany commenced unrestricted submarine warfare with but twenty-one boats, only nine of which were the superior diesel type. To make matters worse, so much time was taken in transit and repair, that only about a third of the total was available to sink ships at any one time.

Like the submarine itself, however, much was concealed beneath the surface of these statistics. Individually, German submarines were proven killers—their torpedoes ran true and were devastatingly powerful; they could lay minefields practically anywhere and remain undetected; the diesel boats had ranges in the thousands of miles and endurance limited only by the staying power of their crews. Technically, U-boats were extraordinarily lethal weapons.

But accumulating enough of them was plainly a problem, though not necessarily an insurmountable one. Initial production was ragged; there were problems with diesel design and fabrication, and inexperienced ship-yards were continually behind schedule. Only eleven boats were delivered in 1914. But, from this point, production began to ramp up until it had attained considerable momentum. In 1915 a total of fifty-two new submarines were added, and between January and August 1916 a further sixty-one were commissioned. Meanwhile attrition remained very low, since the Royal Navy had little in the way of defenses.

The initial English efforts against the submarine bordered on the laughable. Picketboats armed with blacksmiths' hammers were sent out to smash periscopes; attempts were made to catch submarines with nets like cod; sea lions were even trained to seek out unwanted submerged intruders—none of which met more than the slightest degree of success. It took until July 1915 and the formation of the Board on Invention and Research before the English made a wholesale effort to generate effective countermeasures. Even then progress was slow. Only in June 1917 were sufficient quantities of hydrophones (the first workable acoustical detection system) and depth charges available for surface ships to menace submarines consistently. Before that, success against them remained highly problematic. From the beginning of the unrestricted campaign to August 1916, Germany lost thirty-three boats, only eighteen of which were confirmed kills. For the fifty-one months of the First World War (including the later stages when defenses were better) the exchange rate was 29.67 merchant ships, or 69,015 tons sunk per U-boat lost. This amounted to a very substantial advantage, which allowed the German Navy to build up U-boats quite rapidly, until their total in August 1916 stood at 111, with an average of 68 submarines available for the nineteen months beginning in February 1915—probably enough to do the job. But they were not allowed to, and this was a matter of politics.

Unrestricted submarine warfare was undertaken by the German leadership with barely any consideration of what the American response might be. They were in for an unpleasant surprise. Woodrow Wilson immediately denounced the decree, threatening to hold the German government "strictly accountable" for the loss of American lives. Nothing of great significance happened until early May, when the Lusitania (no longer flying an

American flag) was sunk by a U-20, killing 1,198, including 128 Americans. Wilson responded with a series of increasingly truculent notes, which culminated in an implied threat of war if the unrestricted submarine campaign persisted. This led directly to the suspension of the program in September 1915. Most historians have judged the Germans prudent and Wilson to have been on firm ground in making the threat—especially considering the decisiveness of America's ultimate intervention.

Yet the state of the United States as a potential belligerent in the summer of 1915 argues strenuously in the opposite direction. While the influence of domestic political disunity and pacifism easily can be exaggerated, it is hard to overestimate the military unpreparedness of the United States at this point. The army was tiny and ill-equipped; the navy focused on relatively useless dreadnoughts; realistic battle plans were lacking; and the arms industry was incapable of producing modern heavy weapons. All of this could be righted, but it would have been time consuming. Even with the benefit of a gradual but significant Preparedness campaign, it required more than a year after the United States' declaration of war in April 1917 before American troops began making a significant difference on the Western Front. In 1915 it would have taken considerably longer. So Wilson's threat was without real substance. America could very well have declared war; but all it had to offer the Allies was a vast pool of untrained bodies. And the Germans should have known as much. The future chancellor, Franz von Papen, an energetic military attaché in Washington at the time—he was soon to be expelled for his espionage activities—was disdainful of America and the threat it posed. While he plainly overestimated the degree of pro-German sentiment, he had access to a network of informants and must have been aware of the true state of American military weakness. It was obvious.

Yet on the other side of the Atlantic, German decision-making was hermetically sealed, far more subject to influence than information. The key was the kaiser, who retained ultimate authority over all decisions relating to foreign and military policy. But Wilhelm was at this point a pathetic figure, still pompous, but terrified of losing his throne and ready to jump at the advice of the last courtier who caught his ear. Bethmann-Hollweg, on the other hand, knew exactly what he wanted and was a master of isolating his prey and enforcing his opinions. Not only was he convinced that the submarine campaign could not prove decisive against England; but he was certain that it would draw the United States into the war, with inevitably disastrous consequences for Germany. He may well have been correct on the issue of America going to war; but there is good reason to believe his judgment was seriously flawed on the technical matters of the submarine's capabilities and the potential U.S. impact on the battlefield. Meanwhile, he was virtually without allies. The press, the public, and the Reichstag were solidly behind unrestricted submarine warfare. And among the inner circle, where it really mattered, his only support came from Admiral Georg Alexander von Muller, the chief of the Naval Cabinet, a secondary figure at best. Nonetheless, Bethmann-Hollweg, through sheer force of personality, managed to win over Erich von Falkenhayn, the all-important chief of staff of the army, and then use him in a successful assault on the pliant kaiser. It was a virtuoso performance, and also an unlikely one. Germany, already up to its neck in blood and desperation, allowed itself to be shorn of its most valuable weapon—which, after all, killed only in the thousands rather than the millions already lost on the Western Front—all because of the persuasiveness of a single individual who took advantage of a closed decision-making process, a weak monarch, and arguing on the basis of questionable information. Without Bethmann-Hollweg, everything might have been different.

So, as the basis of our counterfactual analysis, Bethmann-Hollweg will be removed from the scene on May 10, 1915—a victim at age fifty-nine (he actually died only six years later in 1921) of a fatal heart attack brought on by overwork and, suitably enough, concern over the *Lusitania* sinking. Among the inner circle, only Muller's dissenting voice is left, Falkenhayn and the kaiser remain on board, and the campaign rolls on with no apparent source of opposition.

Success follows in its wake. Backed by unwavering support, monthly scores could be expected to have accelerated from 127,000 tons in May (actual) to around 250,000 tons in August (183,000 actual). At this point the total of boats stabilized at around 58 until the first part of 1916, so it makes sense to keep the scores steady at a quarter million ton per month for the remainder of 1915. Since the next eight months roughly doubled the flotilla to 111, a steady increase in kills up to 550,000 tons seems reasonable. (If these figures seem high, it should be remembered that actual U-boat sinkings peaked in April 1917 at 860,000 tons, achieved with a flotilla of 156 submarines.) The net result from this nineteen-month campaign would have been roughly 5.3 million tons sunk.

Yet based on the actual facts, the British reaction can be projected to have been fatally sluggish. The admiralty had only a vague idea of the shipping situation, since it failed to keep the necessary statistics. Hence, it remained blissfully unaware of both the precipitous drop in replacement merchant ship construction during the 1915–16 period and the submarine-induced congestion in ports, which was estimated to have reduced the annual carrying capacity of the ships affected by as much as 20 percent. (The submarines never posed an effective challenge to the transport of troops to the Continent, since the English Channel was well patrolled, heavily mined, and blocked by obstacles such as nets.) The added pressure of a truly unrestricted submarine campaign might have added to an intuitive sense of a brewing crisis; but, without access to the necessary figures, the admiralty would have had little way of understanding how truly desperate their situation was becoming. To further compound matters, British naval authorities could be depended on to have refused to take the critical step necessary to save themselves, the introduction of merchant convoys. Prior to the Battle of Jutland on the last day of May 1916, the combat readiness of the battleships of the Grand Fleet at Scapa was universally considered vital. Therefore, any request to detach even some of its seventy to eighty destroyers for convoy escort duty would have been summarily rejected. (Even after the disastrous month of April 1917, the admiralty only reluctantly acceded to convoys on the insistence of Prime Minister David Lloyd George.) So the noose would have tightened silently and rapidly around the condemned, with little prospect of the rope being broken.

Meanwhile, the sheer futility of the war's major events during the first six months of 1916 take on added significance, hammer blows to the morale of all participants. Although the United States declares war against

Germany at the beginning of January, it refuses to send troops immediately and has virtually no impact on the conflict during the months that follow. The horrific stalemate at Verdun softens up not only the French but the Germans, who are led to believe victory is imminent. For the British population the news of the disappointment of July 1, 1916, at the Somme, coming on top of the letdown of Jutland, is just too much. The combination of a diminished food supply and widespread hoarding results in a sudden perception of mass starvation. On July 6, food riots break out in Liverpool and spread quickly to every major urban center. Looting follows; martial law is declared, and 350 are shot by the Home Guard on the night of July 7. Two days later a general strike paralyzes the country and then spreads to the troops on the Somme, who stage a passive mutiny; plans for a renewal of the offensive are cancelled. On July 14 Prime Minister Herbert Asquith informs the king and the Russian and French ambassadors that Britain can no longer continue the war, upon which the Cabinet resigns. The king promptly asks David Lloyd George to form a government and then charges him with negotiating a peace settlement. Reluctant to give up the ghost on Bastille Day, the French hang on one day longer, declaring a unilateral cease-fire beginning on July 15. The Russians follow suit on July 17, and the czar abdicates. One week later progressive forces in the Duma form a provisional government dedicated to democratic principles under liberal Prince Georgi Lvov. Aleksandr Kerensky is appointed chief of the peace commission. In Washington, Woodrow Wilson declares the Great War "effectively over," and offers his services to preside over the formation of a "just and lasting peace"—a proposal for which there is little enthusiasm elsewhere.

Germany stands victorious on all fronts; yet events prove it to be in no mood to ratify its peace plans. On July 19 the kaiser and the high command outline their terms, which include the annexation of Belgium, painful territorial concessions by France and Russia, the partition of the British Empire, and in particular, a German mandate over Canada—this last thrown in by the kaiser. To ensure their acceptance, German troops are ordered to ignore the cease-fire and ready themselves for a "crushing offensive." Instead, they are swept by a sit-down strike, which the officer corps proves unable to quell. Fraternization between German and Allied troops becomes general, and within a week the various fronts cease to exist. A general strike sweeps Germany, and on July 25 the Social Democrats publish their own peace terms based on status quo antebellum and an immediate national referendum. The kaiser orders Philipp Scheidemann and the Socialist leadership arrested, but instead is himself forced to flee the country.

With progressive elements in power among all the major belligerents, the so-called Third Hague Conference proves remarkably free of recriminations. Although it is later seen as postponing the inevitable, the general principle of "no territorial gains" prevails. Initially, there is strong sentiment for arms limitation, but only chemical warfare is banned. Overall limitations on the size of armies and navies are stipulated, but these are so generous that no European power ever actually exceeds them. American president Woodrow Wilson comes to the conference with high hopes and proposals for an international governing body and diplomatic negotiations open to public scrutiny. But the United States' marginal role in the fighting ensures he will be roundly ignored. To compound Wilson's humiliation, in the midst of the conference he is voted out of office and returns home a bitter and defeated man. His replacement, jurist Charles Evans Hughes, divorces himself from the proceedings and the United States never signs the treaty.

On the basis of such a denouement, the subsequent course of the twentieth century might well have looked a good deal different—still turbulent but not nearly so cataclysmic. Arguably, the net effect of the Great War would have been not simply the deromanticizing of militarism, but the spread of democratic regimes robust enough to resist its siren song. Very likely the process in Russia would not have been smooth, especially given the probability that major parts of the former czarist empire, such as Poland and the Ukraine, would strike for independence. Nevertheless, the Bolshevik revolution almost certainly would not have happened, effectively aborting international Communism as a philosophy of the underdog. In the Middle East the survival under the secular Ataturk of a greater Turkey that would still encompass much of the old Ottoman empire might have more effectively spread modernization, representative government, and, down

WHAT IF? 2

the line, headed off Islamic fundamentalism. Further west, it becomes possible to draw the rapprochement of a politically and economically stable
France and Germany back from the 1950s and '60s to the '20s and '30s. The
breeding ground for general war is transformed into a pillar against it, and
Adolf Hitler, World War II, the Holocaust, and even nuclear weapons fade
from the pages of history. Meanwhile Britain, the Great War's biggest loser,
very probably would have been forced to face up to the incongruities of its
imperial system and begun the process of decolonialization much sooner,
forcing the other European powers to follow suit. Without these burdens,
the English might have avoided or, at least, mitigated the half-century economic funk from which they have only recently emerged. Certainly, not
having to fight World War II would have helped.

Of course not everything would necessarily have turned out for the better. America, thwarted by its experience with European politics, likely
would not simply have turned inward. Rather, it might have looked southward and laid a heavier and not necessarily more beneficial hand on Latin
American developments. Almost certainly its gaze would have been focused on the Far East and Japanese military expansion. Given domestic attitudes and the aggressiveness of Japan, a major military confrontation
seems almost inevitable—perhaps as soon as the 1930s. The United States
would have won, but also found itself thrust in the midst of turmoil, as an-
ticolonialism and nationalism worked its way across the Asian rim. Under
the circumstances, it follows that Americans would have been perceived as
imperialists and suffered consequences not so different from what actually
happened in Korea and Vietnam. Yet Americans would not have been
alone.

Overall, it is logical that a different end to the Great War only would
have hastened a fundamental North-South split, instead of an East-West
one. The absence of a Second World War and more uninterrupted economic growth in the North, along with hastened decolonialization and nationalism in the South would have fostered and intensified perceptions of
exploitation and racial tension. In the absence of Marxism-Leninism, leaders of the South would have had to look to another source for a unifying de-
velopmental philosophy. Were we all to have been very lucky, it might

have been Gandhi—but the alternatives are mostly far less benign. Meanwhile, all of us would still be faced with the underlying problems of the North-South relationship: overpopulation, gross inequality, and ecological degradation. A better end to the Great War might have taken the edge off the rest of the twentieth century, but we would not have escaped its most profound contradictions.

GEORGE FEIFER

NO FINLAND STATION

A Russian Revolution without Lenin?

Vladimir Lenin's domination of the Bolsheviks he led to power—"willed" might be a better word—was total, and in a way that had never been known before. "No other political party," the historian Orlando Figes writes, "had been so closely tied to the personality of one man." Impatient and acerbic, perpetually angry, Lenin did not tolerate dissent: There was no way but his. Moral choice (or immoral, as the case might be) was resolved by force of character—his. He was never one to mix personal feelings with impersonal fact. "I can't listen to music too often," he once commented mirthlessly after he had been forced to sit through a concert. "It makes me want to say kind, stupid things, and pat the heads of people. But now you have to beat them on the head, beat them without mercy." He trafficked in abstractions and treated human beings, indeed entire populations, as if they were boxcars in a switching yard. And yet this man of few contradictions was a natural leader, whose obsession would sweep along hundreds at first and, eventually, millions. Lenin's single-minded inflexibility would influence the future of most of the world, now almost entirely to its regret. Can history demonstrate a better example of winning through intimidation?

Had there been no Lenin, or a Lenin who showed up in St. Petersburg late, there might have been no Bolshevik revolution of October 1917, and perhaps no revolution ever. Whenever events center on a single individual, the counterfactual scenarios multiply. In Lenin's case, most center on timing, both before his arrival and after. Once the czar abdicated in February, to be replaced by a democratic

210

provisional government, Lenin's dilemma was how to get from his base in Zurich to the Russian capital: Hundreds of miles of Germany and Austria-Hungary, Russia's enemies, intervened. The professional revolutionary, who had spent more than a third of his life in exile and had not been in Russia for eleven years, considered his options, none of them satisfactory. Should he attempt to go via England? That scenario he ruled out because the British had a record of detaining Russian Marxists. He even considered hiring a plane to fly him to the homeland he barely knew any longer. He abandoned the idea as being too impractical and dangerous. Lenin, who thought nothing of condemning others to death and who would soon institute a system of state terror, was something of a coward—as one associate put it, he had "an anxiety for self-preservation." Here the Germans came to the rescue with their famous "sealed train." What if they had not done so? Or if the Provisional Government had rejected its notorious passenger before he reached St. Petersburg's Finland Station? What would Russia (and by extension, the whole world) have been like if Lenin had been delayed until the time was no longer ripe for his messianic vision?

GEORGE FEIFER is the author of eight books on Russia, including *Justice in Moscow, Moscow Farewell,* and *Red Files.* Since his first visit in 1959, he has lived there extensively; he spent a year as a graduate student at Moscow University. His most recent book is *The Battle of Okinawa.*

The comrades all groped about in darkness until Lenin's arrival.

　　　　　　　　　　　—Bolshevik Ludmilla Stal, 1917

*The uprising's object is to seize power. Its political task will be
clarified after the seizure. . . . The people have the right and
duty to solve such questions not by voting but by force.*

　　　　　　　—Lenin, shortly after returning to Russia in 1917

VLADIMIR LENIN may be said to have lived his forty-seven years for
his return to Russia in 1917. A week before departing, the reckless extremist, as most of the few Russians who knew of his existence regarded
him, had been stewing in frustration some 1,500 miles from St. Petersburg,
with a huge obstacle in between. Stuck in Zurich, the Bolshevik party's
founder and guiding spirit had every reason to bite his nails in fear of missing an opportunity of which not even he, the supreme political fantasist,
had dreamed mere years before. The route devised for slipping him through
the mighty obstacle and into the Russian capital's ferment was a highly
risky gamble—and even if it paid off, his further plans hung on extremely
doubtful chance.

His last visit to St. Petersburg had been during the 1905 Revolution.
Slinking back to Western Europe in its embers, the master of splinter-group
polemics spent the intervening dozen years dispatching fierce but insignificant denunciations to less relentless Continental revolutionaries. (He was
utterly alone in visualizing backward Russia, rather than the most advanced European powers specified by Marxism, serving as the spearhead of
the world's proletariat.) Unable to handpick all his lieutenants from his
refugees in exile, the lover of absolutes and controller of his fringe movement's every possible aspect greeted those who had managed to make their

way out of Russia with bullying attacks on any deviation from his views. *Renegades! Traitors!*

What if he'd lived amid the give and take of Russia's rapidly changing political and social realities instead of watching from a distance that inevitably simplified them? Actually, his brief Russian stay from 1905 to 1906 was his single break in seventeen years of foreign exile, beginning in 1900. For years before the outbreak of World War I, the dogged political Quixote wondered whether he'd ever again set foot on Russian soil. His chances of doing that seemed as slight as his ideas were cosmic. But now, after three years of that calamitous war and the revolution they triggered—the one that toppled the czar and his government in February 1917—the prophet tasted validation and power. His primary instinct—to snatch the latter as quickly as possible, *then* carry out his program—would astonish even his closest collaborators. It set him apart from all other revolutionary thinkers, especially after taking him from scholarly/journalistic disputation to chiefly *doing*, and in the most opportunistic ways.

The gaping obstacle on his return route was the Germany that couldn't be fully trusted even in her exhausting third year of war with his Russia. Imperial Germany's military and civil burdens had become enormous. The kaiser, his ministers, and the General Staff had ever more reason to see the fighting on two fronts—in this case, both hugely draining—as the long-predicted national disaster.

Yes, good things were happening on the Eastern one. The Romanov dynasty had collapsed, and the Russian army, whose 1916 "Brusilov offensive" had at last threatened, albeit momentarily, to become the feared "steam-roller," was disintegrating. That was what had delivered the final blow to the disastrously inflexible Nicholas II, who abdicated when popular opposition to him gained an unstoppable momentum. But the Reichswehr, well aware of Russians' ability to endure and prevail even after ghastly losses, remained apprehensive, all the more because the new St. Petersburg government was sworn to continue fighting. Thus the obvious motive for permitting and facilitating an enemy national's travel through the German heartland: Lenin, who called himself a "professional revolutionary," might serve a subversive purpose.

THE GOD THAT ALMOST FAILED

Vladimir Lenin addresses a crowd, in a painting that has less to do with real-
ity than iconography. Luck had been on his side, in the form of the German
government's decision in the spring of 1917 to whisk him on the famous
"sealed train" from his Swiss exile to Petrograd.

(Alexander Gerasimov, 1881–1963, *Lenin at the Tribune*. Tretyakov Gallery, Moscow. Scala/Art Resource, NY)

But what if Berlin had made a more enlightened decision? What if the
government there *hadn't* permitted his return to St. Petersburg in the celebrated "sealed train" because it had thought more carefully about Germany's future? World War II's devastation and the Cold War's rending
would remind succeeding generations of suffering Germans that subver-

sion, like poison gas, tends to spread beyond its intended limits. The ultimate goal for Russia of a German government that took that menace into account would have been nearly opposite: a *stable* state with which to negotiate and settle conflicts peacefully and efficiently. But wartime Germany had neither the luxury nor the foresight to act in its long-term national interests. Instead, it opened a switch to Lenin that otherwise would have been carefully closed: a gift of chance in what would become an implausible series of them.

In the late winter of 1916 to 1917, secret exchanges between Wilhelmstrasse, its ambassadors in Bern and elsewhere, and the General Staff confirmed, as one put it, that "We must now definitely try to create the utmost chaos in Russia. . . . Our support of the extreme [Russian] elements is preferable, because that way the work is done more thoroughly. . . . According to all forecasts, we count on the disintegration being so far advanced in three months or so that our military intervention will guarantee the collapse of Russian power." An official deal was therefore struck with St. Petersburg to exchange German nationals interned in Russia for Marxist exiles in Switzerland, who were given the permission and means for transit.

But there are of course two sides to every bargain, and this one was clearly unappealing to Russia. What if her new government hadn't entered into it? More experienced leaders probably wouldn't have. Nor less idealistic ones. A tad more caution might have kept them from authorizing the return of the exile whose intentions they knew far better than any German did, thanks to czarist police reports. Nevertheless, they threw open another switch for Lenin's revolutionary fervor, thanks not only to the paralysis that often overcomes democratic politicians who are faced by the old and enduring dilemma of what to do with people who advocate nondemocratic methods. That was stiffened by the lifetime of repression by czarist officials that made their replacements particularly loath to limit Russia's new freedoms of travel and speech. Another circumstance, another chance. Besides, the new government believed it had little to fear from the impossible zealot, especially because his enemy-assisted journey would surely put him in disgrace with a population whose wartime suffering had intensified its enmity toward Germany. And in addition to everything else, the government's authority and power were challenged by a rival Russian body, as we're about to see.

None of that, however, spared Ilich, as hundreds of millions would soon call him in reverent tenderness, from apprehension that the switches were being opened to a trap and imprisonment rather than to the political battleground he yearned to enter. His rail journey in a single-carriage train—its "sealed" label applied because the German authorities accepted his demand that no outsider enter for any reason—would take him from Gottmadingen near the Swiss border almost due north to Frankfurt, then northeast to Berlin, and further up to the Baltic coast. The "bald, stocky, sturdy" man whose forehead reminded Maxim Gorky of Socrates wore a three-piece suit and bowler hat that spoke of the comfortable birth he shared with many other revolutionaries. Leaving Bern on April 13 [April 1 according to the Russian calendar then in use], he remained on guard throughout the two-day trip, and not only against external enemies, for his personal habits were worthy of the keenest missionary. Detesting the corridor drinking and singing of some of his thirty-odd fellow exiles, he permitted his small entourage to smoke only in the lavatory, use of which he gave priority to the nonsmokers. Such dictates, a fellow Bolshevik would quip, prepared him to assume the leadership of the Russian government.

But the exiles went unchallenged during their uneventful trip across much of Germany's north-south axis. (To keep it smooth, a train of the crown prince was delayed some two hours near Berlin.) Continuing over water by ferry, they proceeded up to neutral Sweden for their route's final leg, which was again northeast, via Finland. An advance welcoming party met the new train at the Finnish border. It included Lev Kamenev, who would become deputy chairman of the USSR Council of People's Commissars before Stalin had him executed in 1936. Now Kamenev was high on the editorial board of the formerly underground *Pravda*, the ban on which had been lifted a month after the February Revolution and a month before now, as Lenin's return neared completion. The star passenger hardly resumed his seat in the carriage before chiding Kamenev for his insufficiently revolutionary line. The party newspaper, operating beyond Lenin's control, had been cautious. With the Bolsheviks so outnumbered—no more than 40,000 adherents nationwide—Kamenev, like all other party leaders to one degree or another, advocated cooperation with other Socialist parties while revolutionary prospects ripened, as they were expected to do. Ilich, however, saw that as heresy. Cordial as he was to the comrades who'd come to greet him, he seethed internally. For it was time, as he'd written just before embarking on this unlikely trip, for the Russian proletariat to seize power, "with the people armed to a man."

If that daring now sounds unremarkable, even expected as a core assumption of Marxism-Leninism, it is thanks only to the inevitability that historical events acquire when viewed in retrospect. To those who read it then and there, the call to armed action was outlandish, even in that day when street orators touted all manner of weird delivery from Russia's troubles. Her other political activists, somber and discordant as many were, believed in an entirely different approach. Apart from the extreme right that aspired to restore the monarchy, they were struggling, among other things, to become practicing democrats by *sharing* power.

Whether they'd have succeeded if not for Lenin will of course never be known. But if they had, the rewards would have been huge. Alexis de Tocqueville, the author of the justly acclaimed *Democracy in America,* had reasons to predict that a second country, although started from a very different place, seemed headed toward great prominence among nations. While freewheeling America was tackling the frontier, slovenly Russia was bogged down in autocracy—yet she too showed immense promise during the late nineteenth and early twentieth centuries. Compared with Western Europe, the Empire remained retarded in many ways, especially in its political social development, which the benighted czar was sworn to thwart. But it's not too much to speak of an explosion of energy in other areas. Literacy was soaring, along with education in general and commercial development, particularly industrial. With no help from the throne, the judicial system operated independently and reasonably well. Russia had surged to the forefront—or was making her way in that direction—in literature, the visual arts, music, theater, film, and ballet. Her resources were vast and creative talents remarkable; her scientific, technological, and industrial capacities revealed ever more potential as they raced ahead. Full of excitement despite the proverbial Russian passiveness and restraints—or because of them, thanks to the zest that can follow awakening—the country had taken off toward almost certain realization of de Tocqueville's vision.

It "only" remained to establish and secure a suitable political structure and civil society—the chances of which were fair to good, despite the hugely divisive pressures generated by the staggeringly costly Great War. So suggested the course of Russian history until now, especially after the lifting of the Romanov burden, because it resembled Western Europe's, however much delayed, in certain critical ways. The rooting of the education, training, and ideals of the great majority of Russian leaders and opinion-makers in European patterns and standards also justified guarded optimism. Enormous social and economic rewards beckoned if the country could keep to its present road, curvy and unfamiliar as it was. That road not taken remains among the great might-have-beens of the century just ended.

It also explains a good part of the bewilderment prompted by Lenin's summons now, in 1917. Didn't he understand, for a start, from *whom* he proposed seizing power? Not from the wholly discredited Nicholas II or his ancien régime, because those old oppressors had been gone since February. Free of the autocracy at last, the new Russia was enjoying elements of the democracy of which all progressive and radical parties had dreamed seemingly forever. That was why the infant republic, wobbly as it was in its attempts to establish a better new order, emanated more promise than foreboding. Leon Trotsky, the brilliant writer and orator who had played a larger role in the 1905 Revolution than Lenin (whose dictatorial qualities he criticized at the time, before he himself became a ruthless Leninist) called her the freest country in the world.

That freedom was much enhanced by governmental omission and contradiction, for this was the curious "dual power" interval, when its two fragile sources lived in a kind of uneasy truce, now competing, now cooperating. One of them, the Provisional Government that had "graduated" from the Duma (parliament) witlessly hobbled by the fatally obscurantist Nicholas, met in the Marinsky Palace. To the degree that anything was strictly legal in the transition to undetermined permanent arrangements, that generally centrist coalition was the czarist government's legitimate successor. The second source, the predominantly Socialist Soviet of Workers' and Soldiers' Deputies, was a more self-assertive rebirth of the assembly that had constituted itself, of course without the czar's authorization, during the 1905 revolution, after which it was repressed. Its members were elected by spontaneously formed local councils—"soviets"—that more or less represented "the masses." The Petrograd Soviet, as it was also called, met in the Tauride Palace, less than an hour's walk from the Provisional Government.

Although two sets of rival authorities governing a country so much in flux was confusing, everyone knew the Provisional Government, led largely by liberal Duma veterans, was well to the right of the looser congregation of "the people's" representatives. Therefore, it's no surprise that Lenin's revolutionary presumption was anathema to the former body—but it also shocked its much more radical sibling. Virtually everyone in the latter, even the Marxists—including the Bolshevik Marxists who'd been working in Russia, beyond the influence of his personal prodding—considered seizing power a foolish daydream. But that left him the passenger in the curious train as undaunted as did the complexities of the maelstrom he was about to enter and long odds against his ambition.

Reports reaching Zurich of prominent Bolsheviks compromising for the sake of Socialist unity had made him squirm. Lenin's long history of excoriating opponents and manipulating followers convinced Georgy Plekhanov, one of the fathers of (nonviolent) Russian Marxism, that he saw all unity as a piece of bread he was swallowing. Now Lenin considered collaboration with anyone not prepared to support immediate revolution fraudulent and impossible. The Volga-born sage had the answer to the old question of "What's to Be Done?" about Russia's backwardness and malaise. His "scientific" vision and unshakable willpower would set the country straight—if, that is, he wouldn't be arrested upon arrival and delivered to the Russian capital's grim Peter and Paul Fortress. That was where his revered elder brother Alexander had been imprisoned thirty years earlier, before being hung for an attempt on the czar's life. (That trauma advanced Vladimir, then seventeen years old, from a dissident to a revolutionary.

What if Alexander's life had been spared and Vladimir didn't swear to take revenge?)

To his relief, nothing of the kind awaited the surviving younger brother now. The Provisional Government had no plans to curtail his freedom, even though it knew he'd accepted German financial aid for his trip (which is not to say, as many historians still do, that he was a German agent).

Lenin's new train pulled into the Finland Station in Petrograd, as the capital had been rechristened in the war-beset Motherland's purging of its German names, in the late evening of April 16 (April 3, old style). The eternal belligerent who had come to preach force was apparently embarrassed by a bouquet of flowers handed him by Alexandra Kollontai, a follower soon to become notorious for championing "free love," as if that were the sum of her political activity. Apart from that, he had utterly no doubt about the country's need—nor, for that matter, the world's. That supreme confidence alone was unique, even—this merits repetition—to his narrow group of relatively disorganized fellow radicals. In fact, that confidence had never been greater. For the relatively inconsequential Marxist theorist was about to metamorphose into a preeminent fighter in the political combat of the here and now. He was ready to "bring down Marxism's ten commandments from Mount Sinai," as an early follower would put it, and hand them to Russia's young. *Action at last!*

Just after 11 P.M., the exhilarated traveler rushed from the train into the station, where Nikolai Chkheidze, the chairman of the Petrograd Soviet—the Provisional government's rival on the left—welcomed his "comrade" on behalf of "the entire revolution." Chkheidze also cautioned, however, that the revolution's chief tasks at the moment were to make common cause to strengthen itself and defend against "every kind of attack, both from within and from without."

Although Chkheidze's work exposing and opposing the woeful czarist government had earned him the title of the "papa" of the February Revolution, it was enough for him to be a Menshevik for Ilich to despise him. The Mensheviks were the Bolsheviks' more moderate and numerous Marxist rivals, although Lenin, with his genius for propaganda, had branded them with their name, which derived from the Russian for "minority." Even worse than being a Menshevik, Chkheidze had been appealing for a closing ranks in defense of "our revolution"—meaning the essentially democratic one embracing all the reformist parties—instead of igniting what Lenin saw as the second one needed to overthrow it. (Alternatively, he sometimes called the February upheaval the "first stage" of the full revolution.) Ignoring the chairman's judicious greeting, he hurried outside to the station square, where Bolshevik colleagues had organized a demonstration of several thousand sympathizers, many waving red flags. A band struck up the Marseillaise when he appeared, then went quiet, the better for a call for the class war on which Lenin had raised himself to resound. Saluting his "dear comrades, soldiers, sailors, and workers," his confident, upper-class stridency leaped to attack "the robbers' imperialist war." "Any day . . . the crash of all European imperialism may come. . . . The Russian revolution you made has begun that and opened a new epoch. Hail the worldwide socialist revolution!"

The worldwide socialist revolution? No participant in the February one saw that as even faintly imminent. A scattering of fellow Bolsheviks did occasionally evoke it as a never-quite-believable goal, but it was always that remote. Still, Lenin pounded his message into his captivated audience. Fight. Fight for the ultimate good, for the great second revolution that would bring the highest human happiness. Ridicule and destroy every less radical approach. Consign even the non-Bolshevik majority in the predominately Socialist Soviet to the class enemy's camp, as if they were no better than czarist minions. Gorky would later write that the deskbound, print-fixated crusader's limitless ignorance of daily existence and sufferings gave him a "pitiless contempt, worthy of a nobleman, for the lives of the ordinary people." Of course the contrary can still be argued: that Lenin's every act, however mistaken or ugly, was motivated by a desire to improve precisely those lives. But Gorky's further observation that "life in all its complexity" was unknown to him is hard to dispute.

The city's Bolshevik leadership had been driven to the square in armored cars decked with red banners. Their crews helped Lenin mount one of them. When its projector threw a beam into the dark night, a witness in whose ears his proclamation of a worldwide Socialist revolution still rang saw the effect as brilliantly symbolic of the arming for which Ilich had called, together with changing the party's name to "Communist."

The Bolshevik party had installed its headquarters in the mansion of a former mistress of the still-uncomprehending Nicholas II, who was now under a kind of house arrest in Tsarskoye Selo, the "Tsar's Village," outside Petrograd. She was Mathilde Ksheinskaya, the glorious dancer. When the same armored car rushed Lenin from the station square to that "satin nest of a court ballerina," to use Trotsky's image of the unlikely site, a national party conference was still in session, having just approved a policy of making common cause with other Socialist parties. From the train to the tussle, to adopt an old Russian saying about newcomers to a crucial scene. Lenin's single-mindedness had never been sharper or more stunning. He rose to denounce the agreed strategy. Bolsheviks should work not for a parliamentary system but for "a republic of soviets of workers', soldiers' and peasants' deputies throughout the land."

A member of another Marxist party, whose invitation that evening represented the kind of discipline breach Lenin detested, was stupefied. The speech "shook and astonished not only me, a heretic accidentally thrown into the delirium, but also the faithful, all of them." It seemed as if a "spirit of universal destruction, knowing no obstacles, doubts, human difficulties, or human considerations" had risen from its lairs. Another distinguished observer felt he'd been "flogged over the head with a flail. Only one thing was clear: there was no place for me, a nonparty man, beside Lenin."

But there was also no place then for most fellow party members. The following day, a conference of Bolsheviks, Mensheviks, and representatives of radical splinter parties convened to consider unifying their actions. When Lenin more or less repeated to the mixed members his summons of the previous evening, an old Bolshevik who'd long supported his hard lines expressed a general outrage by piercingly denouncing "the delirium of a madman." E. H. Carr, historian of the revolution, would call Lenin "completely isolated" at this juncture. Once again, solid Bolshevik opinion opposed what *Pravda* called his "unacceptable" ideas. After discussion, his own party's Petrograd committee rejected them by a vote of 13 to 2. What if that overwhelming majority included someone with enough skill and determination to control Lenin's obsessiveness?

But chance was still favoring him in unpredictable ways. The disapproval by even his own fellow Bolsheviks further dimmed the perception of the danger he posed. It wouldn't have been too late to counter that by expelling or otherwise silencing him. On the contrary, now may have been the best time for that, after his full and blatant profession of outlandish disdain for any kind of accommodation, all forms of the overwhelmingly desired democracy. Besides, his own party's rejection of that might have, at that point, inoculated it against that ultimate, irreversible extremism. But the Provisional Government made no effort to defend itself. Another unpredictable circumstance; another opportunity bestowed on him, this one by default of the opposition—which remained inert in the face of ever-increasing provocation during the following days. For Lenin's answer to *Pravda*'s admonition was to attack the newspaper for failing to understand that the Provisional Government *must be taken down* because it was capitalist.

He kept to his habit of putting his views on paper. Much of the "April Theses," as his "On the Proletariat's Tasks in the Present Revolution" would become known when codified by Soviet rule, was devoted to condemning Russia's "predatory imperialist war," for which no effort and "not the slightest concession" should be made. That went with reiteration of his larger arguments against "the government of capitalists, the worst enemies of peace and Socialism." "The specific feature of Russia's present situation is that it represents a *transition* from the first stage of the revolution ... *to the second stage*, which must place power in the hands of the proletariat and the poorest strata of the peasantry." Thus "no support for the Provisional government; the utter falsity of all its promises should be explained. . . . Exposure in place of the impermissible, illusion-breeding 'demand' that *this* government, a government of capitalists, should *cease* to be imperialist."

Since Russia's future turned almost entirely on whether she could manage to construct a political order the majority would accept and respect, further examination of why other radicals considered such talk utterly wrong seems merited. Writing in exile fifteen years later—and eight before his murder by an agent of Stalin—Trotsky gave the broad answer: "For the others at that time, the revolution's development was identical with a strengthening of the democracy," meaning the fruit of the February Revolution. That went without saying for the conservatives, liberals, and nonrevolutionary Social-ists. But the Marxists' reasons for opposing the use of force to overthrow the government of a country so relatively backward in economic development were even more absolute. For no nation was supposed to have—no, *couldn't* have—a Socialist revolution until capitalism had incubated the conditions for it. That came from Marx himself, after all. It followed from his dictums that every society's "economic structure . . . independent of human will . . . determines the general character of the social, political and spiritual processes" and that "no social order ever disappears before all the produc-tive forces for which it has room have been developed." Of course the Pro-visional Government was "capitalist." Every political system *had* to reflect its economic foundation, just as real life, here meaning the ownership and workings of the means of production, determined political attitudes. Mass allegiance to socialism would surely—but only—be generated by capital-ism's full flowering.

That was central to Marxism's foundation. It was what made the axioms "scientific," the observations and predictions being based not on subjective opinion or wishful thinking but on the undeniable, always-formative real-ity of economic workings and appetites. That wasn't a mere theory, like those that had been advanced and disproved during all of human history before Marx divined the ultimate pattern of its development, but bedrock reality. It was an essential canon of *The Answer* that comforted and inspired Marxists with conviction that socialism was historically inevitable, since "state forms are rooted in the material conditions of life" and the progres-sion to higher and higher stages—from prefeudalism to socialism—was in-exorable just because it was driven by iron *economic* imperatives. But Russia's conditions were far from ready for the final (supposedly easy) shift to socialism, nor had anything remotely approaching a revolutionary majority been massed. That was precisely what Lenin himself had been instructing—years earlier, of course, when all such rumination was profoundly abstract; when a Bolshevik seizure of power in czarist Russia was as likely as a speech from one of the angels who danced on pin heads. And it was hardly more likely now, except to Lenin alone, since more or less liberated capitalism and the "bourgeois-liberal" state that Marxist dogma decreed it must serve had been achieved only two months ago, with the February Revolution.

The April Theses were unacceptable, *Pravda*'s April 21 issue declared, because they "start[ed] from the view that the bourgeois-democratic revolution has ended." That was the argument not of effete liberals but of the stalwarts of Lenin's own grouping. But he didn't care. Infant bourgeois democracy *would* soon be ended—by him. For much as he too believed in "scientific Marxism," he tossed it overboard when he—at that point still alone—glimpsed an opportunity for a shortcut. His impatience to reach "history's highest goal," to put the best light on his deepest intention, or his evangelical arrogance and intolerance, which may have had more to do with it, took over. Or his unconscious yearning for revenge, if that applied.

His replies to the charge of betraying Marx might seem laughable if so much pain hadn't been coming. The sophistry of his justification would matter enormously to the world because it mattered so little to him.

But it didn't yet matter much because his was still a very much minority opinion in a minority party on the periphery of Russian political thought and activity. What if a series of unlikely boosts didn't now advance that still-outrageous opinion? Lenin's attempt to rework Marxism would have never advanced more than it already was from the Finland Station: a matter of inches or feet, metaphorically speaking, in Russia's immense landmass.

As it happened, the seven-month zigzag to the second Bolshevik revolution went far less smoothly than the journey in the sealed train. At first, Ilich pulled a number of people his way, if slowly. He was a mediocre speaker but a bruising debater. His incessant castigation of the Provisional Government—which he called a "stinking corpse," borrowing an admirer's characterization of nonrevolutionary German Social Democracy—began to work on the Petrograd Soviet, especially as resentment grew of the still-sacrificial war against the Central Powers. At the same time, his exhortations and reproaches began drawing Bolsheviks away from the fragmentary Socialist unity the Soviet had so far prided itself on for maintaining.

The first Congress of Soviets—a gathering of representatives of similar councils in various regions—was convened in June, two months after his arrival. During the course of an address, one of its democratically inclined speakers implied that no single party was prepared to assume sole responsibility for governing—to which eager Lenin famously replied "There *is* such a party!" But that too represented his chutzpah more than any reality: The Bolsheviks were still a small minority in that Congress, and even smaller in the country as a whole. Despite their growing popularity, they'd won no election in any city. Much worse for them, Lenin had cause to fear for his life by late the following month.

In July, workers and soldiers, some partially organized by low-level Bolshevik organizations, instigated mass demonstrations. Above all, the so-called "July Days" of feverish protest and violence on the streets were a reaction against the disastrous pursuit of the war. Now Lenin's prospects plummeted. The participation of military units in the disorder boosted ministerial fear of fatal insurrection, while press and popular censure of the Bolsheviks much diminished their appeal. Finally acknowledging the danger Lenin posed to it, the Provisional Government cracked down on his party and ordered his arrest.

What if a more alert police had performed that arrest quickly instead of setting out, or failing to, with hardly uncommon Russian inefficiency? Would the October Revolution have been launched if Lenin were now taken into custody, as lesser Bolshevik leaders were? Very doubtfully, to put it mildly; doubtful even that the party would have continued to consider the "second" revolution. But Lenin slipped the noose, thanks not only to police delay but also a last-minute warning by a sympathizer in the Ministry of Justice. That added a car-chase element to his sequence of "what ifs?": His escape turned on a lost or gained hour, depending on one's view of him.

Disguising himself as a workman, he slipped back into Finland for refuge. Despite his political daring that took people's breath away, the great polemicist wasn't blessed with physical courage. From his new hiding place, he wrote Lev Kamenev to be certain to publish his notebook if he were "bumped off." But although Finland was still part of the Russian Empire, his fear of being hunted down turned out to be exaggerated.

How the Bolsheviks managed to recover enough to accomplish their actual seizure of power three months later is another story, this one full of yet more unforeseeable openings, most provided by disastrous right-wing fumbles. In August, it managed to outdo the left wing's blunder of July. Its purpose was to stem popular hostility to the army and bolster the Provisional Government's crumbling authority. Its method was an attempt to reestablish public order and discipline by General Lavr Kornilov, the army commander in chief. That convinced much of the population, not entirely without reason, that reactionary czarist generals were intent on establishing a military dictatorship and/or restoring Nicholas to power. The Bolsheviks were seen as the best defense against that, just as many would see them as the best resistors to Nazism twenty-five years later.

Although Lenin made no public appearances from July through the October Revolution, he remained the party's unrivaled leader even from his hiding places. Writing furiously, he prodded and browbeat other Bolsheviks toward insurrection, rebuking those who clung to despised "parliamentary tactics." Such people were "miserable traitors to the proletarian cause," especially after the party's popular support grew in reaction to the failed military coup. "We're on the eve of a world revolution!" To wait for action or approval by the Second Congress of Soviets, which would convene in October—and might vote to continue the policies of democratic rule and substantial cooperation with other bodies—would be "utter idiocy or sheer treachery." Missing this perfect moment for armed action would "*ruin* the revolution."

The world would have been incalculably different if the moment for which Lenin had called from his homecoming exhortation at the Finland Station had indeed been missed. To say his role in creating it was utterly critical is not, of course, to prove that a later moment wouldn't have been seized without him; but all the most reliable observers of the time are convinced of that. His greatest contribution to Russian and world history was a sense of destination *now*—and the "hypnotic power," as described by an early collaborator who was soon repelled by his methods, of the sort exercised by many who assume command. "Only Lenin was followed unquestioningly as the indisputable leader, as it was only Lenin who was that rare phenomenon particularly in Russia—a man of iron will and indomitable energy, capable of instilling fanatical faith in the movement and the cause."

Would the country have taken his path without his leadership, imagination, and compulsion? Would other croupiers have appeared to spin the roulette wheel, as a history professor recently asked? Although anything's possible in Kierkegaard's "game of world-history," it's hard to imagine a less likely crucial happening than a Bolshevik revolution without Lenin's "supreme genius of revolutionary leadership," as the historian Henry Chamberlin called it, supporting Gorky's further description of him as "a man who prevented people from leading their accustomed lives as no one before him was able to do." Eager-to-please Stalin—who was nine years younger than Lenin and had considerable underground experience but none of the founder's ability to conceptualize and inspire—originally opposed the "go for broke" gamble. The dutiful executor of assigned tasks was also a member of *Pravda*'s editorial board, having returned from banishment after the February Revolution. Although he quite soon converted to Lenin's side, and later actually admitted the mistake in vision he'd "shared with the majority of the party," he remained too narrow to conceive grand concepts, too cautious for bold action on a sweeping scale, too intellectually limited to bully his fellows with argument, and too uncharismatic to rouse audiences.

Even Trotsky's splendid oratorical, literary, and organizing skills were no substitute for Ilich's obsessiveness and daring. His theory of Permanent Revolution may have helped prompt Lenin's crotchet that Russia *was* ready for Bolshevik rule, since her special case required combining the capitalist and socialist revolutions. Trotsky, however, who had long preached a need for unity among all Social Democrats when Lenin was preaching and practicing the opposite, changed his mind only after his own return from abroad, a month after Lenin's. Even then, he remained quiet about it until

July, following General Kornilov's attempted military coup that sparked the Bolshevik resurgence. After that, and until Lenin considered it safe enough to return from Finland in early October, Trotsky's work was essential, especially in organizing the actual coup as a kind of operations commander and symbolically linking it to Congress of Soviets because its Bolshevik contingent was still small. Nevertheless, he would bow to Ilich, and not only for convening the Central Committee's secret October meeting but also for taking the party's most important decision ever: to prepare for the armed insurrection. According to *The People's Tragedy*, Orlando Figes's authoritative history, Lenin "once again . . . managed to impose his will on the rest of its leaders." It was fitting that the party's inspiration and commander in chief returned to public view on November 7 [October 25 in the Russian calendar that was still in use there], to announce his momentous news to the Petrograd Soviet. "Comrades, the workers' and peasants' revolution, which we Bolsheviks always said must come, has been achieved." But Trotsky's greater praise of Lenin was for having made that possible by "shifting the whole question" from the moment he returned in April.

From the very first, he'd accused the party for not having taken power earlier, and only because it hadn't sufficiently educated and organized the proletariat. (The visionary who *knew* had only contempt for the wishes of other Russians, the overwhelming majority.) The "boldness of his revolutionary grasp, his determination to break even with his longtime colleagues and comrades in arms if they proved unable to march with the revolution . . . [and] his infallible feeling for the masses" were, Trotsky acknowledged, indispensable. He quoted a prominent provincial leader on Lenin's arrival in April. "His agitation, at first not wholly intelligible to us Bolsheviks but seen as utopianism deriving from his long absence from Russian life, was gradually absorbed by us. You might say it entered our flesh and blood."

It hardly needs saying that Ilich wasn't solely responsible for Russia's intensifying disgust with the war and waxing revolutionary mood among the Bolsheviks, let alone the country at large. The Western Allies—Britain, France, the United States—helped with their pressure to keep fighting their nemesis Germany, although the Provisional Government should have withdrawn from the war as quickly as possible. What if it had done so? What if it had taken the disagreeable but utterly necessary step even as late as July, even after its ill-advised, ill-executed, grievously costly attempt at yet another offensive (the Galician fiasco) then launched in aid of the common Allied effort? The democratically inclined parties and personalities would probably have been strong enough to resist the bacillus of Bolshevism, as its enemies were already calling it—even after Lenin had made his escape from arrest. Just as the war did more than anything else to bring down the monarchy—or, more precisely, the revelations of the appalling failures of Nicholas and his servile ministers in prosecuting it—it did the same to the Provisional Government, despite the time its members had had to know better. Having suffered catastrophically, the justifiably demoralized Russian rank and file could not understand why it should continue fighting, and turned against the officers and "statesmen" who urged them to do so.

If only the Allied leaders, Russian *or* Western, had been as astute as Lenin in recognizing that Russia must immediately abandon the war! Still, he saw the withdrawal itself as secondary to using that richest opportunity for, without punning, capitalizing on the discontent. With his singular drive and his intellectual superiority over his opponents, the magnetic man channeled it to *his* revolution, the supposedly proletarian one. A mind "capable at any moment of providing a centralized organization with decisions [and] each individual with detailed instructions" was among his critical assets, Aleksandr Solzhenitsyn would conclude. But his ability to furnish the masses with stirring slogans was equally important.

He of the iron will was also the master of taking uncompromising stances and pushing them upon others, despite everything. Later, he'd permit an occasional slight relaxation, most notably when reviving the economy ravaged by the Civil War. During the struggle for power, however, he hated nothing more than concession and conciliation. If a healthy person hates, an admirer quoted him, "then he really hates." His entire life was animated by a need to lead, not just nourish, the class struggle. Although his sympathy for the downtrodden was no doubt genuine, his animus against the system that had cost him his brother submerged it. ("I'll make them pay for that, I swear I will," he is said to have reacted to the news of the execution.) That, of course, wasn't the *cause* of the October Revolution—but his *sui generis* leadership was its catalyst.

The Provisional Government's stated reasons for ordering Lenin's arrest in July included a charge—supposedly proved by a packet of documents released by the Ministry of Justice—that he was a German spy. Having made the desired injury to his prestige, those dubious materials went on to enjoy a long life among his haters. The weight of the evidence accumulated since, however, strongly suggests that while he indeed took some travel money, as mentioned, he never served as a German agent. In fact, he used Germany more than the other way around, even, in the end, catastrophically damaging her. The kaiser's government helped him return in order to—again quoting a cable to the Foreign Ministry in Wilhelmstrasse—"exacerbate the differences between the moderate and extremist parties because we have the greatest interest in the latter gaining the upper hand, since the Revolution will then . . . shatter the stability of the Russian state." Few diplomatic maneuvers worked better—or worse. Worse because it helped cause Germany's ruin, starting in 1933. Although the factors explaining that progressive, cultured country's descent into Nazism have never been definitively categorized by importance, popular fear of Communism is high on every list. Hitler's revolution surely wouldn't have succeeded without a Bolshevist monster for panicking his audiences.

Then what if Germany *hadn't* permitted Lenin to pass? He might have devised another route, through England, France, or Norway, for example. But he and his agents considered those options at the time and rejected them as impractical or impossible. (A plot to sneak him through Germany disguised as blind, deaf, and mute—Swedish for some reason—was also discarded, his wife joking he'd give himself away by abusing his nonrevolutionary adversaries in his sleep.) The Western Allies, whose chief interest in Russia, as we've seen, was as a second front against the Reichswehr, would have been very reluctant to aid his travel because they had no reason to share Germany's liking for his potentially corrosive opposition to continued pursuit of the war. Besides, other arrangements would surely have taken a month to coordinate—or more, as with England's detention of Trotsky on *his* return to Russia at about the same time. During that critical waiting, the Provisional Government and the Petrograd Soviet might have solidified their positions and status by achieving more cooperation, as members of both bodies were already urging. Ilich, who was uncannily perceptive about many such tactical issues, felt at the time that he had to undermine their foundations before they hardened, leaving the sealed train as *the* hope in his impatient eyes.

If Germany had indeed rejected the scheme, the consequences would have been measureless, and no doubt happily so. Russia's long-planned Constituent Assembly for hammering out a democratic structure for the nation convened in Petrograd in January 1918. Its members had been chosen in remarkably fair national elections—but too late. That the first free, popular referendum in Russian history was held under Soviet rule was tragic as well as ironic. For Lenin, who had previously claimed only the Bolsheviks could be trusted to convene such an assembly, dispersed it after a single session, although, or because, the Bolshevik share of the vote was only 25 percent.

What if it hadn't been dismissed? What if the Bolsheviks didn't have the guns to do that? It's worth repeating that the assembly might not have achieved enough compromise to establish a working system of government that would have commanded popular allegiance, just as the country as a whole wouldn't necessarily have fashioned a functioning democratic civil society. "If Lenin had never boarded that train," a longtime resident of dismal, post-Communist Russia recently mused, "this place would still be a mess." But not the same kind of mess. Pre-Bolshevik Russia wasn't the haunted land of the Marquis de Custine, whose nineteenth-century images of backwardness, suspiciousness, and duplicity still rivet many Western eyes. Despite everything, it had a fighting chance for recovery, prosperity, and respect for civil rights under a parliamentary system Europeans would recognize as more or less "normal." The elections for that Constituent Assembly served as a national poll. The Bolshevik capture of no more than a clear minority, although the party was already in power and manipulating hard, spoke of the strength of the other groups, all of which had more or less democratic instincts. Their leaders' declarations during the single assembly session testified—as had the exchanges and arguments throughout the time of the dual power, even in the Petrograd Soviet—to a general acceptance of parliamentary norms and aspirations. Only Lenin would have scattered that very promising congregation of idealists and reformers, just as only he could have galvanized the Bolsheviks to his goal of seizing power.

If not for his extremism, a Russia still full of creative, productive, rational, and even moderate forces may well have been governed by Socialists for a time, but nothing like the kind who proclaimed a dictatorship of the proletariat, viewed the state as "an organ of class *domination*" (Lenin again, with his italics), and rushed to construct apparata of repression. (Having ignored Marx's prophecy that the proletarian revolution would take place in advanced countries whose workers constituted the great majority, Ilich had to alter the dictum that the state would wither away. On the contrary, a very powerful state was now needed for remorselessly countering socialism's inevitable enemies.) Surely she'd have been spared the concentration of immense power in a militarized party whose world-encompassing ideology was entrenched by a terrorizing secret police.

Whether or not it was inevitable, the house Ilich built was open for Stalin to move in. Although the extent to which he was the rightful heir remains debatable, the latter would surely have remained a very peripheral figure without the former. To put it more simply, no Lenin, no Stalin. That is to say, no Stalin of whom anyone but historians would have heard: a dedicated revolutionary who, however, would have died in relative obscurity.

And also no Russian Civil War? No famines, including the half-intentional ones for forcing the peasantry into collectivized agriculture? And no murderous purges and boundless other misery to fill the vast landmass? Almost certainly not. Almost as certainly, an essentially European civilization would have flowered richly, its blooms not seriously blighted, and in some ways actually fertilized, by elements of Russian mess. The purges and the Great Patriotic War, as Moscow called its death struggle with Nazi Germany, claimed some 40 million Soviet lives. It's hard to imagine a fraction of that loss without Lenin's obsession and legacy.

It's also hard to imagine all-embracing conflict with the West. Twentieth-

century Russia would have become very powerful under any system, probably enough to rival America in economic and political influence, and possibly discomfort Western Europe in the process. Statistical evidence
indicates that her growth, which had surged before 1917 despite all the im-
pediments and restraints, would have been substantially *greater* if she
hadn't fallen to Soviet rule. Without that, however, there would almost as
certainly have been no Cold War either.

Only the Communists, as the Bolsheviks indeed renamed themselves,
could have provoked such Western reaction to threats from the East.
Washington's intentional exaggeration of them and its stooping to the Soviet level brought more responsibility for the Cold War than most Americans like to think. Still, its ultimate cause was the same arrogance that
Lenin, convinced he'd attained supreme wisdom and held the keys to human history and happiness, displayed in forcing his revolution on his unwilling country. Taunting and deriding foreign "bourgeois-democratic"
governments as well as the Russian one, he challenged not only Western
capitalism but also the increasingly liberal democracy in which it func-
tioned. *We know what's good for everyone. We'll do you a favor by helping tear
down your rotten, doomed institutions.* Without that ideology, which Lenin
advanced from theoretical rumination to actual provocation, Russia and
the other countries of Europe and North America may well have engaged
in very serious competition. But surely even the most intense rivalry
wouldn't have come close to Cold War proportions. On the contrary, Russia would probably have been integrated, if slowly and at times painfully,
into what came to be known as the free world.

No Cold War, no girding for outbreak of a shooting one. No draining of
measureless effort, money, and resources by "defense" on virtually every
continent. And no hideous inquisitions, monstrous imprisonments,
grotesque espionage "games." (No bullets in the back of the heads of perhaps 12,000 Polish officers, to take just the single example of the Katyn
Forest massacre among a numbing surfeit of them.) No censorship, twisted
information, and big and little lies employed for and against Communism,
served up by the one side as paradise and the other as hell, with all the re-
ligiouslike righteousness of both sides' leaders. In short, no sundered planet

stumbling in hostility. Of course, Russia herself squandered and distorted more than any other country, but America, whose national purpose largely shrunk to fighting Communism for forty-five years, ran a good second. It's not too much to say that the struggle diminished human life everywhere in the second half of the twentieth century.

In that sense, the hoary Communist slogan that "Lenin Is More Alive Than the Living" is true even now. The burden has lifted but the deformity and impoverishment endure, again most cripplingly in the Russia to which the forty-seven-year-old Ilich returned in his curious way—Germany having actually given his train extra-territoriality—in order to take her down his singular garden path, with its collection of lucky turns for him that proved so unlucky for the world.

GEOFFREY C. WARD

THE LUCK OF FRANKLIN
DELANO ROOSEVELT

Seven might-not-have-beens on
the road to the presidency

Franklin D. Roosevelt, his biographer Geoffrey C. Ward writes, was an extraor-
dinarily lucky man. You might say that he was a case study in might-have-beens
that all seemed to go his way. For FDR, the roads not taken mostly turned out to
be the ones he should have avoided. Decisions that others made, not always fa-
vorable, turned out to help rather than hinder. Early on, for example, the woman
who had been the "loveliest" debutante rejected him: she would have been the
wrong person for his career, and besides, she was a Republican.

Political opponents underestimated him and refrained from all-out attacks:
They lived to regret it. Luck, in the form of a press too discreet to delve into per-
sonal follies, saved him from the broadcasting of an infidelity scandal that easily
could have terminated a promising future in politics. Sickness resulted in options,
not endings. What proved to be a timely bout of typhoid fever when he was an ob-
scure state senator from upstate New York linked FDR with the one man who be-
lieved all along that he had the potential to be president. Even his greatest
misfortune, polio, turned out to be a stroke of luck in political terms (and also
forestalled the certain tarnish of another scandal). But after FDR's election as
president, luck of another sort, his refusal to give in to the importuning of Miami
newsreel cameramen, may have saved his life in February 1933—and spared the
nation the leadership of a man totally unequipped by desire or ability to guide the
United States through its worst crisis since the Civil War.

You have to think of another close call in Manhattan less than two years ear-lier, when a visitor from England, looking the wrong way as he crossed Fifth Av-enue, was hit by an automobile; he almost died. "Those who believe that personalities make no difference to history," Arthur M. Schlesinger, Jr., has writ-ten, "might do well to ponder whether the world would have been the same in the next two decades" if a car had killed Winston Churchill, or an assassin's bullet Franklin D. Roosevelt.

GEOFFREY C. WARD is the author of twelve books, including A *First-Class Temperament*, his account of FDR's early career, which won the 1989 National Books Critics Circle Award and the 1990 Francis Parkman Prize of the Society of American Historians. In collaboration with the filmmaker Ken Burns, he has written *The Civil War*, *Baseball*, and most recently *Jazz: A History of America's Music*.

I T IS ALWAYS risky for a biographer to speculate what might have been—biography is, after all a record of choices made, paths taken, options closed—and it seems especially perilous for a biographer of Franklin Roosevelt to do so since FDR himself always refused to answer what he called "iffy" questions. Still, Roosevelt *mattered*—I wouldn't be interested in writing (and few would be interested in reading) an essay on what might have happened if, say, Franklin Pierce or Benjamin Harrison, had been kept from the White House—and looking back over Roosevelt's life before the presidency, it is hard not to be impressed by the number of moments when fortune seemed to smile upon him with unusual brightness, when things might just as easily have gone the other way and left him more or less what his father had been; an amiable well-respected country gentleman, little known beyond the borders of Dutchess County, New York, and the paneled confines of his Manhattan clubs.

What kind of politician might Roosevelt have become, for example, had his proposal of marriage to a dazzling but conventional heiress been accepted, not spurned?

Roosevelt was an eighteen-year-old Harvard freshman in the autumn of 1900 when he was smitten by Alice Sohier, the tall, slender, high-spirited fifteen-year-old daughter of an old North Shore, Massachusetts, family. Hers was just the sort of patrician clan his mother, Sara Delano Roosevelt, might have picked for him to marry into; Alice's mother was a collateral descendant of John Alden; her father an ardent yachtsman with three elegantly appointed summer homes. And Alice herself was a great beauty—"of all the debutantes [of the year]," FDR recalled long after, "she was the loveliest."

The young Roosevelt pursued her avidly for more than a year, noting his time with her in his Line-A-Day journal: "To see Alice Sohier"; "dance with Alice Sohier"; "A.S. for supper"; "To Sohiers in the evening." And at some point during the spring of 1902, he evidently made an impetuous of-fer of marriage. He and Alice were still very young. She already had other suitors. And the young Roosevelt's raw ambition had struck her parents as bumptious, even unseemly; when he told the Sohiers one evening at din-ner that he was planning a political career and thought that he, like his hero and distant cousin, Theodore, might even become president one day, an older cousin of Alice's had asked "Who *else* thinks so?" and the whole family had burst into laughter. But beyond that, he confided to Alice, he had ambitions for his future wife, as well: He'd felt isolated as an only child, he explained, and wanted six children, the same number that tumbled across TR's lawn at Oyster Bay. Alice Sohier was flattered by FDR's atten-tion but appalled by his plans for her: in the end, she told a confidante many years later, she had rejected Franklin Roosevelt's suit because "I did not wish to be a cow." (She would later marry an insurance executive, re-main a lifelong Republican, and profess always to be grateful that she'd never become "the president's lady.")

A mournful FDR saw her off on a trip to Europe in October of 1903. Just five weeks later he found himself a fellow-guest at the New York Horse Show at Madison Square Garden with his shy cousin Eleanor and began to turn the full blaze of his charm on her.

Alice Sohier had largely been satisfied with the world as it was. Eleanor Roosevelt never was—and set out to see to it that her future husband should not be either. In later years, she loved to tell of how, during their courtship, she deliberately arranged for him to pick her up in the evenings at the Lower East Side settlement house where she served as a volunteer. Once, after helping to carry a sick child up several flights of tenement stairs to the fetid one-room flat that housed his whole family, FDR emerged pale and shaken. "My God," he said. "I didn't know anyone lived like that."

"I wanted him to see *how people lived*," Eleanor Roosevelt would say, smiling at the memory. "And it worked. He saw how people lived, and he *never* forgot."

It seems likely that Franklin Roosevelt would have succeeded in politics no matter whom he married. He entered his very first race—for the New York State Senate in 1910—already armed with gifts that would be the envy of everyone who ever ran against him: good looks and boundless charm, genuine interest in people, almost manic energy, plus personal wealth and a celebrated name. But it is hard to see how, without Eleanor Roosevelt's consistent, if sometimes tactless goading, her relentless appeals to his better nature, he would ever have moved far enough beyond the benign insularity of his parents and the other river families among whom he had grown up to have become the sort of president who could say to his secretary of labor, Frances Perkins, "What we are doing, Frances, is trying to build an America in which no one is left out."

How might Roosevelt have fared in politics had a long-forgotten New York reformer named Thomas Mott Osborne been more successful? Or if he had himself not fallen victim to typhoid fever in the midst of his first campaign for reelection?

The young state senator brought political weaknesses as well as strengths with him to Albany. He still often seemed disdainful of people whose upbringing was less patrician than his own. (A good many of his fellow Democratic legislators saw him simply as a snob.) And he was altogether too eager to wage noisy battles against Tammany Hall that produced plenty of headlines but precious few results. And, while he was blessed from the beginning with an uncanny ability to absorb and marshal disconnected bits of information, he also had a short attention span and intensely disliked detail work.

It was Louis Howe, the seasoned but threadbare Albany newspaperman with progressive tendencies and a fierce desire to wield political power behind the scenes, who famously did the most to set him straight, but it has largely been forgotten that Roosevelt was not the first charismatic New York reformer whose career Howe attempted to shape.

In 1906, Howe had attached himself to the magnetic former mayor of Auburn, Thomas Mott Osborne, then engaged in a struggle to deny the Democratic nomination for governor to William Randolph Hearst. Osborne was handsome, eloquent, and high-minded (he would become the best-known prison reformer of his day), but he was also vain, bombastic, and gratuitously insulting—he refused even to parley with the "dogs" and "curs" who he said ran the Democratic machine—and he was badly beaten. Howe believed Osborne had a great future in politics, nonetheless, and clung to him for six more years, acting as a secret operative and using his credentials as a supposedly objective journalist to garner information about party regulars for his boss. In 1912, he quit his newspaper job to work for Osborne full time, confident that his employer would one day ascend at least as far as the governorship and that he himself would rise with him.

Then, without any warning, Osborne withdrew from politics altogether. Howe was out of work and desperate that fall when Eleanor Roosevelt telephoned him. Her husband was in bed with typhoid fever, she said, far too ill to run personally for reelection to the state senate. Would Howe be willing to take over his stalled campaign? Howe gratefully signed on, began addressing Roosevelt privately as "Beloved and Revered Future President," and remained at his new boss's side until his own death in 1936. It is hard to see how FDR could have risen as far as he did without Howe's inbred caution and unswerving loyalty, his insider's perspective—and his willingness to see to all the burdensome details.

What would have happened to Roosevelt had he worked during his years at the Navy Department for a superior less forbearing than Josephus Daniels?

FDR brought enormous vitality and remarkable administrative ability to the job of assistant secretary of the navy before, during, and after World War I, and he was almost always courteous when in the presence of the avuncular North Carolina newspaper editor who had invited him to Washington at thirty-one despite the prescient warning of an old friend that "Whenever a Roosevelt rides, he wants to ride in front."

Daniels's affection for the youthful Roosevelt had been "love at first sight," he liked to say. FDR's feelings about his boss were more complex: There were genuine differences of both substance and style between them. Roosevelt had yearned to be part of the navy since boyhood; Daniels was wary of the military and suspicious of admirals. FDR believed America was sure to be drawn into World War I; Daniels did not. Daniels was slow-moving, courtly, and cautious; Roosevelt was impatient, brash, eager for action.

FDR was given the freest possible rein; no assistant secretary of the navy had ever been given more responsibility. It was never enough for Roosevelt. He had been taught since birth that no man should be his chief, that he and no one else was supposed to be in charge. "I am *running* the real work," he claimed in a letter to his wife in 1914, "though Josephus is here! He is bewildered by it all, very sweet but very sad!" He portrayed his boss and benefactor as a countrified naif so frequently at Washington dinner tables that a close friend took him aside and told him he should be ashamed of himself. He kept right on doing it, anyway. He also leaked damaging information about Daniels to hostile newspapermen, lobbied to replace him at the top, and conspired with several of his chief's enemies—including the archenemy of the Wilson administration in which he served, Theodore Roosevelt. That Daniels seems not merely to have liked but actually to have *loved* Franklin Roosevelt, in spite of all this, is one of the enduring puzzles of American political history. Anyone but Daniels, it seems to me, would have delighted in sending Roosevelt back home to Hyde Park before he'd been on the job six months.

Would FDR ever have had a national political career had Theodore Roosevelt still been alive in 1920?

In later years, FDR liked to say that it had been his vigorous record as assistant secretary of the navy that had won him the Democratic nomination for vice president in 1920: "They chose me," he told one early biographer, "because my name had become known during the war." In fact, he was chosen in large part simply because he bore the same last name as the late Theodore Roosevelt.

It would be hard to exaggerate the importance of TR's example in FDR's life. It was he who had first demonstrated, in Sara Delano Roosevelt's words, that a member of the family "might go into politics but not *be* a politician." At Groton, fourteen-year-old Franklin adopted pince-nez because his fifth cousin had worn them when he charged up Kettle Hill in Cuba. At Harvard, FDR joined the Republican club and marched through the rain in support of his hero. His love for Eleanor Roosevelt was genuine but the entrée she provided to her uncle's circle at Oyster Bay was a considerable part of her dowry, nonetheless. The fact that TR had four sons, any one of whom then seemed more likely than he to inherit the Roosevelt political mantle, may have helped persuade FDR to enter politics as a Democrat in 1910; there seemed to be no future for him as a Republican, and his unexpected victory for the state senate that same year was largely a result of the split in GOP ranks engineered by TR's progressive followers. Theodore Roosevelt hoped to wrest power back from the Republican bosses and make himself the party's presidential nominee in 1920; hundreds of thousands of his admirers were awaiting word from him to enlist once again in his cause when he died suddenly in January of 1919.

Franklin Roosevelt was only thirty-eight and looked still younger when he traveled west with the New York delegation to attend the Democratic National Convention in San Francisco the following summer. Once he had made a good impression on the crowd by seconding Al Smith's nomination for president, all the excitement seemed to be over for him. But it took forty-four ballots before the exhausted delegates picked the third-term governor of Ohio, James Cox, as their presidential nominee and when it was over, the governor turned to the young Roosevelt as his running mate. As an eager young supporter of Al Smith, Cox told his startled aides, Roosevelt might help carry New York without which victory in November would be impossible. But above all, he said "his name is good," by which he meant that it would appeal to progressive Republicans sickened by the nomination of Warren G. Harding and still mourning Theodore Roosevelt. The newspaper headlines that appeared the following morning echoed Cox's thinking: Franklin Roosevelt's Career Parallels Cousin Teddy's . . . Liken Career of Roosevelt to Cousin's . . . Cousin of TR Is Picked for Second Place . . . The Democrats Hope Name of Roosevelt Will Draw Votes . . . All the World Loves a Roosevelt.

The Cox-Roosevelt ticket was crushed by Harding and Coolidge that fall and the Roosevelt name was not enough to carry a single New York county. But party professionals did not blame Franklin Roosevelt. Millions of voters now considered him not merely a pale reflection of his late cousin but a vigorous, attractive personality in his own right.

Would FDR ever have reached the White House if the press of his era had approached candidates with the intractable cynicism and obsession with personal scandal that seems so pervasive in ours?

There is no clearer evidence of how different the age of Roosevelt was from our own than the ease with which the complexities of Roosevelt's private life were concealed. To begin with, there was FDR's early romance with Lucy Mercer, widely known among his contemporaries in Washington but never so much as hinted at in print during his lifetime. Once Eleanor Roosevelt discovered it in 1917, her cousin Corinne Alsop remembered, "everybody behaved well and exactly as one would expect each of the protagonists . . . to behave." Eleanor offered Franklin a divorce. His mother said that if her son chose divorce he could expect to be overlooked in her will. Lucy Mercer, a practicing Catholic, agonized over whether or not she could marry a divorced man. And Louis Howe counseled that if FDR allowed his heart to rule his head he could say good-bye to politics. Divorce would be political suicide.

In the end, Howe's view prevailed. It is impossible to know what would have happened to the presidency, to the country, or to the cause of freedom itself had Franklin Roosevelt divorced his wife, married Lucy Mercer, and thereby ended his political career. But the late Murray Kempton once offered a memorable "fugitive fantasy" about Roosevelt and his second wife. The two would have retreated to the Hudson Valley, he suggested, and there "endure in the imagination, growing old together, say near Newburgh, he languidly farming and drawing wills and litigating country quarrels and she stealing now and then into the dreary little church to grieve a while for the spiritual loss that had brought their happiness. The Depression is hard on him; but when he dies he has managed to recoup by selling his remaining acres for a postwar housing development. His obituary is exactly the size the *Times* metes out for former assistant secretaries of the navy who had been nominated for vice president of the United States in a bad year for their party."

Roosevelt had other closely guarded secrets that responsible newspapermen and women of his time simply considered none of the public's business, including his closeness to his unmarried secretary, Marguerite Le Hand, and the fact that once their children were grown, he and his wife lived apart for all but ceremonial purposes, maintaining separate residences when away from the White House, surrounding themselves with separate circles of friends, rarely even dining together unless guests were present.

The fact that Roosevelt was a paraplegic after polio—and not merely "lame" as *Time* magazine reported and most Americans believed—was also tactfully concealed by mutual agreement between him and those who covered him. If there had not been such an unspoken pact—had photographers and newsreel cameramen routinely shown him being carried from place to place, unable to take a step unaided or even rise from his chair—it is hard to see how a country already grievously disabled by Depression would ever have elected such a man to lead it. (Nor do I think things have changed much over the intervening years: Were some other candidate, equally well qualified but no less physically impaired, to try to win the nation's highest office today, television's unblinking, unforgiving omnipresent eye would make his or her election impossible.)

What would have happened to Franklin Roosevelt had he not contracted infantile paralysis in 1921?

As late as the 1920 vice presidential campaign, his loyal press secretary, Steve Early, once confided, FDR was "just a playboy" who "failed to take life seriously enough . . . [and] couldn't be made to prepare his speeches in advance, preferring to play cards, instead." The late Franklin Roosevelt, Jr., once told me more or less the same thing: his father had been "a playboy in politics" before the onset of his illness, he said, "living off his cousin's name and his mother's money." And FDR Jr. further believed that his father's illness, ghastly as its physical impact was, had also turned out to be still another "stroke of luck" in political terms. It taught him patience, he said, and, more important, it kept him from "making a fool of himself" by running for the presidency in the hopelessly Republican twenties, before he was ready for the job or the country was ready for him. FDR Jr. overstated his case—Al Smith would likely have remained New York's favorite son in 1924 and 1928 whether or not FDR had remained able-bodied—and the son's harsh portrait of his youthful father may have been colored in part by raw memories of his own repeated disappointments in political life.

Still, polio did indirectly save FDR from the one threat that really might have cut short to his career—the controversial part he had played in what came to be called the Newport scandal. In the spring of 1919, Secretary Daniels had sailed for Europe to attend an Allied naval conference, somewhat nervously leaving the Navy Department in the hands of his eager young assistant secretary, with instructions not to sign anything really important until he got back and they could talk it over. As always, Roosevelt reveled in being in charge: "You ought to see the change in the carrying on of the department work," he boasted to a friend who had worked there with him. "I see civilians in the old building from 9 A.M. to 10:30, then I see the press, and then dash down to the new building in a high-powered car, and from that time on—11 A.M.—see no outsiders, congressmen, senators, or anybody else. The department mail is signed at regular hours and absolutely cleaned up everyday, with the result that nothing is taken home, mislaid, lost, et cetera, et cetera." Among the documents to which both he and his chief would later wish he had never affixed his bold blue signature that spring were several orders setting up a top-secret intelligence unit, to be attached to his own office, whose purpose was to end homosexuality on and off the naval base at Newport, Rhode Island. In that time there was nothing especially remarkable in working toward that goal: Both military and civilian law then held homosexual acts to be criminal.

It was the *methods* employed that came close to derailing Roosevelt. For under his at least tacit approval, young sailors were recruited with instructions to become sexually involved with homosexuals "to the limit," in order to obtain evidence against them. Among those arrested was a prominent Episcopal clergyman whose arrest made national headlines and whose lawyers, understandably enough, charged entrapment.

There were two separate investigations of the incident, one by the navy, the other by a Senate subcommittee. FDR angrily denied everything. He couldn't recall even *reading* the letter he'd signed setting up the secret squad, he claimed, had never been told how it gathered its evidence, and had never asked.

Hadn't it been his duty to do so? No it had not, he answered under oath. He was a busy man. Only results had mattered to him.

The navy court of inquiry eventually let him off with a gentle reprimand. But the Republican majority on the Senate subcommittee dismissed Roosevelt's testimony as "unbelievable" and "incredible." They had him coming and going: If he *hadn't* made it his business to know what sort of dirty work was being directed from his own office then "he was most derelict in the performance of his duty," they said; and if he *had* ordered "the use of enlisted personnel for the purpose of investigating perversion"—and the Republican senators were convinced he had—then that decision should be "thoroughly condemned as immoral and an abuse of the authority of his high office."

The degree of Roosevelt's actual culpability in this sordid business is impossible to assess all these years later, but he seems to have been less complicitous than oblivious, signing the orders in his superior's absence without much thought, probably relishing the air of importance that surrounded a clandestine investigation but too busy or too distracted to learn the day-to-day details. In any case, it certainly *looked* bad, and some newspapermen—with encouragement from Republicans eager to write an end to the young Roosevelt's promising political career—looked forward to probing the part he'd played still further.

Here, Roosevelt's illness turned out to be an unlikely boon. The Senate subcommittee's charges had just surfaced on the front page of the *New York Times*—which had headlined its story "Lay Navy Scandal to F. D. Roosevelt" and then made things look even worse than they were by declaring its details "Unprintable"—when he sailed for Campobello and his rendezvous with infantile paralysis in the summer of 1921.

After Roosevelt was stricken, even his most implacable opponents saw nothing to be gained in doing further damage to a now-helpless man whose political race had so obviously been run. The story was allowed to die away. Still, back in politics and running for president eleven years later, Roosevelt remained so worried about its potential for political damage that he and Howe insisted that Earle Looker, his first campaign biographer, include in his book the complete text of the lengthy press release FDR had issued in his own defense in 1921; in the finished volume, it took up eight of the eighteen pages devoted to his years at the Navy Department.

The Republicans who dropped the Newport scandal because they believed FDR no longer a threat to them were joining a long line of people who lived to regret having underestimated Franklin Roosevelt. That line began forming early, with his classmates at Groton and Harvard, who could never quite understand how the glossy youth they remembered as altogether too easy to please could possibly succeed in the sweaty world of politics. And it stretched on to include the Roosevelts of Oyster Bay, who thought that in marrying him, Eleanor Roosevelt had married beneath herself; the Dutchess County Democratic bosses who picked him to run for the State Senate in what had been a hopelessly Republican district mostly in hopes of tapping into his mother's fortune; the Tammany bosses who thought they had permanently put him out of business when they trounced his candidacy for the United States Senate nomination in 1911; and finally Al Smith, who in 1928 thought Roosevelt a lightweight in frail health and therefore believed it safe to ask him to return to politics and run for governor.

Wasn't he raising up a dangerous rival? an old ally named Dan Finn asked Smith.

"No, Dan," the governor replied confidently. "He won't live a year."

He lived another seventeen years, of course, and would spend the last twelve of them in the White House. But before he could move in, he would be favored by fortune one more time.

What if Giuseppe Zangara's bullets hadn't missed?

At seven in the evening on February 15, 1933, Vincent Astor's yacht, the *Nourmahal*, docked at Miami, Florida. Among the passengers on deck was the president-elect, FDR, tanned and rested after a Caribbean fishing trip.

His inauguration was only seventeen days away. The mayor had organized a welcome-home rally at the Bayfront Park amphitheater, and thousands of people had already gathered there to see and hear him. Among them—in the second row, just thirty feet from the spot where the president-elect's open car was to stop so that he could speak to the crowd—was a delusional Italian immigrant named Giuseppe Zangara, wracked with pain from peptic ulcers and consumed with rage at all the "people who run the government . . . [and] suck the blood out of the poor." He had a .32 revolver in his pocket. He had once hoped to kill Herbert Hoover. Now, Roosevelt was his intended target; if he didn't get a clear shot at him here he planned to travel to Washington and shoot him during the inaugural parade.

The president-elect's car nosed its way through the cheering crowd and pulled to a stop at about seven-thirty. As well-wishers closed in around it, FDR hoisted himself up onto the back of the car seat so that people could see him while making a few cheery, inconsequential remarks into a microphone—so few remarks that by the time a newsreel crew got ready to start filming, the president-elect had already slid back down into his seat. The cameraman begged him to climb back up again and repeat his words for the newsreels. Roosevelt gently demurred. "I'm sorry," he said. "I just can't do it." At that moment, Zangara, frustrated that his target had dropped from sight before he could get a clear shot at him, clambered onto a metal chair and started firing. He managed to get off five shots, hitting five people—including Mayor Anton Cermak of Chicago, who subsequently died of his wound—before members of the crowd hurled him to the ground.

Somehow, FDR remained untouched. Had Zangara reached Bayfront Park early enough to find a place in the front row of the crowd instead of the second, or had FDR given in to the importuning of the newsreel crew, things might have been very different. It is impossible to know what would have happened next, except for one thing: under the new twentieth amendment, the presidency would have passed to the vice president–elect. John Nance Garner of Texas would have found himself faced with the gravest crisis since the Civil War—the Depression.

There was precious little to suggest that he was interested in breaking "foolish tradition," as Roosevelt had promised *he* would do, no hint that

Garner came to the job equipped with the kind of fresh ideas needed for what FDR had called "unprecedented and unusual times." Born in 1868 in a log cabin at Blossom Prairie, Texas, he was the son of an ex-Confederate cavalryman and a mother whose earliest memories were of fortifying the family cabin against Comanches. He had walked three miles each day to a one-room schoolhouse, first won local fame as the star shortstop for the combined Blossom Prairie–Coon Soup Hollow baseball nine in its annual battles with a team fielded by neighboring Possum Trot, and he learned his law, just as Abraham Lincoln had learned his, in a small-town law office. He passed the bar at twenty-one and in 1893, after a doctor suggested he might be developing tuberculosis, he set up shop in Uvalde in the dry-ranch country west of San Antonio. There, he rode the circuit over nine counties, sometimes accepting cattle and mohair goats for his services instead of cash, married a rancher's daughter whose considerable inheritance helped him build a fortune as a rancher, pecan-grower, and small-town banker, and got himself elected to the state legislature where, as chairman of the committee on redistricting, he saw to it that the map of Texas was redrawn to ensure him a safe seat in Congress. He went to Washington in 1903 and, through persistence, seniority, and shrewd parliamentary astuteness, rose steadily to the Democratic leadership. When the Democrats took over the House in 1931, he became Speaker. He remained an unreconstructed Jeffersonian: "The great trouble today," he said in the third year of the Depression, "is that we have too many laws. I believe that primarily a government has but two functions—to protect the lives and property rights of citizens. When it goes further than that, it becomes a burden." (As late as April of 1937 he would argue in Cabinet meetings that many of the nation's problems could be solved if city dwellers could only be persuaded to move en masse back into the countryside.)

His presence on the 1932 ticket had been the price Roosevelt had to pay for Texas support at the convention. Garner would have much preferred to remain Speaker. "The vice presidency," he once told a reporter, "isn't worth a pitcher of warm piss"—and when the newsman changed it to "a pitcher of warm spit" for public consumption, Garner privately called him a "panty-waist." Only lifelong devotion to party unity persuaded him to run.

A RELUCTANT LEADER?

*FDR's first vice president, John Nance Garner of Texas—"Cactus Jack"—
posed for a formal portrait in 1934. A year earlier, only a would-be assassin's
wild shot kept this profoundly negative man from becoming president during
one of the greatest crises the United States ever faced.*

(Culver Pictures)

He barely knew FDR and made only a single campaign speech before
hurrying home to Uvalde to await the results. It was probably just as well.
He was an unprepossessing figure: short—just five-foot-one—red-faced,
and faintly redolent of bourbon, with close-cropped white hair and formidable eyebrows ("like two caterpillars rasslin'," he himself once said) and a

dead cigar perpetually stuck in the corner of his tiny mouth. He was also a dreadful speaker. In his safe, Democratic district there had been no need for speechifying and he had seen little need for it in the House, either. His standard counsel to new congressmen was to keep quiet and get things done behind the scenes. "It was a good many years before any remarks of mine got into the [*Congressional*] *Record*," he told his successor in Congress, "and I hope you won't make a damn fool of yourself either." An America desperate for reassurance on inauguration day in 1933 was unlikely to have gotten much from the taciturn Texas politician who had once been pleased when the press called him "the Texas Coolidge."

Garner opposed none of the bills proposed by the president in his first one hundred days, granting Roosevelt more power than any chief executive in history—though he privately thought the NRA "a moony adventure." Even he believed that desperate times demanded desperate measures and he used his position as presiding officer of the Senate to slam them through. "After a bill was read," his friend and chronicler, the veteran newspaperman Bascom Timmins, remembered, "and before a senator had time to clear his throat, adjust his papers and call for recognition, Garner in rapidly tumbling words would say: 'The question is: Shall the bill be engrossed, read the third time and passed? There being no objection the bill is passed.'" Senators too slow to react were out of luck. Still, as early as 1934, the journalist John Carter Vincent would suggest that the Texan was "as out of place in the New Deal as a dead mouse in a mince pie. . . . The epitome of the Western middle class: a big farmer, a banker, and a businessman, the individual entrepreneur who has made a conspicuous success under the old rules of the old game. He is against Big Business, but only because it interferes with small business, and if the New Deal should ever fall into his hands, God save the New Deal and Heaven help the country."

Garner remained adamantly opposed to deficit spending of any kind: Mrs. Garner had never had a "charge account," he once said, and he saw no need for the country to have one, either. His views on labor were out of sync with his times, as well. His own fortune was built in part on cheap labor: while union carpenters in Texas got a dollar and a quarter a day, those who worked for Garner got only the quarter; the Mexican-Americans who gathered and shelled him pecans for a penny a pound "are not troublesome people unless they become Americanized," he unwisely confided to a visiting reporter from Philadelphia. "The sheriff can make them do anything." Sit-down strikes, he told the Cabinet, constituted simple thievery.

He was also utterly uninterested in foreign affairs. It had been his hostility to the League of Nations and his interest in his "own people" and "his own country" that had made him William Randolph Hearst's first candidate for the Democratic nomination in 1932. He opposed FDR's recognition of the Soviet Union in 1933 and was at home in Uvalde feeding his chickens later that same year when, after five Cuban presidents in a row had been overthrown by coups, the president called to consult him on whether the United States might have to intervene to protect U.S. interests on the island.

"What do you think we ought to do, Jack?" FDR asked.

"I'd keep out of Cuba."

"But suppose an American is shot?"

"I'd wait," Garner answered, "and see which American it was . . ."

The Nazis didn't worry him much, either. When someone at an early Cabinet meeting worried aloud that the new Hitler regime seemed serious about persecuting the Jews, according to John Carter Vincent, "Garner— perhaps remembering the effect of fifty years of Northern moral indignation with the Southern treatment of Negroes—tartly reminded his colleagues that the internal politics of Germany were none of the business of the American government, and hopefully suggested that the hotter the Nazi excesses, the sooner they would burn out." In 1938, he told the Cabinet he hoped Britain never paid its war debt because then it could borrow no more money. As late as midsummer of 1939, he refused to believe a European war inevitable, let alone concede that America might become involved if one started. Secretary of State Cordell Hull, who detested him, told Interior Secretary Harold Ickes that Garner saw all international relationships in the light of Uvalde, Texas. That evidently went for some domestic issues, as well: when Marion Anderson sang at the White House for the visiting king and queen of England in 1939, the vice president alone among the guests assembled in the East Room refused to applaud.

No one can tell how much of the New Deal might have been enacted without FDR or how close we would have come to revolution from the right or left had his unshakable, contagious confidence in America's ability to solve even its most serious problems not spread among its people. Nor can we know whether without him Americans would have awakened in time to meet the Axis threat. But it seems clear that the thirties would have been a far grimmer time for America and the world a far more frightening place had Franklin D. Roosevelt's extraordinary run of luck ended on that warm winter evening in Miami.

WILLIAMSON MURRAY

THE WAR OF 1938

Chamberlain fails to sway
Hitler at Munich

If there is a single enduring image of the Munich Pact of September 1938, it is of the British prime minister Neville Chamberlain emerging from a plane and waving a clutch of papers that, he said, assured "peace in our time." The British and French had just allowed Hitler to annex the Sudetenland, those large portions of Czechoslovakia with a predominately German population (as well as the Czech version of the Maginot Line). Hitler claimed that this would be his last demand: Six months later he swallowed up the rest of Czechoslovakia. Munich, the historian Norman Davies has written, "must qualify as one of the most degrading capitulations in history."

Chamberlain's defenders have long claimed that the unfortunate pact gave Great Britain needed breathing space, in which it had time to build up its defenses, the RAF especially. In Williamson Murray's view, that is nonsense: Not England but Germany benefited most from the remission. Hitler almost threw that advantage away. He was determined to go to war against Czechoslovakia and would have done so within days of the last-ditch Munich meeting of September 29 and 30, when Chamberlain unexpectedly caved in. Even as the talks went on, troops were moving up to the Czech border. "Until his dying days," Murray writes, Hitler "remained bitterly disappointed that the British had deprived him of the opportunity of launching the Wehrmacht against the Czechs."

What would have happened if a major European war had broken out in the autumn of 1938? Its results, in Murray's view, would have been very different from *what actually happened. Germany in 1938 was simply not prepared for a conflict of any duration. The problem for Hitler was not taking Czechoslovakia: Though his armies and air force would have been roughed up, the entire campaign would have lasted no more than a month, about the time needed to roll over Poland the following year. More to the point, what would have happened afterward, when Hitler's armies would inevitably have been forced to turn westward? To consider that prospect, Murray argues, is to understand how unfortunate was the respite that Neville Chamberlain bought.*

WILLIAMSON MURRAY, a senior fellow at the Institute for Defense Analyses, is a professor of history emeritus at Ohio State University and, with Allen R. Millett, the author of *A War to Be Won: Fighting the Second World War.*

O N SEPTEMBER 29, 1938, Adolf Hitler, führer of Nazi Germany, Benito Mussolini, duce of Fascist Italy, Edouard Daladier, premier of France, and Neville Chamberlain, prime minister of Great Britain, met in the Bavarian capital of Munich and agreed to a peaceful settlement of the Czech crisis that the Nazis had manufactured over the course of that summer. That agreement sealed the fate of Czechoslovakia. Yet only the day before the conference convened, German troops had been rolling up into their jump-off positions against a mobilized and deployed Czech Army, while the Luftwaffe was completing deployment of its aircraft onto bases in the immediate vicinity of the Czech Republic. Determined to crush the Czechs by war, Hitler had created a crisis that seemed headed toward war. Only at the last moment, for reasons that still remain inexplicable, had the führer backed off.

The Munich conference resulted from the course of German military and diplomatic policy throughout 1938. Nazi strategy had in turn resulted from a number of factors, the clearest being Hitler's implacable long-term aim to destroy the European balance of power and replace it with a German hegemony that would stretch from the Urals to the Atlantic. Coming to power in January 1933, the führer had immediately launched a massive program of rearmament for the war he saw as inevitable. But by late 1937 the Reich's rearmament remained incomplete, while the German economy appeared headed toward bankruptcy, pressures of a serious economic situation, combined with Hitler's unwillingness to abandon his goals, led the führer to determine on a riskier approach in 1938.

The Austrians were the first to feel the pressures of Nazi expansionism in early 1938. Confronting the severe economic problems occasioned by his massive rearmament program and a political crisis occasioned by his firing of the army's commander in chief, Werner von Fritsch, on trumped-up charges of homosexuality, Hitler moved against the Austrians. While Hitler browbeat the Austrians into submission, the major European powers backed away from the crisis and abandoned Vienna to its fate. In mid-March 1938 the Nazis overthrew the Austrian government, and the Wehrmacht occupied Hitler's native land.

If the Europeans thought that the *Anschluss* (the union of Germany and Austria) would relieve international tensions, they were quickly disabused of that notion. In May 1938 the Czechs, alarmed at German propaganda in their borderlands—the Sudetenland, largely inhabited by Germans—mobilized and placed their frontier districts under martial law. Outraged that the Czechs had taken matters into their own hands, Hitler ordered his military planners to begin immediately drawing up plans for an invasion of Czechoslovakia on October 1, 1938. At the same time he had his propaganda minister, Joseph Goebbels, unleash a massive propaganda campaign to justify such an invasion. As storm clouds gathered in the summer of 1938, the French and British desperately attempted to divert Hitler from an attack on Czechoslovakia. They had reason to do so; the Franco-Czech alliance directly committed the French to intervene on the side of the Czechs, were they attacked by the Germans. But the British, with close ties to the French, were also desperately afraid that in the case of a major European war, unleashed without justification by the Nazis, they too would inevitably be drawn in at the side of the French. Thus, throughout the summer, Chamberlain made desperate efforts to appease the Germans. In September, having never flown before, he undertook two journeys by air to Germany. Only at the last minute did the führer back down and agree to a conference at Munich, where he obtained all of his demands. But Europe had perched on the edge of a major war—one that would have occurred under very different circumstances from those surrounding the one that began in September 1939.

Almost from the moment of the signing of the Munich Agreement, the arguments of contemporaries and then historians have swirled around the issue of whether the military weaknesses of the Western Powers justified the surrender or whether war in 1938 would have more readily and quickly resulted in Nazi Germany's demise than the war that broke out a year later.

HITLER'S INVASION OF CZECHOSLOVAKIA, OCTOBER 1938

ARMY DESIGNATIONS

Army

Divisions:
Infantry
Mountain
Motorized Infantry
Armored
Light

HUNGARY

POLAND

Kraków

CZECHOSLOVAKIA

SILESIA

Breslau (Wrocław)

Brünn (Brno)

Bratislava

Danube River

Vienna

Prague

Pilsen

Dresden

GERMANY

Danube River

N

© 2001 Jeffrey L. Ward

On one side, Winston Churchill, speaking before a hostile House of Commons in 1938, warned that the British people had "sustained a defeat without a war, the consequences of which will travel far with us along our road; they should know that we have passed an awful milestone in our history, when the whole equilibrium of Europe has been deranged, and that the terrible words have for the time being been pronounced against the Western Democracies: 'Thou art weighed in the balance and found wanting.'" On the other hand, the British chiefs of staff, just a few weeks before Munich, had warned that the military situation heavily favored Nazi Germany. The argument has continued unabated since.

What matters in thinking about war in 1938 is the actual balance of military, economic, and political forces in the fall of that year and the possible outcome of a major war. As was not the case in the other crises of the 1930s, Hitler had every intention of fighting; he had created a situation that would have forced the Western Powers to intervene, if the Wehrmacht had attacked Czechoslovakia. The brutal, aggressive behavior of Nazi Germany in the face of Neville Chamberlain's extraordinary peacekeeping efforts had finally resulted in a fundamental shift in British and French public opinion in favor of standing against Hitler's unreasonable demands. Until his dying days he remained bitterly disappointed that the British had deprived him of the opportunity of launching the Wehrmacht against the Czechs.

In thinking about a war in 1938, one simply cannot point to a replay of the Battle of Britain. First, the Germans were not yet in a position to achieve the kind victory that would have destroyed the French Army on the Continent and secured the air bases on the Channel coast that made the Battle of Britain possible. Second, in 1938 the Luftwaffe possessed none of the prerequisites for such a battle. In fact, a war in 1938 would have looked nothing like the war that actually occurred in 1939 and 1940.

In considering the German Army's development in the 1930s, it is difficult to avoid considering the impression created by its later victories. In 1938 its forces still possessed considerable weaknesses. Re-armament had built the army up to forty-eight regular divisions, only three of which were panzer, four motorized infantry, and four light divisions (which consisted of a mixed bag of motorized, mechanized, and cavalry units), while the remainder were World War I–style infantry units, their equipment largely drawn by horses, and most with considerable shortages in artillery and other weapons.

Moreover, German rearmament had yet to establish any depth; there were few reserves except for Landwehr divisions consisting of overage and out-of-shape World War I veterans. Even the three panzer divisions had considerable weaknesses; their equipment consisted entirely of six-ton PzKw Is and ten-ton PzKw IIs, the former a glorified tin can. The result was that the existing armored forces possessed little hitting or staying power.

But the real weakness in the army lay in the quality, training, and skills of its junior officers and NCOs. The army's growth from the minuscule Reichswehr of 1933 had resulted in an officer corps that had expanded far too rapidly. Consequently, the Germans still confronted two crucial problems in 1938: Not only did the army's combat potential suffer from real deficiencies in training and leadership, but the reserve forces on which Germany depended to defend its western frontier and take part in any sustained combat, did not yet exist.

Thus, the strategic demands of a war in 1938 would have been beyond the army's manpower, equipment, and resources. Because the Germans could not trust the Poles, three divisions had to remain in East Prussia (separated from the rest of the Reich by the Polish Corridor), whatever the strategic situation. Five of the army's regular divisions had come directly into the army as a result of the *Anschluss* and fully reflected their heritage in the Austrian Army. By the fall of 1939 the Wehrmacht managed to correct those deficiencies, but in 1938 they remained quite apparent. As one senior general noted, the difference between Austrian and German units was the difference between night and day.

In planning *Fall Grün* (Case Green, the attack on Czechoslovakia) the OKM, or Oberkommando des Heeres, the army high command, allocated thirty-seven divisions for the campaign. After the subtraction of three divisions in East Prussia, there remained only eight for the defense of the west, Pomerania, and Silesia against the French and Poles. Backing up this scanty operational reserve were fourteen Landwehr divisions, all under-

trained, underequipped, and unprepared for combat. In nearly every respect, the army was not ready.

There was also considerable political dissatisfaction among senior officers over Hitler's handling of the Fritsch/Blomberg crisis during the winter
of 1938. Even pro-Nazi officers like Heinz Guderian were angered by the
phony charges of homosexuality that the SS had manufactured against
General Werner von Fritsch, the army's commander in chief. Only the
stunning success of the *Anschluss* that March prevented a simmering crisis
in civil-military relations from becoming a full-blown eruption. In addition, Hitler's war policy toward Czechoslovakia occasioned deep worries
among senior generals. The chief of the general staff, Ludwig Beck, had resigned as a result of his disagreement with Hitler's drive toward war. The
disquiet with Hitler's policies even led a number of senior generals to plot
against the Nazi regime as the crisis reached its height in September. Thus,
the army was hardly the unified, ideologically committed organization it
would be in the early 1940s.

If the mid- and long-term prospects of the German Army in war in 1938
did not look bright, the Czechs also confronted serious problems. They had
begun work in the mid-1930s on a complex series of fortifications to defend
against a German attack from Silesia. While considerable work had gone
forward in creating field fortifications, their defensive works still had serious deficiencies. The old frontier with Austria was particularly vulnerable.
While the mountains and forest ringing the Bohemian/Moravian plateau
offered considerable challenges to an invader, the Germans had the opportunity in the area between Silesia and Austria to cut the Czech Republic in
half—particularly given the lack of fortifications along the Austro-Czech
frontier.

The Czech Army's potential is, of course, difficult to evaluate, since it
would never fight. Its equipment was excellent, a reflection of the up-to-
date, highly efficient armament complexes in Czechoslovakia, the Skoda
works being the most famous. Ironically, those works would turn out high-
quality weapons for the Wehrmacht right through 1945. But the quality of
the army is another matter. The human material from the Czech regions
was motivated and well-educated, but the Czechs only made up approxi-

mately 50 percent of the republic's population. The fighting qualities of even the Slovaks were problematic, while those of the republic's smaller nationalities such as Ruthenians, Hungarians, and Sudeten Germans was almost nonexistent. Generally the officer corps was competent, but senior officers were not a distinguished lot. The operational planning for *Fall Grün* suggests the risks Hitler was running. In the west General Walther von Reichenau's Tenth Army was to break into Bohemia with a blow aimed at Prague. But Franz Halder, Beck's replacement as chief of the general staff, placed the emphasis on General Gerd von Rundstedt's Second Army, which was to attack from Silesia to meet General Wilhelm List's Fourteenth Army attacking from Austria. The aim was to cut Czechoslovakia in half and isolate the Czechs from receiving outside aid.

At the first briefing of invasion plans by Halder, Hitler objected to the OKH's operational conception. He suggested that Rundstedt's attack from Silesia would result in heavy casualties in fighting through the strong Czech defenses in the region; he worried that the fighting might turn into another Verdun. Hitler also demanded that Halder reinforce Reichenau's Tenth Army with panzer and motorized divisions so that German forces could capture Prague early in the campaign and thus deter the French and British from intervening. As Hitler suggested:

> There is no doubt that the planned pincer operation is the most desirable solution [from the military point of view] and should take place. Its success, nevertheless, is too uncertain to depend on, especially as, politically, a rapid success is necessary. The first eight days are politically decisive, in which period of time we must achieve far-reaching territorial gains.

In the end the final plans represented a compromise between Hitler and Halder. Reichenau's Tenth Army received additional divisions, but nothing on the order of what Hitler had initially demanded, while Rundstedt's offensive was to go forward into the teeth of the Czech fortifications. In political terms, Hitler's conception was both daring and offered better prospects for deterring the Western powers. However, the compromise weakened the blow from Silesia without significantly increasing the chances for a successful capture of Prague in the invasion's first days. As he was to do for the remainder of his career, Hitler was ready to take great risks.

The balance in air power between the Czechs and the Germans was relatively straightforward. While the Luftwaffe enjoyed great superiority, it would have confronted some significant problems. Eight of the days between October 1 and October 11 (the first days of the scheduled invasion) had bad weather—the kind of conditions that would have presented an inexperienced air force with considerable difficulties. In retrospect, the Luftwaffe would undoubtedly have played a major role in the conquest of Czechoslovakia, but because of bad weather and its own weaknesses, it would have suffered heavy losses that would have hampered its ability to execute further operations.

The ground capabilities of the other European armies are relatively easy to lay out; in contrast to 1914 virtually everyone was unprepared for another great war. At best the British could have sent two unprepared and ill-equipped divisions to support the French. The Soviets possessed great masses of equipment and huge numbers of soldiers, but Stalin had shot most of the Red Army's senior leadership in the purges that had begun in May 1937. The year 1938 represented the nadir of Soviet preparations for war, as an imaginative and innovative military leadership had given way to the worst sort of sycophants—few of whom knew the slightest thing about the conduct of military operations. The great wild card in the 1938 situation remains the question of what the Soviets, who had little real interest in helping the Czechs, would have done. The Poles represented a more serious military factor, since their army was not nearly as bad as the campaign in 1939 would suggest. In a war in 1938 they could have picked the time and place for military operations against the Germans. German forces in Silesia, tied down as they would have been in attacking Moravia, would have been particularly vulnerable to Polish attack.

In the west the French possessed strong military forces. If confronted with a German invasion, they would have fought well in defense of their homeland. As we now know, French soldiers would fight hard in 1940;

123,000 would die in defense of the republic in that campaign, betrayed by abysmal generalship. The generalship would have been no better the year before, but the German Army would not have been in a position to take advantage of those weaknesses. It is doubtful whether the French would have launched a serious offensive against the Rhineland. But, if presented the opportunity, they would have acted against the Italians, whom they regarded with reason as ill-trained and ill-prepared. Of all the armies in Europe, Italian ground forces were the least effective. The cause of this state of affairs had nothing to do with the bravery of Italians—over 600,000 had died in the Alps in some of the worst battles of World War I—but because of a general staff and leadership that displayed not a hint of serious military professionalism. The megalomaniacal tendencies of Mussolini's regime only served to exacerbate the incompetencies of generals like Marshal Rudolfo Graziani, who commented at the last crown council immediately before the war that "when the cannon sound, everything will fall into place."

The European naval and air balances underline how much weaker the Germans were in 1938 than they would be the next year. On the naval side, the Kriegsmarine was categorically not ready for war. It had yet to complete any of the major fleet units laid down under the Nazi construction programs. Neither *Scharnhorst* nor *Gneisenau*, the first battle cruisers, had yet to complete fitting out or working up. There were no heavy cruisers, no aircraft carriers, only seven destroyers and three "pocket" battleships (glorified heavy cruisers). Even more glaringly there were only seven oceangoing U-boats available for service in the Atlantic. Consequently, the Germans were hardly in a position to protect their own coasts, much less execute a war on Allied commerce in the North Atlantic. As a result, the Western Powers could have concentrated their naval resources in the Mediterranean, where the Italians were even more vulnerable.

The air balance was, of course, one of the crucial elements in the strategic equation of 1938. One of the most persistent myths in the post-Munich literature has argued that Chamberlain saved Britain at Munich from defeat at the hands of the Luftwaffe and won time for the RAF's Fighter Command to win the "Battle of Britain." Supposedly, the year's grace provided by the Munich surrender allowed the RAF to equip its fighter squadrons with Spitfires and Hurricanes and extend the radar system and sector stations to cover the whole of the British Isles. In fact, the Luftwaffe was completely unprepared to launch a strategic bombing campaign against the British Isles.

The persistent belief in the possibility of a German air campaign against Britain in 1938 is the direct result of the massive disinformation campaign the Germans waged in 1938 to persuade their potential enemies of the Luftwaffe's terrifying capabilities. Charles Lindbergh was to mar his reputation for the rest of his life by the gullibility with which he swallowed the propaganda line that Hermann Göring and other Luftwaffe leaders fed him during his visits to Germany. But the chief of staff of the French Air Force, General Joseph Vuillemin, was no more perceptive during a visit to Germany in August 1938. He returned to France to fill the highest councils of the French government with reports about the terrifying capabilities the Luftwaffe possessed. Astonishingly, a number of historians, without the slightest reference to German records, have projected German capabilities from such disinformation.

By September 1938 the RAF's rearmament program had made little progress. Reequipment of fighter squadrons was only beginning, while Bomber Command had no modern aircraft in production. Instead of the fifty fighter squadrons considered the minimum for Britain's air defense, only twenty-nine existed. Of these only five possessed Hurricanes and none Spitfires. Even the Hurricanes could not operate at altitudes above 15,000 in combat, since they had no gun warmers. The remaining squadrons possessed obsolete Gladiators, Furys, Gauntlets, and Demons, none of which could catch the newest German bombers.

But the Germans were no better off. For most of 1938 the Luftwaffe was exchanging its first generation of aircraft for newer models with which it would eventually fight much of World War II. Fighter squadrons were receiving Bf 109s in place of obsolete biplanes, but in fall 1938 there were no more than 500 Bf 109s in front-line squadrons. Virtually all the fighter squadrons transitioning to Bf 109s ran high accident rates, as inexperienced pilots struggled to handle the aircraft's high performance and narrow undercarriage. In the bomber squadrons, neither of the models in production, the Do 17 and He 111, possessed the range or load-carrying capacity to act as "strategic" bombers. The Luftwaffe was waiting for the introduction of the so-called *Schnell* (swift) bomber, the Ju 88, which would not arrive for another year. From bases in Germany the available bombers could have only carried minimal bomb loads against targets in Britain. The *Knickebein* blind-bombing system that used radio beams to guide bombers to their target was not yet deployed. In effect the Germans could have done little against British targets in 1938 and 1939. As it was, introduction of technologically complex, high-performance aircraft occasioned serious problems in the Luftwaffe's maintenance and supply organizations. The chief of the Luftwaffe's supply branch characterized the Luftwaffe's state in the fall of 1938 in the following terms: "The consequences of these circumstances [the Czech crisis] was a) a constant and, for first-line aircraft, complete lack of reserves both as accident replacements and for mobilization; b) a weakening of the aircraft inventory in the training schools in favor of the regular units; c) lack of . . . reserve engines, supplies for the timely equipment of airfields, supply services, and depots both for peacetime needs as well as for mobilization."

Thus, there was no possibility of conducting a successful strategic bombing campaign in 1938 due to the state of the Luftwaffe's armament and support structure. Moreover, Luftwaffe planning staffs had only recently begun thinking about such a possibility. In August 1938, the Luftflotte 2. (Second Air Force), which had responsibility for operations over the North Sea and Britain, characterized its combat capabilities as no more than the capacity to launch pinprick attacks against the British Isles. The command emphasized that German ground forces would have to seize Belgium and Holland before the Luftwaffe could attack targets in Britain. General Helmuth Felmy, commander of the Luftflotte 2., warned the Luftwaffe's high command in late September 1938 that "given the means at his disposal a war of destruction against England seemed to be excluded."

The basic strategic problem for Germany was that an attack on Czechoslovakia would not have remained a limited war, and the more the war spread, the more critical Germany's strategic situation would have become.

In Eastern Europe the attitude of the Soviet Union and of Poland would have been crucial in determining the course of a Czech-German war. Yet Stalin's purge of most of his officer corps and Soviet actions in late September, which aimed at paying the Poles back for their invasion of the Ukraine in 1920, suggest the Soviet Union would have been a doubtful participant, at least in providing significant help to the Czechs. Significantly, the Soviet Union had no frontier with either Germany or Czechoslovakia, so that it is difficult to visualize exactly what help the Soviets might have provided.

The Poles would have been a more important strategic player in a 1938 war. Józef Beck, their foreign minister, believed the Czechs would not fight, the West would refuse to take a stand, and Poland must remain implacably hostile to the Soviet Union. Still, he indicated that if the British and French intervened on behalf of the Czechs, Poland would support the Czech Republic. The great question in the 1938 confrontation, however, was whether the Poles could have intervened against the Germans or whether a Soviet attack on Poland under the guise of forcing the Poles to allow the Red Army to cross Polish territory to aid the Czechs would have forced the Poles to look east.

The most important difference between 1938 and 1939 was the fact that the overall strategic situation in the Balkans and Eastern Europe was far more favorable to the West. In 1938, whatever the Red Army's military capabilities, the Soviets would not have been the willing allies of Nazi Germany. Thus, the Germans would not have received the flood of goods they received from the Soviets after the signing of the Nazi–Soviet Non-Aggression Pact the following year. Equally important, the Germans in 1938 had not yet succeeded in overawing the Eastern European nations. The Yugoslavs and the Romanians gave tacit support to the Czechs during the crisis, while the Romanians went so far as to warn the Germans in late September 1938 that they were about to cut off petroleum exports to the Reich. Such an action would have had enormous implications for the effective functioning of the German war machine, not to mention the Reich's economy.

While the Germans confronted serious difficulties in the east, things were not much better in the west. With only eight regular divisions and a number of weak Landwehr divisions in that theater, the Germans were in a weak position. Only in March 1938 had the Germans begun major work on the Westwall—a chain of fortified bunkers along the Reich's frontier with France. The Czech crisis, which began to heat up in May 1938, then led Hitler to undertake a massive program of construction. But most of this effort was eyewash, because there was not sufficient time for concrete to set, while many of the fortifications were badly sited. The Westwall's weaknesses and the few troops available led the chief of staff of the armies in the west to declare to Hitler that the French would penetrate deep into the Rhineland within three weeks of the start of hostilities. With typical aplomb, Hitler declared that the fortifications could be held not for three weeks, but for three years.

The difficulty was that the French had no intention of taking advantage of German weaknesses. As Charles de Gaulle, still a relatively junior officer, put it to Leon Blum: "It's quite simple. . . . Depending on actual circumstances, we will recall the . . . reserves. Then looking through the loopholes of our fortifications, we will passively witness the enslavement of Eastern Europe." The visit of Maurice Gamelin, the French commander in chief, to London on September 26, 1938, underlines the accuracy of de Gaulle's appraisal. Gamelin indicated to his British hosts that after mobilization, the French Army would attack. But what he meant by attack was not exactly what the Germans meant by that word. He suggested that while there were advantages to an offensive, it might be more prudent to allow the evacuation of Paris. He then wondered how soon the Germans might begin transferring troops from east to west. When the Germans began that transfer, he admitted, his plan was for the French Army to "retreat strategically in the manner of Hindenburg in 1917 to their fortifications in the Maginot Line, devastating the territory as they went." This was surely a recipe for doing nothing, which was exactly what Gamelin did in 1939 and 1940.

Serious problems for the Germans in a war in 1938 would also have risen in the Mediterranean. No one in Italy yet understood the extent of German irresponsibility. Thus, throughout September Mussolini made a number of strong speeches declaring his intention to stand by his fellow dictator. It would have been difficult for the duce to disavow such statements, had a war over Czechoslovakia broken out. An Italian declaration of war would have been a disaster for the Germans. Italy's participation in the war would have harmed the Reich in a number of important respects. It would have increased the effectiveness of the Allied blockade. The burden of supplying Italy as well as the German war economy with raw materials from the limited resources available might have strained the German economy to the breaking point. Considering British and French naval superiority in the Mediterranean, there is no doubt that Allied navies would have quickly cut supply lines to Libya and bombarded the Italian coasts. With reason, the French were optimistic about prospects both in the Alps and in Libya. As one French staff officer commented, the Allies could have scored major successes against Italy in the Mediterranean within the first two months of the opening of hostilities.

But of all the adverse factors confronting the Germans in a fall 1938 war, the most serious lay in the economic sphere. Although the *Anschluss* and the seizure of Austria's gold and foreign exchange reserves had temporarily improved Germany's economic situation, these gains had proved to be wasting assets. Over the summer of 1938 a combination of the massive rearmament program, construction on the Westwall, the initiation of a drastic program to increase production of synthetic fuels (from coal) and munitions, and the mobilization of hundreds of thousands of soldiers created a serious economic crisis. Four-year-plan experts admitted among themselves that in the last half of 1938 the German economy had faced "undreamed-of difficulties. The strongbox was empty, industrial capacity was committed for years to come." Construction on the Westwall compounded all these problems.

Signs of an economic crisis appeared throughout the fall of 1938 in the German economy. The economic strain was so bad in October 1938 that the Reich's Defense Committee reported that "in consequence of Wehrmacht demands [occupation of the Sudetenland] and unlimited construction of the Westwall, so tense a situation in the economic sector occurred . . .

that continuation of the tension past October 10 would have made an [economic] catastrophe inevitable." One month later at a sitting of the same committee, Göring admitted that the strain on the economy had reached the point where no more workers were available, factories were at full capacity, foreign exchange was completely exhausted, and Germany's economic situation was desperate.

The German economy in 1938 did not possess the strength to support a breakout from the Reich's constrained economic base, as occurred in spring 1940. Not only was the production of synthetic fuels, synthetic rubber, and munitions substantially lower than in 1939, but the Germans could expect no help from the Soviet Union and little from the Balkan states. The crucial problems in 1938 were the consistent and endemic shortages of raw materials and the lack of foreign exchange to increase imports, all of which disappeared when the Germans conquered Western Europe and opened the floodgates of Soviet support. Most probably the German economy would not have suffered a catastrophic collapse had war broken out in the fall of 1938. Instead, the situation would have resembled Germany's situation in 1917 in the midst of World War I, after which a slow, steady economic disintegration took place. In a war starting in 1938, the Germans would have had to resort to a series of expedients to meet present demands, and then only at the expense of future requirements. As production decreased and raw materials became in shorter supply, the Wehrmacht's fighting capabilities would have suffered a corresponding decline. Once this vicious cycle began, there would have been little chance that Germany could have escaped the inevitable consequences: defeat.

The German invasion of Czechoslovakia was scheduled to begin on October 1. How might it have unfolded? As was to be the case the next year against Poland and then against France and the Low Countries, the Luftwaffe would have begun operations with a massive strike at Czech air bases and transportation centers. However, the bad weather would have severely limited the impact of the first attacks, particularly on the Czech ground defenses. It is also clear that the Germans would have lost heavily in the opening attacks, as they did in France in 1940. Thereafter, the Luftwaffe would have gained a measure of air superiority, but given its inexperience at a heavy cost in terms of pilots and air crews.

The most important drive would have come from the Tenth Army. Most probably, it would have broken through the Czech defenses confronting Bavaria and onto the Bohemian plain. But it is unlikely that Reichenau's troops would have captured Prague in their first rush. The Czechs had a second line of field fortifications in front of their capital and substantial reserve forces available to support the fight to protect Prague from an attack from the west. Moreover, Reichenau possessed only one panzer division and one light division; the bulk of his motorized strength was concentrated in three motorized infantry divisions. In effect the Germans were not yet able to put a single panzer corps into the field. Thus, even if the Germans had achieved a breakthrough of the Sudeten frontier, Tenth Army did not possess the armored strength to exploit that opening.

The OKH divided the other two panzer divisions between List's Fourteenth Army and Rundstedt's Second Army. Rundstedt's forces confronted the daunting task of fighting their way through the strongest Czech fortifications. To help in the effort the Germans planned to drop what airborne forces existed behind Czech defenses at Bruntal, south of Silesia. (After the Czechs evacuated the area in early October, the Germans actually did execute the planned drop in a major exercise. The test was a shambles; transport aircraft dropped the paratroopers all over the landscape including many too close to the main fortifications; engineers failed to clear landing fields for follow-up troops; and much of the heavy equipment failed to arrive on schedule. The exercise suggested the attack would have been a catastrophe, had it taken place under combat conditions.)

Thus, Rundstedt would have received little help from the paratroopers, and Second Army would have fought its way through heavily fortified positions held by strong Czech forces. The Czechs also had powerful reserves of one mechanized division and two reserve divisions immediately behind the front line, facing Silesia. In the south, the German Fourteenth Army, advancing from Austria, would have confronted a less formidable defensive system. But again the Czechs held strong reserves near the frontier—three regular divisions, two reserve divisions, and a mechanized division. Here the Germans would have run into substantial opposition that would have significantly interfered with closure between Fourteenth and Second Armies. All this suggests that on the tactical level, the Czechs could have put up sustained resistance and inflicted severe losses on the attackers. Because of the shape of their country, the Czechs would probably not have lasted much longer than the Poles did in 1939, three weeks at the maximum. But they would have inflicted heavier losses on the Germans, who had no prospect of gaining the kind of operational freedom that proved so devastating in the 1939 campaign, because Czechoslovakia's mountainous terrain was so much more defensible than the plains of Poland.

Equally important for its long-range impact on the Wehrmacht's buildup would have been the fact that a sustained campaign would have destroyed virtually all of the Czech Army's equipment. Those arms fell into German hands in undamaged condition in March 1939 and provided the equipment for four Waffen SS and eight army divisions, and tanks for three panzer divisions. Bombing attacks and deliberate sabotage by the Czechs would also have wrecked much of Czechoslovakia's armament potential—which the Germans would take advantage of throughout World War II. The most significant strategic factor is that sustained Czech resistance would have forced the British and French to declare war. However, the French would have failed to launch any kind of a serious offensive against the weak German defenses and forces in the west, whatever was happening in the east.

A Polish entry into the conflict with a limited attack on Silesia would have placed Rundstedt's forces in a dangerous position. Limited attacks on Pomerania and East Prussia would have added to the difficulties the Germans confronted. The critical element in Poland's decision would have been how quickly the Western Powers would react to the Nazi attack on the Czech Republic—the slower the Western response, the more unwilling the Poles would have been to act. However, the Soviets might well have taken advantage of a German attack on Czechoslovakia to settle scores with the Poles. Whatever the Soviets did, however, would have achieved minimal success, given the disastrous impact of the purges on the Red Army's officer corps.

But for the Germans, the Poles would have represented only one of many strategic worries. The economic situation would have been even more desperate than it was to be in the fall of 1939. And German economic difficulties a year later almost forced Hitler to move against the almost unanimous advice of his generals. Hitler would have confronted the strategic and economic problems raised by an economy starved for raw materials and by oil stocks at minimum levels. In addition, there were no obvious sources to replace those blocked off by an Allied blockade, as there would be in 1939 and 1940, when the Soviets so enthusiastically stepped in to help the Germans.

Exacerbating German difficulties might have been a coup attempt. Two senior officers, Erwin von Witzleben and Erich Hoepner, both had committed themselves to removing Hitler should he provoke a war with Czechoslovakia. Halder was also dabbling in the plots that were constituting and then dissolving according to the political situation in September 1938. Considering the inept effort that took place in July 1944, one cannot place much confidence in these efforts by a variety of plotters. In the summer of 1938 Beck had even suggested arresting Hitler's advisers, but leaving the führer in charge!

Unfortunately, most of the junior officers and enlisted men remained solidly behind the regime. But if ever there was a time when a coup might have succeeded, it would have been in the fall of 1938, when there was enormous dissatisfaction in the German population over the prospect of another great war. Nevertheless, even had a coup failed, it would have further shaken the confidence of a population dubious about the prospect of war.

Moreover, the Nazi leadership would have had to confront the problem of what next after Czechoslovakia? A Luftwaffe that had suffered heavy losses against the Czechs would not have had sufficient strength to launch a major air campaign against France, much less Britain. Even had the Germans possessed sufficient aircraft, there were two daunting problems: insufficient fuel and the bad weather that cloaks Europe from October until May. In such conditions, there was no possibility the Luftwaffe could have hit major targets on a sustained basis. Even as late as the summer of 1939, the future field marshal Albert Kesselring admitted that his bomber crews were incapable of hitting targets accurately in such conditions.

If the Luftwaffe could not solve Germany's strategic problem, Hitler would have had to turn to the army. With Germany's economy in serious difficulties, the pressure would have been to settle matters with the French before the British arrived in strength. Over the winter of 1939–1940 the Germans delayed their attack through the intervention of fortuitous (from their point of view) bad weather; in 1938 the exigencies of the situation— i.e., their desperate economic situation—would have forced them to seek a decision in the west. Here their prospects would have been most uninviting. German mechanized forces would have consisted of three badly battered panzer divisions, three light divisions in not much better shape, and four motorized infantry divisions. The rest of the attacking force would have consisted of regular infantry divisions, most of which would also have suffered heavy losses against the Czechs. The Germans would have also disposed of the fourteen Landwehr divisions, most of which would have been moved east to occupy the conquered portions of Czechoslovakia and protect the frontier with Poland.

As in October 1939, the Germans would have confronted the problem of how to defeat the French. Since we know that the OKH had no advanced planning available for a Western campaign in October 1939, we can assume that the Germans would have had no extant plan in the fall of 1938. The planning for a war in the west that did exist consisted of efforts aimed at defending the Rhineland against a combined French/Belgian offensive. Thus, the Germans would have had to cobble together a plan for a campaign against the west, one that would have looked quite similar to what Hitler and the OKH put together in October 1939: a great offensive to take Holland, Belgium, and northern France to the Somme. But unlike the situation in 1939, there would have been greater pressures, particularly considering a desperate economic situation, to attack in the winter. Thus, there would have been no time to consider the Ardennes alternative—and even if the Germans had hit upon that possibility, they did not have the armored forces to create and then exploit a breakthrough along the Meuse.

What then would a straight-out infantry offensive against the Low

Countries and Northern France have looked like? The attacking force would have resembled those it was attacking far more than in 1940. The Germans would not have had time to absorb the lessons of even the campaign against Czechoslovakia. Their opponents would clearly have been ready for such an attack, as they were in May 1940. The Dutch would probably have been the least effective in resisting a German offensive, although it is unlikely that there were sufficient German paratroopers to achieve the stunning success of May 10, 1940, nor would the Germans have had a panzer division to drive deep into Fortress Holland. Instead, they would have had to take Holland by an infantry assault on the Dutch fortifications.

The problem would have been the same in the assault of northern France and Belgium. The Germans would have been advancing into the teeth of their opponents' defensive strength. Conceivably, the Germans might have taken the Belgian fortress of Eben Emael by a *coup de main,* but thereafter, it is difficult to see much opportunity for the Germans either to achieve a breakthrough, or had they done so, to exploit such an opportunity in the fashion they were to do in the spring of 1940. The campaign then would have turned on a World War I–style infantry battle. It would not have been a battle of trench lines, but rather a war of movement that characterized the fighting after March 1918. Here the Germans would have had some advantages. Both in terms of doctrine and training, they were far in advance of their French opponents. But unlike 1940, these advantages would not have been sufficient to achieve a decisive breakthrough. And they would have involved heavy casualties: The German attacks in the spring of 1918 that returned maneuver to the battlefield also proved very costly. The German losses for the four months from March through June 1918 were double the British losses at Passchendaele—nearly one million casualties.

At best the Germans would have gotten to the Somme, but no further. The French would also have suffered heavy casualties, but as suggested above, even in 1940 under impossible circumstances, they suffered heavy casualties in defense of their homeland. A 1918-style infantry battle in the fall of 1938 would have been precisely the one that the French high command had prepared to fight; and if the French generals did not have the skill to fight that battle in a flexible fashion, at least their men would have fought the battle tenaciously.

Reaching the Somme with a burned-out army would have solved none of the Reich's difficulties. The Germans would still have confronted their problems in the east, while they might have also faced the collapse of their ally in the Mediterranean. There, a declaration of war in support of the Germans by Mussolini would have opened a Pandora's box of troubles for the Italians. With no fleet to speak of (two of Italy's four battleships were in dockyard, undergoing refit, and none of the new battleships were yet complete), the Italians would quickly have come under assault by sea. The Royal Navy and the French Navy would have had a field day, particularly since there was so little for them to do in the Atlantic. The Regia Aeronautica (the Italian Air Force) had neither aircraft nor training to support the Italian fleet, while the army was in even worse shape than two years later. Allied successes, of greater magnitude than in fall 1940, would only have encouraged the British and French to further action. And the Germans would have been in no position to provide assistance, given their own troubles.

It is difficult to carry the scenario for the war over Czechoslovakia out much further than the above discussion. But at a minimum the strategic situation for Germany's opponents would have been far more favorable than would be the results of the first nine months of the conflict that actually occurred. And the ensuing conflict would have resulted in far less destruction and fewer deaths. It would also probably not have resulted in the Holocaust, although Europe's Jews, and German Jews in particular, might well have suffered onerous persecutions, given the racist climate of the time. There are a number of imponderables that must remain unanswered: Would Hitler and Stalin have made a deal? Would Hitler have survived? How effectively would the Poles have intervened against the Czechs and Germans? Would a Soviet-Polish War have resulted from the German attack on Czechoslovakia? How effective might the German opposition have proved, had things gone badly for the Reich in the course of the war's first months? Would the British and French governments have displayed the toughness to take advantage of German troubles?

A close analysis of the military balance in the fall of 1938 suggests that the Germans would have emerged from their attack on Czechoslovakia weakened rather than strengthened, as would be the case in 1939. In that weakened condition the Germans would have had to launch the Wehrmacht west with little prospect of gaining a decisive victory, much as had been the case in March 1918. The result would have been that there would have been no Norwegian campaign, no catastrophic defeat of France, and certainly no Battle of Britain.

What the historian can suggest from the available evidence is that the strategic situation in 1938 was far more favorable to the Allies than it would prove the following year. Tragically, in mid-September the British tried and failed to grapple with the question of whether the loss of Czechoslovakia to the Germans might fundamentally alter the European balance of power in Germany's favor were war to break out in 1939. The evidence clearly indicates that it did, and that a major factor in the catastrophic German victories of the spring of 1940 resulted from the additional year and a half the Germans had to prepare. Winston Churchill quite accurately described Munich as a "defeat without a war." The tragedy of European history was the fact that the one great risk Hitler decided at the last moment not to take was the one risk that might well have ended the terrible adventure before it had begun.

ANDREW ROBERTS

PRIME MINISTER HALIFAX

Great Britain makes peace
with Germany, 1940

Six decades after Winston S. Churchill became prime minister of Great Britain in May 1940, it is easy to forget that he was hardly a universal favorite: not quite a choice by default but almost one. Many of his fellow Conservatives distrusted him because Churchill had on occasion crossed party lines. His stability was questioned. And many too blamed the first lord of the admiralty in Neville Chamberlain's government for the looming disaster in Norway. Few probably saw that Churchill possessed (as the American novelist James Gould Cozzens once put it) "greatness's enabling provisions—the great man's inner contradictions; his mean, inspired inconsistencies; his giddy acting on hunches; and his helpless, not mere acceptance of, but passionate, necessary trust in, luck."

As it became ever more obvious that Chamberlain had lost the confidence of the nation and his party, the choice of a replacement narrowed to Churchill and the foreign secretary, that tall, slope-shouldered scarecrow in a derby hat, Lord Halifax. The former viceroy of India was widely admired but deeply associated with Chamberlain's failed appeasement policies. Think of him as a British Herbert Hoover, a man whose credentials were impeccable but who lacked the one ingredient most needed in a crisis: the ability to inspire. "A tired man," the indefatigable diarist Harold Nicholson called Halifax. But he was plainly Chamberlain's preference.

The prime minister made one final attempt to stay in power, inviting the leaders of the Labour party into his government; they declined. On the afternoon of

May 9, Chamberlain met with Churchill and Halifax. As Churchill later re- membered, he wanted to know "whom he should advise the king to send for after his own resignation had been accepted." There was a long silence. "Then at length Halifax spoke. He said he felt that his position as a Peer, out of the House of Commons, would make it very difficult for him to discharge the duties of prime minister in a war like this. . . . By the time he had finished it was clear that the duty would fall on me—had in fact fallen on me." The next day, May 10, Hitler invaded the Low Countries and the king summoned Churchill to Buckingham Palace.

That is what did happen. But Andrew Roberts, one of the foremost authorities on this period, wonders how the next months and years would have played out had Halifax not taken himself out of the running. His speculation is hardly outlandish: As late as the weekend of Dunkirk—the beginning of June—some members of Churchill's cabinet, including Halifax (who had stayed on as foreign secretary) were seriously discussing the possibility of making a deal with Hitler, going through Mussolini, who was not the tragicomic figure he would presently become. Churchill, it should be noted, stood firm in his determination to resist. But Roberts here presumes that Churchill's star was already waning and that there would be no Dunkirk, no "Finest Hour."

ANDREW ROBERTS is the author of a biography of the Earl of Halifax, The Holy Fox; Eminent Churchillians; and a biography of the Victorian prime minister the third marquess of Salisbury, Salisbury: Victorian Titan, which won the Wolfson History Prize and the James Stern Silver Pen Award for nonfiction. His latest book is Napoleon and Wellington: The Long Duel.

HITLER'S LIGHTNING ATTACK on Denmark and Norway on April 9, 1940, as successful as it was unexpected, severely unnerved the British people and political class. Only a few days earlier the British prime minister, Neville Chamberlain, had reassured the country that "Hitler has missed the bus." Yet by April 14, the Royal Navy had to be dispatched to the west coast of Norway, where an expeditionary force failed to take Trondheim due to lack of air power. Only two weeks later, on May 2, British forces had to evacuate Norway altogether, adding a military humiliation to the long list of diplomatic defeats the government had suffered at the hands of Adolf Hitler.

The whole northern flank of the Western alliance had collapsed in a matter of days, and a significant body of members of parliament in the British House of Commons were now in a mood to exact vengeance on Chamberlain, the man they blamed for displaying a lack of grip and determination in his conduct of the war.

The four men who met in the Cabinet room at Number 10, Downing Street on Thursday, May 9, 1940, were under no illusions as to the gravity of their deliberations. The previous night had seen the climactic conclusion of the adjournment debate in the House of Commons, which had turned into an issue of confidence in Neville Chamberlain's Conservative-dominated National Government. The government's majority had fallen from around 200 to only 80, the result of widespread abstentions and no fewer than 41 defections. The prime minister was under enormous pressure to resign and allow a coalition government to be formed, which would include the Opposition parties. Yet who would succeed him?

The only two serious candidates were Lord Halifax and Winston Churchill, and the decision could easily have gone either way. The following presupposes that it did not go Churchill's:

Present in the Cabinet room were Chamberlain himself, the foreign secretary Viscount Halifax, the Government chief whip David Margesson, and the sixty-five-year-old first lord of the admiralty Winston Churchill. The last had clashed violently with Labour MPs at the end of the debate, in which he had stoutly defended the government's record over the recent conduct of military operations in Norway, for which his own department had been largely responsible.

After a short discussion about the possibility of Chamberlain staying on, which was conclusively ended by Margesson stating that the Labour party leader, Clement Attlee, was known to be unwilling to enter a coalition government under the present prime minister, Chamberlain bluntly asked the two candidates whom they thought ought to take on the premiership? In his memoirs, Churchill records how "a very long pause ensued. It certainly seemed much longer than the two minutes which one observes in the commemorations of Armistice Day."

After Halifax had judged that Churchill had had enough time to make a statement of self-abnegation but had failed to do so, the foreign secretary pressed his claim, adamant that he was the best candidate. He pointed out that he was senior to Churchill, was trusted by the Lords and Commons, was the preferred choice of the king and queen, and enjoyed good relations with the Opposition. While Churchill had been antagonizing Labour during the General Strike in 1926, he pointedly remarked, he had been *hors de combat* as viceroy of India.

Halifax fully admitted that he was no military expert, but a German attack had yet to materialize on the Western Front. Churchill could anyway, as minister of defense, take over the day-to-day running of the war, albeit with a chiefs of staff committee to ensure that no "disastrous flanking operations were decided upon unilaterally," a clear reference to Churchill's role in the planning of the Gallipoli campaign a quarter century before. The primary task of a wartime premier, Halifax contended, was to keep national morale high, which required avoiding "histrionics" on the wireless and in Parliament. Churchill winced as each dig went home.

With Churchill still silent, Margesson then added that Halifax's undoubted moral stature would be invaluable in rallying the country, and that

PRIME MINISTERS IN WAITING

In a 1938 photograph, Winston Churchill (left) strolls with Lord Edward Halifax, that gaunt, dapper figure in a bowler hat, who seemed destined to become prime minister. Had this consummate politician not taken himself out of contention when Neville Chamberlain resigned on May 10, 1940, Halifax and not Winston Churchill would have led Great Britain.

(Hulton-Deutsch Collection/CORBIS)

only that very morning a letter had appeared in the *Times* written by the Labour-supporting Oxford All Souls fellow A. L. Rowse, suggesting that Churchill should be minister of defense in a Halifax Cabinet, an arrangement that the senior Labour leaders Hugh Dalton and Herbert Morrison were also known to support. Margesson added that his whips had ascertained that the vast majority of the Conservative party, which was preponderant in the Commons, wanted Halifax. Almost rubbing the matter in, Margesson added that Churchill's support was confined to a tiny minority of MPs thought to number little over thirty, a hodgepodge of politicians with no one other than Anthony Eden of any great weight. Churchill, knowing this to be true, stayed silent.

Chamberlain then spoke about the constitutional difficulty of having a peer as prime minister, debarred from sitting in the House of Commons. He revealed that the previous December he had asked the parliamentary legal adviser, Sir Granville Ram, whether "as a special ad hoc war measure" a peer could be allowed to sit—speak but not vote—in the Lower House. Ram had answered that all that was required would be a resolution in both Houses, which in emergency circumstances could be effected in an hour or two.

The prime minister then spoke of the wider implications of Halifax succeeding him. He pointed out Halifax's superior qualifications for the post, above all the trust the Conservatives placed in him and his good relations with the Opposition, who had already let it be known that they would serve under him in a coalition government. Grand strategy could be left to Churchill for the duration of the war, but as everyone who had watched his career during the Abdication Crisis, the Sidney Street Siege, the Gold Standard issue, the India Bill debates, and the General Strike attested, the cool judgment required of a prime minister was not Churchill's strong suit. Instead he was considered by many to be overly romantic, prone to bombast, and exceedingly ambitious. Yes, Chamberlain fully admitted, Churchill had been proved right about the true nature of Hitler and the inadvisability of appeasement, but now was not a time to look back to the past and, anyhow, the Munich agreement had bought the crucial year of peace with which Britain had boosted her air defenses.

"Stick to the war, Winston," seemed to be the united cry of the outgoing premier, the royal family, the majority of the Cabinet, senior Opposition figures, *The Times*, the Tories, the House of Lords, the city, and the higher reaches of society. Most importantly, though, it was emphatically Halifax's view also. Churchill knew that were he to refuse to serve in a Halifax ministry he would be accused of putting his personal ambition before his patriotic duty at a time of grave national crisis.

Churchill had been advised by Anthony Eden and the lord privy seal Sir Kingsley Wood to stay silent at the meeting and thus effectively to stage a coup, but the plan had hopelessly backfired. It was clear that the premiership was Halifax's for the taking and the best he could do was to haggle for a powerful Defense Ministry with all-pervading powers over the Admiralty, War Office, and Air Ministry. He also tried to ask for jobs for some of his supporters such as Alfred Duff Cooper, Lord Beaverbrook, and Brendan Bracken. Halifax, with a perceptible tone of relief, agreed to the Defense idea, but said he could not commit himself to finding posts for all the more outré of Churchill's friends. Churchill shrugged glumly; he had done his best.

Saturday, May 25, 1940, is undoubtedly the most controversial date in contemporary British history, being the day on which the Butler-Bastianini Pact was signed, bringing Britain's participation in the second Franco-Prussian War to an abrupt end. Depending on your viewpoint, it was the day that the Halifax government saved the British Expeditionary Force (BEF) from almost certain capture at Dunkirk and brought it safely home, or the day when a craven peace was signed that betrayed Britain's allies. Yet whichever view one takes, the facts are clear.

The story of the Wehrmacht's vast flanking attack around the Maginot Line at dawn on May 10, knocking the Allies back with its revolutionary Blitzkrieg tactics, is well-recorded. By May 24, all objective military analysis agreed on the likelihood of the BEF, then in full retreat toward the Channel ports, being doomed. It has since been suggested that Hitler was about to halt his panzers on the ridge above Dunkirk the following day, which might have allowed the BEF a temporary respite, but that was obviously not known in London at the time.

At a special Cabinet meeting at nine A.M. on Saturday May 25, the new prime minister Lord Halifax announced a surprise development. (He had been encouraged to set up a small War Cabinet but had resisted, realizing it would only have strengthened Churchill's position vis à vis his own.) Halifax, who had retained the Foreign Office portfolio for himself, handed the discussion over to his undersecretary for foreign affairs R. A. B. Butler. To general astonishment, Butler informed their colleagues that he had entered into advanced, fruitful discussions with the Italian ambassador, Giuseppe Bastianini, about an immediate armistice and that subject to Cabinet approval it would be declared effective from noon that day.

The terms negotiated by Mussolini's foreign minister and son-in-law Count Ciano in Rome, in close consultation with Ribbentrop and Hitler in Berlin, could hardly have been more favorable to Britain. In return for a complete cessation of hostilities and the signing of a ten-year nonaggression pact, Germany would allow the BEF to return to Britain unmolested, seek an armistice with France based on the occupation of Paris but not much further south, and would guarantee the British Empire against attack from any third party. In return, Britain would return those African colonies confiscated from Germany by the Versailles Treaty and would demilitarize Malta and Gibraltar.

After a brief but vitriolic exchange of views, in which the word "traitor" was leveled at the prime minister, Churchill, Eden (minister for war), Ernest Bevin (minister for Labour), A. V. Alexander (first lord of the admiralty) and Duff Cooper (minister of information) walked out of the Cabinet and wrote vituperative letters of resignation.

The Halifax Government nonetheless survived, with the Labour leader Clement Attlee and the Liberal leader Sir Archie Sinclair viewing the Pact as not particularly noble but the very best terms that could be obtained under the extraordinary circumstances. Had the BEF been captured wholesale, as seemed the most likely outcome, it was feared that any future terms from Hitler might call into question the existence of the Royal Navy or even the very independence of Britain herself.

This view was echoed by the media, especially by *The Times,* which was edited by Halifax's close friend Geoffrey Dawson and by the state-controlled

BBC, which kept anti-Pact propagandists such as the National Labour MP Harold Nicolson resolutely off the airwaves. The noisy support the Pact gained from the British Union of Fascists leader Sir Oswald Mosley was an embarrassment for Halifax, but the diaries of King George VI, Sir Alec Cadogan (permanent undersecretary at the Foreign Office), Sir Henry "Chips" Channon MP, Victor Cazalet MP, and many others testify to its grudging acceptance generally, especially once the boys in khaki began returning home safely. After a famously bitter debate in the Commons, in which Churchill made one of his best speeches claiming that "this might have been our finest hour," the Pact was approved 420 to 130.

The war over, it was incumbent on the government to hold an immediate general election, the first since 1935. Of course it turned into a virtual referendum on the Pact and was won by the National Government with a majority of 60, nothing like the landslides of 1931 and 1935 but enough for Halifax to govern comfortably.

In the wider world, the Pact had tremendous strategic implications. American support and sympathy for Britain, lukewarm in the Phoney War, had been growing in the fortnight campaign between May 10 and 24, but fell away sharply once the Pact was announced. The war in Europe over, American attention increasingly focused on the darkening situation in the Pacific.

Meanwhile Hitler was able, once Paris was occupied and the Reynaud Government signed their own peace agreement, to concentrate on the East without any fear of having to fight a war on two fronts. His new Western provinces were held with relatively few divisions, the only continental opposition to the peace being articulated by a Colonel de Gaulle, who found it impossible to raise French enthusiasm for a war of *revanche*. German factories hitherto dedicated to U-boat production were reconditioned to build the tanks and aircraft Hitler now required for a final settling of accounts with Bolshevism.

Without any British-backed provocation in Yugoslavia and Greece, Hitler felt no inclination to divert his attention toward southeast Europe before unleashing Blitzkrieg on Russia. He duly launched Operation Barbarossa on April 22, 1941, as soon as the roads across the steppes were dry and long before the Russian winter could be mobilized in Stalin's support.

The Butler-Bastianini Pact also had profound implications for the continental alliance, which Halifax had painstakingly built up during his foreign secretaryship. The French, not unnaturally, ascribed their humiliation on betrayal by "perfidious Albion." King Léopold of the Belgians even broke off diplomatic relations with Britain for their "treacherous" failure to warn him before the Pact was signed. On the other hand, most of the British Commonwealth dominions applauded the Pact, especially South Africa, which had been deeply split over the conflict, and Australia, which was looking toward her domestic defenses against an increasingly aggressive Japan.

When, in December 1941, Japan simultaneously attacked the U.S. naval base at Pearl Harbor and the British possessions in the Far East, Germany— in accordance with its undertakings to guarantee the Empire—declared war against Tokyo. This was a mere pro forma declaration but President Roosevelt nonetheless made known his appreciation of German effective neutrality in the conflict.

With no European war to mobilize American public opinion behind close Anglo-American cooperation the United States and Great Britain fought essentially separate campaigns in defense of their Indian and Pacific Ocean interests. Failing also to pool their knowledge in the field of atomic research, the war against Japan was fought out, island by island, until the final, costly victory in August 1949.

As befitted a Christian gentleman, Lord Halifax steadfastly stuck to the spirit and the letter of the Pact, whilst prudently maintaining high defense spending on all three services. The loss of the bases on Malta and Gibraltar severely stretched Britain's Mediterranean fleet, which had to use Cyprus as its main center of operations. When battle was joined between the German Fatherland and Russian Motherland, Britain and America stayed resolutely neutral, refusing to help either side even covertly in the struggle.

The result was, of course, that when the Soviet forces finally prevailed there was no Anglo-American presence in Western Europe when the triumphant Red Army marched on Berlin and beyond. Although the Wehrmacht had taken Moscow—which the Russians evacuated and burned as in 1812—and captured Stalingrad and subjected Leningrad to a grueling thousand-day siege, the final outcome was not in doubt. The combination of overlong German supply lines, appalling Russian winters, and dogged Soviet resistance, with manpower easily replaced wherever it was lost, meant that Stalin triumphed in the end, albeit at the cost of nearly 40 million Russians dead.

For all Hitler's strategic and matériel advantages in 1941–42, the sheer size of Russia and her army, and the willingness to accept any privations rather than surrender began to tell against him by 1944–45. The watershed year came in 1945, and by January 1946, the Wehrmacht was in full retreat back to Germany's borders.

Stalin felt no compunction to stop his march westward once Hitler had committed suicide in the ruins of Berlin in April 1946 and the Third Reich lay crushed beneath the Soviet heel. Indeed the lack of any help from Britain or America in his struggle, and their complete military absence from the European theater, probably goaded him on. In the spring of 1946, Stalin picked up the rest of Hitler's Western spoils. Communist-led resistance movements in Northern France, Denmark, Norway, Italy, and the Low Countries welcomed the Red Army into their countries, lynching the quislings who had administered their countries for the Nazis. Opponents of Communism, such as Colonel de Gaulle in Bordeaux, were arrested and executed; and there were several unpleasant instances of British businessmen having their heads forcibly shaved.

Stalin celebrated May Day 1946 at Versailles. Even Czar Alexander I in 1815, *Pravda* declared, had not entered Paris in such glory. Stalin was soon planning how to settle his score with General Franco on his new southern border. With 100,000 Spanish Republican refugees in southern France he could be assured of an enthusiastic campaign.

It was against this backdrop that the renegade Conservative backbencher Winston Churchill made a speech entitled "The Sinews of War" at Westminster College in the small Missouri town of Fulton. At the age of seventy-one he had been written off by most in British politics as a has-been and warmonger, but still retained an American following due to his opposition to the appeasement first of Hitler and now Stalin. In the past seventeen years since losing the chancellorship of the exchequer in 1929, Churchill had only held office for eight months between the outbreak of war in September 1939 and the coming of peace in May 1940. For a man of his undoubted talents it was a sorry record. Indeed it was considered a gracious act that Halifax had not had Churchill expelled from the Tory party despite his opposition to the central plank in the government's foreign policy.

"From Narvik in the North Sea to Toulon in the Mediterranean," thundered Churchill, "from Calais in the English Channel to the very heights of the Pyrenees an iron curtain has descended across the continent. Behind that line lie almost all the capitals of the ancient states of Europe. Warsaw, Berlin, Prague, Vienna, Helsinki, Budapest, Belgrade, Bucharest, Rome, Athens, Sofia, Paris, Brussels, Oslo, Copenhagen and The Hague, all these famous cities and the populations around them lie in what I must call the Soviet sphere."

Churchill's speech went largely unrecorded. He was known not to speak for the British government and anyhow he was only stating the obvious. Historical records show that on the day the speech was delivered, Stalin was not even informed of it. Instead that same day the Russian dictator had another, far more important file in his in-box. The debriefing of German scientists, his NKVD agents reported, had revealed that they had been working on a very interesting project to do with the military use of nuclear fission. The file was codenamed Tube Alloys and it did not take long for Stalin—by then the undisputed master of Europe with ambitions now stretching further afield—to recognize its potential significance.

JAMES BRADLEY

THE BOYS WHO SAVED AUSTRALIA, 1942

Small events can have large results

In the first months of 1942, Americans were consumed by dire "what if?" sce-narios that, for the moment, were not altogether fantastic. NOW THE U.S. MUST FIGHT FOR ITS LIFE, *read the lead headline of the March 2 issue of* Life. *Less than three months after Pearl Harbor, the world was collapsing before the twin on-slaughts of the Germans and the Japanese, and the United States seemed as vul-nerable to Axis attack as the Philippines or the Soviet Union. The invasion fears were well-founded. When the war began, there were only 100,000 troops to guard the entire Pacific coast and precious little ammunition to arm them with. Major General Joseph W. Stilwell, who in December 1941 was charged with de-fending central and southern California, noted in his diary, "If the Japs had only known, they could have landed anywhere on the coast, and after our handful of ammunition was gone, they could have shot us like pigs in a pen."*

The same March 2 issue of Life *served up a chilling menu of invasion schemes, and to make the peril more graphic, the magazine provided a series of artists' con-ceptions of how the Battle for America might unfold. Those pictures showed U.S. demolitions men blowing up the San Francisco Bay Bridge just as a Japanese troop-ship arrived; the city was burning in the background. Lines of Japanese troops plod-ded by Mount Rainier and tankmen joined in a firefight at a southern California filling station. Indeed, these scenes perfectly suited the plans Japanese strategists had for their suddenly expanding Pacific empire. Overcome by what was known in Japan as the "victory disease," they contemplated sweeping through the Indian*

Ocean to Africa, capturing Australia, New Zealand, and Hawaii, as well as invading Alaska and thrusting southward along the Pacific coast of Canada and into the U.S. Northwest. And while they were at it, they would take over all of Central America (including the Panama Canal), Colombia, Ecuador, and even extend their domain to Cuba.

If the United States was as edgy as it was unprepared, Australia faced a prospect that was even more dismal. By the end of the spring, Japanese troops had established themselves on the north coast of New Guinea, only a few hundred miles away from the island continent. Invasion seemed likely in a matter of months, and there was little that could be done to prevent it. The results of a Japanese beachhead could have drastically altered the way the Pacific war was played out. Why that invasion did not happen is one of the seldom-remembered episodes of World War II—except, of course, in Australia. The battle for the Kokoda Trail over New Guinea's Owen Stanley Range and the Japanese attempt to reach and take Port Moresby, the settlement that would be the staging base for their Australian operation, had an undeniably epic quality. Though it is generally thought that the Battle of Midway in the first days of June marked the beginning of the end for the Japanese empire, the struggle for the Kokoda Trail and the bravery of a handful of young Australians may have been equally important in the reversing of what had seemed an irreversible tide. Only a few thousand men may have been involved on both sides, but the Kokoda Trail was a perfect example of what has been called the minimal rewrite rule of counterfactual history: that small events can have great consequences.

JAMES BRADLEY, the son of one of the six flag-raisers of Iwo Jima, is the author (with Ron Powers) of the best-selling *Flags of Our Fathers*. A movie producer and motivational speaker, Bradley is currently at work on his second book, *Flyboys*, about World War II carrier pilots.

B Y THE SUMMER of 1942, Japan had conquered the largest and most populous empire in the history of modern warfare. With shocking ease, its army had overrun Hong Kong, Singapore, the Philippines, Burma, the Solomons, much of China and what is now Indochina, Malaysia, and Indonesia. Hitler's empire at its greatest extent would fit comfortably into a corner of Japan's vast new imperial map. The Chinese, Dutch, and British had been humbled. In the Philippines, the emperor's troops had handed the United States Army its most costly defeat ever. Only Australia remained to be subdued and its prospects seemed bleak.

To invade Australia, Japan needed an air base and harbor from which to launch its attack. Port Moresby on the southeast coast of New Guinea was the obvious choice. From there, it was just a short hop across the Coral Sea to the peninsula of the province of Queensland. The Japanese came close to that goal at the beginning of May 1942. They dispatched troopships with aircraft carriers to cover them: Their intention was to land at Port Moresby and capture it. But they headed into the Coral Sea, between Australia and the eastern end of New Guinea, and they ran into an American carrier force. In the Battle of the Coral Sea (May 3–8), the Japanese sunk one carrier and badly damaged another; but their own losses forced them to turn back. For the moment Port Moresby was safe.

It would be a brief respite. A little more than half a year after Pearl Harbor, elite Japanese troops landed at Gona, on the north coast of New Guinea. They prepared to trek over the Owen Stanley Range to seize Port Moresby, following a route called the Kokoda Trail. It is true that those 130 history-changing miles passed through some of the most difficult terrain any army has ever stumbled over. It is true that almost no one except the native cannibals had penetrated the darkness of this mountainous, equatorial nightmare. And it is true that the combination of heat, humidity, altitude, and tropical disease sapped a man's strength and began to eat away at his body the moment he dared to set foot on a trail that hardly qualified for the name. The Kokoda Trail is a muddy track just a few feet wide in its good spots. To traverse the Owen Stanleys involved climbing switchbacks with precipitous drops and crossing bridgeless streams.

Japanese soldiers would be swept away in those streams, which could rise nine feet in an hour. Not a few who strayed from the track were felled by blow darts of Stone Age headhunters, men who still seek human heads for trophies. Others succumbed to bizarre unnamed diseases or plummeted to their deaths because they stepped a few inches too far or slipped off the cliff-hugging trail. But what finally did them in was an unlikely force that seemed to conspire with nature—a group of young Australians, many of whom were still teenagers. On the Kokoda Trail, the Japanese Army would experience a land defeat for the first time in the Pacific War.

July 21, 1942, was a bad news day for the Bataan Bunch. That was the derisive name Australians used to refer to Douglas MacArthur and his advisers who had fled to Australia four months earlier after their defeat in the Philippines. Australia had turned over command of their paltry armed forces to MacArthur. With most of their best fighting men away in North Africa or in Japanese prison camps after the fall of Singapore, he seemed the country's last hope. Now the shocking news had reached Allied headquarters that the Japanese had landed in northern New Guinea and were on their way to invade Australia.

Australia was almost completely undefended, ripe for invasion. During the 1920s and '30s she had systematically disarmed as Great Britain, her colonial ruler, assured her that the impregnable "Rock" of Singapore and the Imperial Fleet would shield her from any attack. The fleet had lost a battleship and a battle cruiser in the opening days of the war. And thousands of British soldiers had surrendered when the Japanese surprised the Singapore defenders by not attacking from the sea as anticipated, but had come through the wide-open overland back door instead. There would be no reinforcements. The British were fighting for their own survival against Hitler.

Australia may have been a country of rugged individualists, but that was

PACIFIC THEATER, 1942

EASTERN NEW GUINEA, 1942

© 2001 Jeffrey L. Ward

little help when there were not enough rifles to arm volunteers, not enough bullets for the few available rifles, and only enough shells to keep field artillery in action for a day and a half. The Australian Cabinet hoped that MacArthur had the clout to focus America's attention on their plight. But U.S. troops and planes were mostly still far away and the Japanese were threateningly close.

The Pacific War would be largely a battle for island airfields and Port Moresby was the airfield closest to Australia, the one piece of real estate that would guarantee Japan's ability to invade. After the Japanese Navy's failure at the Battle of the Coral Sea, the Japanese Army decided to take matters into its own hands. It would land unopposed on the north shore of New Guinea and then hurry along the Kokoda Trail to seize the prize from the land side.

The Americans had been reading coded Japanese military messages all along and in May had learned of the Japanese plan. MacArthur refused to believe the scoop his intelligence people had handed him. MacArthur's chief of Intelligence wrote, "An overland advance in strength is discounted in view of the logistical difficulties, poor communications, and the difficult terrain." The Owen Stanley Range was thought to be so impassable that the Allies didn't even bother to order a reconnaissance of the Kokoda Trail.

If you were to search for the most inhospitable territory encountered in all of World War II, New Guinea would be at the top of the list. New Guinea is the world's second largest island and had been known to Western settlers for 400 years, but few explorers had penetrated its miserable mysteries and no maps existed of its interior. There were no roads and no towns. New Guinea is geologically new, with numerous volcanic peaks. A thousand-mile-long spine of mountains reaching as high as 16,000 feet creates a barrier between north and south. Rivers with their innumerable tributaries bar movement between east and west. New Guinea lies just eleven degrees below the equator, and heat combined with moisture creates a giant sauna. In the highlands, however, travelers may shiver from frost and hail or be drenched by downpours so violent that an inch of rain has been known to fall in five minutes. The climate that allows the jungle to flourish is also home to a bewildering variety of microorganisms, many of them harmful to man.

In general, gold mining will tame any country, no matter what the climate. In the 1930s gold was discovered in New Guinea, but a road just seventy miles long was deemed impossible to build and planes had to ferry supplies in and ore out.

New Guinea was the green armor that protected Australia and MacArthur assumed it would prove an effective barrier against Japanese invasion. But Hirohito's troops had other plans.

MacArthur and his staff thought in Western terms when evaluating the needs and capabilities of an enemy. They could not imagine that they were facing an army that in all ways was composed and balanced differently than any troops Westerners had ever encountered. Western armies want their troops to survive. Japanese soldiers sought glory in death. The Japanese army fought with fewer rations than their counterparts, believing that it could live off the land. Japanese soldiers required fewer clothes and demanded less in the way of shelter, transport, and creature comforts than Westerners.

In their swift victories in Malaysia, the Netherlands East Indies, and the Philippines, the Japanese had proved themselves expert jungle fighters, the best in the world. They had learned how to operate in small, self-sufficient units. They were trained to move silently through the jungle. As one observer later wrote, "They could conceal themselves like leaf insects and move with the silence of a cat."

Although Port Moresby on the south coast of New Guinea was the obvious base from which to launch an invasion of Australia, the Japanese had telegraphed their intention to take it with the attempted naval assault, and the Allied command had intercepted Japanese army messages detailing their invasion plans, MacArthur had stationed only a ragamuffin outfit to defend it.

Militia troops, akin to the U.S. National Guard, who thought their job was to defend the homefront, were sent to New Guinea. They were called up from stores, factories, and farms and received only perfunctory training. Clad in ill-fitting khaki, they were issued weapons they hardly knew how to fire. Once they arrived, these raw troops were given almost no training in jungle fighting but were employed in Port Moresby mostly to dig trenches. A visiting Australian general on an inspection tour gave them an "F" rating and proclaimed them to be "quite the worst regiment in the Australian army."

On the other hand, Japan had sent their best. For the all-important task of securing the Australian invasion base, Major General Tomitaro Horii had assembled an elite formation of shock troops designated as the South Seas Detachment. They were hardened veterans flushed with success from victories throughout Asia.

General Horii's plan depended upon two factors: time and *Yamato Damashii* (Japanese Spirit). He landed with 6,000 troops and relatively few supplies. His hope was that his lightly provisioned troops could race across the Kokoda Trail, beat back any opposition, capture provisions, and then seize Port Moresby. His soldiers would have to achieve victory with only the food and ammunition they could carry on their backs: Food supplies had been sacrificed in the interests of mobility. The trail could not accommodate vehicles or even beasts of burden. The whole plan depended upon surprise and audacity.

A full month after the invasion, Allied intelligence still refused to believe the Japanese would attempt the Kokoda Trail. The Japanese objective, they insisted, was to only build an airfield at Buna. Finally bestirring himself, MacArthur ordered members of the militia to investigate. An Australian general assured the raw troops that all they had to do was get to a "gap" in the range and hold on. One of those Australian boys, Ken Murdoch, remembers that company commanders were told that they were to "rush forward and sit on 'the Gap.' One platoon could stop an army there. The Owen Stanleys are impassable."

The boys carried no maps or surveys. They knew only that somewhere along that jungle trail they would collide with the enemy. Worse, they were being sent into a green wilderness with khaki clothing that was fine for the Australian or North African deserts, but screamed "shoot me" against the deep green of the jungle. They wore leather boots with smooth leather soles, the worst possible footgear for climbing wet, slimy trails; moreover, the leather began to rot. They were issued only World War I vintage rifles and carried no heavy mortars. By contrast, the Japanese wore jungle boots with treads that gripped the soil, green camouflage uniforms, and steel helmets garnished with camouflage leaves that blended into the surroundings. They carried abundant supplies of ammunition, a machete for clearing the jungle, and specially designed easy-to-assemble mortars.

After a short trek from Port Moresby the Australians encountered what came to be known as the "Golden Stairs," slippery steps crudely cut into the mountain. "Don't tell me about the Golden Stairs," remembered Geoffrey Lyons. "We started in the morning and I finished about nine at night on my hands and knees. But we made it."

Ralph Honner, another veteran of the Kokoda Trail, recalls: "I saw what the country could do to raw troops. A detachment came in behind us in full marching order. Most of them were big men and were fit by normal standards. They made the last few hundred feet of the climb out of the valley in five- and ten-yard bursts. Half of them dropped where they stood when they reached the plateau. Their faces were bluish with strain, their eyes staring out. They were long beyond breathlessness. The air pumped in and out of them in great, sticky sobs. And they had a hundred miles of such traveling ahead."

The Australian boys soon learned the quality of counsel they had received from their superiors back in Port Moresby. The narrow "Gap" where they were told to head off the Japanese was a valley seven miles wide.

Neither side realized that sending men up the Kokoda Trail was like sending them into another world, a different planet with different physical rules, with changes as severe as those experienced by a deep-sea diver who plunges 100 feet below the surface. One who survived the Kokoda Trail remembered how "We slogged through continual rain, which made the trail a muddy river. Our ankles were twisted by tangled roots concealed beneath the deep mud. The feeling was eerie in that dark moss forest, with the water dripping on us." During the day the humidity-amplified heat sapped their strength and at night they shivered in the cold high-altitude damp.

And as Eric Bergurud writes in *Touched with Fire*, "Mud bothers all armies, but the rain and mud here took on a different dimension. To begin with, they were always present. There was no genuinely dry terrain in the theater. Volcanic soil, so common in the South Pacific, turns to an ugly grey slush when rained upon, creating some of the most noxious mud on the planet."

Frank Taylor, a present-day guide on the Kokoda Trail, talks about the difficulties: "The physical exertion is continuous. You're never walking on a flat surface. You can only take boot-length steps going up. Going down you have to go sideways, switching from one side to the other. It's a constant physical strain, the lactic acid builds up. You are quickly so tired you make mistakes. One foot placed not perfectly and you fall. You fall at least three times a day."

"It is difficult to describe the abysmal depression that had me in its grip," wrote Oscar White. "The rain did not vary in intensity for as much as a minute—an endless, drumming, chilling deluge. It roared and rustled and sighed on the broad leaves of the jungle top. It soaked through the green pandanus thatches of shelters and spilled clammy cascades upon the bowed backs of exhausted men. It swamped cooking fires. Creeks ran in every hollow. One's very bones seemed softened by the wetness. For long stretches the trail was precipitous—no more than a muddy cleft in a clay cliff, down which one swung on lawyer vines and supple branches made ragged and greasy by thousands of pairs of clutching hands."

Japanese tactics called for a spearhead to encounter the enemy with leading scouts running forward, sacrificing their lives so that their fellow soldiers could identify and target the Australian positions. The Japanese out-ranged the Australians with mortars, heavy machine guns, infantry support guns, and mountain guns; the Australians possessed nothing larger than Bren light machine guns.

The Australian boys may have been outclassed, but they had a motivation that the Japanese lacked: They understood that they were fighting for their homeland. "I looked around at my mates," recalled Jack Manol, twenty-one years old at the time. "They all had yellow, malarial skin, eyes back in their heads, all scruffy, and I thought to myself, 'Christ, there's no one between us and Port Moresby. If the Japanese get through us, Australia's gone.'"

Men on the other side recognized that determination. As a Japanese lieutenant named Onogawa wrote in his diary: "Although the Australians are our enemies, their bravery must be admired." At one point there were only about 480 Australians holding off over 2,000 Japanese troops, yet a report to General Horii stated: ". . . We are engaged in a battle with 1,200 Australians and have suffered unexpectedly high casualties."

The boys held out for thirty days. They were making what they assumed to be their last stand against a numerically superior force when reinforcements finally arrived. Raymond Paull describes what the replacements witnessed: "The morale of officers and men was as high as their physical appearance was low. They resembled neglected scarecrows—gaunt, unkempt, and ragged. They had lived for weeks without a change of clothing, and the musty smell of the jungle clung about them. Their boots were grotesque leathery objects of gaping holes and sagging soles. The constantly damp climate had rusted their weapons. Their food was monotonous and not always plentiful. Malaria and dysentery scourged them. Although the rain poured continuously upon them, and the nights were cold, most men had no shelters, no blankets, and many had no ground sheets."

So now there were a few more Australians on the trail, including regular army troops, but still there was no place to make a stand, not even a clearing to gain a foothold. Vastly outnumbered, all the Australians could do was hit out and withdraw, then hit out and withdraw again: Unable to defeat the Japanese, they hoped only to slow their advance. The generals in Port Moresby and back at MacArthur's headquarters could not fathom the conditions on the trail and were dismayed by the battle reports they were receiving. A visitor to MacArthur's headquarters found him beside himself at the Japanese advance over the Kokoda Trail and "obsessed by a plan he can't carry out, frustrated, dramatic to the extreme and even shell-shocked."

Assuming just the opposite of reality, that the Australians had the upper hand in numbers, MacArthur repeatedly demanded aggressive action. Safe in his Brisbane headquarters, far from the misery of the Kokoda Trail,

MacArthur radioed the beleaguered troops: "Operation reports show that progress on trail is *not* repeat satisfactory. The tactical handling of our troops in my opinion is faulty. With forces superior to the enemy we are bringing to bear in actual combat only a small fraction available strength enabling the enemy at the point of actual combat to oppose us with apparently comparable forces." Unable to face reality, MacArthur sent a wire to Washington: The Australians, he said, lacked fighting spirit.

In fact, with bad advice from their superiors, inadequate armaments, and few supplies, fighting spirit was all the Australian boys had. Charles McCallum was wounded three times but still managed to cover the withdrawal of his mates. With two machine guns, he fought off scores of Japanese who fired from unseen positions in the thick foliage. At one point the enemy was so close that one of them wrenched away the utility pouches on his chest in an effort to seize him. He shot the man. It wasn't until the wounded had been carried out and his comrades called to him that they were clear that McCallum swept the area in a final defiant gesture. Witnesses claimed he killed forty Japanese in the brief action; he was later awarded the Distinguished Conduct Medal.

Keith Norrish fought on even though a pink froth covered his upper lip and chin like a moustache and beard. It was aerated blood coming up from his lungs. Keith had been shot four times in the chest and had three broken ribs. "The medic stuffed sulfaminde tablets into the holes, wrapped it and that was that," he remembered. Why didn't Norrish die? "I had no intention to. We had spirit. It never entered our heads that we would fail. Defeat was never an option."

Jim Moir was twenty-two when he got shot from behind. "I was shot in the hip. It hit the main bone and exploded out my groin. It burst out between my thigh and genitals. I was paralyzed from the waist down. I thought I was dying, such a mess in front of me. The stretcher bearers got me on the track and into the jungle. The chaps who were carrying us were getting so far behind that the CO decided that we should be left behind. I had no medication in those thirty-one days. We had to let the blowflies get to our wounds. They eat rotten flesh, which prevents gangrene. I had no pants on and half a blanket. You wanted to get away from those wriggling maggots on your body, but you had to let them eat. I spent thirty-one on the same stretcher with no medication. Just lying on that stretcher." He later completely recovered.

Charles Metson's leg was shattered by a Japanese machine gun. Offered a stretcher, he refused, explaining, "It will take eight of you chaps to carry that thing," he said. "Throw it away. I'll get along somehow." He crawled down the muddy trail, dragging his useless leg, his knees and hands wrapped in bandages to protect them from the sharp rocks that lay beneath the mud of the trail.

Chester Wilmot, an Australian journalist who later wrote a memorable history of World War II in Europe, was so appalled by the fighting on the Kokoda Trail that he wrote a secret report and presented it to the prime minister of Australia in person. For his efforts, his press credentials were withdrawn and he was prohibited from publishing his findings.

Time now became the Japanese Army's enemy. The Australian holding actions had played havoc with General Horii's plan of a rapid advance and a quick conquest. Japanese troops had indeed captured provisions abandoned by the retreating Australians, but the Australians had punctured cans and left the bags slit open to make sure they would be spoiled. Now the Japanese were dogged by hunger and dysentery. The emperor's finest made it to within thirty miles of Port Moresby; they could see the twinkling lights of their prize. But they had been fighting for too long. Three months of battling the Australian defenders had ravaged the Japanese.

And then in mid-September the order came from Tokyo. Imperial Headquarters had lost patience with General Horii's campaign in New Guinea and ordered him to retreat, using his depleted South Seas Detachment to reinforce besieged troops in Guadalcanal.

The Australian boys had worn down the best the Japanese could throw at them. Now it was the turn of the Australians and Americans to pursue and harass the Japanese as they tried to reach the safety of the northern coast. The campaign ended when the Australian 7th and American 32nd divisions overran Buna and Gona at the end of January 1943.

. . .

The Australian defense of the Kokoda Trail marked the first check on land suffered by the Japanese. Obscure events can have big consequences. A Japanese victory would have changed the entire calculus of the Pacific War. Once they had taken Port Moresby, an invasion of the almost unpopulated northeastern peninsula of Australia, just a few hundred miles away from Port Moresby, would have been impossible to stop. It would have forced the United States to divert its resources, still fairly negligible in mid-1942, to the defense of the island continent. (This was a time when more American soldiers—close to 20,000—were in Japanese POW camps than were available to fight.) Landings on islands like Guadalcanal and Bougainville would have to be postponed, as would any thought of an island-hopping strategy. Where could the Allies begin their opening thrust? Even if Japan could not conquer the entire continent, a substantial foothold would have been enough to provide a southern anchor for its empire. Imperial forces would have the Pacific battlefield bracketed by the Australian and Chinese landmass. Moreover, the securing of the Australia–New Guinea flank would have allowed the Japanese to cut off American aid to Australia and to initiate an island-hopping strategy of their own, with Hawaii as their ultimate goal.

The war may have turned on the struggle for the Kokoda Trail as much as it did on the more heralded June naval victory at Midway.

For their heroic defense the Australian boys were vilified. Australian commanders, bending to MacArthur's will, criticized them for their masterful defensive withdrawal. The officers who led the defeat of the Japanese were demoted and reassigned as punishment for not following the ruinous orders of an out-of-touch command.

But through the years the truth of Australian bravery on that wretched trail has come out. Every year Australia now celebrates Kokoda Day, August 29, as a national holiday. It's a day that recalls not generals or government ministers, but a handful of boys who fought against all odds to keep the enemy from their shores, those boys who saved Australia.

DAVID KAHN

ENIGMA UNCRACKED

The Allies fail to break the
German cipher machine

The clandestine success of the Allies in breaking Axis codes has been called the greatest secret of World War II after the atomic bomb, but it was a secret that would remain largely unrevealed until 1974. Great Britain, it turned out, had its own version of the Manhattan Project. Bletchley Park was an ugly late Victorian mansion north of London whose gardens had been replaced by rows of wooden barracks, where code breakers worked, as many as 10,000 by the end of the war. It was a veritable factory of intelligence. The object of all this effort, directed by mathematicians and cryptographers, was the German Enigma machine. The machine was about the size of a typewriter. The cipher clerk pressed the letters of the original message on the Enigma's typewriter-like keys and noted which cipher letters lit up on an illuminable board. The machine enciphered the letters by passing them through an electrical maze that consisted of three wired codewheels. They were selected from a set of five (for the army and Luftwaffe) or eight (for the Kriegsmarine). The choice of codewheels, their starting positions, and the connections of plugs to them were changed at least daily.

The Germans believed that the Enigma codes were unbreakable. But in fact the Poles had broken the code in 1930 and given their solution in 1939 to their allies, the British and the French.

With the fall of Poland and France, England became the code-breaking center of the shrinking Allied world. British cryptographers took over and improved on the high-speed calculating machine known as the Bombe that the Poles had invented, a code-breaking aid that was a forerunner of the computer. Machines were now being used to break into and neutralize other machines, a first in history. The Germans constantly improved the Enigma, "not because," as David Kahn has written, "they thought it had been compromised but because they feared that growth in communications might produce a leak." There were periods when the Allies could not read Enigma messages. But the code breakers of Bletchley Park always managed to catch up in time. Code breaking by itself did not win the war, but it gave the Allies advantages that helped them to win.

Kahn is the world's foremost authority on the history of codes and code breaking, and in the chapter that follows he speculates on what might have happened if the Allies had not broken the Enigma codes. Had the Allies not read the U-boat messages during the Battle of the Atlantic, their efforts to return to the Continent in the Normandy invasion would have been set back. Less important but immediately more dramatic was the desert war in Africa. What would have happened, Kahn asks, if intercepted Enigma messages had not led to the sinking of tankers carrying the fuel that Field Marshal Erwin Rommel's Afrika Korps so urgently needed? Could that gas have carried his panzers to Cairo and beyond? And how far?

DAVID KAHN is the author of The Codebreakers and Seizing the Enigma.

THE ALLIED DOMINATION of enemy secret communications is universally regarded as an important contribution to their victory in World War II. In the Pacific, American solution of the Japanese naval code JN-25b enabled the U.S. Navy to spring with surprise upon the Imperial Combined Fleet at Midway and all but destroy it, turning the tide of the war in the Pacific: Japan never again advanced, but only retreated. In Europe, the Allies' reading of German cryptosystems—code-named ULTRA—helped them win victory after victory. In the battle of the Atlantic, the most fundamental struggle of the war, their knowledge of the location of U-boat wolfpacks let convoys steer around them, avoiding crippling losses and helping bring men and material to Britain. Later, in the great invasion of Europe that conquered Hitler's Reich, solution of German messages helped the Allies to foresee and ward off counterattacks and drive more successfully through German weak points toward the Ruhr and Berlin. Soviet code breakers, too, exploited German communications intelligence to help win the war in the East.

But what if the Allies had not been able to crack enemy communications? The question cannot be answered with a single response. The Axis utilized many different communications systems. The Japanese, for instance, depended not only on its chief naval code, but also an administrative code, a flag officers' code, an army transport code, air codes, and many low-level military tactical codes, to mention only some. The Germans likewise used not only their famed Enigma cipher machine but also the tactical double-square cipher, whose key changed every twelve hours, two different on-line teletypewriter cipher machines, the naval dockyard cipher, a plenitude of constantly changing ground-to-air systems, and some local cryptosystems. Even the Enigma was used in a variety of ways. Each service gave each of its communications nets its own key for the Enigma. Every corps in the army, for example, had one. The Kriegsmarine in particular divided its Enigma settings keys between U-boats and surface vessels and between various coastal commands. Solution of messages in one key did not automatically give the Allies access to messages in other keys. And some Enigma messages, like those used by the Luftwaffe, were relatively easily and almost constantly solved, while others, like those used by the U-boats, sometimes were solved and sometimes were not.

As a consequence, even a question that can be put simply—What if the Allies had not cracked Axis codes?—is complex. It hides many parts. The answer depends upon the cryptosystem under consideration. The matter may be simplified somewhat by eliminating the Japanese. This is fair because Japan's codes were not modern mechanical marvels but old-fashioned book codes. Such codes and their ancestors had been solved since the Renaissance. Thus, though Japan changed its codes at intervals, the new ones were constantly being solved on the basis of widely known principles of cryptanalysis. There was little chance that the Allies would entirely lose that source of information. This situation differs from that of the Enigma. Though the Enigma was employed with different keys and in slightly different ways in the several services and their various communication nets, it remained a single machine cloaking a great many medium- and high-level operations in all theaters of war. And its solution rested in the end upon a few ingenious ideas that applied to all its uses. If Marian Rejewski in Poland in 1931 and Alan Turing and Gordon Welchman in England in 1939 had not had those ideas, the Enigma might well not have been solved. So the suggestion that the Allies may not have cracked Enigma is not a blue-yonder possibility but one that enjoys substantial probability.

Again, the question—What if the Allies had not cracked the Enigma?—hides many parts. Which Enigma is being talked about? When and where was it used? Managing the question means reducing it to a single case. And that case must be relatively simple. To ask what would have happened if the Allies had not cracked the U-boat Enigma engages so many other factors as to make it all but unanswerable. Were there so many U-boats in the North Atlantic that convoys could not divert around all of them? Conversely, was air cover so complete that even if the Allies steered right

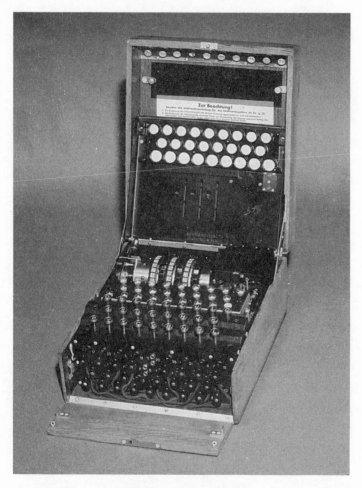

THE PERFECT MACHINE

This photograph of a German Enigma cipher machine shows the typewriter-sized device with the interchangeable rotors. The Nazis, who used it to send top-secret military orders, believed that its codes were all but unbreakable. But the British, employing thousands of code-breakers and primitive computers, managed to crack the codes.

(Hulton/Archive)

through wolf packs the U-boats would not attack? And it must not be forgotten that the enormous successes of the U-boats off the eastern coast of the United States in the first half of 1942 owed nothing to the temporary inability of the Allies then to read Enigma. Rather that so-called "killing time," just after the United States had entered the war, came before convoys had been introduced and while the seaboard cities still blazed with lights, silhouetting tankers and making them easy targets for submarines, who often sank their targets in sight of watchers on the beach.

Still, though numbers cannot easily be attached to the question of what effect the Allies' reading of the U-boat Enigma had, a vague answer can be: It helped. It reduced the number of U-boat sinkings of Allied cargo vessels and so raised the quantity of supplies that crossed the Atlantic from America to Britain. This meant that the buildup of ammunition, guns, fuel, food, and the other necessities of war proceeded more rapidly than it otherwise might have. As a consequence, the invasions of North Africa, Sicily and Italy, and Europe itself were not delayed and had a greater chance of success than if ULTRA had not worked its wonders on the Enigma messages.

One case, however, permits a relatively straightforward response. What if the Enigma messages that told the Allies where and when ships would carry fuel to Rommel's forces in Africa had not been solved? For those solutions enabled the Allies to sink many of those vessels and choke off the fuel that was critical to his motorized campaign.

Rommel's panzer army used 300 tons of gasoline on quiet days for supply deliveries and other routine activities. In battle, it needed 600. This came to him by tanker across the Mediterranean from Italy. It had fueled his race hundreds of miles across the desert by the end of October 1942, ending near a railroad stop called El Alamein. A glorious prize glittered ahead: Cairo, the Suez Canal, and the gates to the Middle East. He wanted to leap forward. But the advance had exhausted his gasoline stock. As the enemy fortified the ridge of Alam el Halfa, Rommel felt that he had enough fuel only to advance thirty miles. On October 24, he was informed that he had only enough for three days' battle. One reason was the sinking of the tanker *Panuco*, which had been carrying 1,650 tons of gasoline. One of his staff officers demanded another tanker immediately and insisted on being told when it would arrive. Headquarters in Italy enciphered a reply in Enigma and radioed it to Africa: "Tanker *Proserpina* sailing evening 21st with 2,500 tons army gasoline, arriving Tobruk early 26th. Tanker *Luisiana* ready to sail with 1,500 tons army gasoline on 25th; if tanker *Proserpina* arrives, tanker

Luisiana will sail with tanker *Portofino* from Taranto evening of 27th, put into Tobruk approximately 31st. *Portofino* has 2,200 tons army gasoline."

But the British code-breaking establishment at Bletchley Park, sixty miles northwest of London, had solved a message of Rommel's reporting that his fuel consumption had exceeded his resupply and that he had enough fuel to last only until August 26. Based on this information, the British chiefs of staff instructed the forces in the Mediterranean to do all they could to interrupt Rommel's fuel supply. And they did. Ship after ship was sunk—either by Royal Air Force bombers or by submarines based in Malta. Rommel's fuel situation grew tighter and tighter, limiting his ability to maneuver and to fight. Thus, when General Bernard Law Montgomery fell upon him at El Alamein, Rommel could do little more than put up an ineffectual defense—and retreat. It was, as Churchill said, "the end of the beginning."

But imagine that Britain cannot learn of Rommel's precarious supply situation and that Enigma solutions do not let her partially choke off his fuel supply? Of course, some of the tankers are sunk even without that information, but the panzer army is now not thirsting for gasoline. Rommel, no longer restrained by fuel problems, has the freedom to continue the advance that had taken him so many miles along the coastline of North Africa.

He is aided in this advance by a useful bit of German codebreaking. They had broken the U.S. military attaché code, named the black code for the color of its binding, and were reading the messages of the American observer in Cairo, Colonel Bonner Fellers.

Fellers was an intelligent, energetic officer. He sought to send home information that would enable his army to learn the lessons of desert warfare. And the British, who desperately wanted American help, gave him access to almost everything. Visiting the British front, he discussed the capabilities of their forces, analyzed tactics, revealed their strengths, weaknesses, and expected reinforcements, even foretold plans. He dutifully encoded his messages in the black code and sent them through the Egyptian Telegraph Company by radio to the War Department.

So rich, so full of information were these messages that the Germans assigned two radio intercept posts, one at Treuenbrietzen and one at Lauf-an-der-Pegnitz, to pick them up to make sure that they missed not a precious word. The solutions were then radioed to Rommel, encrypted in Enigma. He called them his "good source," for, coming from an observer who had unparalleled access in the enemy camp, they gave him fabulous insight into his foe's intentions. Hitler himself commented that he hoped "that the American minister [attaché] in Cairo continues to inform us so well over the English military planning through his badly enciphered cables." Rommel probably had the broadest and clearest picture of enemy forces and intentions of any Axis commander during the war.

Early in 1942, for example, he was getting information like this from the Fellers intercepts:

Jan. 23: 270 aircraft being withdrawn to reinforce Far East

Jan. 29: List of all British armor, including number in working order, number damaged, number available and their locations

Feb. 6: Iteration of British plans to dig in along the Acroma–Bir Hacheim line

This helped him rebound in the seesaw desert warfare starting January 21, 1942, with such vigor that in seventeen days he threw the British back 300 miles.

Momentum hurls him along. His new adversary, General Bernard Law Montgomery, does not have time to build up his defenses at El Alamein, much less prepare an offensive. Rommel sweeps the few score miles into Cairo. Fellers flees but his intercepts are no longer needed. The British destruction of bridges across the Nile does not slow Rommel; he throws pontoons across and sends his tanks rumbling across their shaky spans. The populace cheers its relief from the hated British colonizers, who run south, to Ethiopia, which they had liberated in 1941 from its Italian conquerers. Rommel, with greater visions in mind, ignores the remnants of Montgomery's army. Wearing his goggles atop the visor of his cap as he rides a scout car, he waves back at the Arabs. Mussolini sits atop the white charger he has had flown in for his entry into the capital of a country that was bounded south (until recently) and east by Italian territory and that, he believes, naturally belongs to the ruler of the Mediterranean. He thinks himself a successor of the emperors who 2,000 years ago rode in golden chariots through the triumphal arches of ancient Rome, captive kings and lions crouching before them.

He and Rommel then drive the eighty miles to the Suez Canal. They watch amazed as vessels, behind the levees that hold the water higher than the desert, seem to sail through the sand. No Royal Navy warships, no freighters flying the red ensign of the British merchant marine will henceforth take that shortcut from India and the dominions beyond the seas. They will have to steam around the Cape of Good Hope, adding weeks to their voyage and subtracting effective men and supplies from the Allies' armory. The Mediterranean is again for Italy, as it was in Roman times, a *mare nostrum*.

The world is as shaken by the fall of Cairo as it had been by that of Paris two years earlier, and armchair strategists and pundits foretell dire results. But they do not know of all plans. Some things happen that they never foresaw; some that they predicted do not happen at all, and some not when they said. Gabriel Heatter, a newscaster with a lugubrious voice on New York's radio station WOR, forecasts that Spain will soon join the Axis. It doesn't happen. Franco sees no loot to grab, any more than he did when France fell in 1940. He was cooperating with Hitler anyhow, and while Britain was still standing, as was the United States, he sees no reason to stop hedging that bet. Like Switzerland, Spain remains neutral.

Everyone realizes that Malta, though it had bravely withstood Luftwaffe air attacks, is now utterly isolated, with support possible only from Gibraltar through a hostile sea. Emotionally, Britain would have liked to sustain its faithful colony, and militarily it would have liked to retain its powerful naval base there. But to what end? What could its ships do from there? Harass the Italian fleet, perhaps, only to be sunk by overwhelming Axis naval and aerial forces. Could help be sent? Churchill would dispatch neither ships nor men on a suicide mission that could bring no hope of positive results. He abandons the island. Hitler, who had promised Mussolini to invade Malta and then postponed doing it, recognizes that he can redeem that promise the easy way. He will let the isolated island wither. Il Duce is happy to get a coveted new possession so easily.

Momentous as is the fall of Cairo, it cannot stop other events that have
been set in motion. The United States and Britain have been planning for
months finally to shift to the offensive. Convoys had sailed even as Rommel and Mussolini were marching through Cairo. And on the night of November 7 and 8, American and British troops come ashore at Oran and
Algiers and western Morocco. The areas are poorly or not defended at all
and the Allies are soon lodged on the continent of Africa—their first holding beyond the island of Great Britain.

It worries the Axis not at all. To them, it is a mere pinprick, and in their
rear at that. It cannot stop their march of conquest. Rommel dispatches a
corps—infantry, not panzer—to stop the silly, inexperienced Americans.
And for a few months, at Kasserine Pass in Tunisia and elsewhere, he does
so. Meanwhile, true to the German tradition of aggressive action, he fo-
cuses on his next advance. Where will it be?

The decision, of course, is not his alone. It will be made in Berlin. And
Hitler must choose between two axes of advance. One is east. It would
strike through Arabia and its oil toward Iran; it would sever the Allied supply lines across Iran to Russia and across India to China. The Germans
would shake hands with the Japanese advancing from Burma and outdo
Alexander the Great. The other axis drives north. Rommel would roll
through Palestine and Iraq to bite the underbelly of the Soviet Union and
shake neutral Turkey into the Axis camp. Oil does not figure into this scenario because Hitler is confident that Army Group B, driving southeast
through the Ukraine, though temporarily slowed at Stalingrad, will soon
capture the fields around Baku on the Caspian Sea. Moreover, the Axis
control of Egypt means that Allied bombers will no longer fly from there to
strike the oil fields of Ploiesti in Romania. In the end, Hitler decides on the
northern advance. It will speed the defeat of the Soviet Union, both
through the German invasion from the south and Turkey's attack on its old
enemy Russia. The Mideast oil is far away and not immediately available.
Moreover, with the Soviet Union gone, Iran, which cannot defend itself, even with British help via the Persian Gulf, will submit to Hitler's
demands.

With the British neutralized in the Mediterranean, Hitler can send major reinforcements to Egypt.

After a short rest and refitting, Rommel's panzers mount up, and, gas tanks full, thunder into the desert east of Cairo in December. They cross the canal and traverse the top of the Sinai Peninsula, then turn north through Palestine and northern Transjordan, across Iraq to Kirkuk, and then north again through the outliers of the Caucasus to enter the Soviet Union through Armenia. As the armored columns pass threateningly close to Turkey, that country, bordered by Axis partners or conquests, seeing no option other than cooperation, and hoping for the destruction of Russia, jumps onto the Axis bandwagon. It doesn't gain the advantages it hoped. Armenian troops, remembering the massacres of their fathers by the Turks during World War I and resisting the invasion by Turkey's new allies, fight hard for their homeland. They cannot turn back Rommel's armor and battle-hardened troops. But they delay them. And while they do so, Army Group B gets stopped at a city of rubble and doom and glory named Stalingrad. Rommel indeed reaches Baku at the end of the winter of 1943. The German troops that reached the western Caucasus the previous summer have already been forced to retire. Soviet troops keep Rommel from driving the 600 miles to link up with Army Group B. And then what? He is stuck. He can't get the oil out. Hitler's grand plan has failed. To save himself, Rommel turns tail and returns home to Africa—a wornout corps, with no mission, no heroes, and no future.

In western North Africa, meanwhile, the Americans have learned to fight better, and their greater material strength—more men, more airplanes, more tanks, more ammunition—is gradually telling. They are advancing more and more against the battle-tested but now battle-weary Germans. In the months that Rommel has been away, the Allies have pressed eastward. The British forces in Ethiopia are reinforced from India, Australia, and New Zealand and move northward to squeeze the Germans out of Africa. This takes time, of course, and Rommel and his troops escape to Greece and Italy. By 1944, the Allies hold all of North Africa. They consolidate and consider invading Italy.

The Russians slog forward in the bitter, ideological, racist war that Hitler forced upon them. They are helped by their code breakers, who frequently resolve German tactical cryptosystems. It is often noted that Russians are good in music, mathematics, and chess—three characteristics that seem to predict ability in cryptanalysis. But no more than the Western Allies can they achieve a general solution of the Enigma. At best, they occasionally capture a machine with its associated key lists and read messages during the key's validity. Throughout 1943 and 1944 and into 1945 they bleed as they advance against the Wehrmacht. And they scream for a second front.

They are not alone. The American and British publics call for the same thing. Why haven't we invaded northern Europe, they cry? That is the only way to drive a stake through Hitler's Reich. But the buildup for that operation lags, as the U-boats take their toll on the growing number of Liberty ships and sometimes troopships that lumber into packs of submarines. Direction-finding is not precise enough to locate these underwater fleets. The Allies indeed intercept the reports from the U-boats and the directions for their attacks from Germany. The code breakers count the letters in the messages, seek repetitions, analyze them, hypothesize, but hammer futilely upon the impregnable walls of the Enigma. Occasionally they read a cryptogram or two, when a code clerk errs and resends one plaintext twice, each at a different machine setting, giving them an isomorphism that they use to pry open the pair. But most messages remain unreadable. The U-boats roam at will. The Allies seem unable to get enough men and supplies to Britain to mount a successful invasion.

Then suddenly it is all over. A new weapon, in which something too small to see makes the biggest explosion men have ever seen, obliterates Berlin. That nuclear flash makes code breaking unnecessary. World War II in Europe ends.

ROBERT KATZ

PIUS XII PROTESTS THE HOLOCAUST

Could the wartime pope
have prevented the Final Solution?

The one person other than Hitler who might have had the power to stop the Holocaust was the wartime pope, Pius XII. That he chose not to use it and to remain
silent has become part of the ongoing debate both worldwide and within the
Catholic Church itself over the movement to elevate him to sainthood. There are
some who would argue that the compromising of the future pope began with the
Concordat of July 1933, which the then papal nuncio, Eugenio Pacelli, negotiated
with the just-installed Nazi government of Adolf Hitler. The Concordat guaranteed the freedom of the Catholic religion in Germany and the right of the church
"to regulate her own affairs." But there was a price: a tacit admission that the
Church would not resist the power of the Nazi state. Indeed, many historians
regard the Concordat as a major building block of the Holocaust. Once war
came, Pacelli, now Pope Pius XII, took the position that his greatest strength lay
in the neutrality of silence: How else could he maintain a role as a genuine
peacemaker? "An attitude of protest and condemnation," a later pope, Paul VI,
put it, ". . . would have been not only futile but harmful." Such is the broad outline of the case for Pius XII—though, as the scholar Susan Zuccotti has written in
Under His Very Windows, "the Church has not yet completed the process of
dealing honestly with its history during the Holocaust." Pius XII himself would
openly denounce Nazism as "the arrogant apostasy from Jesus Christ, the denial
of His doctrine and of His work of redemption, the cult of violence, the idolatry
of race and blood, the overthrow of human liberty and dignity." But these strong

317

words were uttered in 1945, after Nazism had been crushed, too late for several million souls.

In the view of Robert Katz, who has frequently written about Rome in this period, Pius XII had two golden opportunities, about a year apart, to speak out against the deportation and murder of Europe's Jews, and indeed came close to doing so. If he had, would Hitler have scaled back the Final Solution, saving countless lives in the process? What would have happened if the pope had put his own life at risk? Would his action have ended the war in the West sooner, the very thing Pius XII most devoutly hoped for?

ROBERT KATZ is the author of twelve books, including *Death in Rome*, a study of the World War II Ardeatine Caves massacre; *Black Sabbath*, the story of the roundup and deportation of the Jews of Rome; and *Days of Wrath*, a report on the terrorist kidnapping and murder of the Italian statesman Aldo Moro. Katz divides his time between New York and Tuscany.

W HAT IF, in the darkest days of World War II, the Vicar of Christ
had raised his voice against the perpetrators of the horror of horrors
of this or any other age?

The great debate that has accompanied Pope Pius XII throughout the
second half of the twentieth century—and seems destined to intensify
rather than recede as he continues to be moved by the Vatican along the
road to sainthood—concerns the position he took when faced with the unspeakable evil of Hitler's systematic extermination of Europe's Jews. There
is no dispute, however, about what choice he made. He would remain publicly silent, never once uttering the word "Jew" in his many lamentations
over the death and destruction caused by the global war. "There where the
Pope would like to cry out loud and strong," he confided to the Catholic
bishops in Germany early in 1943, "it is rather restraint and silence that are
often imposed on him."

This policy of silence had not been lightly assumed and it went beyond
the Holocaust. He was among the first to learn that reports of Nazi genocide were not Allied propaganda, as many believed. Maintaining silence,
however, was thought to be an imperative of his strategy: to be seen by both
the Western Allies and Germany as an impeccable neutral and so play a decisive role as peacemaker. Pius's view that Stalin's Russia was a greater menace than Hitler's Germany and that he sought a general rapprochement in
the West to contain if not roll back godless Communism are elements of
the controversy also not in dispute. Nor does anyone deny that the Church
worked behind the scenes to provide sanctuary to persecuted Jews in religious institutions, including the Vatican itself. The number of lives saved
remains hotly contested, ranging from a documentable few thousand to
much higher figures still lacking substantiation.

But the question to ask, and herein lies the rub, is not about the thou-

THE FATAL CHOICE

One man—Eugenio Pacelli, Pope Pius XII (shown in a 1945 photograph)—had the moral authority to check the Holocaust. Why didn't he exert it? The great debate about Pius's role in World War II, Robert Katz writes, "concerns the position he took when faced with the unspeakable evil of Hitler's extermination of the Jews."

(Hulton/Archive)

sands who to their great fortune found a rare hiding place in a Vatican enclave but about the millions who were sucked into the machinery of death
and came out corpses at the other end. What did papal silence mean for
them? One cogent answer—"the long and the short of the matter," its author called it—was provided in 1963 by Pope Paul VI at the time of his ac-
cession to the Chair of St. Peter and it set the tone for all subsequent
defenders of Pius XII. "An attitude of protest and condemnation," he said,
". . . would have been not only futile but harmful"; the wartime pope would
have been guilty of unleashing "still greater calamities involving innumerable innocent victims, let alone himself." Of equal pithiness, but never on
so high an authority, has been the irremovable reply of Pius's detractors,
who have argued that in the historical context of how the Holocaust unfolded it is all but impossible to conceive of anything worse than what actually happened.

Both of these positions had solidified by the mid-1960s. They had arisen
in a storm of polemics let loose by the 1963 appearance of a play, *The
Deputy*, a dramatization of the papal silence written by a young German
playwright named Rolf Hochhuth, whose raw outrage caught the world's
attention. Before long, however, one of the subtlest of the pope's critics, the
historian Leon Poliakov, declared that one could go on forever debating
whether Pius's policy caused more harm than good or vice versa. He noted
that the only thing certain was the silence itself "at the most tragic moment
of modern history." The pope, he suggested—later to be joined by some
Catholic writers—should have lifted his voice simply because it was
morally the right thing to do whatever the consequences; he left it to historians of the future to make better-informed judgments once the archives
of the Vatican were opened. That meant waiting out the Vatican's fifty-year
rule for unsealing its documents, but so intense was the clash of indignation
that Pope Paul announced in 1965 that *all* of the archives concerning
World War II would be made public, and a period of watchful expectation
brought a measure of calm to the fray.

Over the next twenty years thousands of wartime papers were indeed
published in a collection of eleven volumes that completed the project,
though even the Vatican admits that the work was selective, "edited," one

spokesman assured us, "according to exact scientific standards." Meanwhile, independent researchers produced a concurrent and far more voluminous outpouring of scholarly works and analyses of more or less exactitude on both sides of the issue. In any event, those future historians, now filling the empty chairs of the old debaters, came brimming with new information, but were still a long way from ready when the matter flared up again in the '90s. In a major policy departure, Pope John Paul II, in 1996, acknowledged and later apologized for a failure in which the number of Catholics who opposed the Nazis was "too few," but he went on to formulate the strongest defense of Pius XII yet by advancing the case not only for his earthly ministrations but for his canonization as well. He had in fact planned Pius's beatification—the penultimate step to sainthood—as a central event of the Holy Year 2000, but because of the new uproar concluded that it would be more prudent to postpone the event for a lower-profile moment after the Jubilee.

As for Poliakov's future historians, they were left in limbo. At this late date the issue of whether the papal silence was more harmful or less, when based on the thrust and parry of mere documents, seems thoroughly exhausted no matter how many secrets are still to be unlocked from the Vatican's archives. The reason is clear. The fine-tooth comb had already been applied for more than three decades: the strongest documents in support of Pius surely have already seen the light of day and if there had been anything irreparably damning, it would have long ago sapped the powerful forces within the Church seeking Pius's sainthood. John Paul II is nobody's fool and he has staked his legacy on his predecessor's elevation. On the other hand, today's information-loaded historians, and for that matter, playwrights and ponderers in general, are in a more advantageous position than ever to wonder in the sublime arena of "what if?"

Rather more information is extant, for example, about the two known crisis moments in which it appeared that Pius XII, taking pen in hand, would in fact speak out, only to revert to silence in the end. If ever public protest would have made a significant difference in the outcome of events, its greatest impact would have probably been felt in either of those two situations.

Testimony before the Vatican secret tribunal examining the case for Pius's sainthood provides a vivid account of the first of these two crises. It was given by Mother Pasquilina, the German nun who was Pius's longtime housekeeper and confidante both before and during his papacy.

It is the summer of 1942. There has already been a series of Nazi atrocities in Eastern Europe, the work of the Einsatzgruppen mobile killing units. Indeed, well over a million Jews are already dead, and though the events, not to speak of the figures, are imprecisely known to the outside world, the Western media have been reporting eyewitness accounts of hundreds of thousands slain (*The Boston Globe*, June 26: "Mass Murders of Jews in Poland Pass 700,000 Mark"). Nevertheless, the "Final Solution," the actual decision to exterminate all of Europe's eleven million Jews, is only months old. The vast bureaucratic matrix as well as the state-of-the art technology of cost-efficient genocide, though in prototype stages for years, has taken all this time to gear up. The newly built killing centers—the six camps designed as assembly-line, death-only facilities—have just begun to run at capacity, feeding on the July-August deportations from France and the Netherlands. An assembly-line machine has been invented and is running: You get off a train in the morning and by nighttime the ashes of your existence are dumped in a river and your clothes are packed for shipment to Germany, not to mention your hair and gold fillings. In short, the world is on the cusp of what in the coming months will become the bloodiest time in all of history. In the outside world by now, the size of the deportations can no longer be kept secret and the fate that awaits the victims is becoming less and less blurred—to all but the victims. Inside the Vatican, that fate is known.

The pope, according to Mother Pasquilina, has just received word that in response to a fiery protest by the Dutch bishops against the deportations, the Nazis have retaliated by rounding up 40,000 Catholics of Jewish origin. "The Holy Father," she stated, "came into the kitchen at lunchtime carrying two sheets of paper covered with minute handwriting. 'They contain,' he said, 'my protest [to appear] in *L'Osservatore Romano* this evening. But I now think that if the letter of the bishops has cost the lives of 40,000 persons, my own protest, that carries an even stronger tone, could cost the lives of perhaps 200,000 Jews. I cannot take such a great responsibility. It is better to remain silent before the public and to do in private all that is possible.' . . . I remember that he stayed in the kitchen until the entire document had been destroyed."

I suspect that many historians when reading this testimony, released in 1999, felt a bit of a cringe, uncomfortable with the improbable touches of domestic color and the overly formal kitchen-talk attributed to the pope. Some who looked back at the record found both figures cited wildly wrong: the 40,000 Catholic-convert deportees of Mother Pasquilina's recall, for one, were at that time actually 92 and never more than 600. Nevertheless, the incident of the bishops' protest has long been known and there is no reason to doubt Pius's most informed advocate, Peter Gumpel, the Jesuit historian constructing the case for beatification for the Vatican's Congregation of the Causes of Saints, when he tells us that the pope, on that occasion, was indeed on the verge of issuing a public protest against the persecution of Jews. At the last moment, says Gumpel, when news reached him of the Nazi response to the Dutch bishops' initiative, he concluded that public protests only aggravated the plight of the Jews and he burned the only copy of his text, four pages long, he says, not two.

Before rescuing that text from the flames of reality and sending it on to the Vatican newspaper, *L'Osservatore Romano*, for publication to see what might have happened next, let us review Pius's second chance. Now it is a year and a season later, October 1943. The overall peace-seeking strategy, including the policy of silence, has not gone well for the pope, and he has seen or heard unimpeachable reports that Jews are being put to death at the rate of 6,000 a day. The Allies, with the war turning in their favor, are all but ignoring Vatican diplomacy, toughening not softening their stance on Nazi Germany. There can be no separate peace in the West, they have repeatedly proclaimed, only unconditional surrender. Worse, in terms of the papal strategy, Mussolini has fallen, arrested by the king; the new Italian government has switched to the Allied side, and Hitler, enraged as never before, has sent twelve divisions down the peninsula, blasting his way into Rome to occupy the city. Although the Holy See has received assurances from Berlin that its extraterritoriality will be respected, the periphery of the Vatican city-state is ringed with German troops. Still worse, Rome's Jews have been targeted for deportation to Auschwitz and the pope, though not the target, knows it. The policy of silence is about to be put to its severest strain.

On October 16, Adolf Eichmann's raiders strike at dawn in the very heart of Rome. In a house-to-house sweep of the ghetto and twenty-five other Nazi-designated "action-precincts," 365 SS police, over the next several hours, seize more than a thousand Jews, many carted off in the line of sight from the pope's own windows. Never before has a Supreme Pontiff been so affronted. In an unprecedented diplomatic maneuver, hastily arranged that very morning, Pius authorizes a resident German bishop to threaten Berlin with a papal protest. A letter is drafted for transmission to the Nazi Foreign Office, in which the prelate appeals with "great urgency" for an immediate suspension of the roundup. "Otherwise," he warns, "I fear that the Pope will take a position in public as being against this action." The explicit threat, again unprecedented, is delivered that afternoon by the pope's personal liaison to the occupation High Command. Although at this hour, the raid is in fact over, a follow-up dispatch—solicited by Pius's secretary of state—is sent by the German ambassador to the Holy See. He confirms that the bishop is speaking for the Vatican and recommends soothing the papal displeasure by using the Roman Jews for labor service inside Italy. The confrontation between pope and führer has never been more sharply drawn and all that is left is the question of who will blink first.

One week later, the same German ambassador, assessing the post-roundup mood in the Vatican, reports again to the Foreign Office. "The Pope," he writes, "although under pressure from all sides, has not permitted himself to be pushed into a demonstrative censure of the deportation of the Jews of Rome." Pius, he concludes, "although he must know that such an attitude will be used against him . . . has nonetheless done everything possible even in this delicate matter in order not to strain relations with the German government and the German authorities in Rome." As for the thousand Jews snared in the net, not only have they already detrained at Auschwitz, they are, with few exceptions, already incinerated. Their fate will be shared by another thousand Roman Jews, seized catch-as-catch-can before the occupiers withdraw, but as the ambassador's second dispatch predicted, "this matter, so unpleasant as it regards German–Vatican relations, has been liquidated."

Securely buckled up in our what-if machine, we now travel back first to that awful summer of '42, touching down on the marble floor of the Vatican kitchen. It should not be too hard—knowing all that we do in our time—to respectfully persuade the Holy Father not to set his protest aflame but to let it roar. Having an "even stronger tone" than the Dutch censure, it is addressed to all of the world's Catholics (then a half billion), including of course 35 million Germans. It is a clear denunciation of the deportations and genocidal fulfillment of Hitler's pledge to annihilate the Jews of Europe. Apart from appearing in the *L' Osservatore Romano*, it is broadcast worldwide by Vatican radio and, wherever possible, read by bishops to their congregations, revealing to the world's Christians and Jews—and most importantly, Europe's Jews—that what has been cast by the executioners and their defenders as Allied propaganda is indeed true: A whole people is marked for extinction. Providing credible confirmation of the Holocaust in the making, Pius has thus done what he was being urged to do, particularly throughout 1942, on both sides of the Atlantic.

Moreover, he has transcended the skittishness of the Western powers to take concrete steps to alleviate the effects of the persecutions. With the one-way deportation railroad to the killing camps operating at its peak, movements are under way in the Allied countries to devise means of rescuing the intended victims. They are making little headway, but now that Pius has launched his protest, the escalation of public outrage is manifold, tearing down the wall of apathy. In the United States, for example, the July rally in Madison Square Garden, the December "Day of Mourning and Prayer" and the April 1943 bilateral U.S.–U.K. rescue conference in Bermuda end not in hortatory appeals or, as in the Bermuda event, utter failure, but with specific plans, ranging from relaxing immigration restrictions to bombing the railways to the death camps—and later the camps themselves.

Hitler, to be sure, is incensed. Privately he rages (as he would in fact rage a year later) that he has no qualms about breaking into the Vatican "to clear out that gang of swine." For now, however, the papal enclave, though under the protection of his fellow dictator Mussolini—who will remain in power until July 1943—is well beyond the führer's reach. Any notion of an Italian government, Fascist or not, marching on the Vatican is inconceivable. The führer cannot vent enough of his anger by killing many more Jews than his daily 6,000 (the five-fold increase in the slaughter envisaged by Mother Pasquilina's Pius in the kitchen, or anything like it, is simply organizationally impossible at this or any other stage in the war); nor does the idea of persecuting Catholics solely on the basis of their religion appear very attractive. Roman Catholics, woven in every fold of German society, comprise one-third of the Reich's population, including Hitler himself. He is therefore faced with two choices: either scaling back the Final Solution or ignoring the pope and the mounting cries for rescue. The scaling-back option is not as unlikely as it might seem. In August 1941, after resounding protests by the German clergy, Hitler halted the Nazi euthanasia program—the "mercy" killing of the incurably sick—and since then (and throughout the war), every time high Church officials strongly intervened in specific cases, he took a backward step from the carnage. These precedents, however, fall short of the magnitude of the present provocation, so we must assume that his fury is such that he chooses the second alternative and, while surely increasing his enemies list, he stonewalls.

Whatever additional censorship and psychological browbeating are undertaken by his propaganda minister, Joseph Goebbels, to deepen the benighted isolation of the German people, if possible, the tsunami unleashed by the evaporation of the credibility question cannot be stemmed. Planned Allied airdrops of millions of leaflets over Germany informing the people of the extermination of the Jews now go operational with the substitution of Pius's protest, and any lingering doubts of its authenticity in the minds of Catholics inside the Reich are stilled by the nation's priests. Internal resistance grows. The admonition printed in the paybook of every German soldier to disobey an illegal order begins to take on meaning. The highly placed and unbelievably patient circle of anti-Nazi conspirators, whose various schemes to assassinate the führer are finally being activated, broadens, and is emboldened.

But the greatest service that the pope has performed, earning him everlasting gratitude, is to have sounded the alarm to those Jews most in jeopardy, significantly altering the character of their response. Until now, wherever Jewish communities are threatened, they have almost invariably sent their leaders forward to petition the Nazi juggernaut with feckless strategies aimed at negotiating a less-than-final solution. These often ad hoc Jewish Councils, as they came to be called in many languages, would establish an abysmal record of failure and, in spite of usually irreproachable intentions, bequeath a dark side to the Holocaust, scarred with compliance, assistance, and abject collaboration. One of their most fatal miscalculations is the suppression wherever possible of Jewish armed resistance, but Pope Pius's revelation of what lies in store for all Jews, ranking or otherwise, has not only removed the very rationale of the Jewish Councils but has given life to what our hindsight has shown as the only sensible response to the implacable foe, fight-and-flight resistance.

Thus attempts to crush the 1943 Warsaw Ghetto rebellion and uprisings in the death camps (notably Treblinka, Sobibor, and Auschwitz) are carried out against greater odds and with less resolve, some of the uprisings succeed. Contemporaneously, the Allies, yielding to public opinion, bomb Hitler's death-camp railways and finally the gas chambers themselves. Eichmann's deportation organization bogs down. Warned, Jews wherever possible scatter, taken in by the Allies and neutrals, like Switzerland—all of whom have eased their immigration policies, again, under the pressure of the moral chain reaction begun in Vatican City. Future projects such as the roundup of the Jews of Rome in the presence of this protesting pope are as unthinkable as is the late-in-the-war deportation of 430,000 Hungarian Jews.

In the end, one must speak of *a* holocaust, but the Final Solution has failed. We will not be too far from truth if we adopt an estimate that of the six million Jews it would have claimed and the five million non-Jews—

Gypsies, Jehovah's Witnesses, Russian prisoners of war, and political, homo-sexual, and other declared pariahs—who would die with them, as many as 90 percent have survived.

Say, however, that before setting out for the Vatican kitchen, much to our dismay we discover a glitch in our time-traveling device and we can only go as far back as the scene of our second destination, Rome, October 16, 1943. We are, as already glimpsed, in a very different set of circumstances now. In the first place, this being more than a year later, the number of Holocaust victims is dreadfully higher, perhaps more than three million, and the Eternal City, feeling a lot less so, is securely in the hands of the German occu-pation forces. The Hitler who railed about the Vatican "gang of swine" in July believed that the Church stood behind the king's men who arrested Mussolini and he quickly hatched a scheme to drop a parachute division on the capital, arrest the king and his new government, and, to use Goebbels's phrase, "seize the Vatican." Goebbels recorded that he and others emphat-ically opposed breaking into the Vatican because of its effect "on the whole of world opinion," and later that very day the führer agreed. The coup proved to be logistically unfeasible (though he did manage a daredevil res-cue of Mussolini from captivity). But now, three months later, Hitler is in an unopposable military position to act against the Vatican at will and he is exceedingly more infuriated than he was in July—"betrayed" not only by Italy's September unconditional surrender to the Allies but also by its Oc-tober 13 declaration of war against the Reich.

If we hone in precisely on that standoff moment when Berlin has been threatened with a papal protest over the roundup of the Roman Jews, inside the Vatican—where the pope, again persuaded by what is known in our day, is already drafting his condemnation—the situation is as follows. At least 1,060 of those captured in the morning's raid—one-third of whom are men and two-thirds women and children—are being held less than a kilo-meter from the pope's study, awaiting the train of boxcars that will trans-port them to Auschwitz. For some days now, because of a blunder on the part of a high Nazi diplomat in Rome, the pope has known the exact lan-guage of what lies in store on disembarking. On October 6, the acting head of the German embassy, young Consul Eitel Moellhausen, in a noteworthy attempt to forestall the coming roundup, sent a message to the foreign minister and used the term "liquidate" when speaking of the Jews in question. This was the first time someone in the Foreign Office had used so naked a word in an official document, and news of the consul's misstep has been leaked to the Vatican. The pope is also aware that the train that will carry off the Roman Jews is already in the nearby Tiburtina rail yards being assembled for imminent departure. Seeking maximum effect, he therefore issues his protest now, publishing it in the *L'Osservatore Romano* and all other media at his command.

The impact of a papal protest in the fall of 1943, though obviously not as lifesaving as in mid-1942, has many of the same general features already depicted, thus giving Jews wherever they may be in the remaining danger zones, particularly Hungary, greater chances for survival. Even if it is too late to prevent the departure of those Roman Jews, every one of whom believing that he or she is headed for a labor camp, with the truth out, the several opportunities for escape that arose during their historical five-day journey to Auschwitz are not now completely ignored. The essential difference between the 1942 and 1943 predicaments is the führer's dilemma, the outcome of which will determine the fate of the hero-pope himself.

When Pius's defender, Pope Paul VI, as quoted above, spoke of a papal protest victimizing additional innocents, he included Pius as well ("let alone himself"). He was undoubtedly referring to Hitler's long-known, though weakly documented plan to arrest the pope, some versions of which add a provision for his being "shot while trying to escape." The most recent rendering to come to light lies among the sainthood documents, in an affidavit taken from the former head of the SS in Italy, General Karl Wolff. During the occupation of Rome, he says, he was asked by Hitler to draw up a detailed operation for the pope's arrest and transfer to the Reich, a captivity for which there are in fact two historical precedents (in the fourteenth and eighteenth centuries). Wolff, like Goebbels in July 1943, takes the lion's share of credit for dissuading his führer from implementing such a plan, but neither effort required extensive argument beyond pointing to the inevitable backlash. The present public-protest situation, with the stakes immeasurably higher, is barely comparable to the real event but manifests much greater difficulties in imagining *any* benefit Hitler might derive: only a silent pope can be blackmailed into continued silence. If Hitler manages to douse his fury, he is left in the same position as he was in the 1942 scenario (scale back or ignore), facing more or less the same consequences. If, however, he loses it, so to speak, and kidnaps (not to speak of martyring) this Vicar of Christ, who has lifted his voice and shaken the skies, well, we can feel safe in concluding that the ensuing backlash will make the Ten Plagues that rained down on the pharaoh of Jewish slavery in Egypt look like confetti.

The further out one moves from the single event, historian Stephen Ambrose wrote in his essay in the first volume of the *What If* series, "things get extremely murky, as they always do in what-if history." But that shouldn't keep us, as it did not keep Professor Ambrose, from taking one last look in our clouding crystal ball.

In many ways, anti-Semitism was the glue that held Nazism together. It delivered up the external enemy, "international-finance Jewry," by which the führer succeeded in galvanizing and mesmerizing a Germany feeling itself victimized by otherwise less-definable outside forces. In 1939, Hitler prophesied in the Reichstag that in spite of the "hyenous laughter" of the Jews at his earlier prophecies, now fulfilled, if they were to cause another world war, it would bring on their annihilation as a people. Nobody was laughing at Hitler then or at any time afterward but he was still hearing it in the background of his mind when he repeated the same prophecy during the war. But with the Final Solution laid bare and shattered by a papal protest as early as 1942, or even in 1943, what effect would that have had on the prosecution of the military side of that war? Certainly the internal anti-Nazi resistance, which compromised most of its moral advantage and the cover of secrecy in trying endlessly to negotiate a privileged settlement with the West, would have taken a more aggressive turn, extending its reach through the hierarchy. Could the General Staff have been far behind?

History records that the extermination of the Jews was stopped six months before the war was over, when Reichsführer Himmler, realizing all was lost and contemplating his own survival, ordered the killing machines dismantled. In our conceit of what might have been, not only the Holocaust but perhaps the war itself would have ended sooner. Such an outcome would undoubtedly have rippled through the rest of history, changing it day by day, we dare not ask to what—the murkiness of history's outer space being the price of admission to our game.

CALEB CARR

VE DAY–NOVEMBER 11, 1944

The unleashing of Patton
and Montgomery

The summer of 1944 was the most violent season in human history. In Europe alone, anywhere from a million to one and a half million German troops were killed, wounded, or captured between June and the middle of September. Russian losses in the same period ran into the hundreds of thousands. The combined losses of the Western Allies in all the European theaters was well over 200,000. And we should not forget those who perished in the Nazi death camps, which were working overtime. Germany, which could least afford such losses, had suffered the most. Its cities lay in ruins, its once vaunted air force had practically ceased to exist—and to this was added the turmoil that followed the July 20 attempt on Hitler's life. As Allied armies surged across France and into Belgium that August and German resistance disintegrated, there seemed a very real possibility that the war in Europe would end that autumn.

It didn't, as we know. The Germans would turn and fight west of the Rhine, and there would be savage battles at Arnhem, the Bulge, and the Hurtgen Forest; the war in Europe would go on for another half a year, and the death toll would mount by the hundreds of thousands. Had the prospect of an autumn ending, instead of the May 7, 1945, surrender in a French technical school in Rheims, been a cruel mirage? Of all the questions surrounding the final year of war in Europe, none is greater or more surrounded by controversy.

In the essay that follows, Caleb Carr argues that the failure to destroy Germany that fall was not just a great military blunder but "one of the most serious

333

moral lapses in Western history." The Allies, he believes, unwittingly contributed to the German military renaissance with the "broad front" strategy that took shape in the Supreme Headquarters that August, even as George S. Patton Jr.'s Third Army was racing for the German frontier. What if Patton's gas had not been "turned off" (as the British military historian B. H. Liddell Hart put it)? What if Patton and the British commander, Bernard Law Montgomery, had been allowed to plunge deep into Germany, as they pleaded to do? As Carr writes, "The chance to sow strategic confusion, panic, and despair behind enemy lines— the very essence of blitzkrieg—was present in September 1944, as at no other time during the entire European campaign, and had it been seized, a decisive victory could well have resulted." If the Western Allies had reached Berlin first, Carr asks, how different would the Cold War have been? Would there even have been a Cold War?

CALEB CARR is the author of three bestselling novels, *The Alienist*, *The Angel of Darkness*, and *Killing Time*. He has also earned a considerable reputation as a military historian, notably through his books *The Devil Soldier* and *America Invulnerable* (with James Chace).

CERTAIN SPECULATIVE HISTORICAL questions defy academic detachment. In the case of the whether or not the Western Allies could
have defeated Nazi Germany in the fall of 1944 rather than some eight and
a half months later, the specter of what took place during that additional
time period—the Allied firebombing of German civilians, the vicious combat of the Bulge and Ruhr campaigns, the various and infamous German
executions of Allied prisoners of war and, above all, the drastically increased rate of genocide in the Nazi death camps—adds a terrible human
dimension to the debate, making dispassionate discussion seem merely cal-
lous. If any chance to avoid the ensuing nightmare in fact existed during
that autumn, then failure to seize it represents not only one of the great
military blunders of all time, but one of the most serious moral lapses in
Western history.

Was it possible? Could the Allies have chosen a different strategic course
and brought the conflict to a much earlier end, thereby making at least
some of the horrors of the late winter of 1944 and early 1945 either unnecessary (on the Allied side) or (on the German side) impossible?

In August 1944, the military forces of the Third Reich on Europe's
Western front were in a state of nearly complete disarray and collapse. Having first failed to throw the invading forces of the Allied powers off the
beaches of Normandy and back into the sea on June 6 (as Field Marshal Erwin Rommel had repeatedly declared that they must do), and then proved
unable to stop those same forces from breaking out of their beachheads on
July 25, the German army had stood by almost helplessly as the Allies, particularly the Americans on their left flank, had raced across France toward
the German border with breathtaking speed. Outmaneuvering and encir-
cling huge numbers of enemy troops, the Allies gained ground with a speed
unseen since German armor, moving in the opposite direction, had origi-

335

nally conquered France in 1940. On August 25, Paris was liberated; yet American tanks were already in action far to the east of that city, and by the close of the month they had reached and crossed the River Meuse. Try as they might, the overwhelmed Germans could not cobble together an effective defense: the situation was so bad that it had already caused Germany's highly respected Field Marshal Gerd von Rundstedt, German commander in the west, to answer a desperate query from Hitler's headquarters as to what course to take with the famous remark: "Make peace, you fools! What else can you do?"

Yet mere days after reaching the Meuse, the Allied advance slowed and then came to a virtual halt. The high command had voluntarily applied the brakes to its own troops' progress, giving the Germans a desperately needed respite and ensuring that the European campaign would become a protracted affair. The decision was controversial at the time and has been closely and repeatedly examined ever since; indeed, because of the despicable carnage that followed, as mentioned above, the slowdown of the Allied advance at the German frontier has remained one of the most loaded and passionately argued moves of the entire war. And out of the heat of those passions a set of assumptions have emerged to become something very close to conventional wisdom. They run to this effect:

The very success of the Allied spearheads during August caused their supply lines to become so long that their rapid pace could no longer be supported. And even if it could have been, the political necessity of assuaging both American and British egos by not letting either Field Marshal Bernard Montgomery's British and Canadian 21st Army Group in the north or American General Omar Bradley's 12th Army Group in the south gain a disproportionate amount of ground and glory made it imperative that no individual, decisive stroke into the German heartland be made. Taking these logistical and diplomatic considerations into account, the supreme commander in Europe, General Dwight Eisenhower, formulated the "broad front" strategy, according to which all armies would advance along a linear front and at a roughly equal pace toward Berlin.

This interpretation of events has been supported most vigorously (as might be expected) by the popular and scholarly cult of personality that

VE Day—November 11, 1944

337

formed around Eisenhower following the Allied victory; and Eisenhower's subsequent election to two terms as American president made it almost certain that criticisms of the broad front strategy would never be given widespread credence. Finally, of course, there is the fact that the strategy did deliver eventual victory. Because of all this, over time Eisenhower's (and it was above all Eisenhower's) broad front approach became generally viewed as not only the best solution to the problems facing the Allies in the late summer of 1944, but indeed the only realistic one.

But was it? Was there really no other workable option available to Eisenhower, one that might have allowed the Allies to operate in Germany with the same speed and decisiveness that they had displayed in France? Was the adoption of the broad front strategy really an example of military pragmatism? Or did it in fact represent the reassertion of traditional thinking over a campaign that had, for a few brief, remarkable weeks, defied nearly all of American and British military tradition?

Long before July's Operation Cobra (the plan that called for Montgomery's forces to draw German fire on the Allied left flank in Normandy while the Americans broke through on the right to disrupt the German rear), before even the June 6 Overlord undertaking, Eisenhower and his senior subordinates had expressed severe gloom about the prospects for a rapid and dramatic prosecution of the liberation of Europe. Even should the Normandy invasion prove successful, nearly all senior commanders believed that a return to First World War conditions (in other words, a static battle of attrition fought along a linear front) was inevitable. And although they did not relish the prospect, such was the sort of situation for which those same American and British officers were by training and experience most prepared. The high command did not anticipate approaching the German frontier for roughly a year following the Normandy landings: Their operational and supply schedules were all geared to this estimate, and when their men proved able to cover the distance in a small fraction of that time, none of them was fully prepared—or able to comprehend the opportunity.

The fantastic possibilities inherent in the European situation that summer could only be appreciated by soldiers instinctively appreciative of what the Germans had long ago dubbed *Blitzkrieg*, or lightning war. Operations and lines were utterly fluid; and armored commanders as daring as their German counterparts had long since proved that the opportunities were almost unlimited, as the dash across France made plain. Indeed, some have argued that Eisenhower's orders following the July 25 breakout show that in fact he was, at crucial moments, capable of being immensely progressive, and of giving mobile armored columns their head without worrying excessively about either flank protection or supply (two anxieties that, when excessive, were anathema to the concept of blitzkrieg). But in fact the days immediately following the Cobra breakout only further demonstrated Eisenhower's limited understanding of what was happening. For instead of applying blitzkrieg's most basic rule—that armor should move in force toward one key strategic objective—Eisenhower and his lieutenants (even George Patton, the supposed Allied master of mobile operations) allowed their armored units to attack simultaneously in all directions, including, most egregiously, west toward the ports of Brittany.

Those ports had been labeled indispensable for purposes of supply in the Overlord plan; yet by the time they fell to the Allies the armored spearheads were so far east, and other, more ad hoc methods of keeping the tanks moving had been so effectively deployed, that they were irrelevant. What the Brittany move actually revealed was that Eisenhower was deeply uncomfortable with blitzkrieg as a strategic, rather than merely a tactical, notion. Striking deep into the enemy heartland without having completely secured all flanking territory was truly unbearable to him, and though he tried to give a brave show by letting U.S. armor race forward for as long as he did, he did not devote enough strength to the eastward thrust to make it truly decisive. As even Stephen Ambrose, no Eisenhower detractor, has written of Eisenhower's failure to either secure the Brittany ports right away or support a strategically crushing blow toward Germany, "In effect, he failed everywhere."

Yet he still had an opportunity to redeem that failure in September. In fact, he had two, one offered by Montgomery's 21st Army Group, which might have stormed into the weakly defended and industrially vital Ruhr district, and one by Bradley's 12th Army Group, which could have taken the "indirect approach" into Germany, through the virtually abandoned Saar district and then turning northeast. Both commanders were anxious to make the attempt, especially Montgomery—but what would either of these bold moves have had as its objective? Annihilation of the entire German army in the West was certainly, in September 1944, out of the question; but it was also unnecessary. One goal was paramount, and it was a goal for which the strategy of blitzkrieg was uniquely suited: the severing of all road, rail, air, and radio links between Hitler's headquarters and the German armies in the field.

There was and remains every reason to believe that, whether a deep Allied strike was made along the northern or southern route, Germany's senior commanders would have ordered their men to surrender once they were safely cut off from Hitler's suicidal orders to stand and fight, as well as from the possibility of retributions ordered by the Nazi high command. Isolate Hitler in Berlin, in other words (taking the city would likely not even have been necessary), and German commanders could have been induced to do what Grand Admiral Karl Dönitz in fact did once the führer was safely dead: surrender and spare the German people and fighting forces further suffering. The added incentive of avoiding occupation by the vengeful Soviets, a nightmare to German soldiers high and low, could only have been more pointed in the late summer or fall of 1944, when Russian troops had still not made the dramatic advances that the following winter and spring would see, and more of the Fatherland was available for the saving. But all such scenarios depended first and foremost on Hitler and his high command being cut off from their troops—and only a bold strike into the heart of Germany could have brought this about. In short, the chance to sow strategic confusion, panic, and despair behind enemy lines—the very essence of blitzkrieg—was present in September 1944, as at no time during the entire European campaign, and had it been seized a decisive victory could well have resulted.

Thus the question of whether the strike should have been made from the north or from the south, also much discussed over the years, is almost a secondary point. It is probably true that Field Marshal Montgomery did not possess the daring or the offensive acumen for such an operation; whereas

Bradley's divisional commanders were all quickly learning how to conduct just such a campaign from their colleague, Fourth Armored Division's Major General John S. Wood, the man who had led the way across France and been labeled "the Rommel of the American forces" by Basil Liddell Hart, one of the theoretical godfathers of blitzkrieg during the interwar years. Liddell Hart himself believed that Bradley's army group should have been given the nod in September, and that the war could have ended in a matter of months if it had; and taking into account the statements of German generals on the "other side of the hill"—all of whom confirmed, after the war, the mortal weakness of Germany's defensive forces during late August and early September, and few of whom could believe that the Allies paused at their frontier before even attempting a coup de grâce—this assessment is to difficult to argue.

Except if one fails, as Eisenhower and his staff so thoroughly failed, to understand the principles of, and opportunities offered by, modern, mobile, mechanized warfare. Such critics have continued to argue that the supplies for a deep strike were simply not available, failing to appreciate that Eisenhower's worries over supply had proved destructively excessive throughout the French campaign, during which units such as the Fourth Armored Division had stripped down, improvised, and scrounged to such an extent that they were able to move quickly without either major ports behind them or the rather luxurious amounts of supplies that the supreme commander's staff said an American armored division required. The Eisenhower camp has gone on to complain that even if supplies could have been delivered and a Berlin strike effected, much of the German army would have been left undestroyed; and it is here that they betray their most fundamental misunderstanding of blitzkrieg, and unintentionally highlight Eisenhower's own.

The supreme commander often stated his belief that "freedom of action" could only be gained "through destruction of a considerable portion of the enemy forces facing us"; it was this that led him to focus Allied attention, in July and early August, on slaughtering German troops in the area around Falaise—what became known as the "Falaise pocket"—rather than much more vigorously pressing the eastward advance. But the principal tenet of blitzkrieg was that freedom of action, by creating confusion and panic, would in itself bring about the defeat of enemy forces, and this defeat did not necessarily imply their destruction: surrender was quite sufficient. Certainly this result was available to the Allies in September 1944, and on an enormous, indeed a vital, scale. But the high command lacked the ability to understand either the method or the moment. Like his countryman, Ulysses S. Grant, Eisenhower identified annihilation with victory; the fact that an enemy could be defeated in the field and still left alive was lost on him. And so he collected his forces for the final push along a linear front, giving the incredulous but grateful Germans enough time to recover and mount a coherent defense. Certainly, victory over the Nazi Reich was eventually attained—but at an additional cost that must finally be deemed unforgivable.

As to the political rationalization of the broad front strategy, it can be more easily dispensed with. Certainly, if Eisenhower had elected to let Bradley's 12th Army Group strike toward Berlin while the Canadians and British were again assigned the task of pinning the Germans down along the pivot point of the American swing, both Prime Minister Winston Churchill and Field Marshal Montgomery would have been outraged. But Eisenhower's supporters rarely go on to ask: So what? Exactly what would Churchill and Montgomery have done when they were finished bellowing? Ordered their men to lay down their arms? Withdrawn from the Allied cause? That Eisenhower was keenly sensitive to keeping his allies contented in order to prevent their straying into the Soviet orbit after the war had already been demonstrated by his extreme attempts to placate Charles de Gaulle during the liberation of Paris—but does anyone really think that Winston Churchill was prepared to become a postwar Soviet stooge simply because the Americans were given the more glamorous role in ending the war early? Such questions seem too ludicrous to warrant asking; yet they are no more than the logical extensions of the arguments made by those who support the broad-front strategy.

In short, neither military nor political necessity was behind the Allies' decision to slow and then halt their forces at the end of August: it was sheer timidity and ineptitude. As for what would have happened if the war had ended eight and a half months before it did, the list is almost endless. Certainly, the Allied air forces would not have had to commit mass murder, and the German SS would have seen their own efforts to do so severely curtailed—to say nothing of the soldiers whose lives would have been spared. Politically, many of the European countries that ended up under Soviet domination might not have suffered that unfortunate fate; indeed, the Cold War itself might arguably have been averted, or at least mitigated. As in the case of the Persian Gulf War half a century later, the Allied, and especially American, failure to understand how and why one must strike at the head of a snake rather than along its body if one hopes for swift and complete success ensured that suffering and conflict went on far longer than was necessary. The tools and techniques to avert such a result were readily available, just as they would be in Iraq; the supreme commanders simply lacked the will or the perception to properly use them.

ROGER SPILLER

THE FÜHRER IN THE DOCK

A speculation on the banality of evil

The "what ifs?" of the Second World War in Europe go beyond the possibility, less dim than most would imagine, that Hitler might have won. The Western war was, in fact, very much in the balance until the autumn of 1942, when the British broke through at El Alamein and Hitler squandered his legions at Stalingrad. After that only an Allied miscalculation of Stalingrad-like proportions could have tipped the war in his favor. If the Allies had attempted to invade the Continent in 1943, which the Americans originally pressed for, the result might have been a disaster that saved Hitler and his brief empire. Thereafter the question becomes: What, for the Allies, was the most expeditious way to win the war? As Caleb Carr has argued, the war could have come to an end in the autumn of 1944, with the saving of hundreds of thousand of lives and the prevention of the Cold War. It didn't, and by the dreary winter of 1945, after Arnhem, the Battle of the Bulge, and Hurtgen Forest, setbacks that should never have happened, the question turned to what should be done with Germany and its Nazi leadership in the thirteenth and final year of the Thousand-Year Reich?

Roger Spiller reminds us here that powerful Allied voices spoke in favor of a Carthaginian solution: the complete dismemberment of German industry and the reduction of the country to a permanently impoverished agricultural republic. There would be summary field executions of the Nazi leaders, military and civil. Hitler, the man who had started and led the National Socialist revolution, would be at the top of the list. The assumption was that he would be taken alive (though

344

Hitler had already announced to his intimates in the Berlin bunker that he was prepared to commit suicide if worst came: unlike Lenin, he was not a physical coward). Curiously, it was Stalin, the greatest killer of the twentieth century, who took the most legalistic line: No executions without public trials first. And unlike the Moscow purge trials of 1937, they should not be rigged. That brings us to the most intriguing question of all: What if Hitler had lived? "Hitler," Spiller writes, "could have just as easily decided not to kill himself after all. Change nothing else but this and one changes everything."

ROGER SPILLER is the George C. Marshall Professor of Military History at the U.S. Army Command and General Staff College, Fort Leavenworth, Kansas. He has written and lectured widely on contemporary military affairs and military history in governmental, academic, and public venues. Spiller was the editor of the three-volume *Dictionary of American Military Biography* and *Combined Arms in Action Since 1939*. His most recent published work is *Sharp Corners: Urban Operations at Century's End*.

APRIL 20, 1945: Fifty feet under the ruined city of Berlin, Adolf Hitler marks his birthday, his fifty-sixth. It will be his last.

Allied air raids have hit Berlin more than eighty times in the last three months. Miraculously, some Berliners still live in the wreckage. Hitler's glittering chancellery, the Reichskanzlerei, has been pounded into a smoldering hulk. No birthday parties there. So a small affair has been arranged below ground, in the claustrophobic warren of bombproof rooms and hallways that serves as the Führerbunker.

Naturally, many well-wishers who would have been happily present for such an important occasion now find it difficult to attend. Most of Hitler's intimates are still within reach, however. Reichsmarschall Hermann Göring can be coaxed from his country estate this one last time. Foreign Minister Joachim von Ribbentropp and Propaganda Minister Joseph Goebbels are only a bunker away. The minister for armament and war production, Albert Speer, has a dangerous commute, but he will go to some trouble to attend this meeting. He feels he must tell his führer personally that he will disobey his orders: the so-called Nero Directives—to deny the enemy any fruits of victory by laying the entire Reich to waste. Reichsführer Heinrich Himmler is plotting a separate peace with the Western Allies at the moment, but he will come into the city too. A few more, some of the lesser lights of the fading Reich, contribute their presence to the grimy air below: Martin Bormann, who in the ever-more confined atmosphere of the bunker, is fast becoming Hitler's indispensable man; Artur Axmann, the head of the Hitler Youth, who sees in the coming battle for Berlin a great opportunity for his armed children. Admiral Karl Dönitz and Generals Wilhelm Keitel and Alfred Jodl are in attendance, along with several Berlin area commanders thrown in for good measure. A few days earlier, Eva Braun, Hitler's mistress, arrived without notice to take up residence in the bunker. She seemed an omen. But of what?

As the air raids continued, as the Allied armies fought their way toward the heart of the Reich from virtually every direction, those who remained with Hitler anxiously wondered when he would finally see that it was time to quit the city. He had been heard to say that he would leave Berlin on his birthday, transfer his headquarters to his Alpine redoubt at Obersalzberg, and carry on the war from its mountain fastness. Eva Braun's dramatic arrival cast a new and dreadful light on everyone's speculations. Could it be that Hitler meant to stay to the bitter end? And what would happen then?

Perhaps Hitler knows by now. He is sliding in and out of reality. On occasion he is brutally realistic. The war is lost, so everything is lost. His poisonous worldview tolerates no half measures: success or oblivion, total victory or utter destruction of his nation, its cultural and material wealth, its people, of himself. Then he imagines that the war itself has defeated him, or that the German people have failed him. He wonders whether the German people are worthy of his great ideals. Perhaps he has not been sufficiently demanding. "Afterward," he muses, "you rue the fact that you've been so kind." Then he decides, no. All will go down in ruin, and deservedly so. Even abandoned cities are to be burned.

But in these final days Hitler lives in several worlds. He was a man of whom Lord Tedder would write later that "by ordinary standards would be judged insane." Hitler occasionally dreams that victory may not be lost after all. Burning the cities is not a tacit admission of defeat, but a clever tactical ploy to deny the enemy any possible advantage. Shattered armies can be reconstituted for the final apocalyptic battles on the approaches to Berlin. Seized by imaginings of a rejuvenated Wehrmacht, Hitler visits the front lines for the last time in March 1945, venturing as far east as the Ninth Army's headquarters, then in the castle at Freienwalde. There, the generals and staff officers saw a stooped old man with gray hair and sunken face who occasionally, with an effort, ventured a confident smile. Hitler's old headquarters in East Prussia, at Rastenburg, was the site of the most promising assassination attempt against him, one attempt of forty-two in

LAST HURRAH

In April 1945, Adolf Hitler emerged from his Berlin bunker to award medals to members of the Hitler Youth. It was his last photograph. On the final day of the month, as Soviet armies prepared to swallow the Nazi capital, he would commit suicide.

(Hulton/Archive)

all, by Richard Overy's count. Since the bomb exploded on July 20, 1944, historians have been tempted to see the explosion as the cause of Hitler's mental and physical decline. But neither the danger of assassination nor the bomb were catalysts of his deterioration. One would expect a certain correspondence between wartime stresses and a leader's mental and physical health, but humans do not react so literally to dramatic events. One of Hitler's physicians thought that until 1940 Hitler looked younger than he was, thriving on the stresses and strains of his megalomania. Between 1940 and 1943, he began to catch up with his age. Even his most admiring followers began to see signs of physical and mental decline. Joseph Goebbels rhapsodized that Hitler's face was that "of an Atlas, bearing the whole world on his shoulders."

By 1943, the quack who served as one of Hitler's attending physicians, Theodore Morell, was administering injections of a brew made up of twenty-eight different drugs. Well before the bomb exploded at Rastenberg, his downward slide had begun. His extremities trembled. His left arm and leg occasionally shook so much as to be useless to him. He began to stoop and shuffle as he walked. Some of those who saw him most often thought he might have Parkinson's disease, but these symptoms as commonly described could just as easily have been hysterical paralysis of a type all too common among soldiers in the Great War. What is quite clear, however, is that Hitler's physicians were of no help to him. Quite the opposite. They contributed importantly to their patient's miseries. By the spring of 1944, Dr. Morell had developed the practice of simply giving Hitler's aides and servants bulk supplies of pills—Dr. Koester's Antigas Pills—containing a mixture of strychnine and belladonna, to be taken whenever the patient demanded. How one might gauge the effect of these minor poisonings upon Hitler is a nice question. Too many other factors must be allowed their influence upon his behavior at the time. One cannot imagine that any of these actually contributed to his command of self or state during the final days of the war.

After the commencement of Operation Barbarossa—the invasion of the Soviet Union—Hitler spent less time in Berlin and more time in his headquarters at Rastenburg. By the end of November 1944, Russian advances forced him to abandon East Prussia once and for all and return to Berlin. Toward the middle of December, he ventured to his Western Headquarters at Ziegenberg near Bad Neuheim to lend his strategic genius to the direction of the Christmas offensive in the Ardennes that collapsed into the Battle of the Bulge. By mid-January, he was back in Berlin, and with the exception of his visit to the Ninth Army's headquarters, there he would remain.

The führer's bunker at Rastenberg had been no palace; it was dark, airless, dank, certainly cheerless. Even Hitler's doctors advised him not to return after the bomb of July 20. But the bunker in Berlin was even more confining than the one in Rastenberg. It was hardly a place designed for recuperation. By February 1945, Hitler's doctors were adding to the list of his symptoms an inability to concentrate and a certain forgetfulness—or was this merely indifference? By then, time had turned itself inside out in the bunker. Daily military conferences began very late in the evening and usually were not finished before six in the morning. Afterward, Hitler "with shaking legs and quivering hand," stood to dictate instructions to his secretaries and aides. That done, he would collapse on a sofa and engorge himself with his favorite foods, chocolate and cake. During these gastronomic performances, one of his secretaries remembered, "He virtually did not talk at all." Axmann professed to being shocked by his leader's appearance and manner. Hitler seemed to be in his dotage, yet Axmann thought he exuded "will power and determination" all the same. A much less worshipful description of Hitler at the time comes to us from an "elderly General Staff Officer," who saw a Hitler who "dragged himself about painfully and clumsily, throwing his torso forward and dragging his legs after him from his living room to the conference room of the bunker . . . saliva dripped from the corners of his mouth."

That day's military conference—Hitler's birthday conference—offered no hope at all that Berlin could escape destruction by the Red Army. General Hans Krebs, who delivered the briefing, told Hitler that the capital would be completely surrounded within a few days at most, or at worst, within a few hours. Only a few Wehrmacht and SS formations survived. Military units depicted on Hitler's situation maps were little more than ghosts of their originals. Hitler imagined them as up to full strength and combat power. He began directing movements and concentrations of these phantom units, creating a gossamer defense against the Red invaders. All these units he placed under the command of SS Obergruppenführer Felix Steiner, and in Hitler's mind, if nowhere else, the so-called Steiner Offensive was born, another phantom flitting through a mind that was fast losing its intellectual cohesion.

Swinging back and forth between lucidity and near-stupor, Hitler announced that he would remain in Berlin after all, that he would not remove himself and his entourage to the Obersalzberg. He told one of his adjutants that the coming battle for Berlin "presented the only chance to prevent total defeat," although precisely how, Hitler could not then say. With General Alfred Jodl, Hitler was more forthright: "I shall fight as long as the faithful fight next to me and then I shall shoot myself."

Word of the führer's intentions was not long in spreading beyond the bunker, throughout the city. On that day, all Reich administrative agencies in Berlin and elsewhere closed for good. Shops, streetcars, subways, police, garbage, mail deliveries all quit even the pretense of operating. The Berlin Zoo closed its gates. On April 20, the office of the commandant of Berlin issued 2,000 permits to leave the city. Himmler found reasons not to visit the Führerbunker again. Reichsmarschall Göring discovered "extremely urgent tasks in South Germany," and decamped hurriedly from his estate with a truck convoy full of loot.

Those who stayed behind with Hitler for the cataclysmic battle will watch a man falling inexorably into a self-dug grave. The military situation outside formed the perfect accompaniment to the atmosphere of Hitlerian *Götterdämmerung* in the Führerbunker. "There is only one thing I still want," Hitler cried out: "the end, the end!" He was, in Hugh Trevor-Roper's memorable phrase, like "some cannibal god, rejoicing in the ruin of his own temples." He would not have to wait long: On the morning of April 21, Soviet artillery began bombarding the outskirts of the city.

Of course it was the Red Army that had aimed itself most deliberately at the Nazi capital. Stalin had feigned indifference to the fate of Berlin, going so far as to tell General Eisenhower that the city had "lost its former strategic importance." In truth, Stalin believed no such thing: Berlin was to be where the Red Army's war would end. Eisenhower had agreed with Stalin that Berlin was "nothing but a geographical location" of little remaining military significance. Characteristically, Stalin assumed Eisenhower was as duplicitous as he himself was, and on the following day Stalin told his defense committee, "the little allies intend to get to Berlin ahead of the Red Army."

A race for Berlin had thus begun, but only the Red Army would be running it. Stalin set his two most experienced generals, Georgy Zhukov and Ivan Konev, against one another to see who could whip his soldiers faster through the crumbling resistance put up by the Wehrmacht and the SS. By early April, Zhukov is slightly closer than Konev. Zhukov has amassed four field armies and two tank armies at the Kustrin bridgehead on the Oder River. For each kilometer of his front lines, Zhukov has placed 250 artillery pieces virtually wheel to wheel. Eleven thousand of these wait to be fired at Berlin. Konev's forces were equally strong and lay alongside Zhukov's, just to the south. Combined, the Soviet armies driving for Berlin numbered more than a million soldiers, happily anticipating revenge. "Berlin for us was an object of such ardent desire," wrote Konev, "that everyone, from soldiers to general, wanted to see [it with his] own eyes, to capture it by force of arms."

The question of which of the Allied armies was going to take Berlin having been more or less settled in the Soviets' favor, there naturally arose the question of what to do with the city and its inhabitants once captured. Inevitably, high-ranking Nazis would be swept up in the last great battle of the European war—perhaps even Hitler himself. On this latter question, Allied policy had yet to take shape. In the meantime, Allied opinions differed wonderfully.

Churchill had considered what eventually was to be done with Axis leaders as early as the summer of 1941, when he was heard to wonder if Hitler and his cronies might be exiled to some remote island. St. Helena, Napoleon's old prison after Waterloo, would not do, however; Churchill "would not so desecrate" the place by putting Nazis on it. The most extreme punishment, he thought, should be meted out to Mussolini: that "bogus mimic of Ancient Rome" should be "strangled like Vercingetorix in old Roman fashion." Naturally, such opinions would grow even less forgiving over the course of the war. Axis leaders were storing up credits for beastliness at a pace that quickly outran any impulse of Allied mercy. After D day, Eisenhower startled Lord Halifax one day by arguing that all members of the German General Staff, the Gestapo, and any Nazi above the rank of major should be executed. By the spring of 1945, Churchill and the Foreign Office were of one mind: summary field executions for the highest-ranking Axis leaders.

Although Churchill distinguished between the Hitlerites and the rest of Germany, most of his countrymen did not. Nor did the Americans. Roosevelt most certainly did not absolve the German people of responsibility for Nazism. More than once, FDR suggested mass castration of the Germans once the war was safely over, so as to forestall a resurgence of militarism. The president also agreed, at least at first, with his treasury secretary, Henry Morgenthau, who had a plan to de-industrialize Germany and transform it into a permanently impoverished agricultural republic. These were the provisions that seemed to attract the most attention, but Morgenthau also made recommendations for dealing with war criminals that followed Churchill's line. Once a list of Axis "archcriminals" was drawn up and identities confirmed, Morgenthau's plan called for their field execution by military firing squads. One estimate at the time held that many thousands of war criminals all across Europe would be rounded up by war's end.

The American secretary of war, Henry Stimson, was horrified by Morgenthau's plan. At first, President Roosevelt was attracted to the severity of the plan, but Stimson would not hear of it. The Morgenthau Plan was unbecoming of a truly great nation, Stimson argued. The Allies had sacrificed their lives and treasure in defense of the highest moral purposes. Those sacrifices must not be disgraced by the imposition of a Carthaginian peace. Crude vengeance should make way for higher principles of international law and justice. Only a trial by an international tribunal could be acceptable under these circumstances, Stimson insisted. And in this opinion Secretary Stimson could count on the support of none other than Joseph Stalin himself, as Churchill would discover. On a trip to Moscow in October 1944, Churchill had broached this subject with Stalin, and to his surprise found the Soviet leader taking "an unexpectedly ultrarespectable line." Stalin would not budge on the question, Churchill later told Roosevelt. Stalin said "there must be no executions without trial, otherwise the world would say they were afraid to try them." Confronted by an immovable Stalin and a wavering Roosevelt, Churchill gave in to the idea of a trial for the leading Nazis.

Hitler could not have known of Churchill's concession. He almost certainly did know of the Declaration of St. James, an official pronouncement made three years earlier in London by representatives from the nine European governments-in-exile. Constituting themselves as the "Inter-Allied Commission on the Punishment of War Crimes," the conferees foreswore summary retributions against enemy war criminals, and instead demanded "the punishment, through the channel of organized justice, of those guilty of or responsible for these crimes." The leading Allies would eventually come around to this position as the European War bled to a close. The St. James's declaration of high-minded legal purpose could hardly have made any impression on a dictator who had so thoroughly subverted his own nation's legal system. Anyway, Hitler had long thought himself and his party beyond the pale of any law. On the eve of Germany's invasion of Russia in the summer of 1941, Hitler confessed his feeling that they had all passed a moral point of no return. "We have so much to answer for already that we must win," he told Goebbels. Four years later, an international trial was the most humane fate Hitler might have hoped for, but he was in fact contemptuous of any such prospect. He refused, he said, to become "an exhibit in the Moscow Zoo" for the edification of the enemy's "hysterical masses."

By the afternoon and evening of April 22, such prospects as were left to Hitler were disappearing one by one. At the daily military conference in the bunker, it was clear to all present that the Steiner Offensive would never materialize. By then, every Wehrmacht formation in the path of the Red Army was either disintegrating on the spot or falling back in confusion along the roads to Berlin. Virtually all of Berlin itself was now within range of Zhukov's artillery. The city was being drenched in artillery fire, its muffled thumps now discernible in the Führerbunker. Every notion of retrieving the disastrous military situation, of fending off the enemy's advance into the capital, of somehow wresting the initiative from the Russians, of heroic resistance, all these possibilities were rendered impossible by the few reports still being transmitted from the wreckage of the once-proud, seemingly irresistible Wehrmacht.

Hitler listened sullenly as the reports were briefed to him. All of a sudden, casting off any pretense of composure, he unleashed a storm of hysterical ravings. No one was worthy of his regard. All about him were incompetent, corrupt, traitorous weaklings. And so his fit of denunciations went on for who knows how long, draining all those present of self-regard, energy, any reserve of hope. The historian Joachim Fest depicts a scene worthy of a Wagnerian opera: "He shook his fists furiously while he spoke, tears ran down his cheeks; and as always in the disastrous disenchantments of his life, everything collapsed along with the one hysterically magnified expectation. This was the end, he said. He could no longer go on. Death alone remains. He would meet death here in the city." His outburst was so violent, some present thought Hitler had completely lost his senses. On the day after this near-psychotic episode, a corps commander had been ordered to report to the bunker to receive the hopeless command of Berlin's defenses. General Karl Weidling, was dismayed to see his führer sitting behind a table strewn with maps, his face puffy "with feverish eyes. When he tried to stand up, I noticed to my horror that his hands and legs were constantly trembling. . . . With a distorted smile he shook hands with me and asked in a hardly audible voice whether we had not met before." Weidling noticed that when Hitler sat down again, "his left leg kept moving, the knee swinging like a pendulum, only faster."

If Hitler was frenzied by the state of affairs as he knew them, what he did not then know would have rendered him completely insensible. Two reports in particular, tumbling down the stairs on top of one another, cast an even darker shadow over the denizens of the bunker, if that was possible. Unknown to Hitler, Himmler had entered into secret negotiations with Sweden's Count Bernadotte for a separate peace with the Western Allies. If anything, Himmler was even less in touch with reality than his leader. Presenting himself to Bernadotte as "the only sane man left in Europe," Himmler was at the same time considering how to colonize the Ukraine with a religious sect that had been brought to his attention by his masseur. Of course, the Allies were in no mood to entertain any alternative to unconditional surrender, and Himmler's negotiations went nowhere, except, late in the evening of April 28, to be announced by Reuters news service. Hitler happened to be in a discussion with Ritter von Greim when a valet appeared with the report. Von Greim reported that his führer turned purple.

This news was followed the next day by reports that Mussolini and his mistress had been taken prisoner by Italian partisans and summarily executed in the small town of Mezzagra. Their bodies had been taken to Milan and hanged by the heels in a garage on the Piazzale Loreto, where a mob wreaked its vengeance on the corpses. Hearing this news, Hitler began preparing for his suicide, a final contribution to the Armageddon he had shrieked out for the German nation that had so disappointed him. He would show them, those "petty bourgeois reactionaries" who thought they had defeated him. Without him, Germany would be leaderless, carrion to be picked over by the wretched Allies.

Most accounts given by those present who survived this final day in the bunker agree that, having spent most of the evening of April 29 writing his "Political Testament," Hitler retired to his rooms with Eva Braun, there to receive occasional visitors from among the dwindling population of the bunker. Sometime in the middle of the afternoon of April 30, Hitler and Braun took their own lives. Braun used poison. Hitler used a pistol. Following his last wishes, several of Hitler's underlings carried the two bodies to the surface, where they were incinerated in the ruins of the chancellery garden, and where the Russians discovered the remains several days later.

So did Hitler take his own life, by his own hand and of his own volition? No doubt he was hysterical, but he was not deranged. Neither madness, nor the approach of the enemy then less than half a mile away in the Tiergarten, nor entreaties from Goebbels or his other courtiers, compelled Hitler to take this course of action. Nor did the deeper impulses of culture drive him toward self-destruction. This was not an act of seppuku. He did not aim to retrieve his honor or ennoble his death in any way. His suicide was an act of spite. He killed himself in the same spirit in which he had issued orders to kill Germany itself. He meant to punish history by absenting himself from it.

Goebbels followed his master not long after. "There must be someone at least who will stay with him unconditionally until death," Goebbels wrote in a codicil to the political testament Hitler had left behind. After a half-hearted attempt to negotiate with the Russians, Goebbels destroyed himself, his wife, and their five children. Heinrich Himmler's dalliance with the role of peacemaker came to a similar end, and he killed himself within days of Hitler and Goebbels. Göring, of course, was still alive, soon to be taken prisoner and stand trial at Nuremberg. The whereabouts of Martin Bormann, after Hitler the most powerful politician in Germany, were unknown. He was believed to have been killed while trying to escape the Führerbunker at the last minute, but no body was found there.

Uncertainties about Hitler's fate were not assuaged entirely. When his death was announced over the radio by Admiral Canaris, Marshal Zhukov thought, "So that's the end of the bastard. Too bad it was impossible to take him alive." Stalin did not believe Hitler was dead. The Soviet historian Dmitri Volkogonov depicts a Stalin intensely interested in the fate of his mortal enemy. "Stalin's triumph would be complete if he could take the Nazi leader alive and have him tried by an international tribunal," Volkogonov writes. Even though Hitler's remains had been discovered by Russian troops, Stalin seems to have been unwilling to trust his own forensic specialists. When Stalin arrived at Potsdam in July for the Allied conference, he startled the American secretary of state James Byrnes by suggesting that Hitler was still alive, hiding somewhere beyond Germany. And Stalin was by no means alone in his suspicion. Rumors of escape continued to fly about, not only about Hitler, but about Bormann too. The Nuremberg prosecutors then preparing charges against the Nazi elite, not at all confident that Hitler was dead, just in case added Hitler's name to the list of defendants.

All of which brings us to an uncomfortable, even unwelcome question. If Hitler had chosen to live, what then? Historians usually find these questions tiresome. Some speculation might be in order, they say, but one ought to be cautious. One may go too far too quickly, slide into fantasy. Besides, simply finding out what did happen is hard enough, sometimes just impossible. Why add to the confusions history already throws in our way? Protests of this sort, against the variant that has come to be called "alternative" or "counterfactual" history, might best be seen as reactions to intellectual shock—reactions that cannot bear the weight of much argument.

For, in one sense, alternative history is history. The confluence of human action creates contingencies and uncertainties that often do not yield an authoritative version of process, event, or person. More often than any historian would prefer to think, one is reduced to educated guessing about which of several versions of the story one ought to accept as credible. In the end one must decide even if there is a chance of deciding badly. History—not only the living of it but the writing of it too—is a chancy business in which a certain tolerance for the calculation of probabilities comes in handy.

In practice, historians exercise restraint bordering on abstinence when they encounter an opportunity to calculate alternatives. Their calculations show up, quarklike, as the merest shadow of a regret that events in a certain case did not turn out differently. Others are a bit bolder, registering disapproval or rendering judgments. Thucydides cast his *History of the Peloponnesian War* as a tragedy because he grieved over the death of Periclean Athens. And he leaves no doubt about what he thought of the second-rate demagogues who succeeded Pericles and led Athens to ruin. A kind of standard is set up, against which successors are made to struggle—this is just one of any number of puzzles the historian may pose for the reader. Indeed, the practice of hypothetical, or alternative calculation is so common one might even argue that the doing of history without it is well nigh impossible. As the editor of the present volume has written, "'What if' is the historian's favorite secret question.'"

The obverse of history in Hitler's particular case, therefore, is not at all hard to imagine credibly. Reacting to precisely the same circumstances, acting upon the very same stew of perception and delusion, Hitler could have just as easily decided not to kill himself after all. Change nothing else but this and one changes everything. One might impose a measure of control over any alternative scenario by asking no more of inventiveness than one might ask of a prediction. How far ahead might one justifiably attempt to see in April 1945? Whatever one answers, one should go no farther than that.

In April 1945, some very real and very important questions about the future awaited answers. Statesmen, policy makers, and soldiers the world over had to guess about what would happen in a most uncertain world. But they did guess. We know, for instance, that there was no agreement between the Allies over how to treat the leaders of the defeated Reich, save that they would not be shot out of hand. What that meant was that for the contingent moment the leading Nazis who were within reach were to be scooped up and interned. Once the Allies agreed on questions of international law and jurisprudence, there remained the business of setting the actual machinery in place, and all of this required some time. Göring spent this interregnum with his wife and daughter in the safety and relatively comfortable custody of the Western Allies. Those taken by the Russians were neither so safe nor comfortable.

So if we may imagine a living Hitler, one who survived the battle of Berlin, we can see now that a good deal of this canvas has already been painted for us. We know that at 12:50 in the afternoon of May 2, General Karl Weidling's chief of staff and several other official representatives flew a white flag at the Potsdam Bridge, that they were escorted promptly to General Chuikov's headquarters, and that an armistice was arranged forthwith. We also know that at about the same time Russian troops took the Reichskanzlerei and, after some confusion, finally discovered the Führerbunker itself. We can easily envision a resigned, even an indifferent Hitler, still alive, having ordered General Weidling to seek a ceasefire. Perhaps Hitler might still have harbored a fantasy of a negotiated peace, but of course he had nothing left with which to strike any sort of bargain. We can also see without fear of contradiction that the Russians would not have been in a mood especially conducive to negotiation, having lost nearly 100,000 casualties in the Berlin campaign alone. No, Hitler would have been hustled off to see one of the Russian commanders, Zhukov or Chuikov. Immediately, a signal confirming his capture would have gone out to Stalin, and then, to the rest of the world. In all likelihood, the prisoner Hitler would have been on his way to Moscow before the day was out.

But, we have now reached the outer limits of a reasonably safe scenario. Before going further, we are forced to consider a less plausible, certainly a less attractive, alternative. How likely was it that Hitler chose escape over suicide—precisely what many suspected at the time? Here, our answers need not be so speculative; we have testimony of just what was required to make good such an escape at this point in time. Escape was possible, but only just. In the chaotic final hours of the war, several small groups took their chances outside, in a wrecked city engulfed by artillery and small arms fire. The chances of success were minuscule. In the aftermath of Hitler's and Goebbels's suicides, an ill-assorted bunch of soldiers, secretaries, and party officials, including Hitler's own secretary Martin Bormann, tried to get out through the New Chancellery exits and into the city with the aim of working their way northwest of the city. All were killed or captured. Bormann's body was not found.

But the fortunes of battle favored others. Major Willi Johannmeier, Hitler's army adjutant, was chosen to carry a copy of Hitler's final testament to Field Marshal Schoerner, the newly appointed commander in chief of the Wehrmacht. Two other petty functionaries, Wilhelm Zander and Heinz Lorenz, drew similar missions. This party was rounded out by the addition of a fortunate corporal named Hummerich, presumably assigned to assist Major Johannmeier. Johannmeier, an experienced and resourceful soldier, was detailed to lead the group to the safety of German lines. His skills were about to be tested. The Russians had established three battle lines in a ring around the city center, at the Victory column, at the Zoo station, and at Pichelsdorf. The Pichelsdorf sector was where Johannmeier and his party had to go. At noon on April 29, the four men left the chancellery through the garage exits on Hermann Göring Strasse and struck westward, through the Tiergarten toward Pichelsdorf, at the northernmost reach of the large city lake, the Havel. By four or five in the afternoon, having spent the last several hours evading Russians, the party arrived in this sector. The sector was in German hands for the moment, defended by a battalion of Hitler Youth awaiting reinforcements.

Johannmeier and company rested until dark and then took small boats out onto the lake, making southward for another pocket of defense on the western shore, at Wannsee. There, Johannmeier managed to get a radio signal off to Admiral Dönitz, asking for evacuation by seaplane. After resting in a bunker for most of the day, the small group set off for a small island, the Pfaueninsel, where they would await their rescue by Dönitz's seaplane.

In the meantime, another group of bunker refugees arrived. On the morning of April 29, just as Johannmeier and his party were preparing to leave, Major Baron Freytag von Loringhoven, Rittmeister Gerhardt Boldt, and a lieutenant colonel named Weiss asked and received permission to attempt an escape and join General Wenck's imaginary army of relief. The next day, April 30, they would follow the same but even more dangerous route west as Johannmeier's group. The Russians were as close as a few blocks now, already at the Air Ministry. And they had nearly closed the ring on the Pichelsdorf sector at the Havel. Freytag and his group had set out already when they were joined by Colonel Nicolaus von Below, Hitler's Luftwaffe adjutant. Below seems to have been the last one to leave the bunker before Hitler killed himself.

All of these fugitives collected for a time on the lake, awaiting the salvation of the seaplane. A seaplane did materialize eventually, but owing to the heavy enemy fire, its pilot chose between discretion and valor and flew away before taking on his passengers. Now all were left to their own devices. By ones and twos most of the escapees managed to get away, if only to be taken prisoner later. Johannmeier and his group worked their way down past Potsdam and Brandenburg and crossed the Elbe near Magdeburg. Posing as foreign workers, they passed through enemy lines a few days later. Johannmeier simply continued his journey all the way back to his family home in Westphalia. There in the garden he buried Hitler's last testament in a glass jar. Zander made his escape good all the way to Bavaria, as did Axmann, the chief of the Hitler Youth. Nicolaus von Below enrolled in law school at Bonn University. His studies were to be interrupted by the Allied authorities.

All of these men were considerably younger, healthier, and more physically resourceful than Hitler. The vision of Hitler negotiating all these difficulties is an alternative that is defeated by Hitler's psychological and physical states, neither of which, singly or in combination, conduced to the demands of such a choice. By this time, Hitler simply did not have the physical or mental vigor necessary even to attempt an escape, much less actually succeed in one.

But, as the eminent British historian Hugh Trevor-Roper has reason to know, "Myths are not like truths; they are the triumph of credulity over evidence." Immediately upon the conclusion of the war, Trevor-Roper was given access to Allied intelligence and prisoner interrogation reports for the purpose of disentangling the confusions of Hitler's last days, and, by implication, his ultimate fate. Behind Trevor-Roper's assignment were the rumors that swept Europe in the summer of 1945: Hitler had escaped after all, the rumors said. He had gone to ground in Bavaria. Or he was in the Middle East. Or perhaps he had made for the Baltic coast, there to be rescued by submarine and deposited among sympathizers somewhere in South America. These rumors did not merely enthuse the gullible. Stalin startled the American secretary of state at the Potsdam Conference in July by arguing that Hitler was, in fact, alive and in hiding. Allied prosecutors drawing up charges against the leading Nazis took due care to see that Adolf Hitler was indicted, if only in absentia.

But no, given even the unlikely event of survival, it must be to Moscow that he goes. However, this most plausible of alternatives leads us to an important question straightaway. Does he stay there to stand trial, or is he shipped off to Nuremberg for the main proceedings? The Allies had agreed to locate their war crimes trials there because most of the principal defendants had been captured by the Anglo-Americans. The Russians held only a few for the very good reason that the leading Nazis did their best to flee westward, the least immediately dangerous direction, they thought. But if one adds Hitler to Russia's haul of Nazi leaders, the advantage is not quite so certain. The Russians were not particularly difficult on the question of where the trial would be, so long as there was one. Would the Russians have been so obliging if they had held Hitler in the Lubyanka Prison? Would they have insisted upon a grand show trial in Moscow?

There is no way to know for certain. So, one sees, even the most conservative speculation takes one into the shadows of uncertainty quite soon. From this point on, history will insist that we grant more and more "for the sake of the argument," knowing very well that while history is usually explicable it is often irrational. When dealing with the past, the test of common sense is no test at all.

However, we can be sure enough that a living Hitler would have posed considerable problems for the Allies, assuming he would have been moved to Nuremberg. Most immediately, the question was whether he would have been in a condition to stand trial? Wherever he was imprisoned he would have been treated correctly but certainly not lavishly. Stalin had hoped to put Hitler and fascism on trial, and when the Anglo-Americans finally agreed on the principle of an international tribunal, so did they. A damaged or deranged Hitler would have been less suitable for the event. In prison, no longer in command of his own time, his own diet, or his own medicines, and well beyond the clutches of the malign Dr. Morell, Hitler's physical health might well have improved. Most of the Nuremberg defendants fared well enough. The prison regime even improved the dissolute and rotund Göring. He had been weaned from his addiction to drugs and lost eighty pounds. Had Göring not committed suicide on the day of his execution, he would have gone to the gallows a healthier man.

Imagining Hitler's mental state, once he was captured, is less problematic than one might think. Confinement, in and of itself, could not hold terrors for one who seemed so predisposed to bury himself even when he was at large. As we have seen, first at Rastenburg, and then back in Berlin toward the end, Hitler was downright troglodytic. Of course, Hitler was already familiar with prison life, having served a few months in 1923 for his part in the unsuccessful Munich Beer Hall putsch. This earlier sentence, served no doubt in the presence of admiring wardens, afforded him the opportunity to work on *Mein Kampf*. But even criminals know that every sentence is different. In the event he might have forgotten how to behave in prison, the American Army commandant, Colonel Burton C. Andrus, would have been present to reacquaint him. Andrus imposed very strict rules of confinement upon his charges: only one letter per week, one walk per day, no conversations with fellow prisoners except at lunch, and rations in precisely the same amounts provided to the German refugee population during that severe winter of defeat. What had Hitler done for the past twenty years but write and talk. Denied a freedom of movement, of association, Colonel Andrus would have cast his severe eye over a man who had done little else but talk and write for the past twenty-five years and now was allowed neither. The chances for another *Mein Kampf* would have been very small indeed.

If this strictly regimented environment did not improve Hitler's state of mind, it would not have mattered in the end. Rudolf Hess, whose celebrated flight to Britain in 1941 had shaken Hitler like few other events, arrived in Nuremberg from his wartime confinement as a barely functional amnesiac. He had moments of lucidity punctuated by long spells in which he was detached from reality and barely responsive to social interaction. At first, suspecting him of an elaborate malingering, the Allies subjected Hess to extensive psychiatric examinations and were satisfied that even though he was barely competent he was sufficiently so to stand trial. Hess would spend the rest of his life in Berlin's Spandau Prison. Another defendant, the virulent anti-Semitic propagandist Julius Streicher, scored so low on his IQ tests that he was examined further by psychiatrists. A third defendant, Robert Ley, leader of the German Labor Front, managed to commit suicide after he heard the charges against him. If we require further evidence that the Allies were disinclined to forgive, postpone, or otherwise soften their prosecution of enemy leaders on any grounds whatsoever, we need only recall that Japan's wartime leader, Hideki Tōjō, shot himself in the chest in a botched suicide attempt. He ended up in Tokyo's Sugamo Prison all the same, and at the end of the gallows. Hitler could have expected no less, were he to have stood trial.

Allied officials charged with conducting the International Military Tribunal's business at Nuremberg had any number of worries to disturb their nights. One of them was whether one or more of the defendants would somehow turn the trial to his advantage. More than merely convincing the tribunal that they were not guilty, but by some means of guile or rhetoric, was it within the power of these once mighty and feared defendants to emerge from the ordeal as heroes or national martyrs? In the event, this fear was groundless. The justices on the tribunal exercised strict control over courtroom behavior. Göring was able to mug and scowl and rustle in his chair to indicate his reaction to testimony, but no more. The white-helmeted military policemen just behind the defendant's box would have removed any unruly defendant from the court's presence, had the court's decorum been violated. The behavior of all the defendants, Göring's included, was, like their persons, rather more confined than in ordinary circumstances. Even the most extravagant personality, like the nail that came out too far, would be hammered down. Doubtless, Hitler himself, the most extravagant of these personalities, would have responded along the same lines.

We must return, then, to Hitler himself. Exposed, yet confined in the dock day after day, Hitler, Göring, and the other defendants personified the banality of evil. "There had been quite a metamorphosis," William L. Shirer remembered. "Attired in rather shabby clothes, slumped in their seats fidgeting nervously, they no longer resembled the arrogant leaders of old. They seemed to be a drab assortment of mediocrities." Hitler's mana would have faded to blandness, as if scrubbed by each of the prosecution's witnesses, until he was made finally to disappear. In the early morning hours of October 16, 1946, the death sentences for ten of the twenty-one convicted defendants at the Nuremberg Trials were carried out. Göring, who was to have gone to the gallows first, had killed himself the night before, perhaps with the aid of a sympathetic guard. Hitler might have managed to do the same to avoid what he had cried out for, *das Ende, das Ende!*

In the end, our alternative scenario would have given Hitler a year and a half more of life. If a history would not give him the life he no doubt preferred, it was a great deal more than he had allowed the pathetic millions who died because he lived. One would think humankind would be all too ready to consign Hitler to his well-deserved fate, but as Trevor-Roper has reminded us, "The form of a myth is indeed externally conditioned by facts; there is a minimum of evidence with which it must comply, if it is to live; but once lip-service has been paid to that undeniable minimum, the human mind is free to indulge its infinite capacity for self-deception. . . . When we consider upon what ludicrous evidence the most preposterous beliefs have been easily, and by millions, entertained, we may well hesitate before pronouncing anything incredible."

The scenarios imagined here, though barely plausible, are more than enough to disturb one's quiet moments with a glimmer of anxiety. At any one moment an infinitude of contingencies await History's choice. When History finally chooses we say, yes, that must be fitting or right or appropriate to the case. But humankind has seen History make bad choices too. What if Hitler had lived, what if History had been wrong once more?

RICHARD B. FRANK

NO BOMB: NO END

The Operation Olympic
disaster, Japan 1945

Nearly six decades have passed since the United States dropped two atomic bombs on Japan, but the debate over the morality of Harry S Truman's decision has hardly dimmed. Did ending the war in the Pacific justify the obliteration of between 100,000 and 200,000 lives at Hiroshima and Nagasaki? The horror of what did happen—and those who were wiped out in the first instants were the lucky ones—may blind us to a question that has been too seldom asked: What if the United States had chosen not to drop the bombs? Richard B. Frank is one military historian who has examined in detail the plausible scenarios that would have resulted from not pursuing an atomic conclusion. In this case, as he makes clear, "what ifs?" may give us a better understanding of the unpleasant choices facing American military planners in the summer of 1945. As J. Robert Oppenheimer, the scientific director of the Manhattan Project, later put it, "We didn't know beans about the military situation in Japan."

If the bombs had not been dropped, how much longer would Japan have held out? Could Operation Olympic, the projected November 1 invasion of the southernmost home island, Kyushu, have succeeded? Or would the greatest invasion fleet ever assembled have run into disaster costly beyond the wildest estimates of its planners—or the recent revisionist historians? What about alternatives to the bomb, such as a naval blockade or the destruction of Japan's transportation system? Then there was the true, if unrecognized, wild card in the counterfactual deck, the Soviet Union. What would have been the effect of a Soviet invasion of

Japan? Would, ironically, postwar Japan have been in worse shape if the bombs had not been dropped but hostilities had continued? Would just as many, indeed more, lives have been lost?

In Frank's view, speed was of the essence. The war had to end when it did.

RICHARD B. FRANK is the author of two notable works of military history, *Guadalcanal: The Definitive Account of the Landmark Campaign* and *Downfall: The End of the Japanese Empire.*

THE DECISION TO lash Japan with nuclear weapons stands as the greatest and most enduring controversy of the Pacific War. Its defenders view it, in the words of Secretary of War Henry Stimson, as the "least abhorrent choice." Its impassioned critics argue that history would have taken a more humane and wiser path if nuclear weapons were not available or were not used. Which of these views is correct requires a careful examination of the facts, not the fantasies, about the forces steering events in the summer of 1945.

There can be no meaningful expeditions down the channels history did not follow without first comprehending the realities of power in Japan. Militarists held the destiny of Imperial Japan in a rigid grip. They possessed a legal veto over the formation, or continuation, of governments. Bolstering this formality was the implicit threat of their arms, and a history of terror. Between 1921 and 1944, some sixty-four spasms of right-wing political violence, including the murder of two prime ministers, thoroughly cowed those few individuals franchised to participate in any fashion in shaping the nation's fate.

In Japan's misshapen political structure, only eight individuals exercised any meaningful power of decision. An inner cabinet called the Supreme Council for the Direction of the War constituted ultimate governmental authority, but only if its members achieved unanimity. The contemporary shorthand for this body was the "Big Six": Prime Minister Suzuki Kantaro, Foreign Minister Togo Shigenori, War Minister Anami Korechika, Navy Minister Yonai Mitsumasa, Chief of the Army General Staff Umezu Yoshijiro, and Chief of the Navy General Staff Toyoda Soemu. Only Togo was a civilian. Suzuki was a retired fleet admiral and the rest were serving flag officers. The remaining two men who wielded real authority were the emperor and his intimate adviser, Keeper of the Privy Seal Kido Koichi. Kido's power lay in his ability to sway the emperor, and the emperor's power depended upon the compliance of the government and the armed forces to his orders.

To this day, no pre-Hiroshima document has been produced from Japan demonstrating that any one of these eight men ever contemplated a termination of the war on any terms that could, or should, have been acceptable to the United States and her allies. What history does document about their thinking illustrates just how intransigent they remained as late as August 9. On the day the second atomic bomb struck Nagasaki—and following three years of almost unrelenting defeats, the destruction of Japan's shipping lifelines, the incineration of sixty cities, and Soviet intervention—the Big Six for the first time seriously discussed, and agreed on, a set of terms for ending the war. Three members were prepared to surrender if Japan received a guarantee that she could retain the Imperial system. But the other three insisted on a trio of additional terms: Japan's right to repatriate her servicemen; Japan's authority to conduct "so called war crimes trials" only in Japanese forums; and, finally, no Allied occupation of Japan. Since the Big Six could only act in unanimity, these conditions denominated Japan's position.

And what of the emperor? The Japanese—with American complicity—took pains postwar to depict an image of Hirohito as a "symbol emperor" who reigned but did not rule. He was projected as a man who desired peace, but was barred from imposing his will until an extraordinary impasse in Japanese political structure—the deadlock of the Big Six over the terms for surrender—permitted him to intervene in the "Sacred Decision" to halt the war.

The emperor himself confessed that he actually shared the core convictions of the Big Six at least until June 1945, and he never moved decisively away from that stance. This explains why these men failed to move to end the war and points to what their response would have been in the absence of Hiroshima and Nagasaki. Plainly stated, they believed, and with good reason, that Japan still possessed an excellent chance to obtain a negotiated peace that would maintain the old order in Japan—in which they would be dominant.

In the first three months of 1945, Japan's military leaders forged a strategy they called *Ketsu Go* (Operation Decisive) to obtain the political bargaining chips to terminate the war in a manner they could abide. They were confident that no amount of blockade and bombardment, even if it cost the lives of millions of their countrymen, could compel them to yield. Moreover, they believed an impatient American populace would propel their antagonist to avoid a protracted siege and attempt to end the war swiftly. That dictated an invasion of the Japanese homeland.

Japanese strategists next examined the map in light of American operational habits. The United States could be expected to bring its huge preponderance of air strength to bear in support of an invasion. Land-based aircraft constituted the majority of U.S. air assets and thus dictated that the invasion must fall on an area within range of land-based fighter aircraft. From the positions the Japanese expected their opponent to hold by the summer of 1945, the nearest bases would be Okinawa and Iwo Jima. Okinawa, but not Iwo Jima, could support thousands of tactical aircraft, smaller than the B-29s that were already bombing the home islands. From Okinawa, American flyers could reach Kyushu and parts of Shikoku. Of these two, Kyushu offered the better set of potential air and sea bases from which to mount an attack on the obvious supreme objective—Tokyo, the political and industrial hub of Japan. A simple scan of the topographical map of Kyushu easily revealed to Japanese commanders three of the four chosen American invasion sites. Thus, the Japanese anticipated not only an invasion, but the two most probable invasion areas, the sequence of the two probable invasions, and the exact landing sites on Kyushu.

With a firm grasp of the strategic essentials, Japan embarked on a massive mobilization program. By midsummer there would be sixty divisions and thirty-four brigades mustering 2.9 million men in the homeland. A strict conservation program, plus the conversion of the aviation training establishment into kamikaze units, yielded the Japanese over 10,000 aircraft, half suicide planes, to confront the invasion. These forces were arrayed with primary emphasis on defending southern Kyushu and Tokyo.

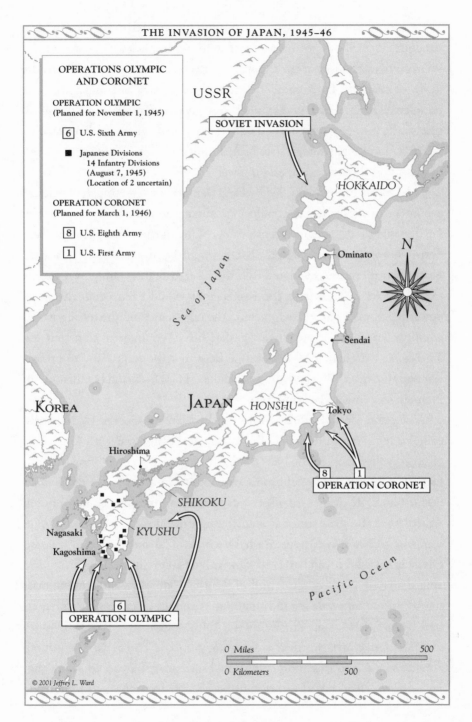

THE INVASION OF JAPAN, 1945–46

OPERATIONS OLYMPIC
AND CORONET

OPERATION OLYMPIC
(Planned for November 1, 1945)

6 U.S. Sixth Army

■ Japanese Divisions
14 Infantry Divisions
(August 7, 1945)
(Location of 2 uncertain)

OPERATION CORONET
(Planned for March 1, 1946)

8 U.S. Eighth Army

1 U.S. First Army

USSR

SOVIET INVASION

HOKKAIDO

Ominato

Sea of Japan

N

Sendai

KOREA

JAPAN

HONSHU

Tokyo

Hiroshima

OPERATION CORONET

8 1

SHIKOKU

KYUSHU

Nagasaki

Kagoshima

OPERATION OLYMPIC

6

Pacific Ocean

© 2001 Jeffrey L. Ward

0 Miles 500

0 Kilometers 500

By comparison to the tortured, military-dominated Japanese political structure, its well-designed American counterpart placed ultimate authority in civilian hands. But those hands changed on April 12, 1945, with the death of Franklin D. Roosevelt, which thrust Harry S Truman into the presidency. Roosevelt signally failed to ready Truman for his responsibilities, so the new president turned to his senior advisers for guidance on political and military strategy. Truman's military advisers, however, were not in accord on the strategy to end the war.

The United States Navy, led by Fleet Admiral Ernest King, had reached a number of fundamental conclusions about the conduct of a war with Japan based on decades of intense study. None of these precepts was more deeply held than the principle that it would be absolute folly to invade Japan. Naval officers calculated that the United States could never mount expeditionary forces across the Pacific that would even equal the manpower Japan would mobilize to defend the homeland and the terrain would wholly negate American advantages in heavy equipment and vehicles. Therefore, entrenched Navy doctrine held that the sound way to bring a war with Japan to a close was by a campaign of blockade and bombardment, including intense aerial bombing.

When the United States Army, led by General George C. Marshall, came to focus attention belatedly on how to bring a war with Japan to a close, it swiftly adopted the view that only an invasion could bring the conflict to an acceptable conclusion. After extended debate over these competing views, the Joint Chiefs of Staff reached an unstable compromise in April 1945. The army secured ostensible approval for a two-phase invasion campaign, code-named Operation Downfall. The first phase, Operation Olympic, set for November 1, 1945, involved a landing designed to secure approximately the southern third of Kyushu. This would provide air and naval bases to support a second amphibious assault, Operation Coronet, set for March 1, 1946, aimed to secure the Tokyo region.

The Joint Chiefs justified this strategy on the basis that the overall American war aim was an unconditional surrender that would assure that Japan never again posed a threat to peace. But history raised formidable doubts about the practicality of that goal. No Japanese government had capitulated in 2,600 years; no Japanese detachment had surrendered in the entire course of the Pacific War. Accordingly, there was no guarantee either that a Japanese government would ever capitulate, or that Japan's armed forces would bow to such a command. Thus, the American nightmare was not the initial invasion of the homeland, but the prospect that there would be no organized capitulation of Japan's armed forces, over four million strong. Indeed, the official rationale for the invasion plan declared that it would be more likely than blockade and bombardment to produce the capitulation of Japan's government, and it would best position the United States to deal with the situation if Japan's armed forces did not surrender.

The navy obtained agreement that the campaign of blockade and bombardment would continue at an accelerating rate for six months prior to Olympic. Admiral King, however, explicitly warned his colleagues on the Joint Chiefs in April that he only concurred that orders for an invasion must be issued promptly so that all the preparations for such a gigantic enterprise could be mounted. He warned that the Joint Chiefs would revisit the necessity for an invasion in August or September.

Radio intelligence proved King prescient. During July and August, ULTRA unmasked for American leaders the ambush awaiting Olympic. The 680,000 Americans, including fourteen divisions, slated for the invasion of Kyushu had been expected to confront no more than 350,000 Japanese, including eight to ten divisions. But decrypted communications identified fourteen Imperial Army divisions as well as a number of tank and infantry brigades—also *at least* 680,000 strong—most positioned on southern Kyushu. Moreover, rather than only 2,500 to 3,000 aircraft to support their ground troops against 10,000 American planes, the ULTRA sources and photographic evidence revealed the Japanese had at least 5,900 to more than 10,000 aircraft, half of them kamikazes, waiting to pummel the invasion convoys.

Only reasonable estimates can be offered of likely casualties in a collision between *Ketsu Go* and Olympic. If the Japanese committed at least a half-million men to southern Kyushu for the customary fight to the death, it is hard to imagine that fewer than a minimum of 200,000 to 250,000 of the emperor's loyal soldiers and sailors would have fallen by the end of the campaign. Moreover, Japan had thoroughly mobilized its adult population, regardless of gender, and organized them into a gigantic militia. Japanese commanders intended to use this sea of erstwhile civilians in a combat support and then combat role, similar to what occurred on Okinawa. According to the 1944 census, the three prefectures over which fighting on Kyushu would have raged contained a population of 3,804,570. If only one in ten of this populace died, a much lower rate of loss than on Okinawa, another 380,000 Japanese would have perished, bringing total Japanese fatalities to the 580,000 to 630,000 range.

When the Joint Chiefs authorized the invasion strategy in April 1945, they formally adopted a planning paper that addressed expected casualties. Rather than a raw number, however, this paper effectively provided a range of possible casualties based upon a pair of ratios derived from European and Pacific combat experience, both in rates per thousands of men committed per day.

	PACIFIC AMPHIBIOUS CAMPAIGNS	EUROPEAN PROTRACTED CAMPAIGNS
Killed in action	1.78	.36
Wounded in action	5.50	1.74
Missing in action	.17	.06
Total	7.45	2.16

A troop list designating the expected number of men committed for the campaign and an estimate of the duration of the campaign permit the application of these ratios. By August 1945, there were two troop lists of 766,700 and 681,000 (apparently differing mainly on the count of support units for base construction). Washington also was projecting a ninety-day campaign (a low estimate before the intelligence revelations). Applying these numbers to the ratios generates in the following range of potential losses:

PROJECTED CASUALTIES FOR OLYMPIC *for 90-day campaign*				
	PACIFIC EXPERIENCE		EUROPEAN EXPERIENCE	
	Troop list case 1	Troop list case 2	Troop list case 1	Troop list case 2
Total Troops	766,700	681,000	766,700	681,000
Killed and Missing	134,556	109,515	28,981	25,471
Total casualties	514,072	456,610	149,046	132,385

Even these terrible numbers are not comprehensive, for they represent only casualties ashore on Kyushu. Kamikaze attacks would produce most naval casualties, supplemented by mines, shore batteries, air crew losses, and losses among naval personnel ashore. Using Okinawa as a reference point, the number of sailors likely to die in suicide plane attacks ranges between about 5,700 to 11,400. If other losses were merely equal to non-kamikaze losses on Okinawa, the additional 1,500 bluejacket deaths would push the range of naval fatalities up to around 7,200 to 12,900. Thus, the overall range of American losses *just to seize one-third of Kyushu* would probably rest between 140,000 to 527,000, including between 32,700 and 147,500 deaths.

But in 1945 American leaders ignored speculation on casualties and focused on the fundamental question of whether Olympic was still rational. A ratio of only one American for every Japanese defender "is not the recipe for victory," warned one intelligence officer. On August 7, General Marshall asked General Douglas MacArthur, the designated army commander for the invasion of Japan, whether he still regarded Olympic as feasible. MacArthur replied that he did not believe the intelligence and therefore he was prepared to forge ahead. After this exchange, however, Admiral King sent copies of both messages to Admiral Nimitz and demanded his views. King knew the answer to the question before he asked it. On May 25, after two months of grueling fighting on Okinawa that generated an

American casualty list exceeding any prior campaign of the Pacific War, Admiral Nimitz privately informed King that he could no longer support an invasion of Japan. King's message of August 9 was clearly intended to bring on a full-scale confrontation over the viability of not only Olympic, but also the whole invasion strategy.

Thus, the first crucial issue confronting American leaders without nuclear weapons would be the prospects for Olympic. While Truman had initially approved Olympic in June, this was before the shocking intelligence revelations on Japanese preparations. Moreover, he singled out the fact that the Joint Chiefs had unanimously supported the operation as a key reason for his sanction. Even with MacArthur and Marshall's obdurate support, if the navy withdrew its endorsement, and the radio intelligence picture appeared so bleak, Olympic could not have survived a second review by Truman. Moreover, the ULTRA portrait of Japanese ground deployments to greet Coronet was equally appalling. Chances are zero that either of these operations would have been executed in 1945.

The two obvious alternatives to invasion were diplomacy and the blockade and bombardment strategy. With the possible exception of Joseph Grew, the assistant secretary of state, however, no senior American policy maker was likely to press for negotiation since the minimum Japanese position involved the preservation of not just the imperial system, but of the old order that produced the war. Intelligence analysts had expressly warned policy makers on July 27 that so long as the Imperial Army remained convinced of its success in *Ketsu Go*, there was no prospect that Japan would yield to terms America could abide. It is vastly more likely that policy makers would have switched their attention to blockade and bombardment and just at that moment they would have learned the prospects for that strategy were waxing dramatically.

In May 1945, a survey team from the United States Strategic Bombing Survey (USSBS) mounted a whirlwind investigation of Germany to derive lessons that could be applied against Japan. The USSBS party concluded that attacks on oil production and the Reich's transportation system had "contributed in decisive measure to the early and complete victory." Added to the very dim American understanding of Japan's war economy, this information triggered a fundamental change in the direction of the strategic bombardment program in the Pacific.

On August 11, 1945, Major General Curtis LeMay, who was then the chief of staff for General Carl Spaatz, the commander of United States Strategic Air Forces, Pacific, promulgated a new targeting directive. Under Spaatz's command were the Twentieth Air Force, based in the Mariana Islands, and the Eighth Air Force, redeploying from Europe to Okinawa. For the over 1,200 B-29s these two air forces would field by October 1, 1945, the directive listed a total of 219 targets. The new blueprint drastically curtailed the program of systematic incineration of Japan's cities begun in March and instead gave top priority to fifty-six railway yards and facilities and thirteen bridges that formed the core of Japan's land transportation system. Then came targets in the aircraft industry, munitions storage, and thirty-five urban industrial centers.

On cursory inspection, this new directive appears far more satisfactory as a means of reducing noncombatant casualties than city burning. But its actual effect would have been to inflict a catastrophic mass famine. In 1945, three of four Japanese resided on Honshu, the largest of the four main home islands. Nearly half the total population clustered in the southwestern half of that island. Japan harvested the great bulk of her food on Hokkaido, northern Honshu, and parts of Kyushu. The annual rice harvest in September and October marked the crucial event in the food supply. A host of factors tumbled the rice production from over 10 million tons in 1942 to only 6.3 million tons in 1945.

Japan customarily bridged the gap between domestic food production and need with imports, but the destruction of her merchant fleet virtually extinguished that source by August 1945. The collapse of the water transportation system threatened even more dire peril. Unlike any other major industrialized nation, Japan relied upon seagoing transportation for domestic as well as international trade. If Japan lacked ships to haul food from surplus to deficit areas, her only alternative was her railway system. That system, however, was limited and extraordinarily vulnerable to air attack. Postwar study by USSBS calculated that a mere half-dozen cuts of the major net along the Pacific coast of Honshu would have incapacitated the whole system. The B-29 force, not to mention carrier-based aircraft, would have inflicted many times this damage in a few days.

Destruction of the railroads would have been cataclysmic. After the surrender in August 1945, as it was, Japan tottered through the 1945–1946 Rice Year in desperate shape. The food ration officially dropped to 1,042 calories per day in Tokyo by May 1946. This was with functioning railroads and a civil administration in place. The effects of the new air-targeting directive would have first struck Japan's heavily industrialized and populated region along the southwestern rim of Honshu. These cities filled the rice needs of their populations with shipments. Tokyo, the worst case, met only 3 percent of requirements from local growers. Without water or rail transportation, these teeming centers would have swiftly depopulated, sending millions of hungry refugees swarming into the countryside. Not only would this have brought the collapse of industrial production, it also would have unhinged the civil government, essential to ration and distribute the available food. By late spring of 1946, all food supplies in the southwestern half of Honshu would have been consumed. This would have compelled the weakened survivors of what was originally half the nation's population to migrate in search of food, or perish.

Within days after the first systematic attacks on Japan's internal rail transportation system, her leaders would have recognized their implications. Moreover, those implications would rip open the key fault line separating the great majority of the leaders of Japan's armed forces from the emperor and a small minority of officers. The former fervently cherished the dogma that the only threat to the old order in Japan was from without. The latter, however, recognized and deeply feared that mass famine and civil disruption would spark revolution from within. To forestall that nightmare, the emperor and those of like insight realized a capitulation might at least maintain some possibility of retaining internal bulwarks to sustain the imperial institution.

But the almost simultaneous Soviet intervention may have obliterated the ability of the emperor to secure a capitulation. Even without the impetus of Hiroshima, the Far Eastern offensive by Soviet forces on August 9 probably would have been set back one or two weeks. Once launched, however, the Red Army juggernaut would have overrun Manchuria, seized all of Korea, and annihilated Japanese units on Sakhalin and in the Kuril Islands.

This was not all. Stalin was poised to launch an invasion of Japan proper in August 1945. Only the delay exacted by the fierce fighting by Japanese troops on Sakhalin that denied the Soviets a key staging area, and Truman's insistence that the Soviets not cross the occupation boundaries fixed at Yalta, halted the thrust into Hokkaido, the northernmost of the four main home islands.

Soviet intervention imposed a horrific cost in human life. Approximately 2.7 million Japanese nationals, about one-third military personnel, fell into Soviet hands. The dead and permanently missing numbered as many as 376,000. If Japanese civilians on Hokkaido fared the same as their compatriots on the continent, at least another 400,000 would have perished.

The more critical effect of Soviet intervention, however, would be in Tokyo. While critics have asserted that the Soviets, not the atomic bombs, triggered Japan's surrender, that view rests upon the thesis that the Japanese recognized the hopelessness of their situation when the Red Army smashed the Japanese Kwantung Army in Manchuria, and thus proved that Japan could not defeat an invasion. But the Imperial Army and other leaders in Tokyo were clueless for several days as to the size and success of Soviet attacks. The Imperial Army—having already written off Manchuria and stripped the Kwantung Army of its first-class units—reacted not with resignation but defiance. Staff officers in Tokyo whipped up plans to declare martial law and to prepare to eliminate all vestiges of authority outside Imperial General Headquarters. This would have eradicated the governmental structure, whose deadlock permitted the meeting before the emperor in which he rendered the "Sacred Decision" to end the war. This alone may have destroyed the chance for the emperor's intervention.

There is, however, a still more fundamental point about why Japan's organized surrender stemmed from the atomic bombs, not Soviet intervention. Halting the war required both the decision of a legitimate Japanese authority that the war must end, and the compliance of Japan's armed forces with that decision. In explaining Japan's surrender shortly after the war, Prime Minister Suzuki testified that Japanese leaders remained devoted to continuing the war so long as they believed that Imperial Army and Navy could ultimately conduct the "decisive battle" against the U.S. invasion. Suzuki confessed that Japan's leaders agreed to surrender only after the advent of nuclear weapons: They recognized that the United States would no longer need to invade Japan. If there was no invasion, Japan had no military and political strategy short of national suicide. The atomic bombs also worked to save face for military leaders since they could claim they only submitted to supernatural forces of the atom, not due to errors of strategy or lack of spiritual stamina.

Therefore, if the emperor and those of like mind had contemplated ending the war even a few days or weeks later, they would have faced two hurdles. First, by that time there likely would have been no remaining governmental apparatus to permit the emperor's intervention in the form it actually took in mid-August 1945. Second, if the armed forces still believed they could execute *Ketsu Go*, they possessed a rational military-political strategy to continue the war—and a reason to refuse to comply with an Imperial order to halt the war. Even as it was, for several days it was not clear to Japanese or American leaders that field commanders would accede to the surrender order. The result could have been that either the emperor would lack the opportunity or the will to attempt to order a halt to the war, or even if he did make such an attempt, that the armed forces would refuse to comply.

The resulting tragedy would have engulfed the Japanese and other peoples in a catastrophe. Millions would have perished in Japan from starvation or disease due to the famine during the 1945–1946 Rice Year. The vastly diminished population of Japan would have been reduced for years to a crude rural subsistence-level existence stalked by the continual ravages of a food shortage. Moreover, all of the Allied prisoners of war and civilian internees in Japan would have perished—as would millions of others. Most, if not all of the two million Japanese under arms outside the homeland would have held out until annihilated by battle, disease, or starvation. With them would have died millions of noncombatants throughout Asia. The Allied prisoners of war and civilian internees would have shared the fate of their peers in Japan, bringing the total deaths in this category to over 300,000.

Soviet intervention would have reshaped the burgeoning American debate over strategy to end the war in August 1945. The most likely result would have been to discard Olympic for a draft plan to invade northern Honshu in an attempt to prevent the Soviets from overrunning more of Japan. Once this operation was complete, however, American leaders would have balked at the prospect of conquering the remainder of the home islands, hole by hole, rock by rock. The devastating results of the blockade and bombardment strategy, as revealed from radio intelligence and other sources, would have argued for the navy strategy of starving Japan into submission. Only the possibility of liberating some POWs and internees would have roused interest in further land campaigns in Japan, so long as they remained limited with acceptable losses. Rising American frustration and fury would likely have sparked the decision to unleash chemical warfare against the 1946 rice crops, as well as succeeding ones—a project under consideration in 1945. The use of poison gas against Japan in support of the invasion had also been under consideration in 1945. The prospect of an endless continuation of the war to annihilate Japanese detachments in the home islands may have lifted that taboo as well. American air power and logistics, but not ground forces, would have aided the Allies in defeating Japanese units on the Asian continent.

The Pacific War would have dragged on for probably two to five more years—perhaps longer. The overall cost would have easily exceeded five million deaths in Japan alone by conservative estimates, and equal or double that number among all the nations and peoples caught in this protracted agony. While there would have been no division of Korea and hence no Korean War, there would have been a sharply divisive Soviet-American rivalry in the home islands to match the one along the uneasy borders of Europe. The surviving Japanese people would have languished in poverty and bitterness for decades. Thus the atomic bomb, for all its horror, was the "least abhorrent choice."

JAMES CHACE

THE PRESIDENCY OF HENRY WALLACE

If FDR had not dumped his
vice president in 1944

Henry Wallace is chiefly remembered today as the vice president who, at the De-
mocratic convention of 1944, was dumped in favor of Harry S Truman. Like an-
other accidental president, Theodore Roosevelt, Truman would go on to become
one of the signal figures of the century just passed. His decision to drop two atomic
bombs on Japan as well as policies that he initiated, such as the Truman Doctrine,
the Marshall Plan, and the formation of NATO, would, by containing the spread
of Communism, go far to alter the historical direction of our times. But for the
behind-the-scenes machinations of a few big-city bosses at the convention, "Give-
'em-hell Harry" would hardly have rated a niche in the American imagination.
The investigations by the senator from Missouri of contract fraud and misman-
agement in the war effort would have remained the fodder of Ph.D. theses.

Instead it is Wallace who became the forgotten man, something few would
have wagered on at the time. Throughout the New Deal era and into the war
years, he was a major player in government and politics. As James Chace writes:
"Henry Agard Wallace—geneticist, agronomist, editor, economist, and busi-
nessman—was the best secretary of agriculture that the United States has ever
had." Even with his shock of graying hair, he remained boyishly handsome; his
ebullience and competence made him the ideal person to replace the dead star of
John Nance Garner on FDR's national ticket in 1940. But Wallace's outspoken
views, in particular his continuing courtship of the Soviet Union, earned him

powerful enemies in the Democratic Party—the very people who were determined to deny him a place on the ticket in 1944, and who succeeded in doing so.

The replacement of Wallace by Truman, Chace reminds us, was by no means a forgone conclusion. FDR waffled. Wallace was enormously popular, and there was a moment at the convention when he seemed about to prevail in spite of his powerful opposition. What if—and it is one of the true might-have-beens of American political history—Wallace had gone on to be renominated? What if, when FDR died of a stroke the following April, he had found himself the thirty-third president of the United States? Would he have ordered the dropping of the bombs? Would his often expressed fears of an arms race that would lead to World War III and his efforts to placate the Soviet Union have prevented the Cold War? Or would they, in the end, only have made it more dangerous? And what about that other ticking time bomb—men marked for prominence in a Wallace administration who had been supplying confidential information to the Soviet Union? Would America have gone through a time even more bitter and tumultuous than the McCarthy era?

JAMES CHACE is the author of *Acheson: The Secretary of State Who Created the American World*, as well as five previous books on international affairs, including *Solvency, America Invulnerable* (with Caleb Carr), and *The Consequences of the Peace*. The former editor of *World Policy Journal*, he is the Paul W. Williams Professor of Government and Public Law at Bard College.

O N Saturday, April 14, 1945, President Harry Truman was driven to Union Station, Washington, along with former vice president Henry Wallace and James F. Byrnes, former supreme court justice and FDR's "assistant president," to meet the train bearing Franklin Delano Roosevelt's body from Warm Springs, Georgia. Either Wallace or Byrnes might well have been in Truman's place; these had been the two main contenders for the vice presidential nomination at the 1944 Democratic convention. Both were better qualified to be president than Truman, a little known senator from Missouri who had gained office there through the support of the Kansas City Pendergast machine.

Eleanor Roosevelt, who had flown to Warm Springs in order to accompany her husband's body, seemed particularly pleased that Wallace was there. As the funeral procession made its way back to the White House, some 350,000 people lined Pennsylvania Avenue to watch FDR's flag-draped coffin pass on a caisson drawn by six white horses. At the White House itself, a simple Episcopal funeral service was held at four P.M. Six hours later the casket was reloaded onto the train for the final trip to the Roosevelt home at Hyde Park, accompanied now by Roosevelt's personal and official families, including Wallace, Treasury Secretary Henry Morgenthau, Labor Secretary Frances Perkins, and Secretary of the Interior Harold Ickes—those who had been with FDR at the creation of the New Deal.

That it was Harry Truman rather than Henry Wallace who had the political savvy and generosity to ask his two former opponents to join him in saluting the martyred president was not inevitable. But if, as the Greek philosopher Heraclitus suggests, character is fate, then Henry Wallace's presence as FDR's secretary of commerce rather than his vice president was due in no small part to Wallace's inability to embrace the role of politician;

on the other hand, Harry Truman's vocation in life was as a politician, and he reaped the rewards, often unsought, by his willingness to play politics.

No more Byzantine game was played than the one that Roosevelt engaged in prior to the 1944 convention. Tired as he was after twelve years as president, his face hollowed out by the wartime cares of office, he might well have retired to his beloved Hudson Valley. But even had FDR been a less ambitious man, he was almost honor-bound to run again unless World War II ended abruptly. Wallace himself believed that Roosevelt would seek a fourth term; FDR's son Elliot said, "Pop has tried for twenty-five years to become president and he is going to keep on being president as long as he can." That supposition struck Vice President Henry Wallace as true.

But beyond winning the war, Roosevelt needed to maintain his influence with Congress and the Democratic Party, and, above all, to ensure that the coalition of Southern Conservatives and urban bosses remained intact. Neither of these groups were particularly friendly to the vice president. But Wallace held a large following among progressive forces—farmers, professionals, and labor—who were the core of his constituency. Moreover, Wallace believed he still had Roosevelt's personal confidence, as he wrote in his diary: "Roosevelt is really very fond of me except when stimulated by the 'palace guard' to move in other directions." As a candidate to be once again FDR's vice president he would simply have to appeal to the people, and he was more than comfortable with this approach. A Chicago politician sympathetic to Wallace offered him the practical advice on how to secure the vice presidential nomination: "Set up an organization with a name like United Nations for Peace to work on his behalf and then line up Democratic National committeemen and potential convention delegates." No, Wallace retorted: "practical politics of this kind simply did not appeal to him."

How did such a man—an American Dreamer, as his biographers have labeled him—become FDR's vice president in 1940? And why did he defy the Democratic Party to run against Harry Truman on a third (or, as it turned out, a fourth) party ticket as the standard bearer of the Progressive

WALLACE TAKES A BACK SEAT

In one of his rare campaign appearances in the fall of 1944, a visibly aging FDR (left) rides with his newly appointed vice-presidential candidate, Senator Harry S Truman of Missouri (center) and the vice president he dumped, Henry A. Wallace. In six months, Roosevelt would be dead; Wallace, who narrowly lost out at the Chicago convention, could have been president.
(CORBIS)

Party in the presidential election of 1948? Had he won that election—an impossible task, as he himself realized—or had he secured the vice-presidential nomination in 1944 and thus inherited the mantle from FDR on the very eve of the Cold War, the conflict with the Soviet Union would have almost surely taken a different course. Could the Cold War, in fact, have actually been avoided? And if not, what would have happened to Wallace, who was so eager to preserve the wartime alliance? To try to answer these questions goes to the very heart of Cold War history.

. . .

Henry Agard Wallace—geneticist, agronomist, editor, economist, and businessman—was the best secretary of agriculture that the United States has ever had. Wallace came from a family of editors from the Farm Belt; his grandfather, the first Henry Wallace, founded *Wallace's Farmer*, a journal dedicated to the propagation of scientific agriculture, which involved not only science but planning and good management. His father, who took over the journal, was appointed secretary of agriculture in Warren G. Harding's administration and turned over the editorship to his son, Henry. When Wallace became editor he was not only committed to the modernization of agriculture, but also to the belief that farmers, who had not shared in the halcyon prosperity of the jazz age, needed federal support to achieve stable incomes. Brought into Franklin Roosevelt's first Cabinet as secretary of agriculture, Wallace became a fervent New Dealer, and, above all, a scientist whose own research allowed him to develop and spread the process of hybrid corn, a process that revolutionized the yield of corn and led to a global agricultural revolution.

In FDR's Cabinet, he concerned himself not only with commercial farming but also with subsistence farming and rural poverty. And he instituted programs for land-use planning, soil conservation, and erosion control. In the twenty-first century, largely as a result of Wallace's reforms and proselytizing, Americans employed in agricultural occupations make up fewer than 2 percent of the population yet produce more than their grandfathers did seventy years ago.

With these successes, it was hardly surprising that FDR picked him as his running mate in 1940. By then Wallace had become, in historian Arthur Schlesinger Jr.'s words, "the unofficial philosopher of the New Deal."

But Wallace was also a man who was privately a mystic, more often than not naive politically, a kind of hero out of Dostoyevsky, an Alyosha or Prince Myshkin, whose work constituted for him a spiritual quest for an enlightenment that went far beyond anything the New Deal could provide. During the 1920s and '30s, he explored Roman Catholicism, theosophy, astrology, and American Indian religions. During his early years as secretary of agriculture, he corresponded with the Russian mystic Nicholas Roerich.

These letters fell into the hands of his political foes and almost became public during the 1940 campaign; portions of them were finally published in 1948, by which time his hidden spirituality seemed a further indication of his political liability.

No vice president has ever enjoyed more power than did Henry Wallace. Roosevelt appointed him head of the wartime Economic Defense Board. By 1942 he was at the zenith of his influence and authority as head of three wartime bodies: chairman of the Supply Priorities and Allocations Board, chairman of the Board of Economic Warfare, and a member of the Top Policy Group that worked on the report to FDR on the feasibility of constructing an atomic weapon.

As James Reston, Washington bureau chief of *The New York Times*, wrote, he was "the administration's head man of Capitol Hill, its defense chief, economic boss and No. 1 postwar planner. He is not only Vice President, but 'Assistant President.'" Yet Roosevelt knew Wallace had his limitations, and so it came as somewhat of a shock to the vice president when FDR appointed Donald Nelson, not Wallace, as chief of the revamped War Production Board. Both Nelson and James F. Byrnes came to play a more central role in the civilian conduct of the war than Wallace—Nelson as a hard-driving former vice president of Sears, Roebuck; and Supreme Court Justice Byrnes, who as a former senator provided Roosevelt with invaluable political assistance.

In wartime, Wallace therefore became the spokesman for a kind of international New Deal: he preached international economic cooperation, an end to imperialism, the abolition of poverty and illiteracy, and a global federation of nations with sufficient power to maintain world peace. All of these aims were shared by Franklin Roosevelt, but FDR was far too much of a realist to expect that all these goals were achievable.

Wallace's vision was most salient in his commitment to progressive idealism as he spelled it out in his speech in 1942 that became identified around the world by its most famous phrase, "The Century of the Common Man." "Everywhere the people are on the march," Wallace said, "The peace must mean a better standard of living for the common man, not merely in the United States and England, but also in India, Russia, China, and Latin America—not merely in the United Nations, but also in Germany, Italy and Japan."

The 1942 congressional elections cut deeply into the Democratic majority in both houses, and FDR had to deal with a coalition of Southern conservative Democrats and conservative Republicans. Wallace, the standard bearer of liberalism, came under criticism from the new conservatives for his unabashed New Dealism. For much of the war, stripped of the power to direct the wartime economy, Wallace concentrated on foreign policy. In particular, he told Roosevelt that "the conservatives in both England and the United States are working together and that their objective will be to create a situation which will eventually lead to war with Russia." He believed that the president seemed to agree with him.

By March 1943, Wallace was even more convinced that a preventive war might be waged by the United States against Russia. Speaking at a conference on world order at Ohio Wesleyan University, he warned: "We shall decide sometime in 1943 or 1944 whether to plant the seeds for World War III. That will be certain if we allow Prussia to rearm either materially or psychologically. The war will be probable in case we double-cross Russia. . . . Unless the Western democracies and Russia come to a satisfactory understanding before the war ends, I very much fear that World War III is inevitable." Although Wallace was severely attacked in the press for asserting that the United States would ever "double-cross" Russia, he continued to believe that he had Roosevelt's confidence.

Roosevelt's chief concern outside of winning the war was to maintain his influence with the city bosses and the Southern conservatives, and while he allowed Wallace to exercise his interest in foreign policy, he kept him out of the domestic war effort. Wallace was very much aware of FDR's political needs, and he therefore concluded that his future rested with his popularity with the people. He had good reason to believe that public opinion was on his side: a Gallup poll in March 1944 showed that Wallace had a "commanding lead" among Democrats over his most likely opponents for the vice presidential nomination. Nationwide, Wallace's approval rating of 46 percent equaled the next three candidates combined.

As the Democratic convention approached, however, Roosevelt granted Wallace's wish to go on a fact-finding, goodwill mission to Soviet Asia and China in May of that year; the trip lasted almost two months. Spending almost four weeks in Siberia, Wallace came back with glowing reports of life in a "collective society." In his report, Wallace described the Siberian port city of Magadan as a "combination of TVA and Hudson's Bay Company." In fact, Magadan was a slave labor camp, which Soviet officials had transformed into a Potemkin village prior to his visit. Watchtowers were dismantled, wire fences removed, and prisoners kept out of sight. (Years later Wallace admitted that "after reading accounts by former slave laborers who had escaped from Siberia [I can see] that I was altogether too much impressed by the show put on by high Russian officials."

By the time Wallace got back, a campaign by Roosevelt's advisers was fully underway to deny him a place on the Democratic ticket in 1944. At the heart of the conspiracy was Ed Pauley, the party's treasurer and chief fundraiser; he was joined by General Edwin "Pa" Watson, presidential appointments secretary, and Robert Hannegan, chairman of the Democratic National Committee, a Missouri man whose career had been promoted by Senator Harry Truman. Big-city political bosses such as Chicago's Mayor Edward Kelly, the Bronx boss Ed Flynn, Frank Hague of Jersey City, and Postmaster General Frank Walker, a former party national chairman, completed the cabal. For these men, Wallace was too radical and too much of a dreamer. And there were others who coveted Wallace's job: Senate Majority Leader Alben Barkley, Supreme Court Justice William O. Douglas, "Assistant President" James F. Byrnes, and House Speaker Sam Rayburn.

In a two-hour meeting with Roosevelt on July 10, 1944, the day of his return to Washington after his Asia trip, Wallace met with two Roosevelt confidants, Interior Secretary Harold Ickes and Sam Rosenman, FDR's speechwriter. Both men urged Wallace not to run. Although they said that FDR preferred Wallace, they implied that the president did not think Wallace could win at Chicago. Wallace discounted their advice, preferring to hear what FDR himself would say. Later that day, he did see the president, who told him that if he were a delegate to the convention, he would vote for Wallace; he also agreed to make a statement to this effect. Nonetheless, he told Wallace that many people had told him that Wallace could not be nominated. Once again, the vice president asked for his support, and FDR gave it to him.

The next day Roosevelt met with the anti-Wallace cabal. None of the bosses wanted Wallace. Nor did they like Jimmy Byrnes, a Southern conservative and a lapsed Catholic, who had converted to Episcopalianism; he surely would be unacceptable to blacks and labor, and could easily alienate both Catholics and Protestants. Despite FDR's preference for him (in 1943, he told Harry Hopkins that if something happened to him, the best man for the job would be "Jimmy Byrnes"), Roosevelt then put forth the name of Justice Douglas. But the bosses saw him, like Wallace, as no party regular. At this point Bob Hannegan floated the name of Senator Harry Truman from his home state, a strong supporter of the president. Roosevelt gave no commitment, but he did say that both Douglas and Truman were good candidates. At the close of the session, Hannegan got FDR to scribble on an envelope a brief message saying that he would be happy to run with either Douglas or Truman. But he did not say he would not run with Wallace.

Neither Wallace nor Byrnes was willing to drop out, even after being told by Hannegan and Walker that the president would prefer others. Moreover, Byrnes persuaded Truman to place his name in nomination, and Wallace flatly declared that he would not withdraw "as long as the president prefers me."

On the eve of the convention, Sidney Hillman, head of the CIO labor union's Political Action Committee, said that labor fully backed Wallace. Philip Murray, president of the United Steel Workers and the CIO, gave a press conference on July 13, at which time he gave an unqualified endorsement of Wallace. A poll among Democratic voters showed Wallace with a 65 percent preference leading in all regions of the country, including the south.

When Wallace took leave of Roosevelt just before the convention, FDR said, "While I cannot put it that way in public, I hope it will be the same old team." Finally, in a letter to Senator Samuel D. Jackson, the convention chairman, to be released on July 17, the president wrote, "I personally would vote for his [Wallace's] renomination if I were a delegate to the Convention. At the same time, I do not wish to appear in any way as dictating to the convention. Obviously the convention must do the deciding. And it should—and I am sure it will—give great consideration to the pros and cons of its choice." This was hardly a ringing endorsement, but it may well have reflected the president's inclination: he was willing to run with Wallace if the vice president could garner the strength needed to put him over the top; otherwise, he would accept another man.

For Hannegan this was not what he wanted, and in a meeting with Roosevelt in Chicago's Rock Island Railroad yards, where the president's private railroad car was sidetracked en route from Hyde Park to San Diego, and where FDR intended to remain throughout the convention, Hannegan pressed FDR to name others who would be acceptable to him. Roosevelt therefore wrote a longhand letter, postdated July 19, the day that the convention was to open, that stated: "You have written me about Harry Truman and Bill Douglas. I should, of course, be very glad to run with either of them, and believe that either one of them would bring real strength to the ticket."

It was not easy to get Byrnes to drop out and Truman to accept the nomination. But Roosevelt did say to both Hannegan and Boss Ed Kelly that the nomination must have the approval of Sidney Hillman—"Clear it with Sidney," he ordered. As Hannegan and his aides conceived it, their strategy was to make Byrnes the front-runner, and then persuade Hillman to back someone other than Wallace to stop Byrnes. Arriving in Chicago, Byrnes was convinced he had the votes for the nomination wrapped up. Moreover, the duplicitous Hannegan had told him that the vice presidency was his, that the "president has given us the green light" to support you.

Once Byrnes learned that the nomination had to be cleared with Sidney, he desperately sought support from Hillman and Philip Murray; he got nowhere. On July 17, according to Frank Walker, when the bosses called Roosevelt on his train somewhere near El Paso, the president told them that Byrnes would be a "political liability" and that Truman was the man.

The next day Hannegan told Byrnes of FDR's wishes and it was over for the "assistant president." That evening Byrnes wrote a letter withdrawing his candidacy.

What was probably decisive in Wallace's inability to secure the nomination was less FDR's refusal to back him from the outset than his own unwillingness to do anything about it. He hated backroom deals, and while he was the nominal chairman of the Iowa delegation he had not even planned to go to the convention. When the CIO bosses set up shop in Chicago, Wallace remained silent in Washington. The so-called Wallace organization was hardly organized: when headquarters in Chicago opened there were neither placards nor floor managers. When his backers finally persuaded him to come to Chicago on July 18, he was surprised at the crowds that greeted him. And when reporters asked him if he would withdraw, he asserted, "I am in this fight to the finish."

On Thursday, July 20, Truman was still balking at accepting the nomination. Hannegan decided he needed Roosevelt's help once again. With Truman present in a hotel room, the party bosses placed a call to FDR in San Diego. Hannegan held the phone out from his ear so that everyone could hear the president's deafening telephone voice. "Bob," Roosevelt boomed, "have you got that fellow lined up yet?" "No, Mr. President," said Hannegan, "he is the contrariest goddamn mule from Missouri I ever dealt with."

"Well, you tell the senator that if he wants to break up the Democratic Party in the middle of the war, that's his responsibility." With that Roosevelt slammed down the phone.

Hannegan looked at Truman. "Now, what do you say?"

"Oh, shit," Truman replied. "Well, if that's the situation I'll have to say yes, but why the hell didn't he tell me in the first place?"

Wallace, unaware of these machinations, gave an electrifying speech at the convention. The bosses were startled. It now appeared Wallace could win, and Roosevelt would do no more to stop it from happening. Hannegan's letter from FDR saying that he would be willing to run with Truman or Douglas was no endorsement of either of them. When Hannegan

finally released the letter to reporters, the letter was seen as only a confirmation of Harry Truman as the bosses' candidate.

At the convention that night, cries of "We Want Wallace" were deafening. Senator Claude Pepper of Florida, Wallace's strategist, tried to get the
chairman's attention in order to have the vote taken that night, in which
case it was certain that Wallace would be nominated. Hannegan saw that
the convention was getting out of his control. Chairman Jackson was unwilling to adjourn the session until Hannegan, desperate to stop Pepper,
shouted at Jackson to cut things off: "You're taking orders from me, and
I'm taking orders from the president." At this, the chairman gave in, and it
was over.

Overnight the bosses worked to defeat Wallace. According to John C.
Culver and John Hyde in *American Dreamer*, their biography of Wallace,
"Ambassadorships were offered. Postmaster positions were handed out.
Cold cash changed hands. Frank Walker was said to have called every state
chairman that night, assuring each one that Roosevelt wanted the Missouri
senator as his running mate."

In the voting that day, Wallace peaked on the second ballot at 489
votes, 100 short of the goal—and then the dam broke. Truman started gaining, and in the gallery box where Truman and his family sat, Boss Ed Kelly
held the senator's hands aloft in a prizefighter's sign of victory. Bob Hannegan later said he would like to have inscribed on his tombstone: "Here
lies the man who stopped Henry Wallace from becoming president of the
United States."

Roosevelt still needed Wallace as the hard-core standard-bearer of liberalism to campaign hard for him in the upcoming election. He offered to
make him secretary of commerce in the next administration, and Wallace
accepted. He knew that Roosevelt could have insisted on his nomination
as vice president at Chicago, and that Roosevelt had capitulated to the
bosses in the name of party unity. But Wallace believed he had to support
Roosevelt, who now stood as the symbol of liberalism to both the nation
and the world. Crowds loved Wallace, and he did not stint in his calls for a
further expansion of New Dealism: for civil rights for blacks and minorities,

a peacetime economy of 60 million jobs, decent health care and housing. It was no surprise to him that the president would win a resounding victory, but in less than six months FDR was dead of a cerebral hemorrhage. A shaken Harry Truman, unprepared for the vast responsibilities that Roosevelt had borne, begged Wallace to stay on. The understanding that Wallace and Truman reached was to continue Franklin Roosevelt's policies, but how they interpreted that legacy was manifestly different. Truman's respect for other professional liberals, as he called them, was dim: he rapidly purged his administration of New Dealers. Within six months only two men who had been part of Roosevelt's team from the outset remained—Harold Ickes and Henry Wallace. And by September 1946, there was only Wallace.

For Wallace, fears of a clash between America and Russia were paramount. But while Wallace remained untouchable politically, he had little effect on actual policy. In the year following FDR's death, the Truman administration had not yet found its course; its foreign policy fluctuated like a compass needle seeking the right azimuth, as it zigzagged between trying to find an accommodation with an increasingly truculent Soviet Union and fashioning tough responses to what it perceived as Soviet attempts at expansion. The reluctance of the Russians to pull their troops out of Iran where they had been stationed during the Second World War met with a sharp American diplomatic note in March 1946, protesting Soviet policy in that region; but Washington also allowed the Russians to have "a graceful way out," in Undersecretary of State Dean Acheson's words. After a tough negotiation with the Iranians, the Russians did withdraw.

But that same spring, when the Soviets began menacing Turkey with hostile troop movements on the Turkish border and demands for basing rights in the Straits of the Dardanelles, no graceful way out was offered them. In August 1946, an American naval task force was sent to the straits. Washington was prepared to risk war if the Soviets did not pull back and abandon any ideas of having a naval or military presence in the straits. Once again, the Russians pulled back. By now Dean Acheson, who had sought cooperation with the Russians—and was seen as a dovish Cabinet member second only to Wallace himself—assumed that the Soviets, like their czarist predecessors, were seeking expansion wherever and whenever the opportunity presented itself.

There was now less and less room for the excessively sympathetic interpretation of Soviet behavior that Wallace espoused. Fearful of an arms race, Wallace was quite prepared to accord the Russians a sphere of influence in Eastern Europe, where, he said, a "complete absence of direct conflicts in national interest" existed between Moscow and Washington. In July 1946, he sent a 5,000-word letter to Truman, stressing his view that Soviet behavior was in no small part a response to American policy. Truman was apparently disturbed at the tenor of the letter but also worried that Wallace might resign from the cabinet, which could hurt the Democrats in the forthcoming congressional elections. He therefore wrote a perfunctory reply, hoping that Wallace would calm down. Wallace, however, was determined to change the direction of American foreign policy by appealing to the larger public.

It was in this atmosphere of growing anti-Sovietism that Wallace came to Truman with a speech he intended to give at a rally on September 12 at Madison Square Garden, New York. He and Truman went over the proposed foreign policy address together, and Truman expressed emphatic agreement with the substance of what Wallace would say. When copies of the speech were handed to the press hours before Wallace was to deliver it, one reporter asked Truman at his press conference that day if Wallace's words "represented the policy of this Administration." Truman responded crisply: "That is correct." He then added, "I approved the whole speech."

The speech, however, was hardly critical of the Soviet Union. On the contrary, it was Britain that Wallace attacked: "Make no mistake about it—the British imperialistic policy in the Near East alone, combined with Russian retaliation, would lead the United States straight to war unless we have a clearly defined and realistic policy of our own."

If this was not enough to undermine the thrust of U.S. foreign policy, what he added was intolerable to Washington's view of the world and American security. "The tougher we get, the tougher the Russians will get,"

Wallace warned. "We have no more business in the political affairs of Eastern Europe than Russia has in the political affairs of Latin America, Western Europe, and the United States." To Wallace, this was an even-handed description of geographical reality. To James Byrnes, now secretary of state and negotiating with the Russians in Paris, this was a direct attack on U.S. policy—which aimed to get Moscow to allow free elections in Poland and democratic norms throughout the rest of Eastern Europe.

When Truman read the newspapers the next morning he realized he had made a grave blunder. Then, when he tried to explain away his error by asserting that he had approved only "the right of the secretary of commerce to deliver the speech," *Time* magazine rightly branded his explanation as "a clumsy lie." Meanwhile, in Paris, Byrnes was threatening to resign in protest, until Truman reassured him that Wallace would never again be allowed to speak out on U.S. policy.

In a meeting on September 18, Truman complained to Wallace that "Jimmie Byrnes says I am pulling the rug out from under him." He told Wallace he could make no more speeches on foreign policy. Then, in a remarkable turnabout, Truman declared that he did not have a get-tough policy toward Russia. He said he liked Stalin personally and thought he could do business face to face with him." He even promised that he would ask for a loan for Russia as soon as the peace treaties were signed. Wallace was stunned and was surprised that Truman insisted he make no more speeches on foreign policy. Reluctantly he agreed and told reporters he expected to stay in the Cabinet.

But two days later, Wallace was in his office when an aide brought in an intemperate letter from Truman asking for his resignation. Wallace promptly picked up the phone and called the president directly. You don't want this letter out, he told him. Truman agreed. After the White House sent a man over to pick it up, Truman destroyed the letter and recognized that Wallace had made a courtly gesture. "He was so nice about it I almost backed out," Truman wrote his mother and sister. But he did not; and Wallace hung up the phone and wrote out his letter of resignation. The break was final, and both Truman and Wallace would pay dearly for it.

. . .

Soon after leaving the government, Wallace accepted the editorship of the left-leaning *New Republic*, but he did little editing. His interest was in writing, and he became a regular contributor to the magazine. But by the end of 1946, he was deeply involved in politics: two political action organizations, the National Citizens Political Action Committee, an offshoot of the labor-affiliated CIO's political action committee, and the independent Citizens Committee of the Arts, Sciences, and Professions, joined together to form the Progressive Citizens of America (PCA). For Wallace, the new organization was a mechanism to push Truman to the left; to others, such as C. B. "Beanie" Baldwin, who was charged with the day-to-day operations of the PCA, it was to become a political party. In the spring of 1947, labor leaders like Philip Murray withdrew support from the organization, which had welcomed American Communists to its ranks.

That year saw the enunciation of the Truman Doctrine of the containment of the Soviet Union. Specifically, Truman asked Congress to appropriate $400 million in military and economic aid to Greece and Turkey. Wallace's response to Truman's speech before Congress, in which the president said that "the policy of the United States [must be] to support free peoples who are resisting attempted subjugation by armed minorities or by outside pressures," came the next day in a radio address over NBC. Wallace asserted that the president had proposed "that America police Russia's every border. There is no regime too reactionary for us provided it stands in Russia's expansionist path. There is no country too remote to serve as the scene of a contest which may widen until it becomes a world war."

Wallace was not far off the mark in predicting the eventual trend toward the *global* containment of Communism, even though the Truman administration intended to send military and economic assistance only to the eastern Mediterranean. The Progressive Citizens of America opposed the Truman Doctrine, as well as Truman's "loyalty" program, which gave government loyalty boards the power to try and dismiss any worker who belonged to an organization deemed subversive by the attorney general.

By summer, Wallace was threatening to run on a third-party ticket; even Truman's support for the Marshall Plan to rebuild Europe, while initially greeted with cautious praise by Wallace, was later repudiated by him and the Progressives after Moscow refused to participate in the plan. Wallace now came to see the Marshall Plan as an instrument in the Cold War that aimed "to revive Germany for the purpose of waging a struggle against Russia." As for the number of Communists who had joined the Progressives, Wallace dismissed their participation by telling Michael Straight, the publisher of *The New Republic*, that the Communists were useful in getting out the crowds.

The near-inevitable clash between Truman and Wallace that led to Wallace's third-party campaign for the presidency took shape in the spring of 1948. Wallace spoke repeatedly in favor of showing understanding for Russian policy. The Czech coup of February 1948, when the Communists took over the government, led Wallace to say, "The Czech crisis is evidence that a 'get tough' policy only provokes a 'get tougher' policy." He even suggested that the Communist coup was in response to a right-wing plot to take over the government.

The Progressive Party mobilized for a presidential campaign in which Truman ran against the Republican standard-bearer, former New York governor Thomas Dewey; "Dixiecrat" candidate Strom Thurmond further split the ranks of the Democratic Party. Of the 3,240 delegates to the Progressive Party convention in Philadelphia, almost half of them were trade unionists; more than a quarter were military veterans. Not surprisingly, Wallace's speech labeled the Truman administration's foreign policy as warlike: Even the 1948 Berlin Blockade, which the Soviets set up to prevent Allied troops from land access to Berlin, was described by Wallace as caused by Truman's "get tough" policy.

Wallace, like most everyone else, believed Truman would be handily defeated by the Republicans. But Truman surprised Wallace by espousing a liberal platform—calling for a higher minimum wage and lower inflation, and for decent housing and universal health care. According to the pollster George Gallup, "as many as one-third of the people who said in late October that they were going to vote for Mr. Wallace shifted to Mr. Truman" during the final ten days of the campaign.

The rout of the Progressives was absolute. Truman received 303 electoral votes to Dewey's 189; Strom Thurmond ran third, with 39 electoral votes. Although Wallace garnered 1,157,063 popular votes, he received no electoral votes. In the entire country, he carried only thirty precincts. Nonetheless, if Wallace had taken just 29,294 votes in Illinois, California, and Ohio, the shift in electoral votes would have given the presidency to Dewey.

In the years to come, Wallace opposed the creation of the NATO alliance and continued to believe that the Soviet Union did not have any greater moral superiority than did the United States; both countries, he believed, should put their faith in the United Nations. As for the Progressive Party, its membership shrank, while its control by Communists and hard-line leftist ideologues grew. Once Wallace clearly saw the direction in which the party was headed, he set forth in its 1950 convention the terms on which he would support the Progressives. The party must demonstrate concretely its independence from Communist control and pledge its support for "progressive capitalism" in the United States.

The outbreak of the Korean War in June 1950 was the turning point for Wallace. The fact that the United Nations endorsed the actions of the Truman administration in opposing the North Korean military attack on the south persuaded Wallace to support the UN response. In a public statement issued in July 1950, Wallace said: "Undoubtedly the Russians could have prevented the attack by the North Koreans and undoubtedly they could stop the attack any time they wish . . . when my country is at war and the United Nations sanctions that war, I am on the side of my country and the United Nations."

On August 8, 1950, Wallace resigned from the Progressive Party. He was sixty-one years old, and for the rest of his life he played no significant role in politics. Living at his farm in New York state, he worked to develop the perfect chicken, which would lay the perfect egg in less time and at lower cost than other varieties. And he remained in constant touch with other scientific farming experts in their efforts to develop new types of high-yielding, disease-resistant corn.

He remained a liberal to the end of his life; in 1952, he came to see the

Progressive Party as little more than a Communist sect and voted for the Democratic candidate, Adlai Stevenson. In 1956, he voted for Dwight Eisenhower, believing that Eisenhower was better able to control the military than Stevenson. On November 18, 1965, he died, and on this occasion his old opponents spoke kindly of him. Harry Truman called him "an asset to the country." But perhaps the most just evaluation came from Lyndon Johnson's secretary of agriculture, Orville Freeman: "No single individual has contributed more to the abundance we enjoy today than Henry Wallace."

If Henry Wallace had indeed become FDR's running mate in 1944—and, as we have seen, this was not beyond the realm of the possible—would the Cold War have broken out? Would the United States and the Soviet Union have composed their differences? Would the United Nations have played the power role Wallace desired of it?

In the light of history, I think that in broad terms the Cold War could not have been avoided. Two superpowers vying for power and influence, espousing radically different ideologies, would surely have become mortal rivals. That said, it seems most likely that Wallace would have made greater efforts than Truman to find ways of accommodation with Russia. Wallace would certainly have pressed Moscow harder to see if Stalin's desire to work with the Allies to set up a neutralized and demilitarized Germany was in earnest.

Like Undersecretary of State Dean Acheson in 1945 and '46, he would have supported the Acheson-Lilienthal plan to put control of the whole field of atomic energy under international authority—from mining through manufacturing. Truman, while voicing support for this approach, nonetheless allowed a hard-line anti-Communist, Bernard Baruch, to shepherd it through the United Nations, which led to a Soviet veto and its ultimate demise. Although as a member of the Top Policy Group Wallace gave his blessing to the project to build the atomic bomb, but by mid-1942, his official involvement in the project came to an end, when FDR put the program under the control of Brigadier General Leslie Groves of the Army's Corp of Engineers. Nonetheless, informally Wallace met with Vannevar Bush, the scientist who headed what came to be called the Manhattan Project, and he was also briefed from time to time by Groves. Although Wallace gave much thought to the need for postwar control of the bomb by some form of international regulation, there is no evidence that he opposed the dropping of the A-bomb on Japan. Indeed, as a strong anti-fascist he might well have endorsed it as a way of saving the lives of American soldiers. But in the aftermath of Hiroshima, aware that there were no scientific secrets as such that could be kept much longer from the Russians, he would surely have pushed far harder than Truman did in enlisting the Soviet Union in a shared arrangement to control the resources needed to build atomic weaponry. Such a stance would surely have confirmed suspicions in Congress that he was dangerously soft on the Soviets: his only alternative at that point would have been to take a far tougher line than he had initially hoped to do, or risk further criticism and the likelihood that his political career would end in shambles, if not threatened with impeachment, as he tried to complete Roosevelt's unfinished term.

Nevertheless, laudable as Wallace's efforts might have proved, it is unlikely that the Soviets would have loosened their grip on the East European satellites; had there been no Truman Doctrine, the Russian's military movements on the border of eastern Turkey might have led to war; the Greek Communists, supported by Yugoslavia's Tito, might well have triumphed, even though Stalin was wary of Yugoslavia's growing influence. Could Wallace have continued his somewhat benign interpretation of Soviet behavior? And could he have rejected the fears of the Allies, in particular Britain and France, that the Soviet Union was bent on establishing a sphere of influence in Western Europe if not actual military occupation? I think not. Wallace may have been a dreamer who shunned power politics, but he was not a fool. Nor did he sympathize with Communist ideology. An emotional man who was often blinded by his own idealism, he was embittered when he perceived that his would-be allies were dangerous to his own hopes and beliefs.

Try as he might to avoid militarizing U.S. foreign policy, he would have almost surely been pushed in this direction, not least by Congress. To do otherwise might have brought about impeachment proceedings, as anti-Communist sentiment—indeed hysteria—swept the nation in 1947 and '48.

Wallace could hardly have avoided being singled out by the House Un-American Activities Committee (HUAC) as a dupe for Soviet agents and sympathizers. According to Christopher Andrew and Vasili Mitrokhin's *The Sword and the Shield*, the secret history of the KGB, Wallace had said that if FDR had died and he had become president, he would have named Lawrence Duggan as secretary of state and Harry Dexter White as Treasury secretary. Duggan, a State Department official who had served as chief of the Latin American division, was almost surely a Soviet agent. Harry Dexter White, a Treasury official who was a key figure in drafting the International Monetary Fund at Bretton Woods, apparently did provide information on U.S. economic policy to the Russians. In 1948, both were publicly named in testimony before the HUAC in 1948 as Soviet agents. White died of a heart attack before he could answer these charges, as he intended to do; Duggan fell to his death from a window in New York City.

There is some dispute over whether Wallace actually declared his intention to appoint Duggan and White to his "Cabinet," but he was known to admire both men, and Wallace would have come under severe fire had he indeed become president and appointed them to his administration. Even if he had been renominated in 1948, Dewey would have had a searing issue with which to destroy him. Such revelations would have surely made the Cold War even more frigid than it was—and perhaps more dangerous.

But even the most naive of men can be stripped of their illusions, and, given Wallace's temperament, the apologist can easily turn into the avenger. Despite his tendency to shoot from the hip, Harry Truman at bottom sought to avoid war; his principal foreign policy advisers, General Marshall and Dean Acheson, promoted a policy of containment, not rollback, and above all, no preventive war against the Soviet Union. With Wallace as president, the militarization of American foreign policy might have well been retarded. But in the end, America and Russia, inheritors of a broken world, would have engaged in the age-old struggle for power, and Wallace, if he were to survive politically, would have had to embrace it.

LANCE MORROW

A TALE OF THREE CONGRESSMEN, 1948

America without Nixon, Johnson,
and Kennedy

Any time in which great changes take place is ripe for counterfactual scenarios. Nineteen forty-eight was one of those crossroads, a year (to use that tautology so beloved by politicians) of "new beginnings." Americans had begun to enjoy the kind of prosperity they had not known since the late 1920s, only spread wider and deeper. There was another difference. The intervention of oceans no longer guaranteed the kind of isolation that had once been almost a birthright. The world was very much with Americans in 1948, and it was not always a friendly or a peaceful place. The end of World War II had only produced fresh upheavals, and like it or not, many had become their responsibility. Meanwhile, old bulwarks like the British Empire were crumbling: England had just pulled out of its largest and richest colony, India, leaving Hindus and Muslims to tear each other apart. It had washed its hands of fractious Palestine, handing the mandate to a U.N. still in its infancy. A new world war, the Cold War this time, was taking shape, and with the threat of subversion at home and Communist power grabs abroad, Americans could no longer feel their familiar insular security. What if there had been no Marshall Plan to rescue Western Europe—or if the Americans and British had flinched when Stalin blockaded Berlin? Would more Communist coups have followed, like the one that drew Czechoslovakia within "the Iron Curtain"—Churchill's phrase, which was barely a year old? Would Greece survive as a Western partner? What if an improvised Israeli army had been unable to relieve a besieged Jerusalem? Would the new Jewish state have been stillborn, a bleak foot-

note to the bleaker text of the Holocaust? And what of China? Did Chiang Kai-shek's Nationalists still have a chance of reversing the red tide of Mao's Communist armies?

That, of course, was the big picture of 1948. But as Lance Morrow reminds us, there were personal crossroads as well. Three would involve the political fortunes of young congressmen whose names would shortly become familiar. Still, in the drama that was 1948, each could easily have traveled different ways to obscurity. But as it would turn out, those would be roads not taken.

LANCE MORROW is University Professor at Boston University and a longtime essayist for *Time* magazine. He won the National Magazine Award for Essay and Criticism in 1981 and was a finalist for the same award in 1991. He is the author of five books.

N INETEEN FORTY-EIGHT was a year of crowded historical conver-
gence—a postwar *annus mirabilis*.

It witnessed the murder of Gandhi, the birth of Israel, the onset of the
Cold War (Communist coup in Czechoslovakia, Berlin blockade and air-
lift, start of the Marshall Plan, Mao's incipient takeover of China), the
liftoff of American television as a mass medium, and Truman's astonishing
victory over Thomas E. Dewey.

And at almost exactly the same moment in August 1948, two young
congressmen, Richard Nixon and Lyndon Johnson, were caught up in dramas that lifted them out of the House of Representatives and propelled
them toward their vexed places in American presidential history. A third,
John F. Kennedy, had just survived one.

If these dramas had not occurred at all, or had come to different outcomes, then Kennedy, Johnson, and Nixon arguably would not have become president. American history in the sixties and seventies (the years of
Vietnam and Watergate) might have taken a different road.

The distinctive, flawed, somewhat mysterious personalities of the three
men shadowed those passages of American history, in the ways we know—
from the aftermath of the assassination in Dallas, on through the Great Society and Vietnam, to Watergate. If presidents other than Kennedy,
Johnson, and Nixon had occupied the White House between November
1963 and August 1974—eventful years—how would history have been different?

In August of 1948, Richard Nixon of Whittier, California—a smart,
young, ambitious freshman working among the comparative dinosaurs of
the House Un-American Activities Committee—was introduced to a senior editor from *Time* magazine named Whittaker Chambers, a disheveled,

evasive, apostate undercover Communist who seemed to brim with dark knowledge about Un-American Activities.

Chambers led Nixon—and HUAC and America—to Alger Hiss, the urbane head of the Carnegie Endowment for International Peace and former high State Department official whom Chambers accused of having been a Soviet agent operating in Washington during the thirties.

Controversy. Headlines. Day after day on the front page. Political liftoff. Nixon became, in a matter of weeks, a familiar national figure—jowly, shrewd, earnest in that darkling way that would become famous later. On the strength of his role in the Hiss case—which until the onset of Joseph McCarthy's anti-Communist career two years later was the focus of American anxieties about the Soviet Union and the deepening Cold War— Nixon ran for the Senate in 1950 in California against the actress Helen Gahagan Douglas and won. In 1952, at age thirty-nine, only four years after the obscure freshman Representative Nixon had met Chambers, Dwight Eisenhower chose the young Californian to balance the Republican ticket (by age, geography, ideology) as his vice presidential running mate.

Eight years as vice president led to the near-miss 1960 presidential race against John Kennedy and, after another eight years of misadventures and Republican missionary work in the political wilderness, to January 1969, when Nixon was inaugurated to succeed the ruined Lyndon Johnson.

It is difficult now to recapture the absorption, fascination, and divisiveness that the Hiss case produced in America when it erupted in August 1948. It was the O. J. Simpson trial of the forties, except that its implications were not only sensational but historic. As with Watergate a generation later, the cast of characters was riveting, the stakes high, and the issues elemental. The details of the story—the Woodstock typewriter, the microfilm hidden in a pumpkin, the prothonotary warbler that Chambers recalled Hiss having seen on the C&O Canal in Washington—were indelible, novelistic. America chose sides.

Chambers seemed at first a squalid, unsympathetic figure—a heavy, dumpy, secretive man with rotting teeth and a melodramatic air, a transplant from Dostoyevsky. Alger Hiss, by contrast, appeared lithe, elegant, patrician, with something of the look of Fred Astaire. To most Americans, he was by far the more credible of the two—at first anyway.

What to make of Chambers? He seemed so melodramatic. Chambers told the committee: "I do not hate Mr. Hiss. We are close friends, but we are caught in a tragedy of history. Mr. Hiss represents the concealed enemy we are all fighting and I am fighting."

Chambers's accusations had been made before. He would say later that his account of Communist activities was "an open secret among government officials and newsmen" before he ever answered the HUAC subpoena.

Chambers told Nixon and the HUAC staff the same story he had given nine years earlier to Assistant Secretary of State Adolph Berle, a member of Franklin Roosevelt's original "Brain Trust" and then the president's ranking adviser on internal security. Chambers described a Communist network, of which he himself had been an important member, that operated in various federal government agencies in the late thirties and that engaged in espionage. As Chambers talked in 1939, Berle made notes about "aerial bomb sight detectors" and "plans for two superbattleships—secured in 1937." In Roger Morris's *Richard Milhous Nixon: The Rise of an American Politician,* Berle is said to have reported Chambers's accusations to Roosevelt over a White House croquet game. "But FDR insouciantly waved aside the whole tale as one more witchhunt to discredit the New Deal, and between croquet shots he snapped angrily at his security adviser. Berle could tell his informer, said the president with unusual vulgarity, 'to go fuck himself.'"

But between 1939 and 1948, much had changed. The Soviet Union, a wartime ally, had become a Cold War adversary. The Soviets, as we know now from the decoded Venona traffic between Moscow spymasters and their agents, maintained an enormous espionage network in America.

Nixon studied Chambers and was, at first, skeptical of the strange man, but gradually was persuaded that he was telling the truth. Nixon, with a sharp lawyer's mind, listened to Hiss, who seemed at first confident in his denials of the Chambers story, and noticed odd notes of prevarication, a tendency to weasel about whether he had known Chambers in the thirties. Fairly soon, Nixon decided Hiss was lying. Nixon's pursuit—of Hiss, and of what he came to recognize as his own future—became relentless and obsessive.

At almost exactly the same moment that Nixon was interrogating Chambers for the first time, Lyndon Johnson was gambling his entire political future down in Texas in a too-close-to-call—in fact, too-close-to-count—race for the Democratic senatorial nomination against a former governor named Coke Stevenson.

The popular Stevenson—a deeply conservative, self-made goat rancher with a spread down on the Llano River, a laconic man in the Gary Cooper or John Wayne style—was running a low-key, traditional campaign. He drove from small town to small town in an old Plymouth, talking quietly to the old boys on the courthouse squares. Stevenson conducted himself with traditional West Texas reserve. He gave an impression of competence and silent strength. If someone asked him a question, he would light up his pipe and squint through the smoke for a minute or two before answering. Bragging was bad form and unnecessary. The voters knew where he stood. It was enough that he showed himself and offered himself for senator, in a manly, understated way.

Johnson's biographer Robert Caro made Coke Stevenson out to be a hero out of the old West, bulldozed by an unscrupulous LBJ. Other historians have portrayed Stevenson as a racist and isolationist reactionary—a "mountebank," in Sam Rayburn's word.

Johnson knew that he was losing the race and knew that his political path ahead, out of the House of Representatives where he had served for fourteen years, was blocked. The Texas governorship was tied up for the foreseeable future, and no other Senate seat would become available until 1954. Now or never. He told a backer: "I am either in the Senate or I'm out [of politics] completely."

In 1948, Johnson invented a frantically efficient, ingenious new way to campaign. Working twenty-hour days, he leapfrogged across Texas in a helicopter—something that had never been done before in a campaign. He covered 118 cities and towns in seventeen days. Johnson's three-passenger Sikorsky S51 would clatter down in remote farming communities—Lyndon ex machina!—the candidate emerging from the chopper to tell astonishing but effective lies about Stevenson (claiming that the arch-Conservative was somehow in bed with big labor, for example, implying that he had made a deal with labor to oppose the Taft-Hartley Act). Sometimes, when he did not have time to land, Johnson would get on the helicopter's loud-speaker and shout down to an amazed farmer: "Hello! This is your friend, Lyndon Johnson . . ."

In the end, George Parr, the "Duke of Duval" and political boss of south Texas, apparently stuffed the ballot boxes with enough illegal Mexican votes to give Johnson the election by eighty-seven votes. Historians and political witnesses seem to agree that Stevenson's people were also stealing votes, especially in East Texas; the trail of evidence has gone cold, and it has become impossible to say which of the men, Stevenson or Johnson, would have won if the race had been honest.

"Landslide Lyndon" shrewdly fought off Stevenson's dogged legal challenges. Once installed in the Senate, LBJ rose with astonishing rapidity to the job of minority, then majority leader, where he eventually became legislative boss to a man to whom he condescended as a feckless puppy dog and playboy, the frequently absent junior senator from Massachusetts, John F. Kennedy.

It was, of course, a surprise to everyone—certainly to Bobby Kennedy and, some say, to John Kennedy himself—when Lyndon Johnson wound up on the presidential ticket in 1960.

None of that would have happened if Johnson had not won the 1948 Senate race. Without that victory over Coke Stevenson, Johnson's political career would almost certainly have ended. He would surely have become a Texas businessman, running the radio stations, or a corporate lobbyist in Washington.

When you embark on fantasies of "what ifs?," you enter into abstract forests of luck and chance, of contingency and probability. Each speculative path opens onto a thousand new possibilities. After venturing down the path of nonfact for a moment, you tend to retrace your steps to the solidity of what actually happened.

Nixon might, of course, have come to the presidency by another route. So might Lyndon Johnson. While drifting in counterfactual speculations around that moment in 1948, one might add a third presidential "what if?"—regarding John Kennedy.

How might history have been changed if Kennedy—another of that generation who had come back from World War II and gone to Congress and later became president—had died the summer before, in 1947, when he was stricken by Addison's disease while traveling in Ireland. A priest gave Kennedy the last rites. A British doctor told Pamela Churchill: "That young American friend of yours hasn't got a year to live."

For the rest of his life, Kennedy lied about his health. He told an interviewer in 1959: "From 1946 through 1949, I underwent treatment for . . . malaria—the fevers ceased—there was complete rehabilitation . . ." After the 1960 election, he declared flatly: "I have never had Addison's disease."

But he did. Addison's—an insufficiency of the adrenal glands, a problem that is often fatal—prompted Kennedy's father to stash supplies of cortisone, the best known treatment, in safe deposit boxes around the United States, in case of emergency while Jack was traveling.

It was in 1948 that JFK adopted his father's patterns of living concealed lives. John Kennedy projected a vigorously glamorous and idealized image of himself in public, in politics, while dangerous truths (his grave illnesses; his reckless, active sex life) remained hidden.

What if Johnson had become a private citizen in 1948? What if Nixon had not met Chambers? What if Kennedy had died?

With Jack Kennedy gone, presumably old Joe Kennedy would have transferred the tribe's presidential ambitions to Bobby—with what result, far down the road, it is impossible to guess. One thinks mordantly, for a second, that RFK might thus have arrived at the same destination, the Ambassador Hotel in 1968, by taking a somewhat different route.

It would be hard to imagine Lyndon Johnson out of politics entirely. If he had become a corporate lobbyist or radio station executive, presumably he would have evolved into a Texas kingmaker, a wheeler-dealer, the political boss of Texas. But he would not have become president. He would not have fused his personality with the power of the White House—and would not have produced the great work he did, especially in civil rights. On the other hand, he would not have been brought to the terrible dilemma of Vietnam, which destroyed him. It is possible that the nation would not have been brought to that dilemma either.

As for Nixon and Chambers: Suppose they had not met. Would Chambers have repeated his story about Hiss to someone else in power? Would that someone else have used the case as the foundation of a political career? Would the Hiss case have arisen in any event, forced to light by the hardening of the Cold War? Without the Hiss case, would Joseph McCarthy have been so important? Would the quality of American anti-Communism have been different, less bitter and divisive?

The decoded Venona papers, released in the 1990s, make clear the extent of Soviet Communist activities in the United States before, during, and after World War II. The 1948 coup in Czechoslovakia, the Communist takeover of China a year later, the Soviet acquisition of nuclear weapons (by way of spies Klaus Fuchs, Julius and Ethel Rosenberg, and others), the invasion of South Korea by the North Korean Communists in June 1950— all these make it likely that the anti-Communist movement in America would have proceeded even without the Hiss case.

If Nixon had not been propelled to national prominence by the Hiss case so early in his career, he would have advanced by other opportunities. He might well have made it to the White House.

On the other hand, suppose that Dwight Eisenhower, surprised by the news in 1952 that his young running mate Richard Nixon had accepted $18,000 in secret donations from wealthy California businessmen, had indulged his famous temper and said, "I will not be fooled by maudlin nonsense about a dog named Checkers. There is something in his character I do not like. I want him off the ticket!"

WILLIAM H. McNEILL

WHAT IF PIZARRO HAD NOT
FOUND POTATOES IN PERU?

The humble roots of history

*A world without potatoes? William H. McNeill asks us to consider some of the
historical landmarks that the starchy tuber, high in calorie yield but low in prestige, has created in the past five centuries. It is as much despised by dieters today
as it was by the soldiers of the Spanish conquistador Pizarro as they brought down
the Inca empire of the Andes in 1531–32. Potatoes are native to the Peruvian altiplano (they did not originate in Virginia, as early Anglophilic historians would
have us believe) and the indigenous peoples of the region depended on the shriveled globules that looked like small rocks and could be stored for years. Pizarro
and his handful of martial thugs had ridden in on a wave of smallpox that had decimated the Inca population and its leadership: they had brazenly manipulated their
disease-borne advantage, which they saw as a token of God's favor. That, and
their greed, is a familiar story. The potatoes the Spaniards called* chuno *"must
have seemed a mere nothing compared with the wealth of booty they seized,"
McNeill writes. "Yet I propose to argue that the humble potato played a larger
part in shaping the subsequent history of the world than did all the gold and silver
that so delighted Pizarro and his successors."*

*But for the potato, what different roads history might have taken? Would
Spain have become such a vast imperial power, presiding over the first empire in
history on which the sun never set? (Its wealth would be rooted in a mound of silver mined by potato-fed conscript laborers.) Would Frederick the Great's Prussia
have survived without the potato in the Seven Years' War (1756–63), paving the*

413

way, ultimately, for the ascension of Germany? How different would the social landscapes of the United States, Canada, and Australia have been without an Irish potato famine? Would Europe's imperial and industrial expansion in the nineteenth century have been possible without the potato? How many crises of the Cold War, one wonders, were fueled by potato-based vodka? And would we now, in a rare interval of relative peace, be appreciating van Gogh's first major, and truly memorable, painting, The Potato Eaters?

This final chapter is one that spans centuries, continents, and natural boundaries—what we might call a counterfactual by subtraction.

WILLIAM H. McNEILL, professor emeritus at the University of Chicago, won the National Book Award for his *Rise of the West*. Among his twenty-six other books are a survey of military history, *The Pursuit of Power*, *Plagues and Peoples*, and most recently *Keeping Together in Time: An Essay on Dance and Drill in Human History*. In 1997, he received one of the most prestigious international prizes for a lifetime of distinguished scholarship, the Erasmus Award.

T HIS QUESTION IS likely to sound strange to most readers and to most historians as well, while Pizarro himself, and the ruffians he led, would have thought such a question absurd. Yet without cheap and abundant food, provided mainly by potatoes, the severe climate of the Peruvian altiplano could not have supported the Inca civilization that so amazed the Spaniards when they climbed into the Andes to conquer it (1531–32). For Pizarro and his followers, the fact that the peoples of Peru did not raise wheat or cattle was a trivial inconvenience, since it meant they had to eat unfamiliar, distasteful substitutes for the bread and meat they preferred. To them that must have seemed a mere nothing compared with the wealth of booty they seized. Yet I propose to argue that the humble potato played a larger part in shaping the subsequent history of the world than did all the gold and silver that so delighted Pizarro and his successors.

In particular, the Spanish hegemony in Europe (1559–1640) could not have been achieved without that humble tuber, for it fed the miners of Potosí, and it was they who produced the unparalleled quantities of silver that allowed the Spanish government to pay its soldiers (at least most of the time) and sustain all the other imperial expenses incurred by Phillip II and his immediate heirs. Nor did world-shaking side effects of potato cultivation come to an end after 1650, when the principal silver lodes at Potosí ran out. Instead, the potato, transferred to Europe, allowed the native Irish to survive efforts of the English government to settle Cromwell's disbanded soldiers on confiscated land after 1652. The same plant rescued Prussian peasants from the ravages of invading armies during the Seven Years' War (1756–63) and their resilience made the survival of Frederick the Great's army and government possible. Then, in the nineteenth century, an expanded supply of calories from potato fields sustained Europe's demographic and imperial expansion by assuring ample labor for factories and other urban occupations, while sustaining massive emigration overseas, as well as overland into Siberia. In short, ever since 1545, when Spanish prospectors discovered the "silver mountain" at Potosí, the military and political history of the world has been profoundly affected by the availabilty of potatoes to fuel human effort, first on the South American altiplano, then in Ireland and across the north European plain, and, with less conspicuous results, throughout other well-watered and relatively cool regions of the earth, most notably in China.

Understanding why requires a bit of explanation. Potatoes, known to botanists as *Solanum tuberosum*, were native to the Andes. They do best in sandy soils with a relatively cool growing season, but adapt readily to diverse latitudes so long as there is enough water in the ground to allow them to form their moist, starchy tubers. Potatoes had several advantages over grain as a food for humans. First and most importantly, in suitably moist soils, the calorie yield from potato fields is usually much larger than what grain produces. This was not true of irrigated rice paddies in East Asia, but in northern Europe, calorie yields per acre from potatoes are between two and four times greater than from grain. Moreover, the tubers have enough vitamin and mineral content to constitute a complete and well-balanced diet when supplemented by the fat, protein, and calcium of whole milk from cows.

On the other hand, potatoes cannot be stored nearly as long as grain. Ripe grain is too dry to sprout without exposure to water. Storage therefore only requires protecting the seeds from water, and from animal and insect would-be consumers. Potatoes, on the contrary, are moist enough to sprout in response to a built-in biological clock that is usually triggered by slight changes in temperature, and do so whether they lie in cellars and storage bins or remain underground where they grow. Stored tubers are also vulnerable to airborne fungi that feed on them as readily as people do; and once fungi start to grow they rot the tubers quickly. Storing potatoes for more than a few months is therefore impractical even today.

Without satisfactory methods of long-term storage, potatoes could not support civilized forms of society as grain did, for it was by taking possession of stored grain and using it to feed urban dwellers that priests and rulers

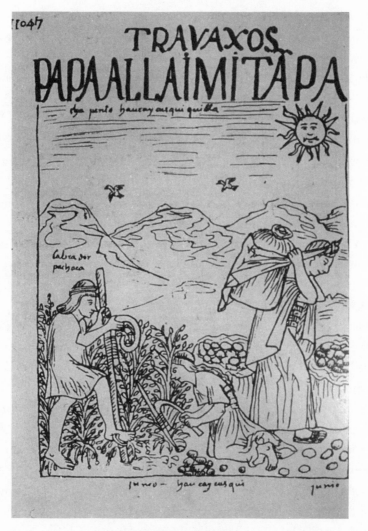

HARVESTING HISTORY

What would the world be like without the potato? The question is hardly a whimsical one: for the past five centuries, the humble tuber has played a considerable role in history. In the drawing above, made by a Spanish colonial artist around 1565, native farmers of the Andes, where the potato originated, harvest the calorie-rich foodstuff that the Spanish called chuno.

(Felipe Guaman Poma, Inca harvesting potatoes, from *El Primer Nueva Corónica y Buen Gobierno*, ca. 1565. Royal Library, Copenhagen, Denmark. Nick Saunders/Barbara Heller Photo Library, London/Art Resource, NY) constructed the earliest civilizations. Rents and taxes, whether in money or in kind, continued to effect the same transfer of grain from farmers to rulers and managers and their urban dependents throughout subsequent millennia of civilized history, and did so until quite recently, when market exchanges between urban and rural dwellers began to dominate the same process.

In their raw form, urban folk could not depend on collecting perishable potatoes from their producers, largely because, since they do not need to be dug from the ground until it is time to eat them, potato gardeners escaped the problem of having to protect stores of valuable food. Grain farmers, on the contrary, were radically vulnerable to armed marauders since ripe grain had to be harvested and stored, and stocks of harvested grain were easy to find and carry away. Civilized rent and tax collectors, who took only part of the harvest, might or might not be able to protect rural dwellers from raids. But it was clearly better for grain farmers to share the harvest with powerful rulers and landlords who had a clear and direct interest in doing all they could to protect those who produced the grain upon which everyone depended. Hence grain farming and civilization went together from the time civilizations arose.

Nonetheless, in their original Andean habitat, potatoes did become the principal food of the Inca empire and its predecessors. That was because the peculiar climate of the South American altiplano made it possible to preserve potatoes by exposing them to the dry night air when, despite Peru's tropical location, temperatures sometimes went below freezing. Shriveled, freeze-dried potatoes, called *chuno* by the Spaniards, were fully equivalent to grain since *chuno* could be stored for years without loss of nutritional value. Hence Inca tax collectors could and did require potato gardeners to supply *chuno* to official storehouses just as they required maize-growers at lower altitudes to hand over corn; and officials could then issue food from such warehouses to maintain the soldiers, public works laborers, and all the household servants, administrators, and priests who combined to make Inca government and civilization what it was.

In 1532 the Spaniards took over this administrative system and after 1545 used it to supply *chuno* to scores of thousands of conscripted silver miners at Potosí. Their efforts, in turn, produced a freshet of silver that sustained Spanish imperial power in Europe and the Americas and, in the course of the following century, inflated prices around the world. Rapidly rising prices, in turn, upset older economic and social relationships in civilized societies everywhere. Thus it was that between 1545 and about 1650, potatoes, processed into *chuno*, fueled an unprecedented scale of silver mining in Peru, provoking worldwide economic and social upheaval, while lifting Spanish military power to new heights in Western Europe. No one understood what was happening at the time; still less did anyone credit *chuno*—a nasty, unpalatable food in Europeans' eyes—with making it possible. Yet so, surely, it was.

But this initial impact on the world's history was only a prelude to what the same plant did when transferred to European soil. How it got there is unrecorded; but plain enough since Spanish ships that entered the Pacific had to stock up on food for their return voyages. Familiar European cereals were not available, so sailors on the way home had to rely on maize and potatoes for most of their calories, which was all that the Pacific coast of South America could supply. We also know for sure that on returning to Spain, sailors carried specimens ashore, and some apparently thought enough of the new foods to try planting them. Most parts of Spain were too dry for potatoes; but Atlantic winds brought enough moisture to the Basque country along Spain's northwest coast for them to thrive there.

Accordingly, within a few decades of Pizarro's conquest, potatoes took root in Basque country, and Basque fishermen soon began to stock their fishing boats with potatoes when setting out for the Grand Banks off Newfoundland. It was they who introduced the crop to the west coast of Ireland, where they habitually came ashore for rest and recuperation on their return voyages. Exactly when potatoes began to flourish on Irish soil remains unknown, but by 1650 the crop was sufficiently widespread in the westernmost province of Connaught to become a lifesaver for the Irish people after their defeat by Cromwell's soldiers (1649–52).

As a result, when the English government undertook to solve its Irish problem by distributing confiscated lands in Leinster and Munster among disbanded veterans while crowding the surviving natives of these provinces into Connaught, the defeated Irish found it possible to survive by planting potatoes on small patches of land, and supplementing this new food with milk from cattle that had long been the principal basis of the Irish economy. Irish soil and climate were such that a single acre of potatoes and enough grass for a cow sufficed to feed an entire family, with enough left over to raise a pig. However monotonous it may seem to us, this diet sustained rapid population growth among a conspicuously healthy Irish population from the time Cromwell's soldiers compelled them to accept it.

English settlers, by contrast, ate bread and cheese and were entirely unwilling to change their habits, even though wheat often failed to ripen in the Irish climate and rye and oats yielded far less per acre and cost more to harvest and process into bread than did potatoes, which had only to be dug from the ground and thrown into a pot of boiling water to be ready for the table. This meant that the Irish could live far more cheaply than the English, and when Cromwell's veterans found that the style of grain farming with which they were familiar in England did not produce satisfactory results in the moister, cooler Irish climate, they sold out to land-jobbers, who soon found that raising beef cattle was the only feasible way to wring cash income from the land.

These upstart landowners needed hired hands to tend their herds and quickly discovered that Irish laborers were experienced herdsmen—and dirt cheap, only needing access to an acre for potatoes and enough grass for a cow. As a result, and despite the intentions of the English government, Catholic Irish laborers and their novel subsistence style of potato cultivation displaced far more expensive bread-eating English laborers from almost all of rural Ireland. Thanks to the potato, therefore, the majority of the population of Ireland remained Irish, except in Ulster, where an earlier rebellion against the English had led to the settlement of Protestant Scots on conflated lands after 1607. Scottish farming, featuring oats rather than wheat, was readily transferable to Irish soil; and since the potato was unknown in Ulster until early in the eighteenth century, the Scots-Irish successfully displaced the Irish in most of that province, with political and social results that still command headlines today.

Then, in the nineteenth century, when faster and larger steamships began to traverse the seas, they inadvertently introduced a South American fungus into Europe that, under wet, cool conditions, proved lethal to the potatoes that by then had established themselves throughout Ireland and across most of the north European plain. The summers of 1845 and 1846 were unusually cool and wet in Western Europe, and the resultant failure of potato harvests brought stark famine to Ireland and serious food shortages elsewhere in northern Europe. In Ireland, more than a million people died of starvation and of infections induced by hunger; while millions of others emigrated during and in the aftermath of the famine. The resulting Irish diaspora altered the social landscapes of the United States, Great Britain, Canada, Australia, and elsewhere. This, perhaps, counts as a second world-changing consequence of potato cultivation, and of an Irish way of life that was dangerously dependent on that single crop.

Nonetheless, the principal impact of potatoes on modern European history was felt on the Continent rather than in Ireland. This story requires backpedaling to the time when Spanish sailors first carried the tubers across the ocean. As we saw, most of Spain itself was inhospitable, but potatoes did well in the Po valley of Italy, which became part of the Spanish empire in 1535. Anonymous sailors must have carried them there, and hard-pressed Italian peasants found them valuable—not least because they escaped taxation since city folk had no use for the new food at first. Potato gardens then spread northward very rapidly, from Italy across the Alps into Franche-Comté, the Rhinelands, and the Low Countries before the end of the sixteenth century.

Potatoes followed this path to the north European plain because it was here that local peasants were regularly exposed to military requisitioning by detachments of Spanish soldiers marching along the so-called "Spanish Road." That, in turn, was because, when Dutch rebels inaugurated eighty years of on-again, off-again warfare against Philip II of Spain and his heirs (1568–1648), their naval superiority made the sea unsafe for Spanish shipping. The Spanish government was therefore compelled to reinforce its armies in the Low Countries by shipping troops to northern Italy, whence they marched northward to the theater of war. From time immemorial, European armies had lived off the land when on the march, since limitations on transport made it impossible for them to do otherwise. Accordingly, Spanish soldiers en route to the Low Countries requisitioned grain from villages along the way, and did so year after year. Under these circumstances, peasants quickly discovered that potatoes were a lifesaver. Simply by leaving them in the ground until wanted for food, they could be sure of having something left to eat even after military foraging parties had carried off all available stores of grain. We can only assume that word of mouth and harsh experience combined to spread news of the lifesaving capabilities of the new crop from village to village, for the spread of potatoes northward from Italy left no trace in contemporary records as far as anyone knows.

Eventually, the existence of potatoes along the "Spanish Road" did come to learned attention, when, in 1588, a botanist who Latinized his name into Carolus Clusius painted a watercolor of a potato plant he had discovered growing in a garden near Mons, Belgium. Clusius subsequently published the watercolor in his book *Rariorum plantarum historia* (Antwerp, 1601) along with a description of what he called "Papas Peruanorum," together with a brief account of what he had discovered about the plant. He correctly reported that it had come from Peru and was "common" in northern Italy, where it was valued both as animal fodder and as human food. This is the first written record of the existence of potatoes on the continent of Europe yet discovered, and a thoroughly believable, but incomplete, description of where the plant initially flourished. To be sure, Clusius quite failed to understand why grain farmers along the Spanish Road were so ready to adopt the new crop, and he knew nothing about Basque fishermens' potato gardens. Their existence can safely be surmised, however, from the provable fact that Irish potatoes derived from Spain and not from Francis Drake's subsequent introduction of a different strain of potatoes into England in 1580. An English botanist promptly took note of the potatoes Drake brought back from his famous circumnavigation of the globe, but though John Gerard chose to make a large woodcut of the new plant into the frontispiece of his *Herball, or General Historie of Plantes* (London, 1597), thereby antedating Clusius's published notice of potatoes by four years, Gerard erroneously named the new plant "potatoes of Virginia," thereby introducing an error into English learning that lingered through most of the nineteenth century.

Until the eighteenth century, potatoes remained only a garden crop, whether in Basque country, Ireland, northern Italy, the Rhinelands, or adjacent areas. Most European grain farmers cultivated strips in open fields, and custom required everyone to plant the same crop in adjacent strips so that subsequent routines of harvesting, gleaning, and plowing could proceed on schedule. This meant that new crops could not ordinarily enter the open fields. Nonetheless, as we just saw, between 1560 and 1700 the spread of comparatively small potato gardens cushioned the customary demographic destructiveness of military requisitioning in some of Europe's most fought-over regions. This was significant, for as the size of European armies increased, rural death by starvation in the wake of marching soldiers became more and more widespread and reached a devastating climax in Germany during the Thirty Years' War (1618–48). Its horrors were long remembered because this was the last time a prolonged war was fought in northern Europe before potatoes became generally available to forestall rural starvation even after grain stocks had all been carried away by foraging soldiers.

That, in turn, became possible because, after 1750, the spread of potatoes across European landscapes ceased to depend on the initiative of illiterate peasants, relying solely on word of mouth. Instead, government officials intervened and set out, first only in Prussia, to propagate potatoes with the deliberate purpose of safeguarding rural taxpayers from wartime famine. This got started when the youthful Prussian king, Frederick the Great, campaigning in the Rhinelands during the War of the Austrian Succession (1740–48), noticed how potatoes permitted peasants to survive military requisitioning. Accordingly, in 1744 he decided to introduce the crop to Prussia, ordering local administrators to distribute free seed potatoes with instructions on how to raise them.

Frederick's initiative paid off handsomely during the Seven Years' War (1756–63) when Prussian peasants endured repeated invasions by Austrian, Russian, and French armies without suffering serious famine. Survival of the Prussian state and army against apparently overwhelming odds depended on the new and surprising resilience of the Prussian peasantry as much as it did on Frederick's famous victories, British subsidies, and Russia's sudden change of sides. It follows that the subsequent history of Germany would certainly have been very different without the presence of potatoes in Prussian fields and gardens during the Seven Years' War. But there is no point in speculating about how the victorious forces of France, Austria, and Russia might have redirected German affairs, forestalling Bismarck's unification of Germany under Prussian leadership in 1870 almost for sure.

Instead, during the Seven Years' War the secret of Prussia's ability to withstand repeated invasions became obvious to the attacking armies, and when peace returned the French, Austrian, and Russian governments all set out to imitate the Prussians by propagating potatoes among their own peasants as a matter of official policy. The French led the way, due partly to the efforts of an army doctor, Antoine Parmentier, who, having encountered potatoes in Prussia, spent the rest of his life investigating their nutritional value and how best to grow them. He published his results in a book entitled *Examen chymique des pommes des terres* (Paris 1774). And on one occasion, official efforts to make potatoes acceptable in France induced Marie Antoinette to advertise the plant's virtues by appearing at a court ball wearing a coiffeur of potato flowers. Austrian and Russian official efforts to catch up with Prussia also produced relatively rapid results, though inertia and the restraints of open field cultivation meant that potatoes remained mostly a garden crop in that part of Europe until the 1820s and 1830s.

By then, in France, the Low Countries, and Germany, potatoes had broken through garden fences and become a field crop, thereby enormously expanding the quantity of calories available to fuel the efforts of rapidly growing populations. To understand the magnitude of this effect one must remember that traditional grain farming in Europe required leaving fields fallow every second or third year. This was needed to clear fields of weeds by plowing the fallow in summer before weed seeds had formed. In potato gardens hoeing by hand was the only way to remove weeds, so from a human point of view potato fields required far more summer labor than did

424

grain, which was too thickly sown for hoeing to be possible. Potatoes could not therefore become a major field crop unless enough labor to hoe the ground they occupied could be found.

But, for reasons still disputed among demographers, Europe along with the rest of the civilized world began to experience sustained population growth after about 1750. Where agricultural land was already fully occupied, the resulting spurt of human numbers meant smaller family holdings and lowered standards of living. Peasant revolts, which began to trouble the Chinese imperial government in the 1770s, registered this unhappy circumstance in China. But across northern Europe, potatoes were available to invade the fallow grain fields, and official governmental policy stood ready to forward the process. Food supplies multiplied accordingly, so that growing numbers of well-fed northern Europeans became available to intensify agricultural, industrial, military, and other forms of organized effort. The rapid surge of northern European nations to world dominion in the nineteenth century depended on this serendipity.

It is easy to understand how the availability of extensive fallow fields allowed a very powerful feedback loop to establish itself in northern Europe after 1750. Simply by planting potatoes on the fallow, a new and enormous supply of food could be produced without the slightest reduction of traditional grain harvests! What a bonanza! Instead of the customary fallowing, a third to a half of Europe's cultivated fields could be planted with potatoes (or other row crops, such as turnips and sugar beets), and as long as the growing plants were hoed by hand once or twice in early summer, weeds were very effectually controlled. Hence potato fields could be planted with grain next year, entirely as usual, while new row crops took over another, no-longer fallow, field. Extra labor was essential for this intensification of European farming; but potatoes, yielding as they did two to four times the number of calories per acre that grain fields did, were instantly available to feed the growing numbers needed for their cultivation. On top of that, leftover potatoes remained for animal fodder and for conversion into vodka, which, in fact, became a very important source of revenue for the Russian government.

Under these circumstances, once potatoes became a field crop, population could and did rise far above older ceilings, and potatoes, being cheap, became the principal food of the poorer classes throughout the north European plain, all the way from northern France and the Low Countries through Germany and Poland into Russia. Bread was never displaced entirely as happened among the Irish, so the impact of the famine years (1845–47), when potatoes failed almost everywhere, was correspondingly diminished on the European Continent (and in England), though the "hungry forties" were long remembered by those who suffered through them.

The potato blight required damp, cool conditions to prosper; and when dryer summers returned to Europe after 1847, the blight diminished or even disappeared. But every so often, cool, wet summer weather, when sufficiently prolonged, allowed the fungus to resume its ravages until the 1880s, when protective chemical sprays were introduced. Shortly before chemical sprays (and artificial fertilizers) began to alter European agriculture, the invention of horse-drawn shufflers reduced or eliminated the need for hoeing potatoes and other row crops, thus releasing a host of rural laborers for industrial employment in the mines and factories that began to sprout near Europe's coal fields while also provoking massive emigration overseas and eastward into Siberia as well.

The effect, therefore, of deliberate official patronage of potato cultivation, pioneered by Frederick the Great in 1744, turned out to be very considerable. First of all, potatoes quickly became a field crop and an increasingly important source of human food throughout northern Europe. Consequently, the intensified warfare attendant on the French Revolution and Napoleon's subsequent career (1793–1815) became bearable for Europe's rural populations thanks largely to the food reserves their potato gardens and fields provided for them. Otherwise European governments could not possibly have mobilized millions of soldiers while continuing to feed their armies in the field in traditional fashion by ruthlessly requisitioning grain and animals from local villagers. But instead of provoking death and disaster on an even greater scale than that of the Thirty Years' War, intensified warfare between 1793 and 1815 wrought only minimal damage to European rural populations.

Then as potatoes continued their expansion into once-fallowed grain fields, and as hand hoeing ceased to be necessary, the European countryside began to empty out. Millions of migrants began to labor in new factories and mines and provided other services in rapidly expanding urban centers, while still others emigrated overseas and eastward into Siberia. The swarming of European peoples in the nineteenth century was indeed remarkable; not least because of the extraordinary fact that first within Europe itself and then overseas and in Siberia, Europeans found empty land to provide their swarming population with adequate, indeed abundant, food.

Elimination of fallowing did the trick across northern Europe itself, and here potatoes played the lead role, as we have just seen. Overseas and in Siberia, it was destruction of indigenous populations by exposure to civilized diseases and the disruption of older ecological balances by civilized demand for furs and a few other commodities that disrupted indigenous societies in Siberian, American, Australian, and other overseas landscapes, opening the way for European settlement. Military conquest merely sealed European emigrants' success in supplanting older inhabitants wherever familiar European crops and agricultural methods proved viable. The resulting cultural and political transformations of the Americas, Australia, and parts of Siberia were drastic indeed, and citizens of the United States and of Russia are today the most conspicuous heirs of this process.

Without the extra food potato fields provided, the swarming of north European populations could not have occurred. Maize also played a similar but less prominent part in southern Europe; but that is another story. Of course much else entered into Europe's rise and recent withdrawal from world dominion; but it is surely safe to say that potatoes from Peru were essential for fueling the swarming human biomass that sustained Europe's imperial ventures. Potatoes thus powerfully affected the general course of world history since 1750. Silver and gold glittered, all right, but potatoes, inconspicuous and unnoticed at first, nevertheless were more important, since they altered the course of human history in far-reaching ways, and did so repeatedly, from the time Pizarro first encountered and disdained them.

So what if Pizarro had not found potatoes in Peru? Our world would be radically different for sure, even though no one can say exactly how very different it would be.